NINJA
ニンジャスレイヤー
SLAYER
KILLS!

ORIGINAL AUTHORS:
BRADLEY BOND + PHILIP NINJ@ MORZEZ

MANGA ADAPTATION SUPERVISION:
YU HONDA / LEIKA SUGI

MANGA:
KOUTAROU SEKINE

CHARACTER DESIGN:
WARAINAKU / KOUTAROU SEKINE

VOLUME
3

FOREWORD

Domo.

I am Truncator.

You have done well to make it this far. You have built your wazamae considerably and may soon yet call yourself a true ninja head. But in truth, your journey has only just begun. The path before you is still fraught with peril, so in the event that your karate is overpowered, I have prepared a haiku for you to read upon your demise.

Struck down I shed free
my mortal coil, my tears
crimson curtains fall

KOTODAMA

What is written upon these pages are more than mere words, they have been brought to life on the breath of those who inhabit the world of Ninja Slayer, and as such, hold power that bring them close to the heart and soul of ninja life. Learn these words as if your life depended on it, for they might be your best weapons in this age of wanton violence and depravity.

BIO-LIFE FORMS

Due to Neo-Saitama's serious pollution problem, most animals have been subjected to genetic modification in order to survive. Yoroshisan Pharmaceuticals owns over 90% of the patents for these animals, including bio-pandas, bio-sparrows, bio-water buffalo as well as bio-unagi (freshwater eel) and most of the Chugoku region is overrun with wild bio-life forms. Animals that have had a high degree of genetic modification performed on them have green blood and a small portion of these animals also require bio-extracts and bio-ingots to support their life.

SURIKEN

A demi-shuriken or small, star-shaped weapon—one of many that may be thrown by ninja. One who possesses considerable ninja soul power will have the ability to generate their own suriken. Ninja Slayer can use his own blood to form suriken.

SEPPUKU

Similar to but different from *harikiri*, this is very simply an act of suicide that is performed by stabbing and slicing one's stomach open. In the Ninja Slayer universe, *seppuku* is considered to be a more ritualistic and spiritual version of *harikiri*. Some ninjas believe *seppuku* and *death-hai-ku* were of extreme importance for the preservation of their souls in Kinkaku Temple.

SUMIMASEN

A ninja expression of contrition that is similar to saying "I'm sorry" or "Pardon me."

NAMU HACHIMAN DAIFUTON

A spell used to seal away great evil by invoking the power of Hachiman, the god of archery and war.

SOMATO RECALL

A phenomenon that occurs near death in which one's life passes before their eyes. The experience is said to resemble the experience of watching a revolving lantern show—a vision of shadowy images passing over a screen lit by the flickering flame of a lantern.

SANSHITA

A small-fry or a weak ninja that lacks refinement . This term is often used as an insult for ninja.

YUKANO

Gendoso's granddaughter. A beautiful ninja who trains hard at the dojo.

DOMINANT

An ambitious young ninja who plots to strengthen his own authority by defeating Ninja Slayer.

FUJIKIDO KENJI

Fujikido is possessed by the wicked Ninja Soul Naraku causing him to be reborn as Ninja Slayer. However, Naraku causes Fujikido to go berserk by taking advantage of his thirst for vengeance. He was stopped by Gendoso, but as a result lost his immense ninja powers.

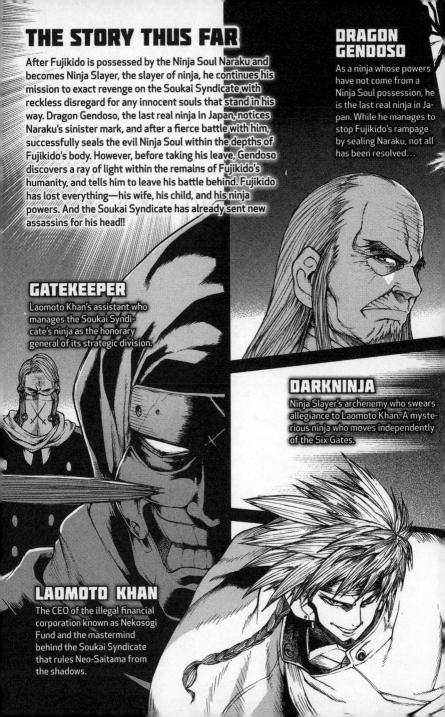

THE STORY THUS FAR

After Fujikido is possessed by the Ninja Soul Naraku and becomes Ninja Slayer, the slayer of ninja, he continues his mission to exact revenge on the Soukai Syndicate with reckless disregard for any innocent souls that stand in his way. Dragon Gendoso, the last real ninja in Japan, notices Naraku's sinister mark, and after a fierce battle with him, successfully seals the evil Ninja Soul within the depths of Fujikido's body. However, before taking his leave, Gendoso discovers a ray of light within the remains of Fujikido's humanity, and tells him to leave his battle behind. Fujikido has lost everything—his wife, his child, and his ninja powers. And the Soukai Syndicate has already sent new assassins for his head!!

DRAGON GENDOSO

As a ninja whose powers have not come from a Ninja Soul possession, he is the last real ninja in Japan. While he manages to stop Fujikido's rampage by sealing Naraku, not all has been resolved…

GATEKEEPER

Laomoto Khan's assistant who manages the Soukai Syndicate's ninja as the honorary general of its strategic division.

DARKNINJA

Ninja Slayer's archenemy who swears allegiance to Laomoto Khan. A mysterious ninja who moves independently of the Six Gates.

LAOMOTO KHAN

The CEO of the illegal financial corporation known as Nekosogi Fund and the mastermind behind the Soukai Syndicate that rules Neo-Saitama from the shadows.

NINJA SLAYER *KILLS!*
CONTENTS

KILLs 012 ✦ BACK IN BLACK PART 3 ——————— 9

KILLs 013 ✦ BACK IN BLACK PART 4 ——————— 43

KILLs 014 ✦ BACK IN BLACK PART 5 ——————— 79

KILLs 015 ✦ NEO-YAKUZA FOR SALE ——————— 111

KILLs 016 ✦ SURPRISED DOJO PART 1 ——————— 137

KILLs 017 ✦ SURPRISED DOJO PART 2 ——————— 171

BONUS EXTRAS 特 烈 收 録

NINJA SETTING DESIGN COLLECTION ——————— 206

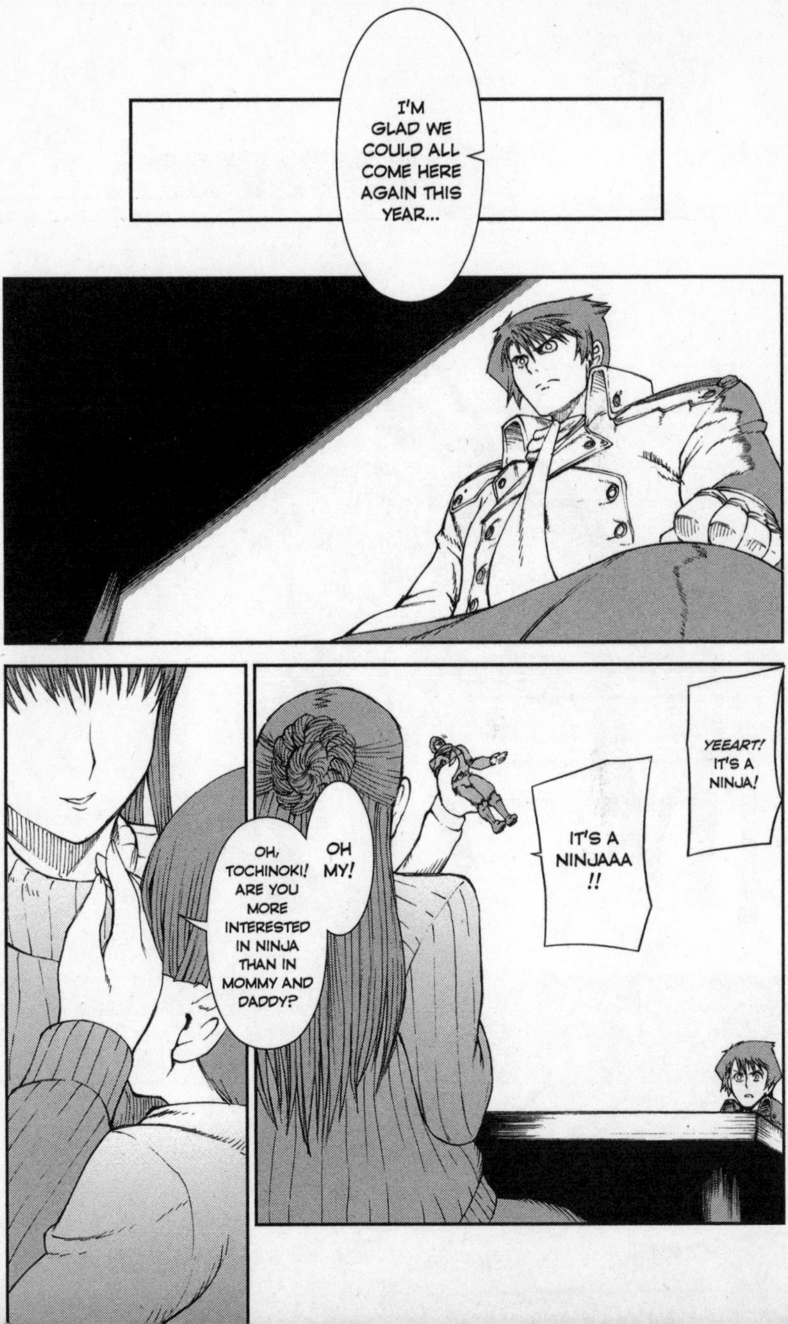
I'M GLAD WE COULD ALL COME HERE AGAIN THIS YEAR...
YEEART! IT'S A NINJA!
IT'S A NINJAAA!!
OH MY!
OH, TOCHINOKI! ARE YOU MORE INTERESTED IN NINJA THAN IN MOMMY AND DADDY?

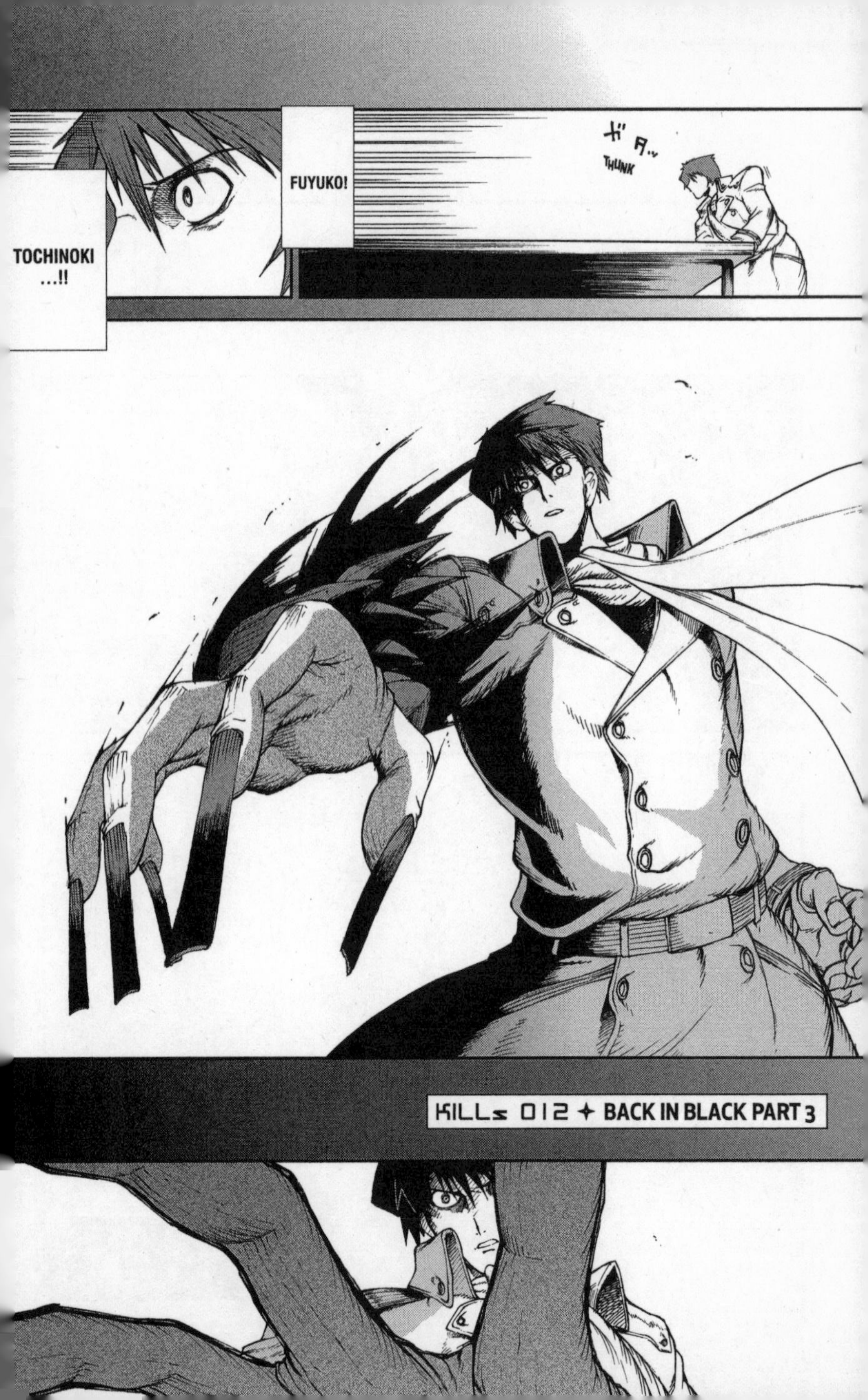

ガタ..
THUNK
FUYUKO!
TOCHINOKI ...!!
KILLs 012 ✦ BACK IN BLACK PART 3

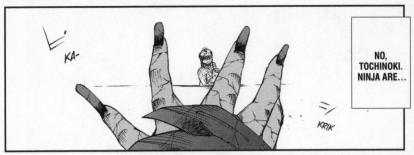

NO,
TOCHINOKI.
NINJA ARE...

NINJA ARE...

11

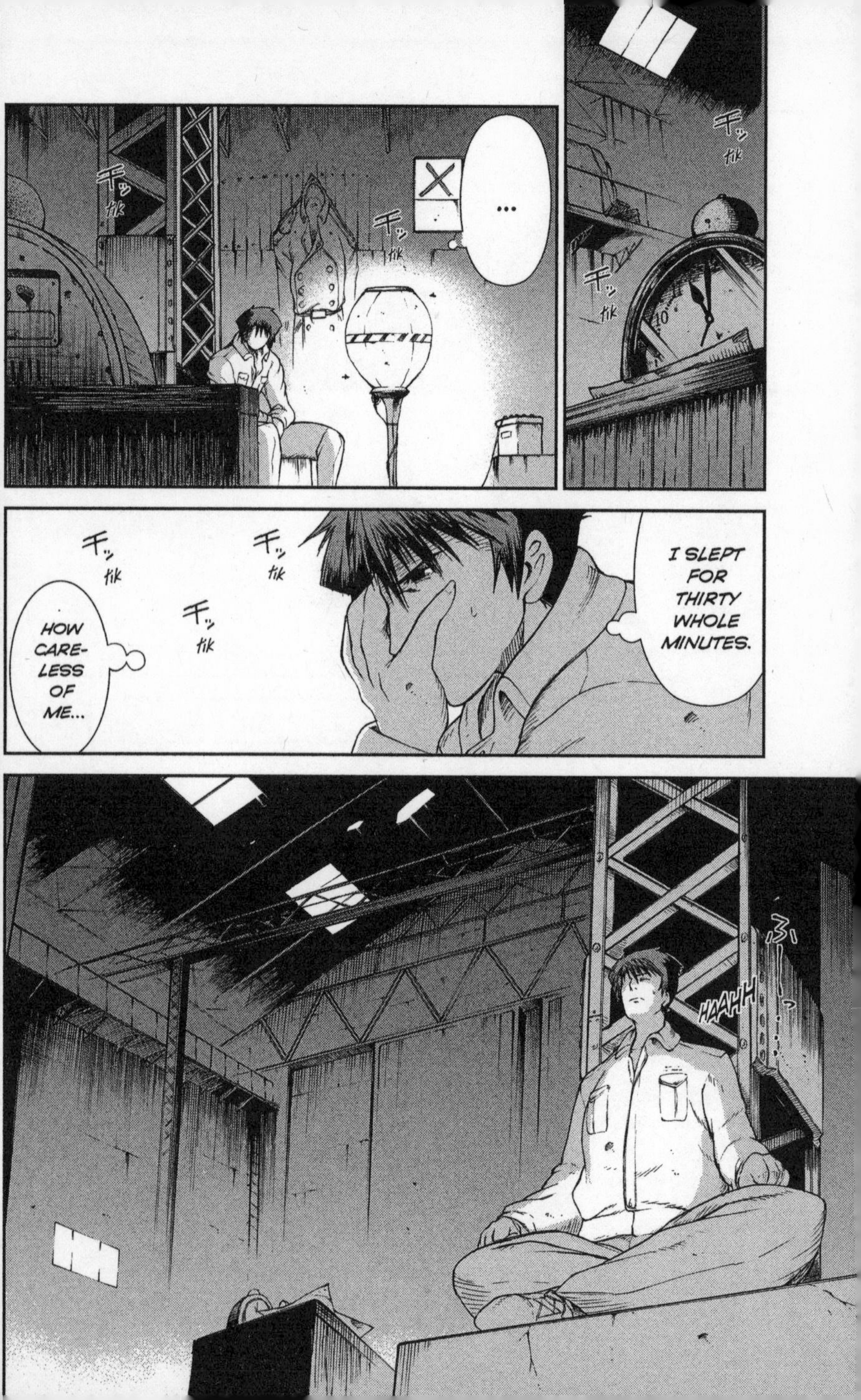

チッ
tik
チッ
tik
チッ
tik
チッ
tik
...
I SLEPT FOR THIRTY WHOLE MINUTES.
チッ
tik
チッ
tik
チッ
tik
HOW CARE-LESS OF ME...
ふー…っ
HAAHH

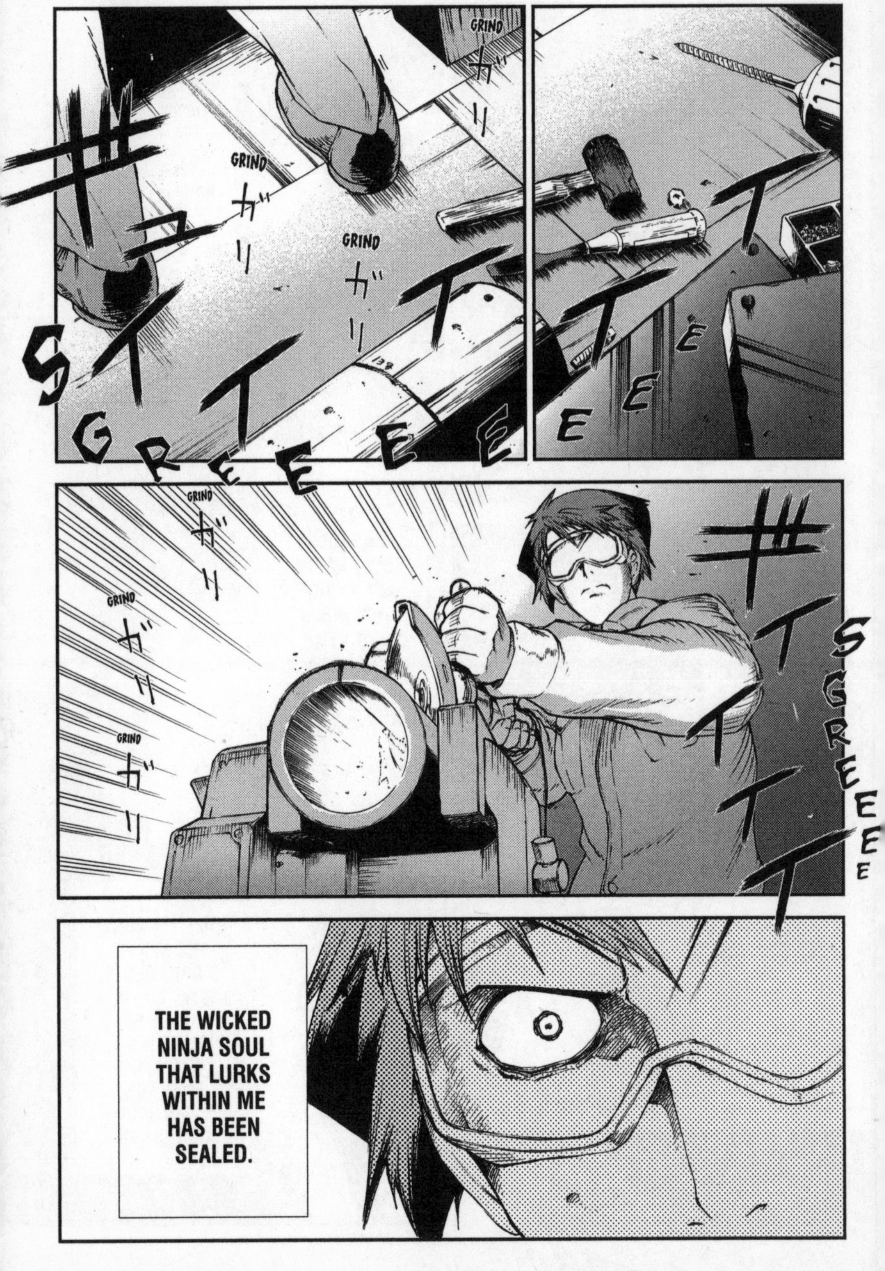
GRIND
GRIND
GRIND
SGREEEEEE
GRIND
GRIND
GRIND
SGREEEEE
THE WICKED NINJA SOUL THAT LURKS WITHIN ME HAS BEEN SEALED.

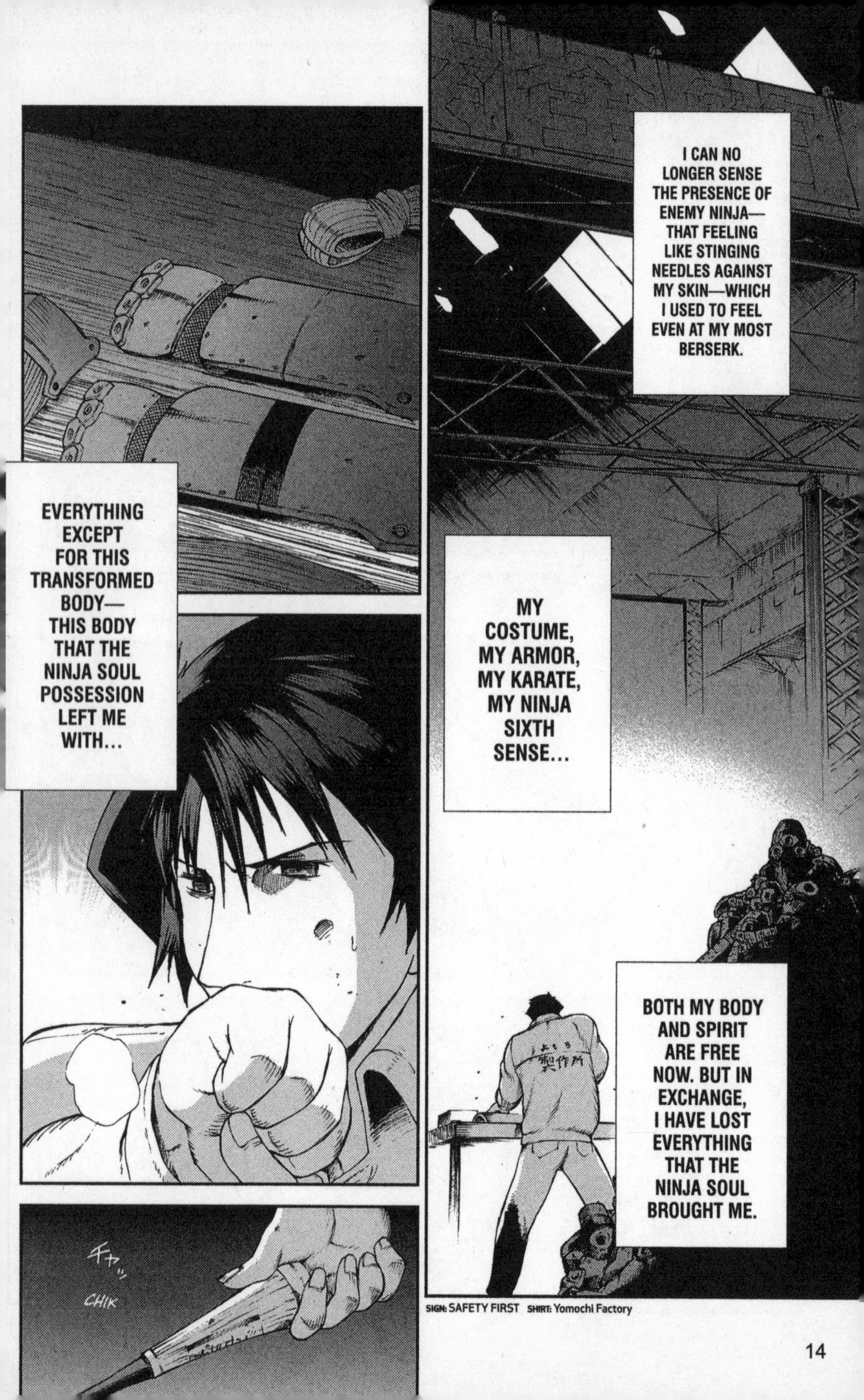
I CAN NO LONGER SENSE THE PRESENCE OF ENEMY NINJA—THAT FEELING LIKE STINGING NEEDLES AGAINST MY SKIN—WHICH I USED TO FEEL EVEN AT MY MOST BERSERK.
MY COSTUME, MY ARMOR, MY KARATE, MY NINJA SIXTH SENSE...
BOTH MY BODY AND SPIRIT ARE FREE NOW. BUT IN EXCHANGE, I HAVE LOST EVERYTHING THAT THE NINJA SOUL BROUGHT ME.
EVERYTHING EXCEPT FOR THIS TRANSFORMED BODY—THIS BODY THAT THE NINJA SOUL POSSESSION LEFT ME WITH...
チャッ
CHIK
SIGN: SAFETY FIRST SHIRT: Yomochi Factory

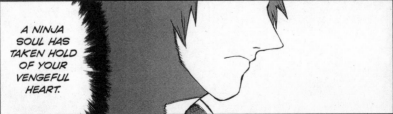

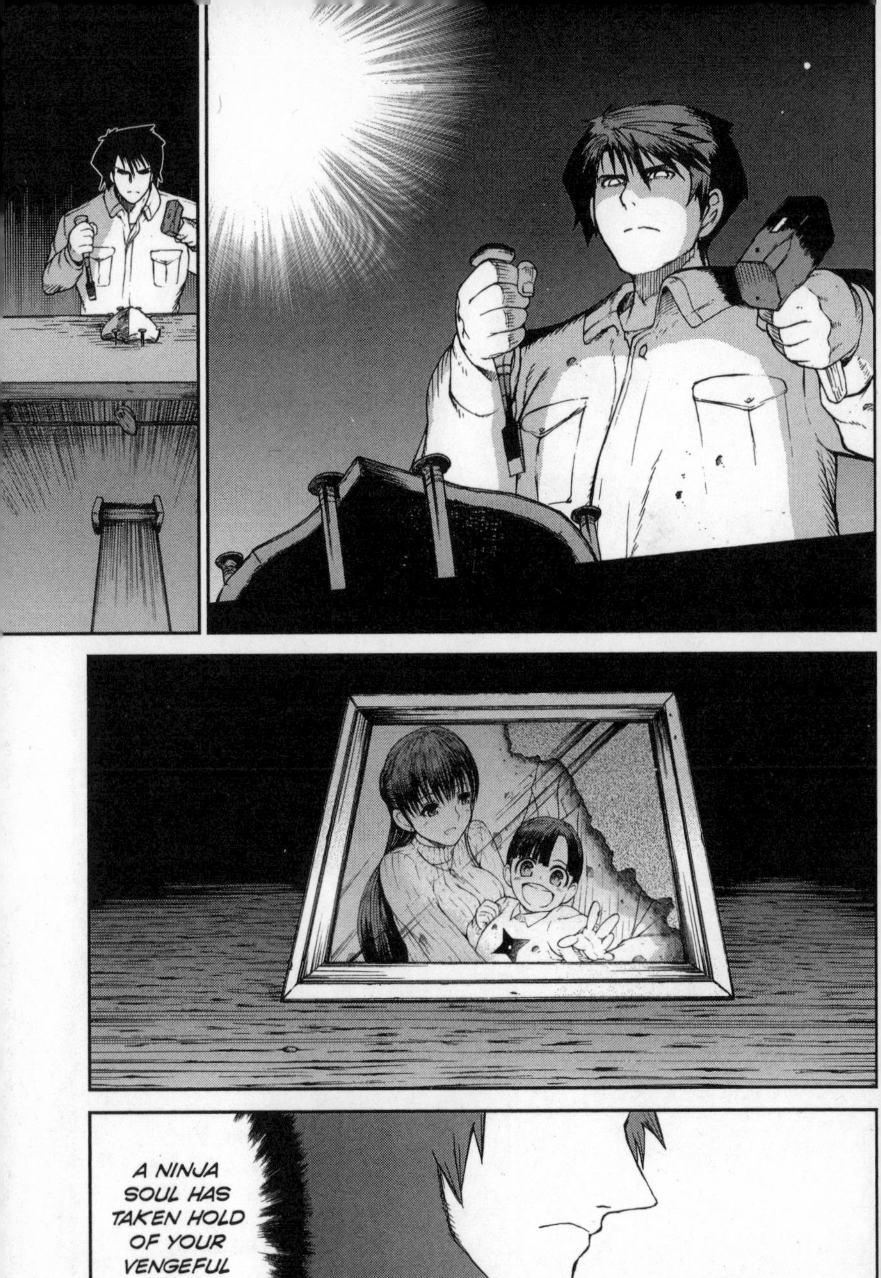
A NINJA SOUL HAS TAKEN HOLD OF YOUR VENGEFUL HEART.

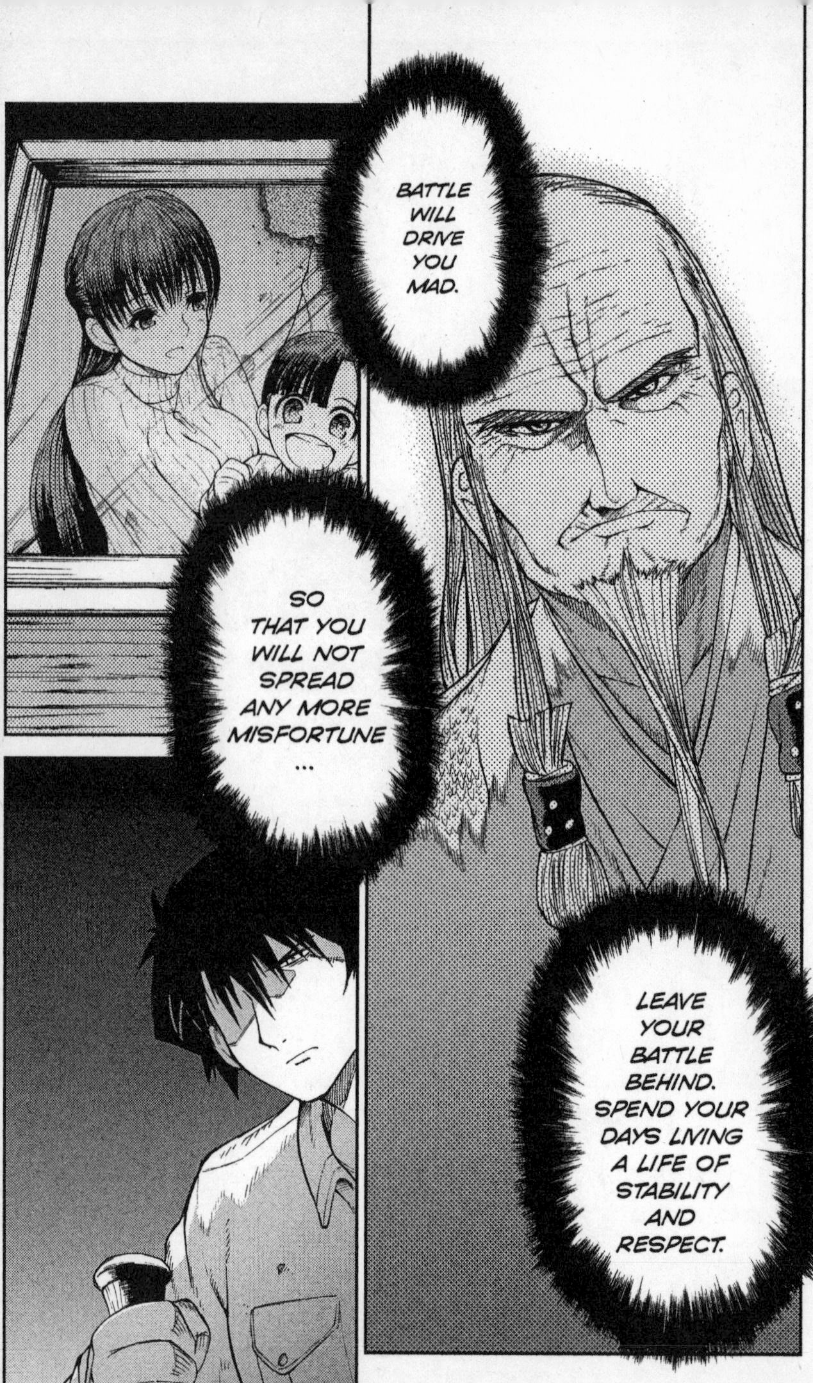
BATTLE WILL DRIVE YOU MAD.
SO THAT YOU WILL NOT SPREAD ANY MORE MISFORTUNE ...
LEAVE YOUR BATTLE BEHIND. SPEND YOUR DAYS LIVING A LIFE OF STABILITY AND RESPECT.

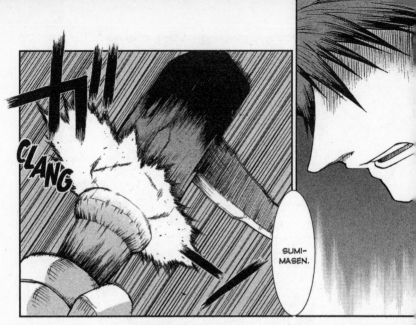

SUMI-MASEN.

WHAT I'M DOING IS SURELY A BETRAYAL OF ROSHI NINJA-SAN, THE MAN WHO SAVED ME.

BUT TO FORGET THE DEATHS OF MY WIFE AND SON AND LIVE AS A RECLUSE?

THERE'S NO WAY I CAN CHOOSE TO DO THAT!

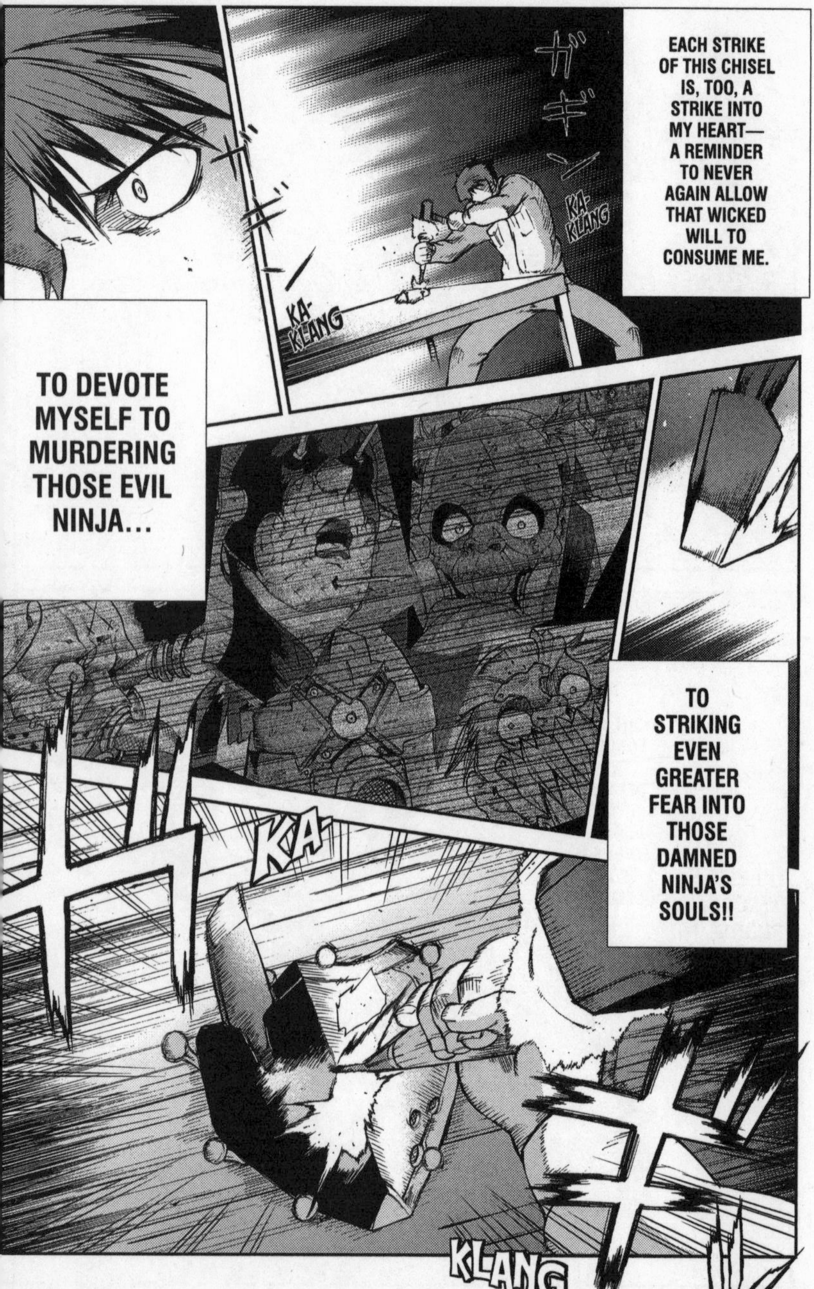
EACH STRIKE OF THIS CHISEL IS, TOO, A STRIKE INTO MY HEART—A REMINDER TO NEVER AGAIN ALLOW THAT WICKED WILL TO CONSUME ME.
ガギン
KA-KLANG
KA-KLANG
TO DEVOTE MYSELF TO MURDERING THOSE EVIL NINJA…
TO STRIKING EVEN GREATER FEAR INTO THOSE DAMNED NINJA'S SOULS!!
KA-
KLANG

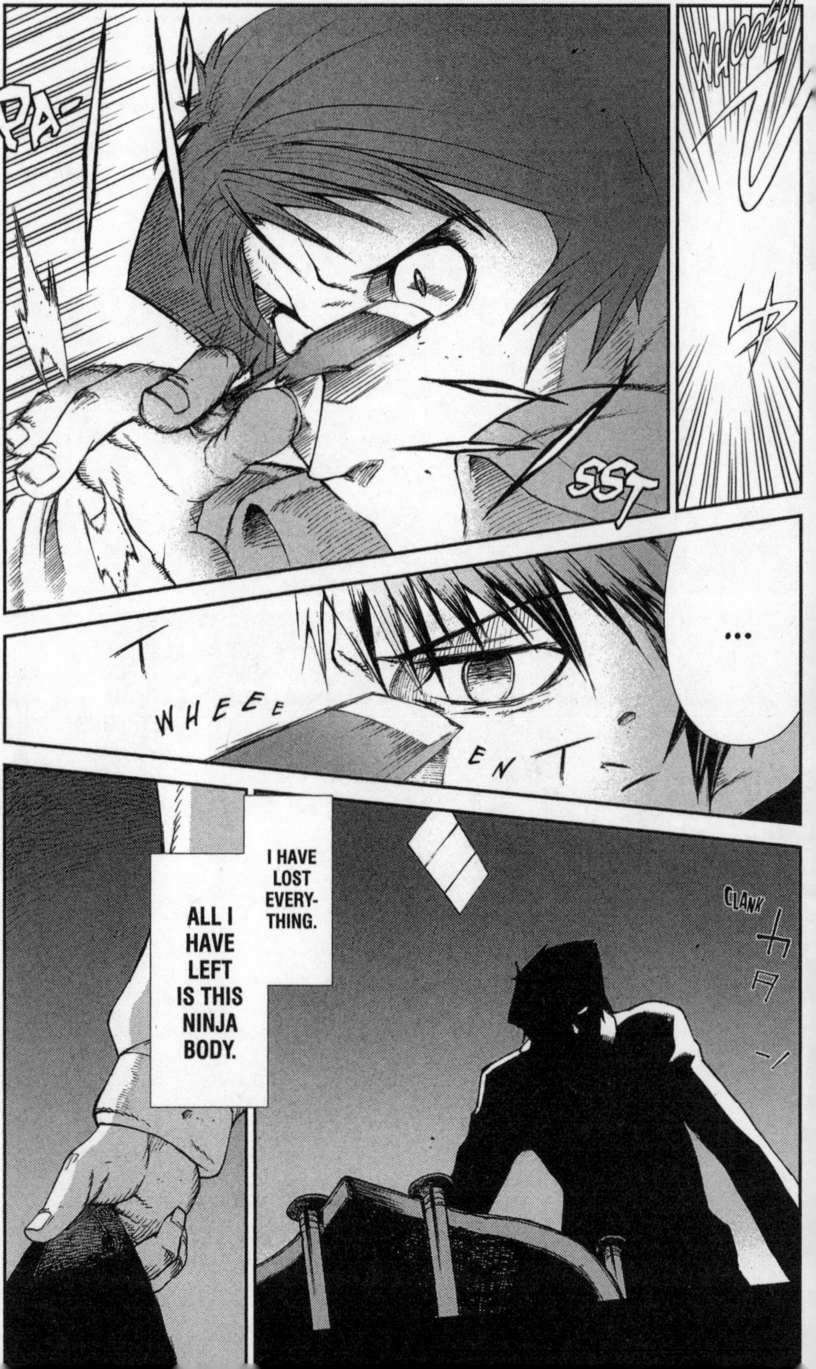
WHOOSH!!
SST
PA-
...
WHEEEENT
CLANK
I HAVE LOST EVERYTHING.
ALL I HAVE LEFT IS THIS NINJA BODY.

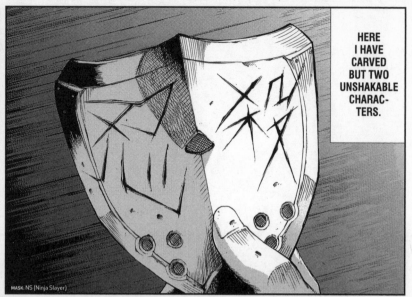

HERE I HAVE CARVED BUT TWO UNSHAKABLE CHARACTERS.

MASK: NS (Ninja Slayer)

SLAY...

...NINJA.

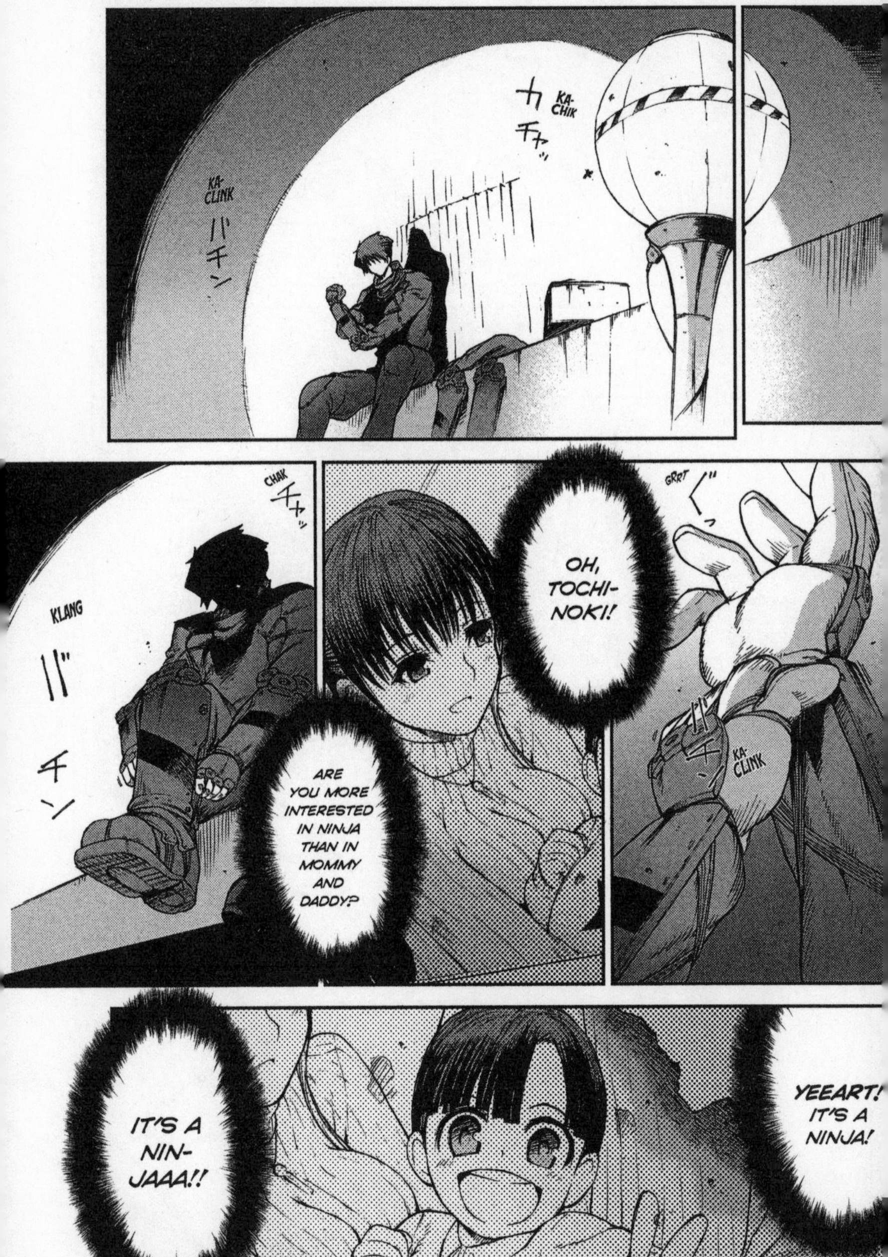
KA-CHIK
カチャッ
KA-CLINK
バチン
GRRT
ぐっ
KA-CLINK
OH, TOCHI-NOKI!
ARE YOU MORE INTERESTED IN NINJA THAN IN MOMMY AND DADDY?
CHAK
チャッ
KLANG
バチン
YEEART! IT'S A NINJA!
IT'S A NIN-JAAA!!

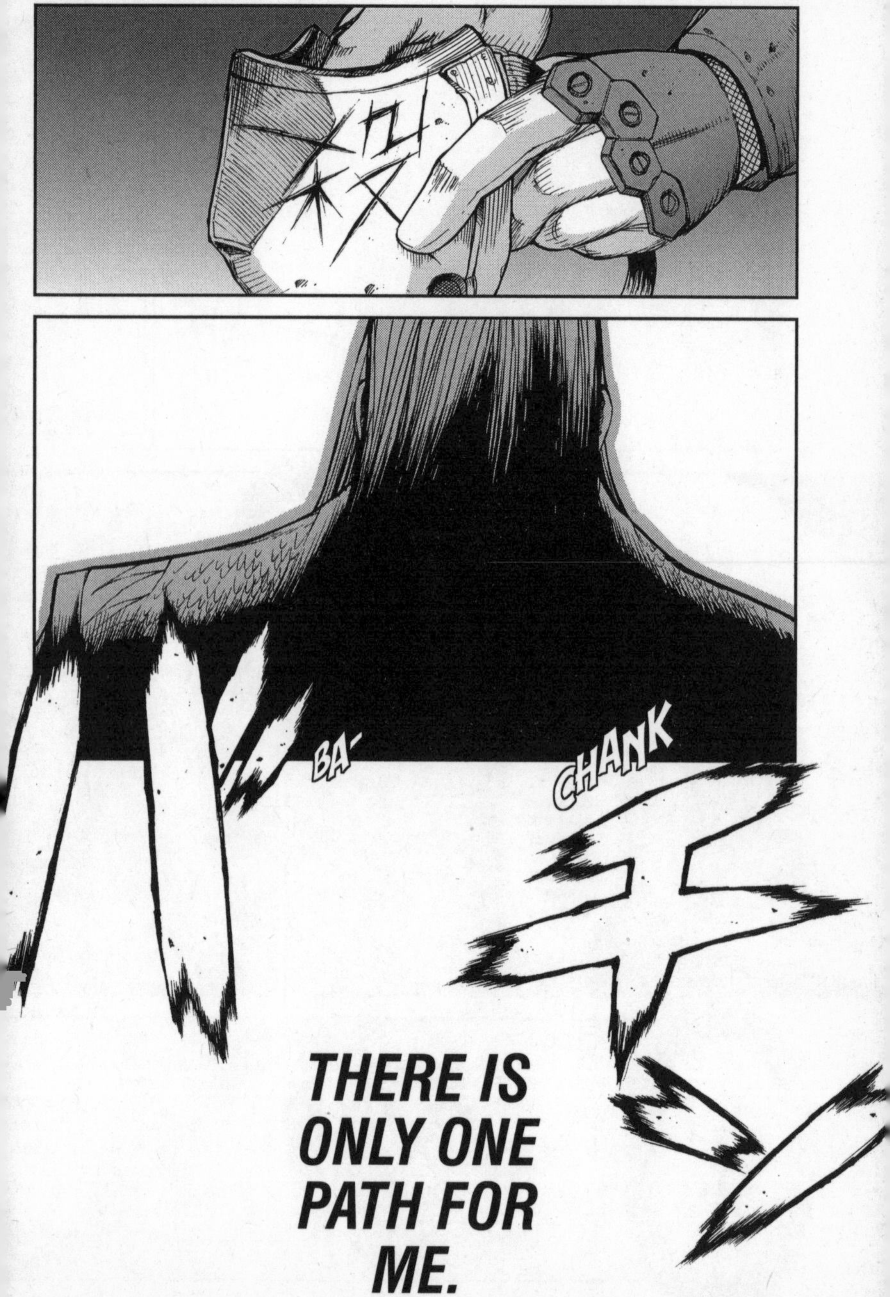
BA-
CHANK
THERE IS ONLY ONE PATH FOR ME.

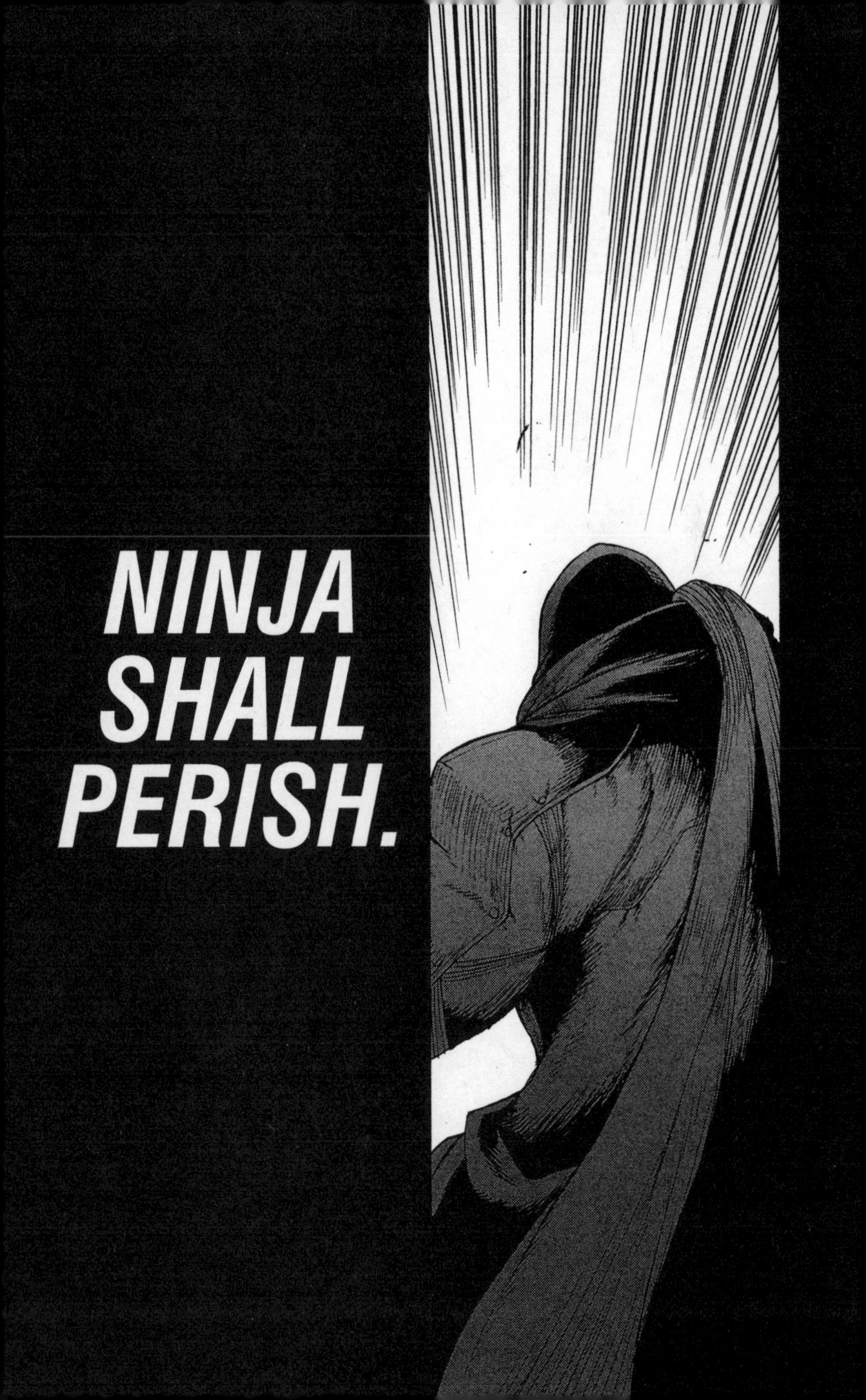
NINJA SHALL PERISH.

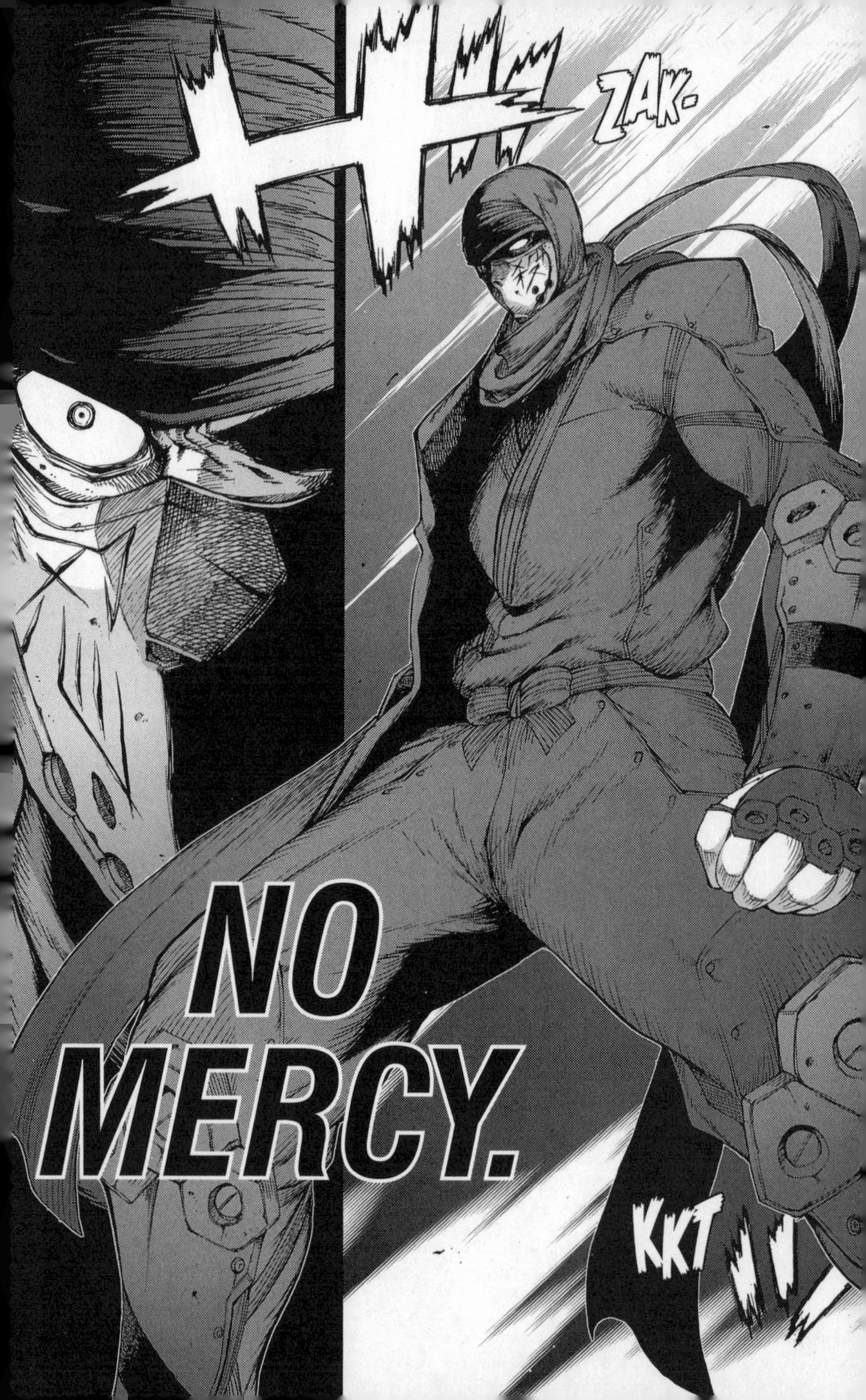
ZAK-
NO MERCY.
KKT

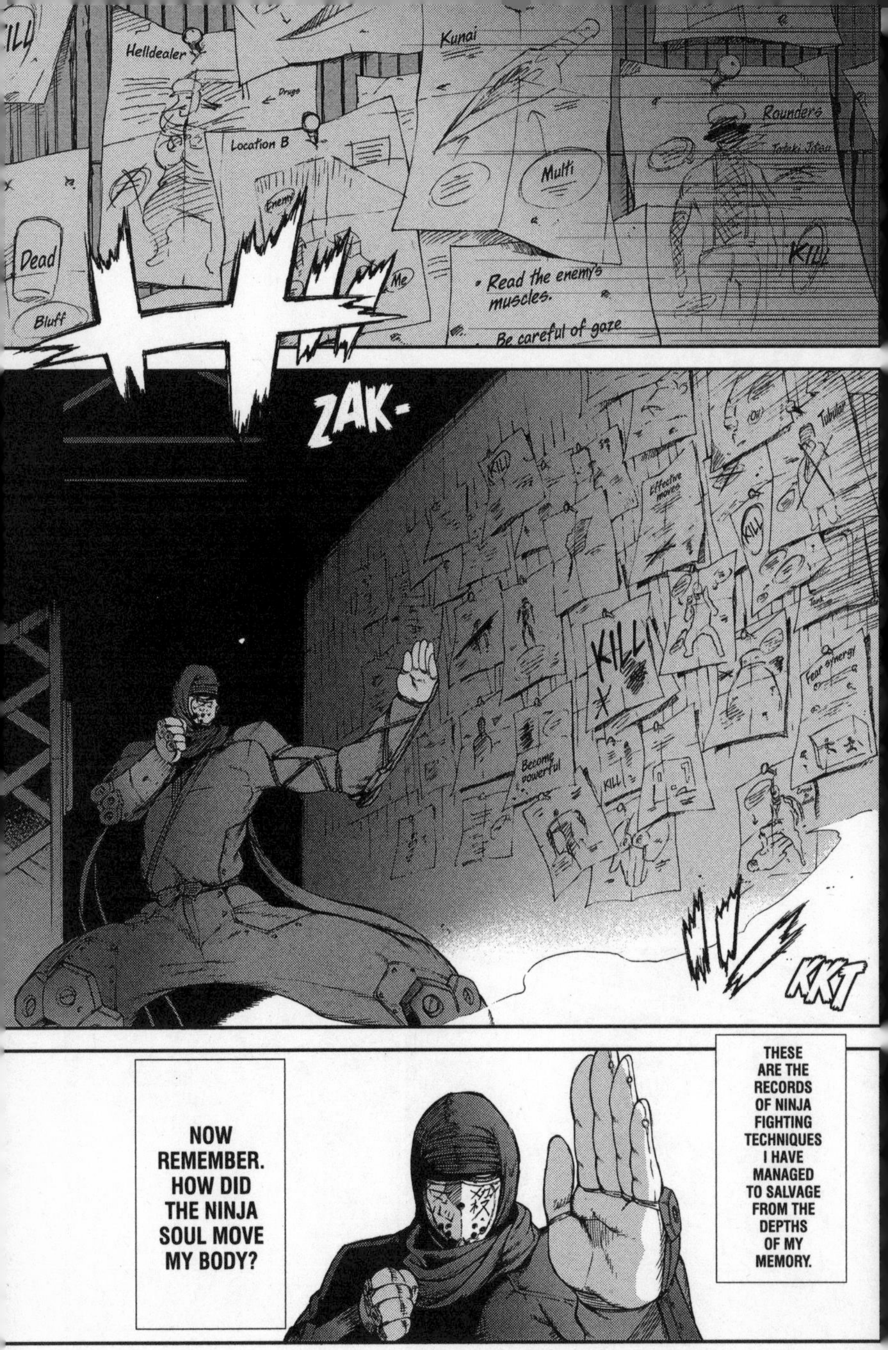

Rounders
Kunai
Helldealer
KILL
Drugs
Multi
Location B
Enemy
Dead
Read the enemy's muscles.
Be careful of gaze
Me
Bluff
ZAK-
Tubular
Effective moves
KILL
Fear synergy
Become powerful
KILL
KKT
THESE ARE THE RECORDS OF NINJA FIGHTING TECHNIQUES I HAVE MANAGED TO SALVAGE FROM THE DEPTHS OF MY MEMORY.
NOW REMEMBER. HOW DID THE NINJA SOUL MOVE MY BODY?

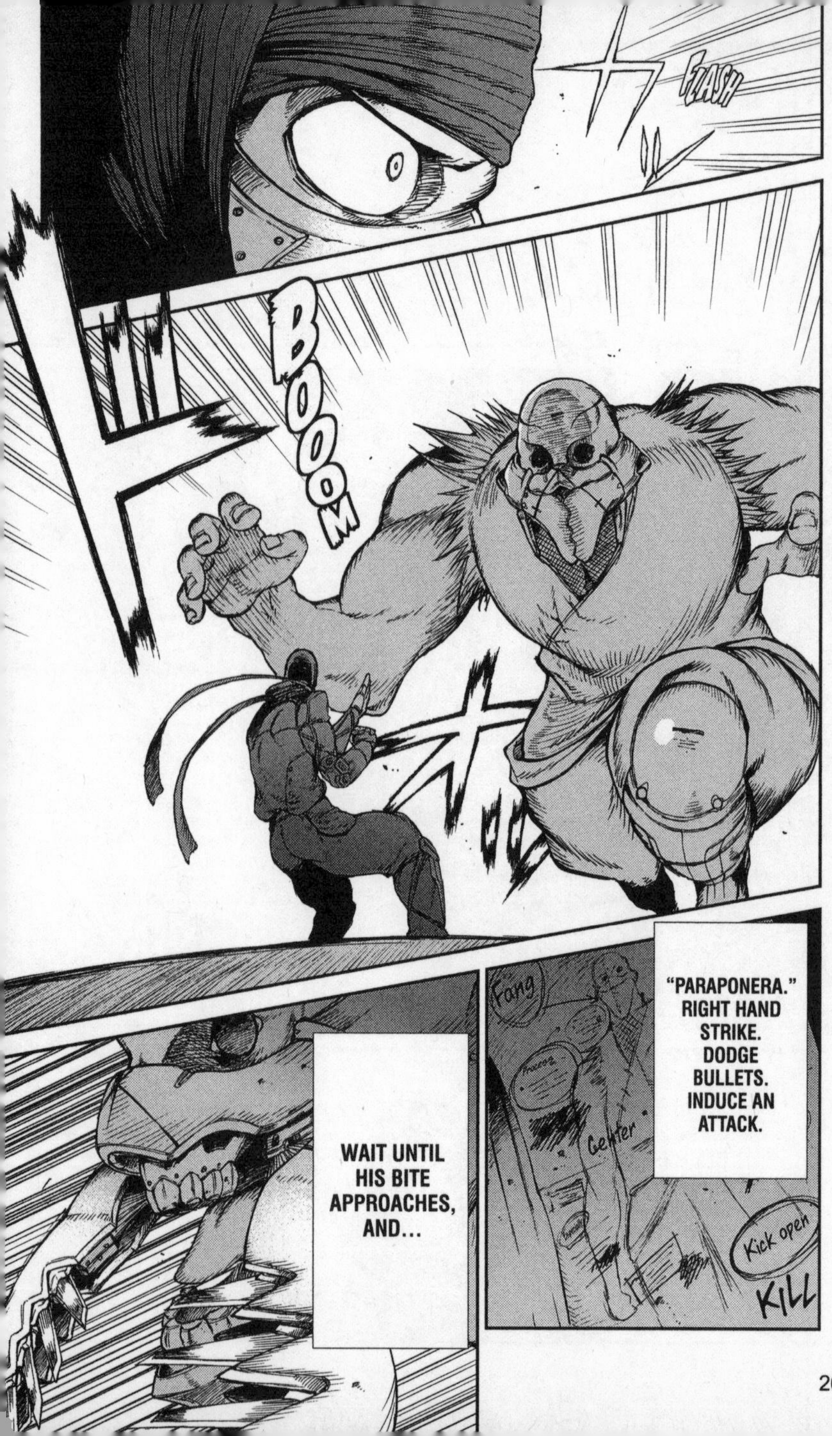

FLASH
BOOOOOM
"PARAPONERA." RIGHT HAND STRIKE. DODGE BULLETS. INDUCE AN ATTACK.
Fang
Kick open
KILL
WAIT UNTIL HIS BITE APPROACHES, AND...

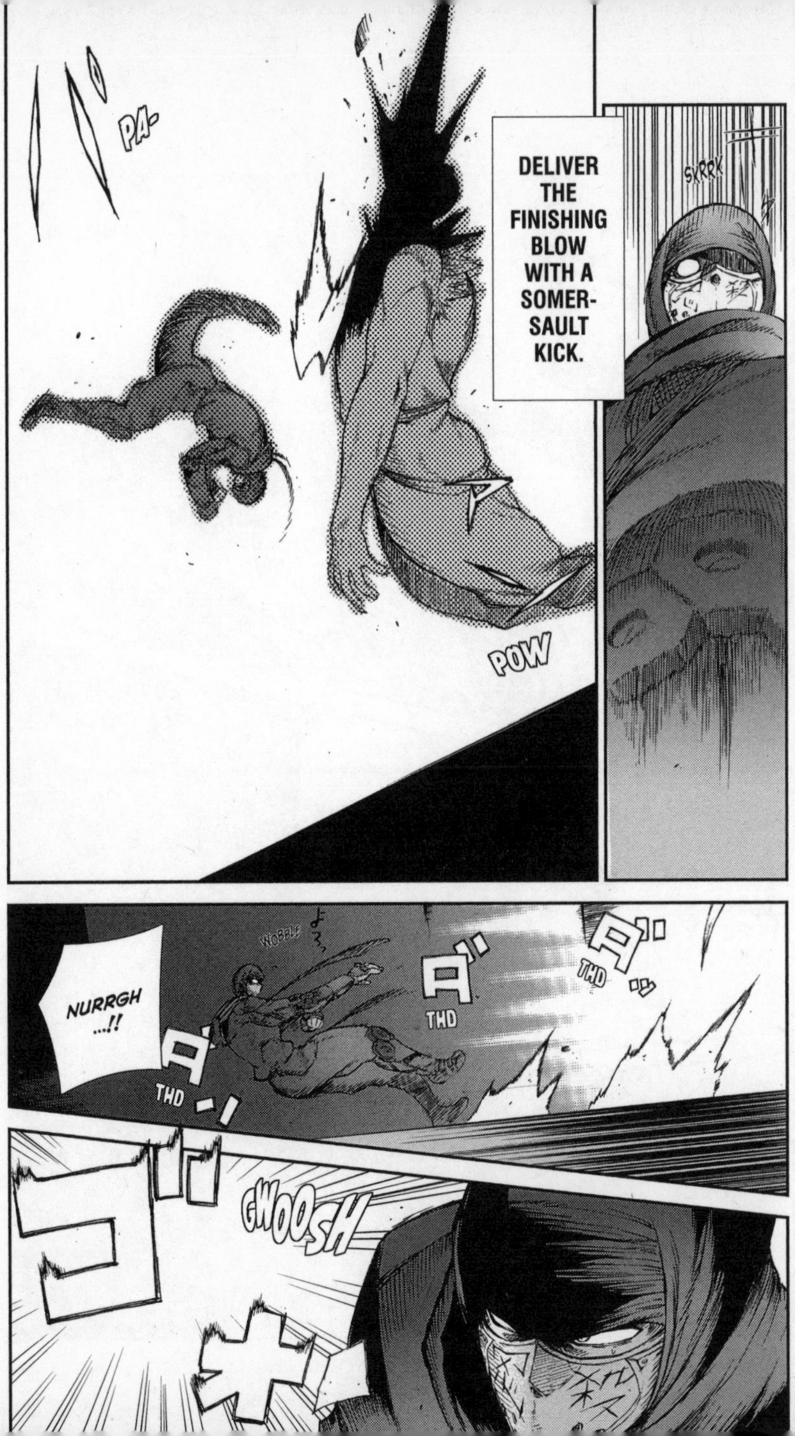
SKRRK
DELIVER THE FINISHING BLOW WITH A SOMER-SAULT KICK.
PA-
POW
THD
THD
WOBBLE
NURRGH ...!!
THD
GWOOSH

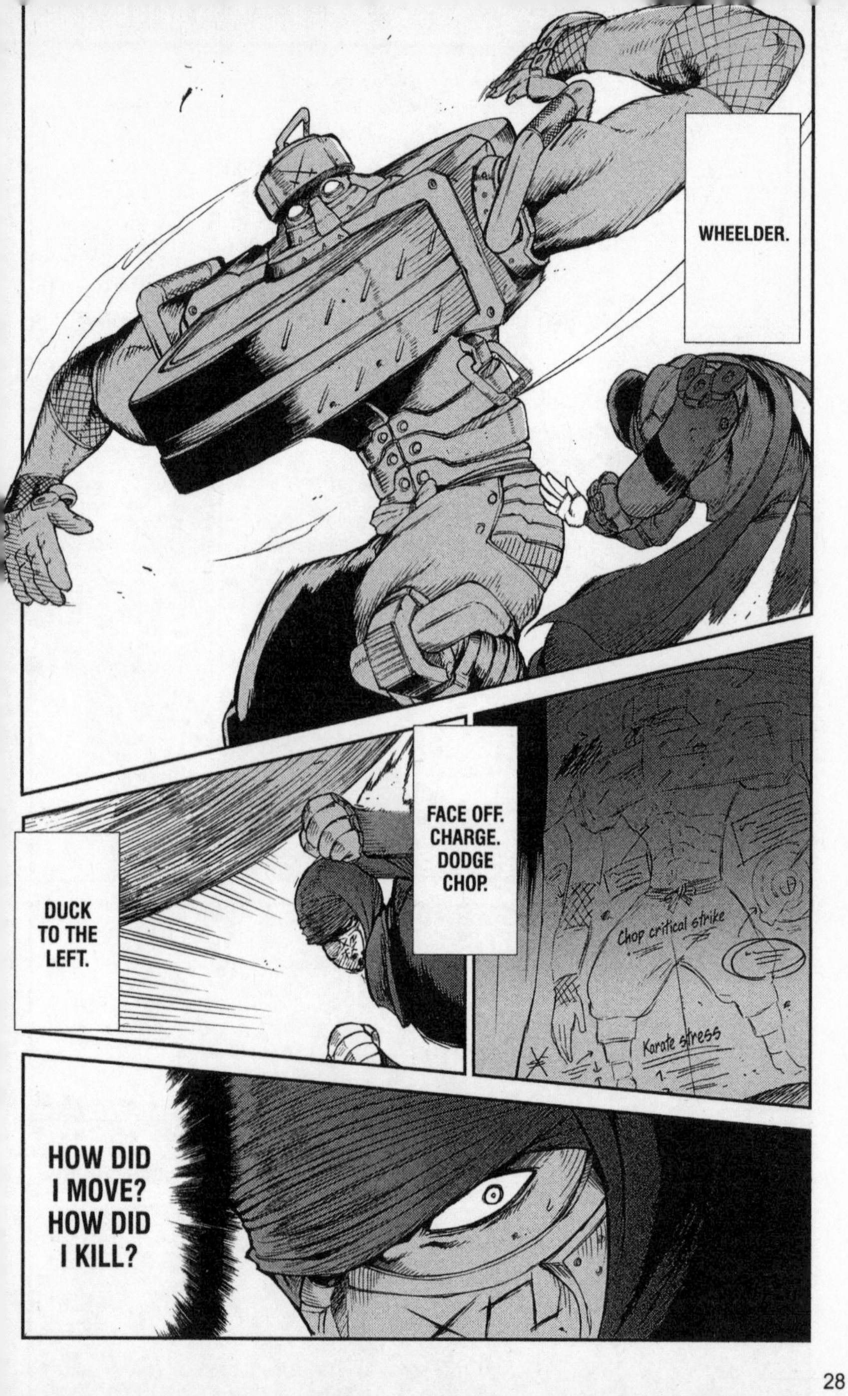
WHEELDER.
FACE OFF. CHARGE. DODGE CHOP.
Chop critical strike
Karate stress
DUCK TO THE LEFT.
HOW DID I MOVE? HOW DID I KILL?

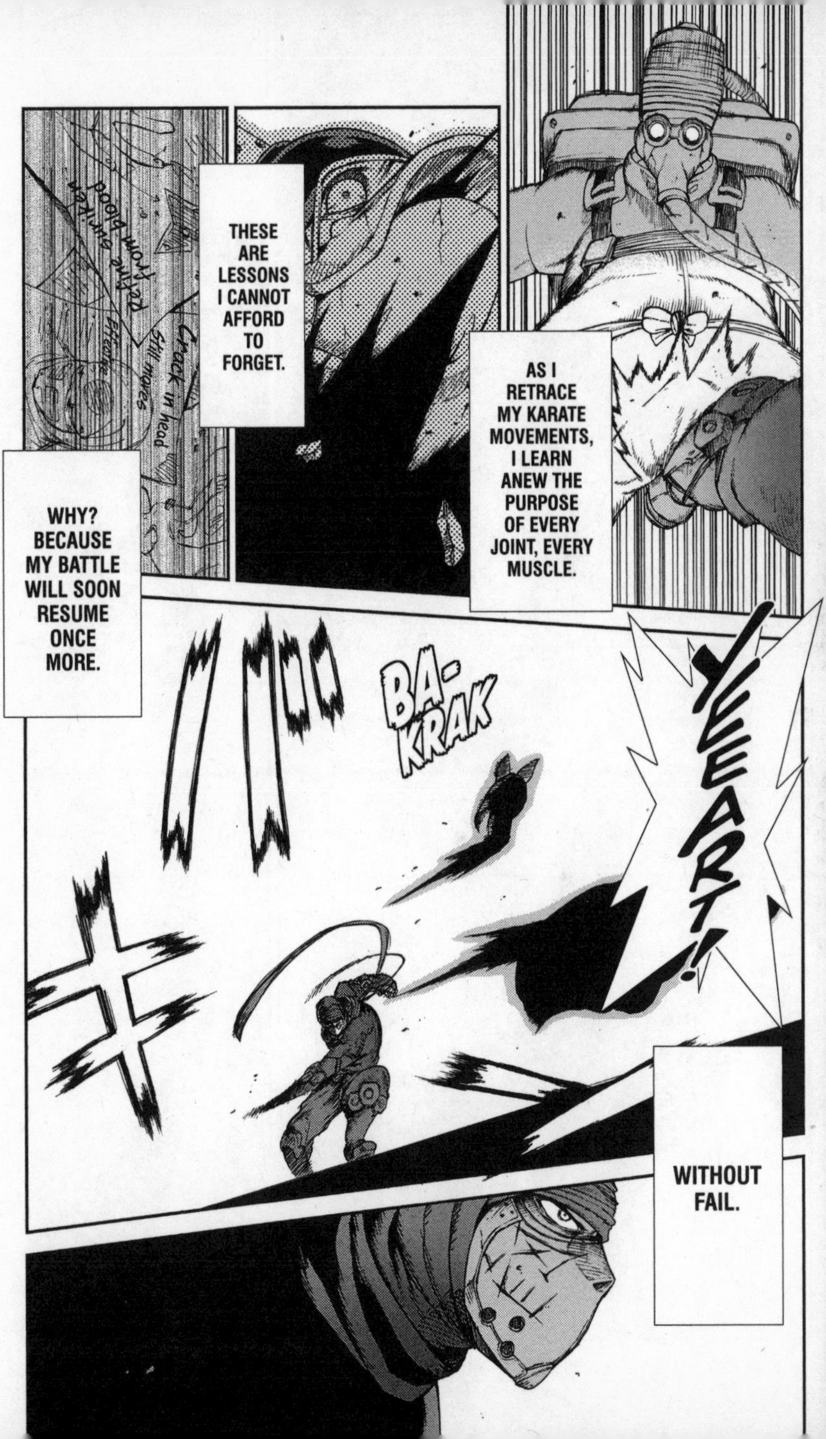
AS I RETRACE MY KARATE MOVEMENTS, I LEARN ANEW THE PURPOSE OF EVERY JOINT, EVERY MUSCLE.
THESE ARE LESSONS I CANNOT AFFORD TO FORGET.
Crack in head
Still moves
WHY? BECAUSE MY BATTLE WILL SOON RESUME ONCE MORE.
YEEART!!
BA-KRAK
WITHOUT FAIL.

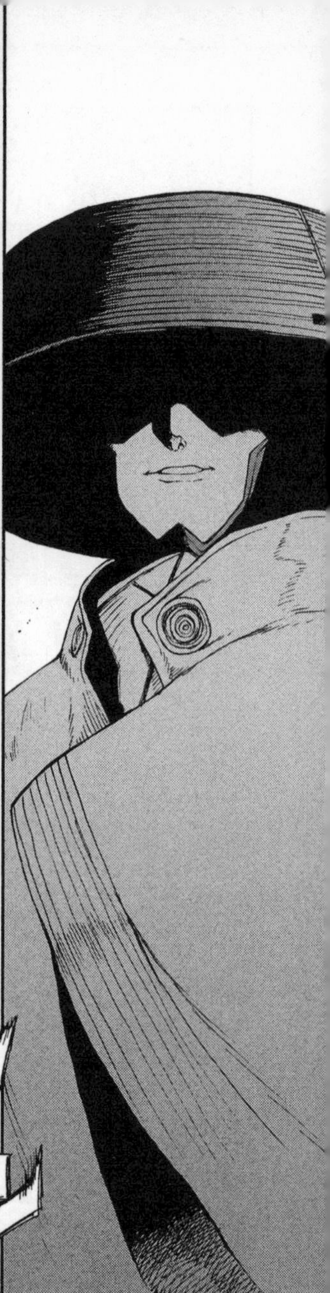

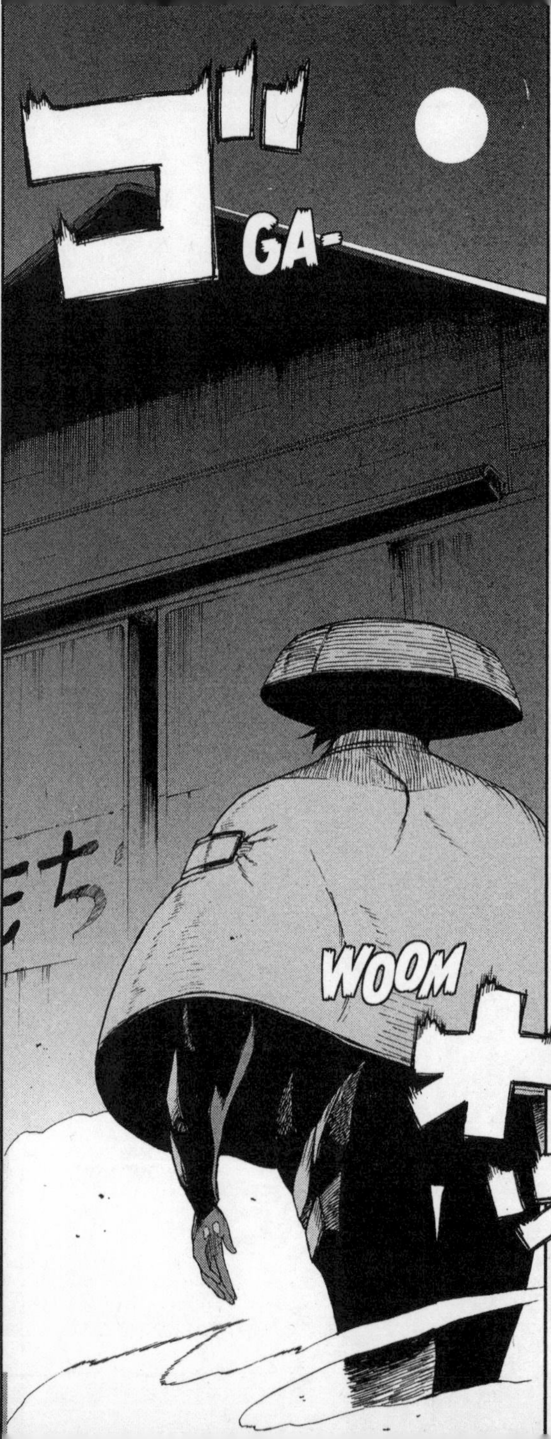
ゴー
GA-
WOOM

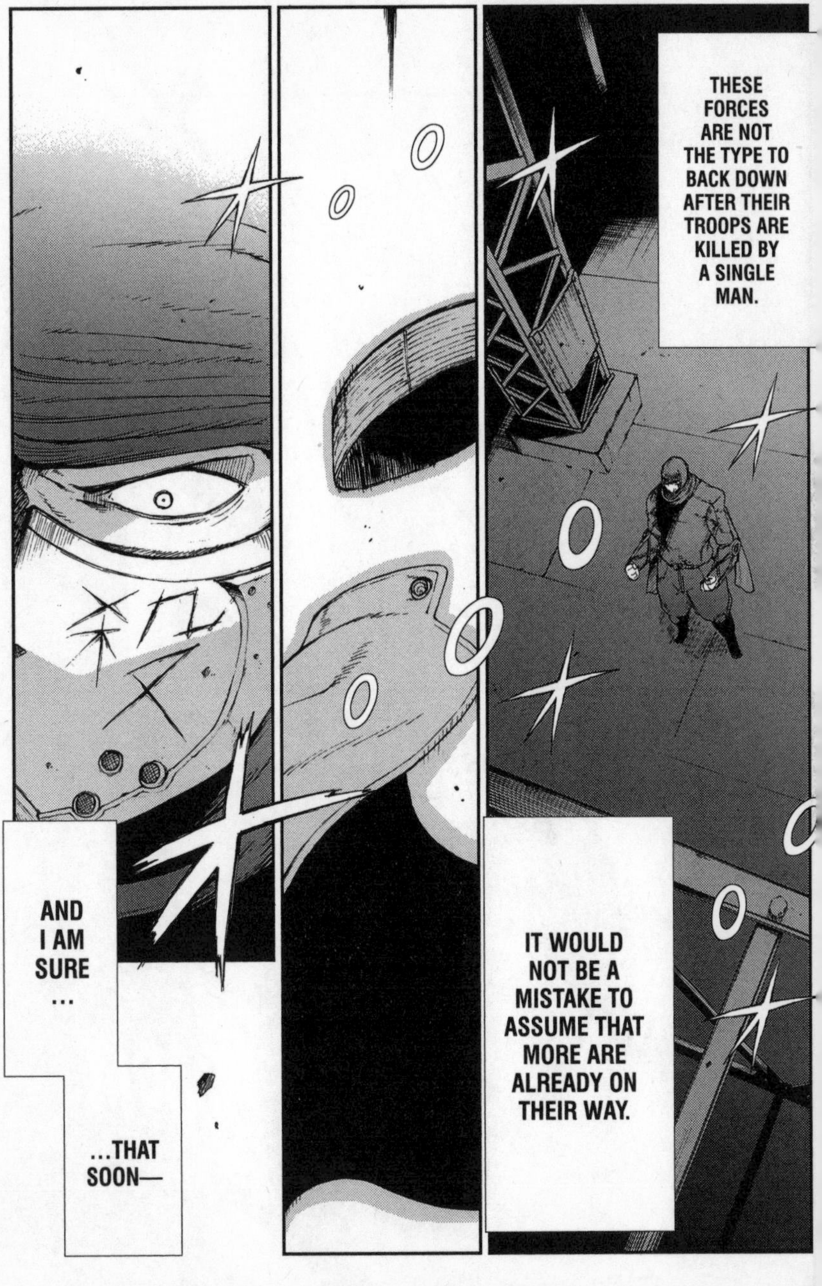
THESE FORCES ARE NOT THE TYPE TO BACK DOWN AFTER THEIR TROOPS ARE KILLED BY A SINGLE MAN.
IT WOULD NOT BE A MISTAKE TO ASSUME THAT MORE ARE ALREADY ON THEIR WAY.
AND I AM SURE …
…THAT SOON—

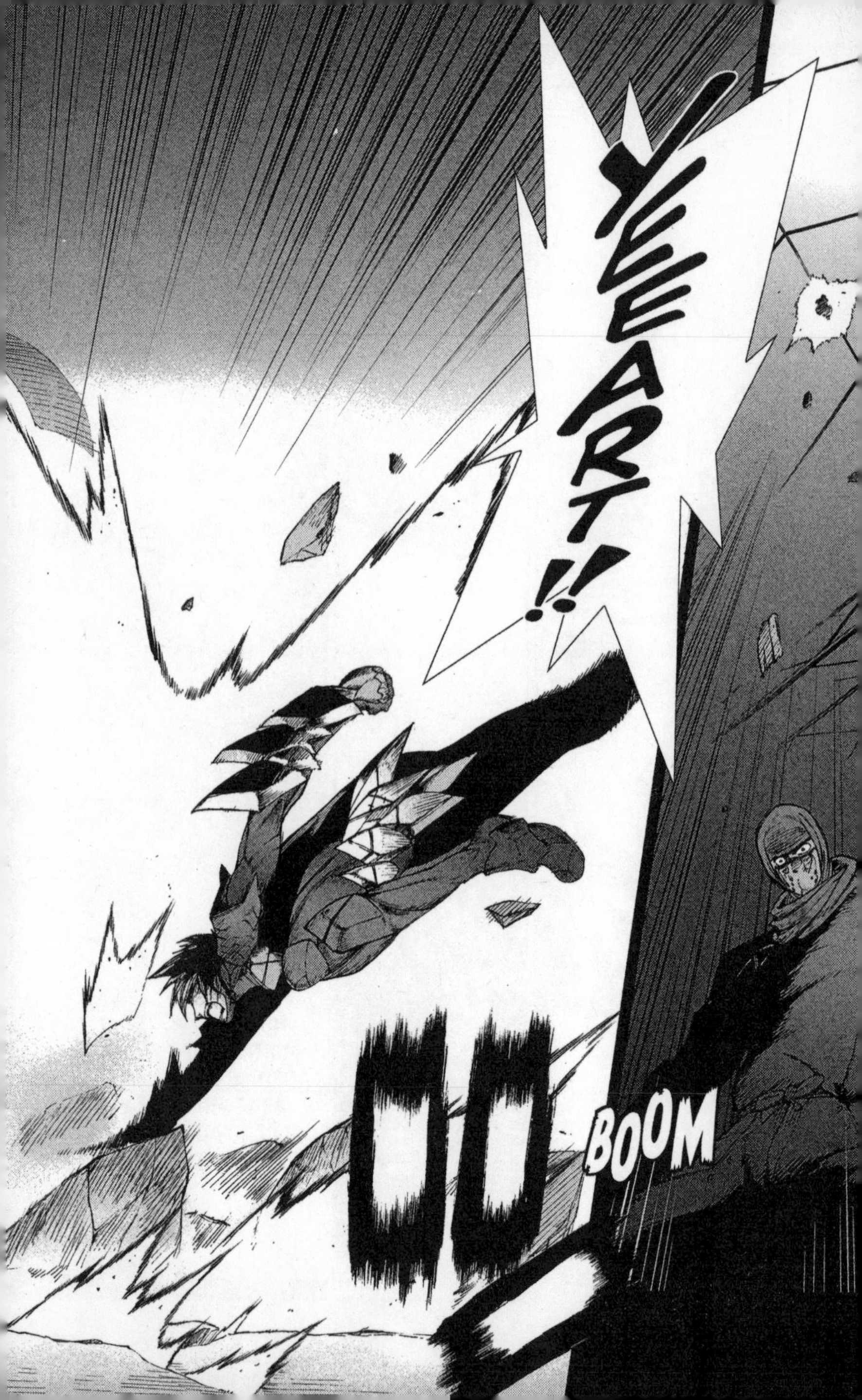
YEEART!!
BOOM

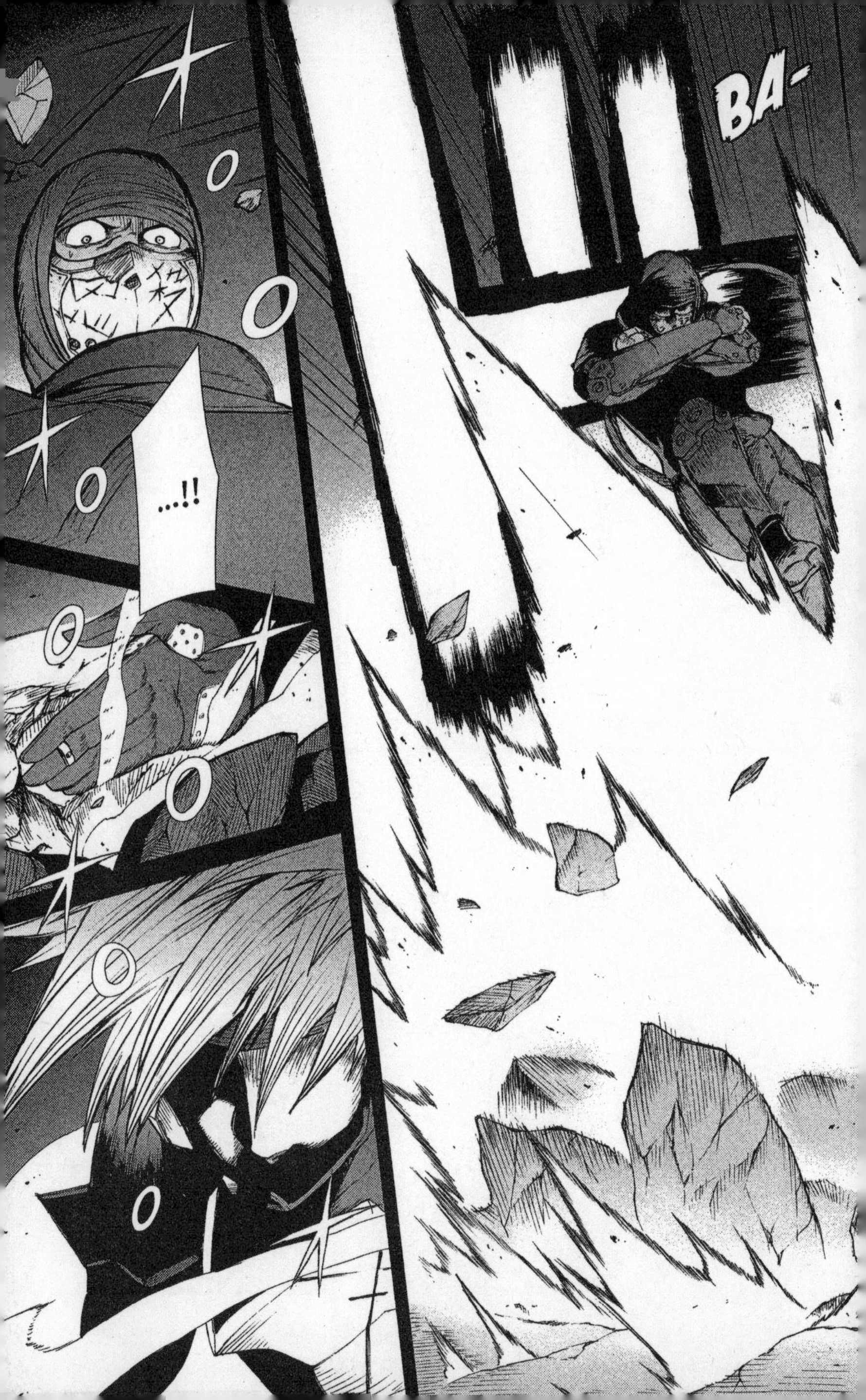
BA-
...!!

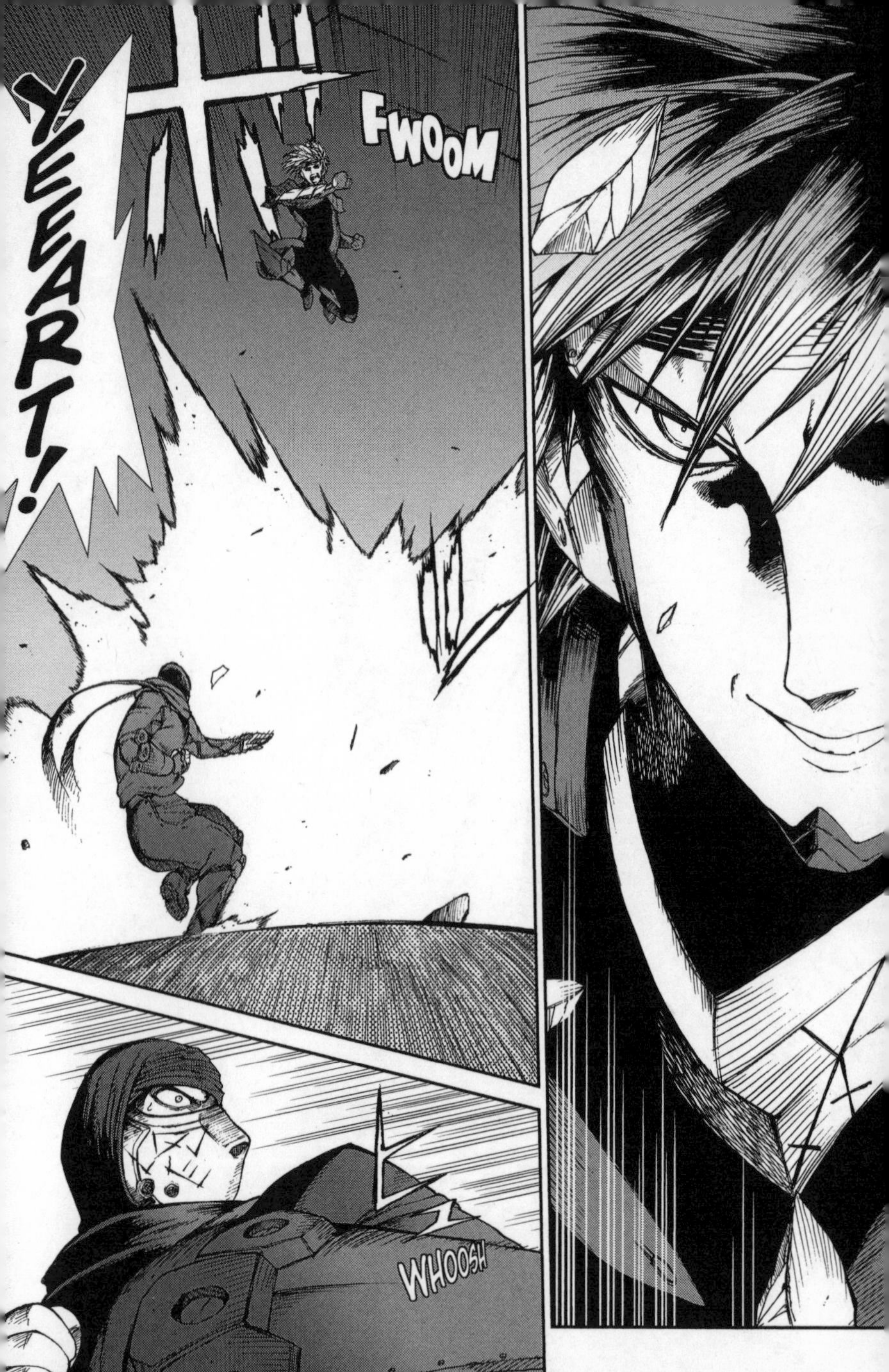
FWOOM
YEEART!!
WHOOSH

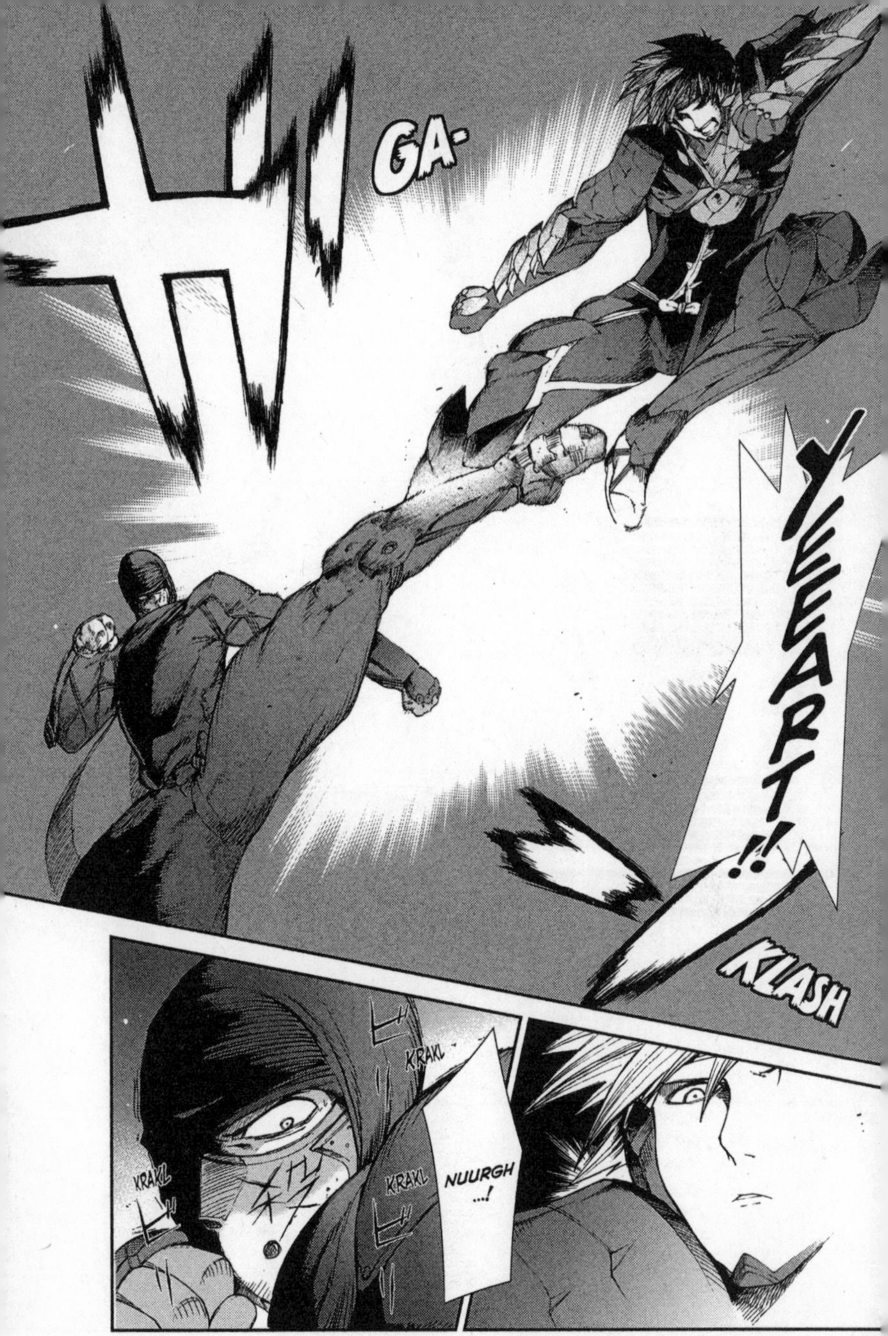
GA-
YEEART!!
KLASH
KRAKL
NUURGH ...!
KRAKL
KRAKL

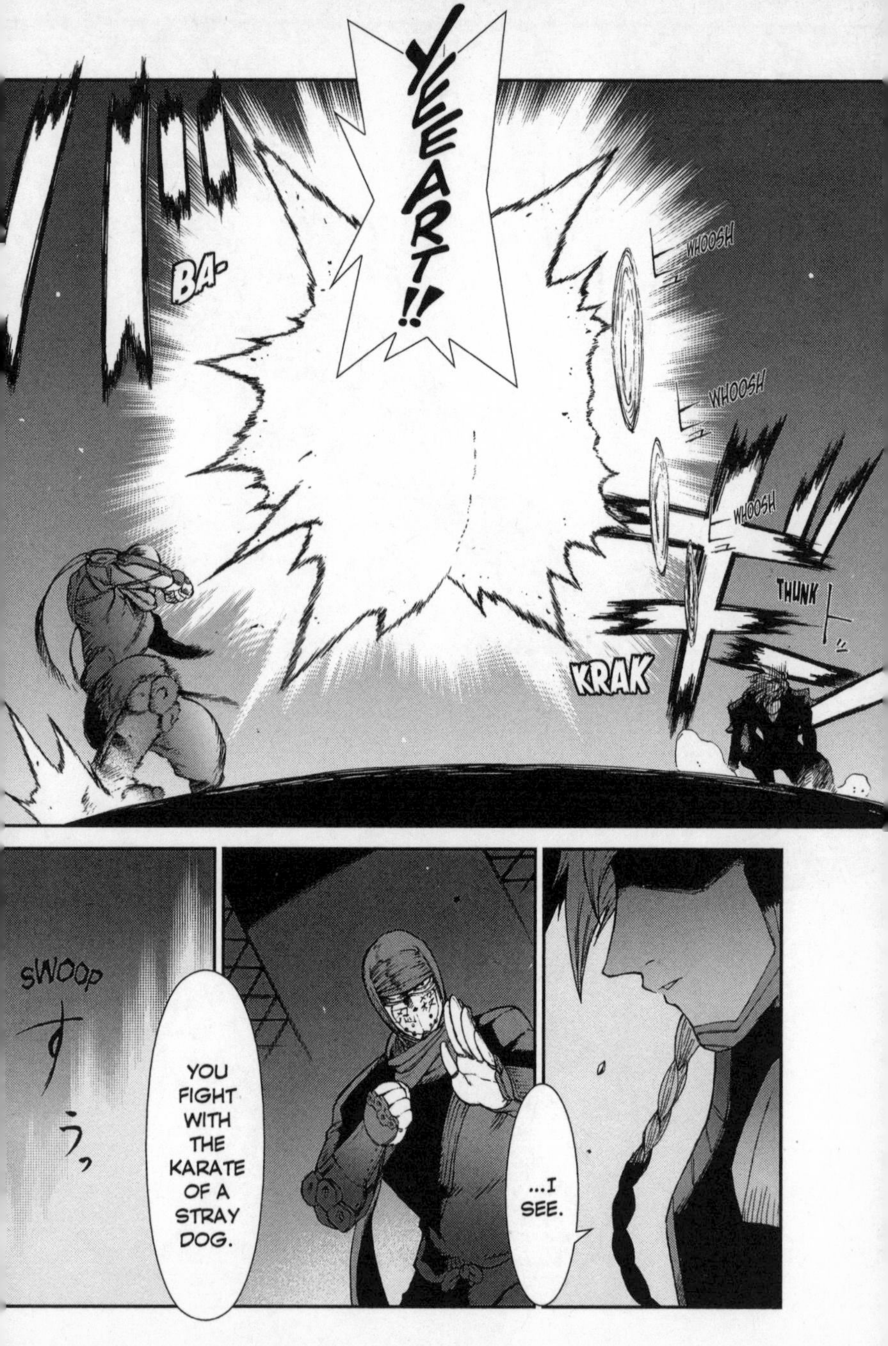

YEEART!!
WHOOSH
WHOOSH
WHOOSH
THUNK
KRAK
BA-
...I SEE.
YOU FIGHT WITH THE KARATE OF A STRAY DOG.
SWOOP

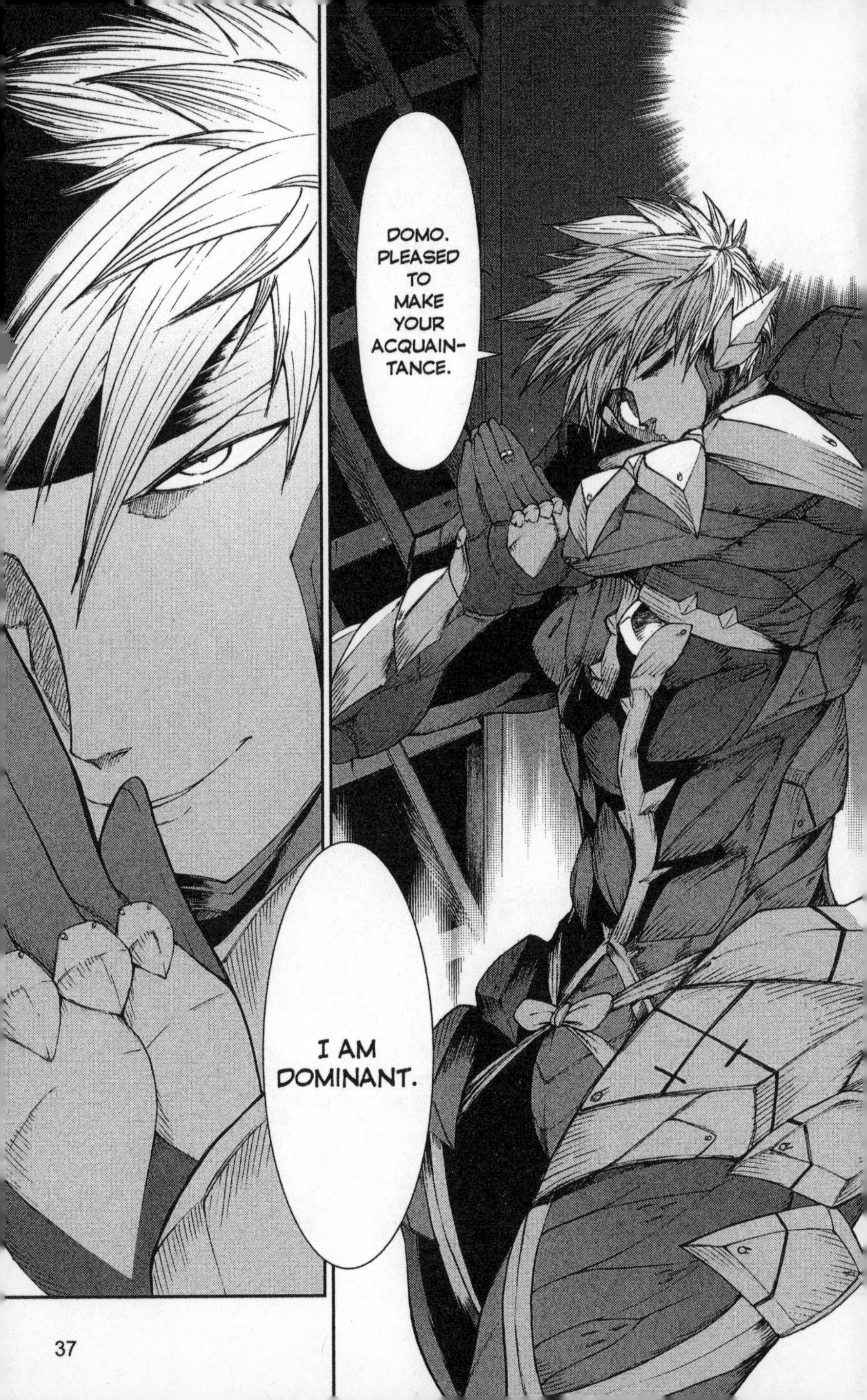
DOMO. PLEASED TO MAKE YOUR ACQUAIN-TANCE.
I AM DOMINANT.

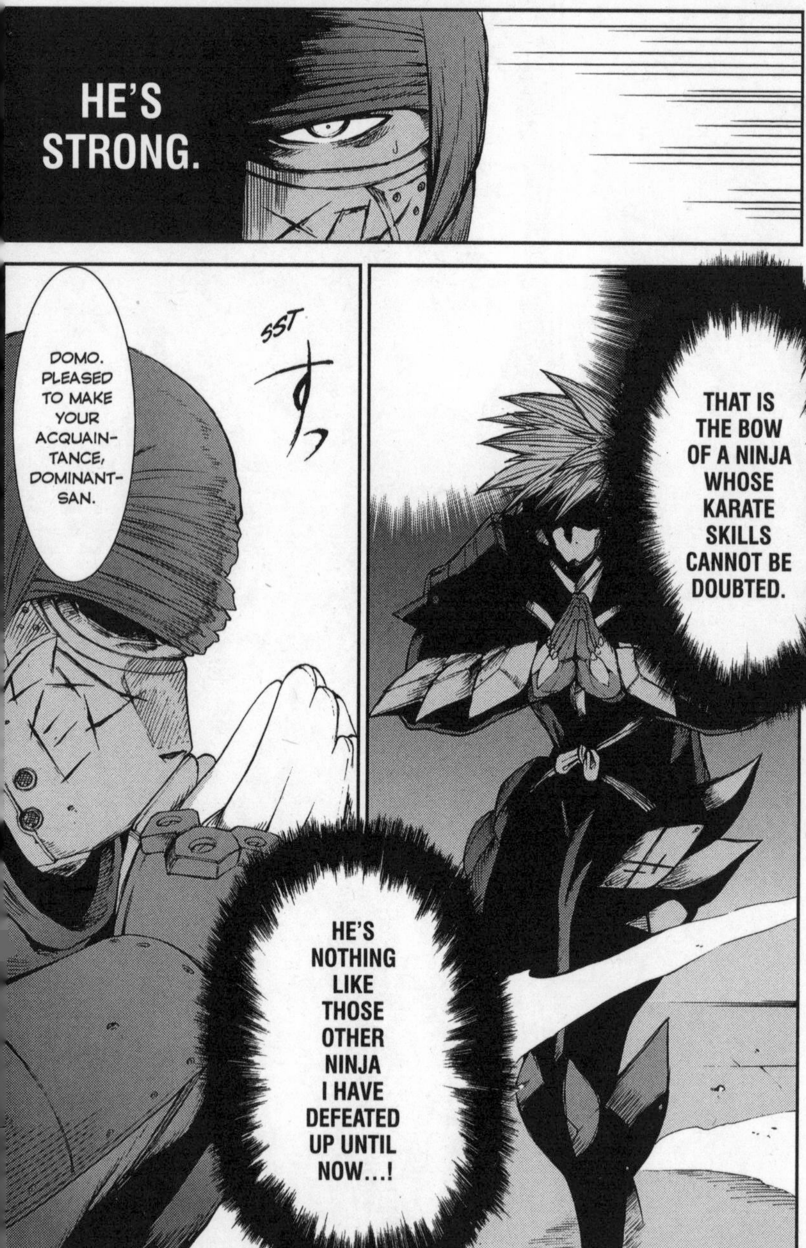
HE'S STRONG.
THAT IS THE BOW OF A NINJA WHOSE KARATE SKILLS CANNOT BE DOUBTED.
SST
DOMO. PLEASED TO MAKE YOUR ACQUAIN-TANCE, DOMINANT-SAN.
HE'S NOTHING LIKE THOSE OTHER NINJA I HAVE DEFEATED UP UNTIL NOW...!

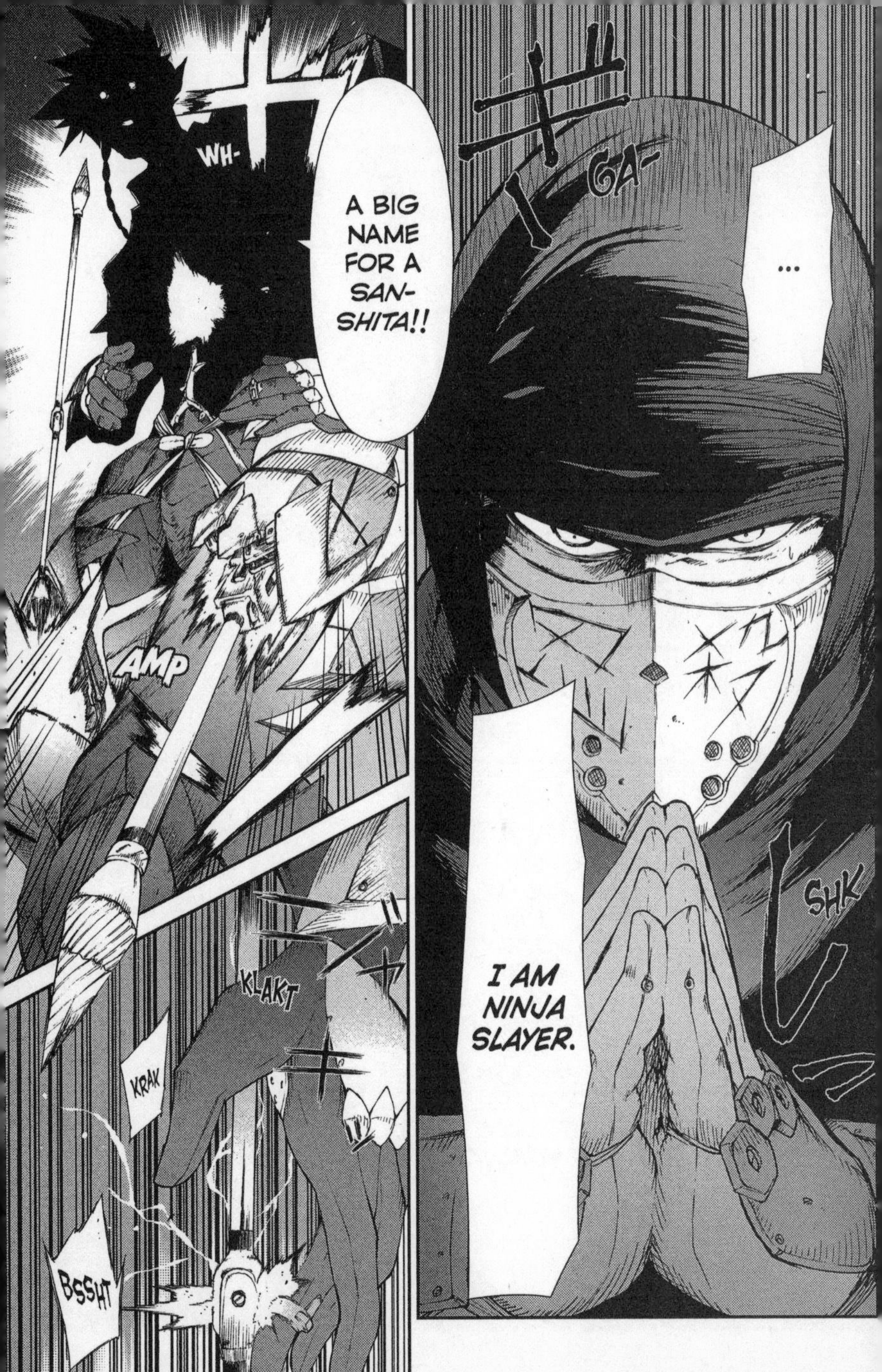
...
GA-
SHK
I AM NINJA SLAYER.
A BIG NAME FOR A SAN-SHITA!!
WH-
AMP
KLAKT
KRAK
BSSHT

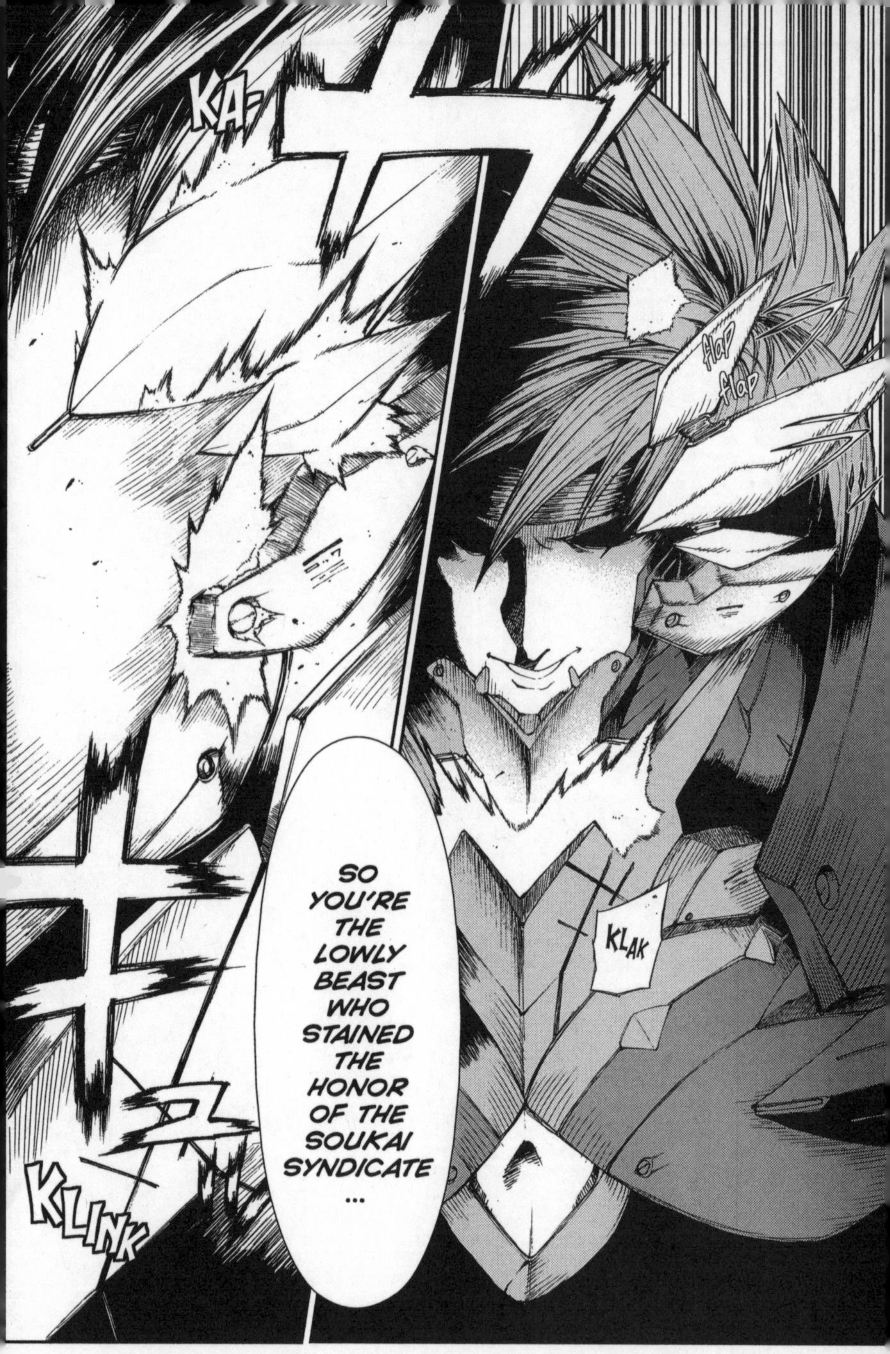
flap
flap
KA-
KLAK
SO YOU'RE THE LOWLY BEAST WHO STAINED THE HONOR OF THE SOUKAI SYNDICATE ...
KLINK

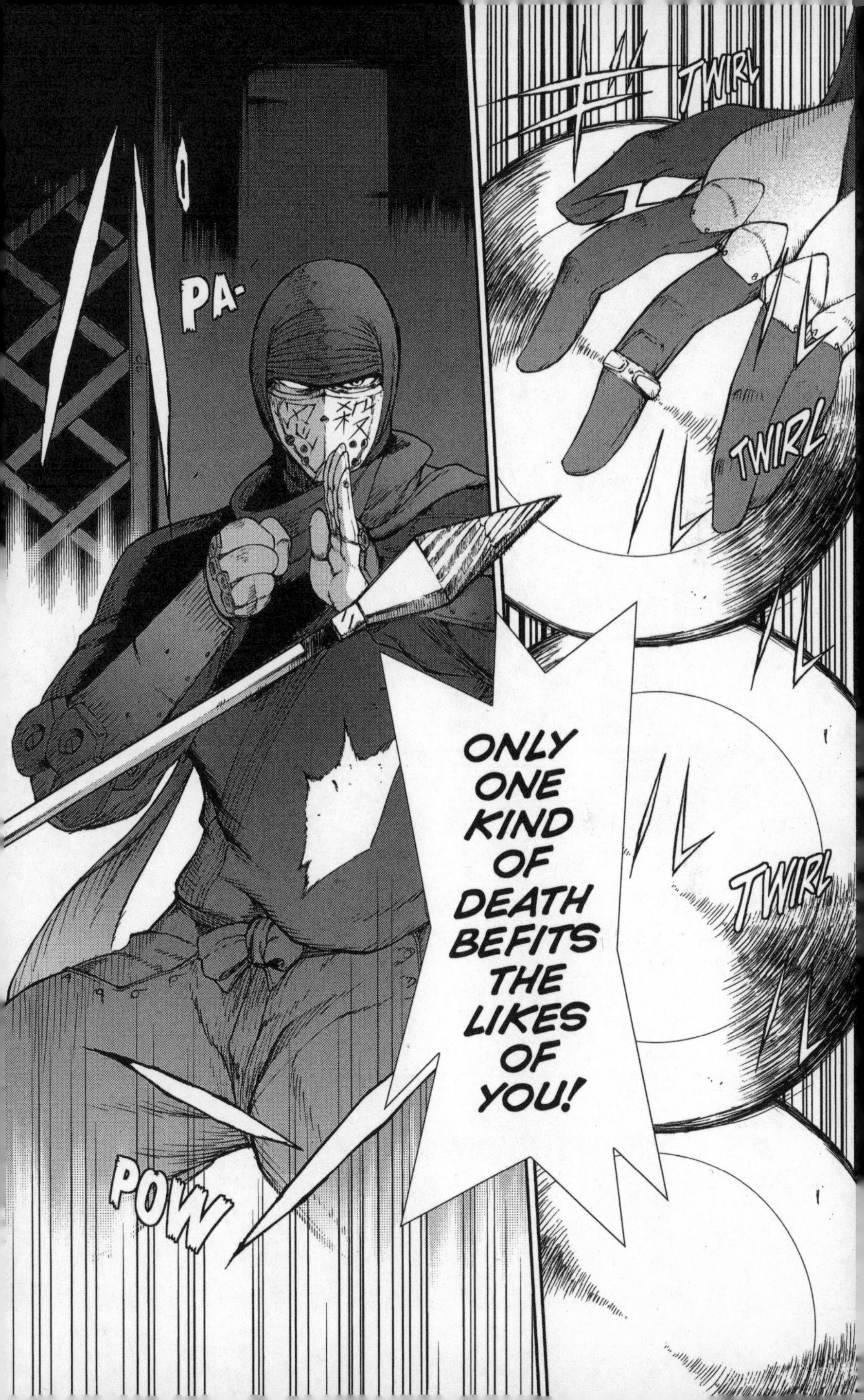
TWIRL
TWIRL
TWIRL
ONLY ONE KIND OF DEATH BEFITS THE LIKES OF YOU!
PA-
POW

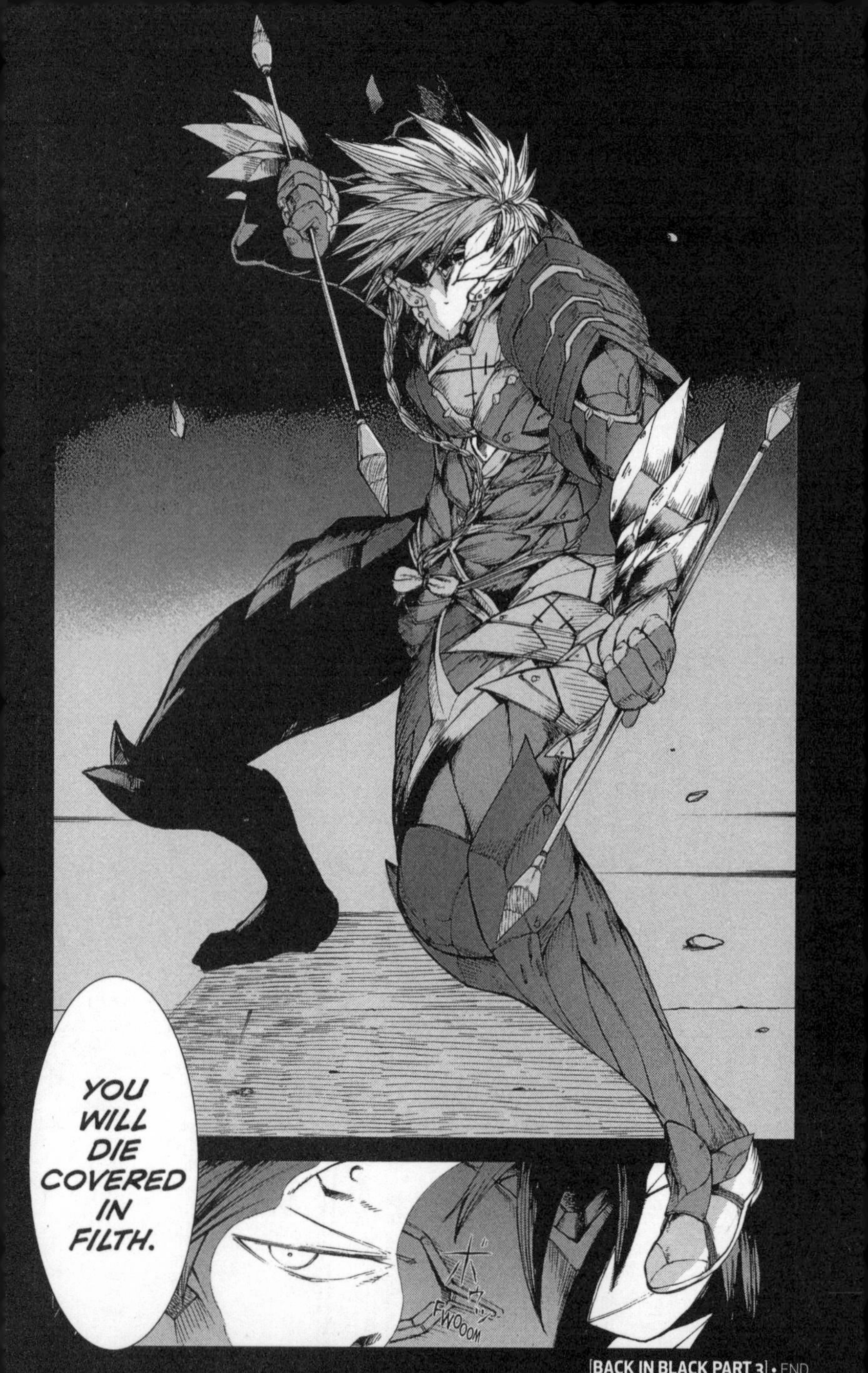
YOU WILL DIE COVERED IN FILTH.
FWOOOM

[BACK IN BLACK PART 3] • END

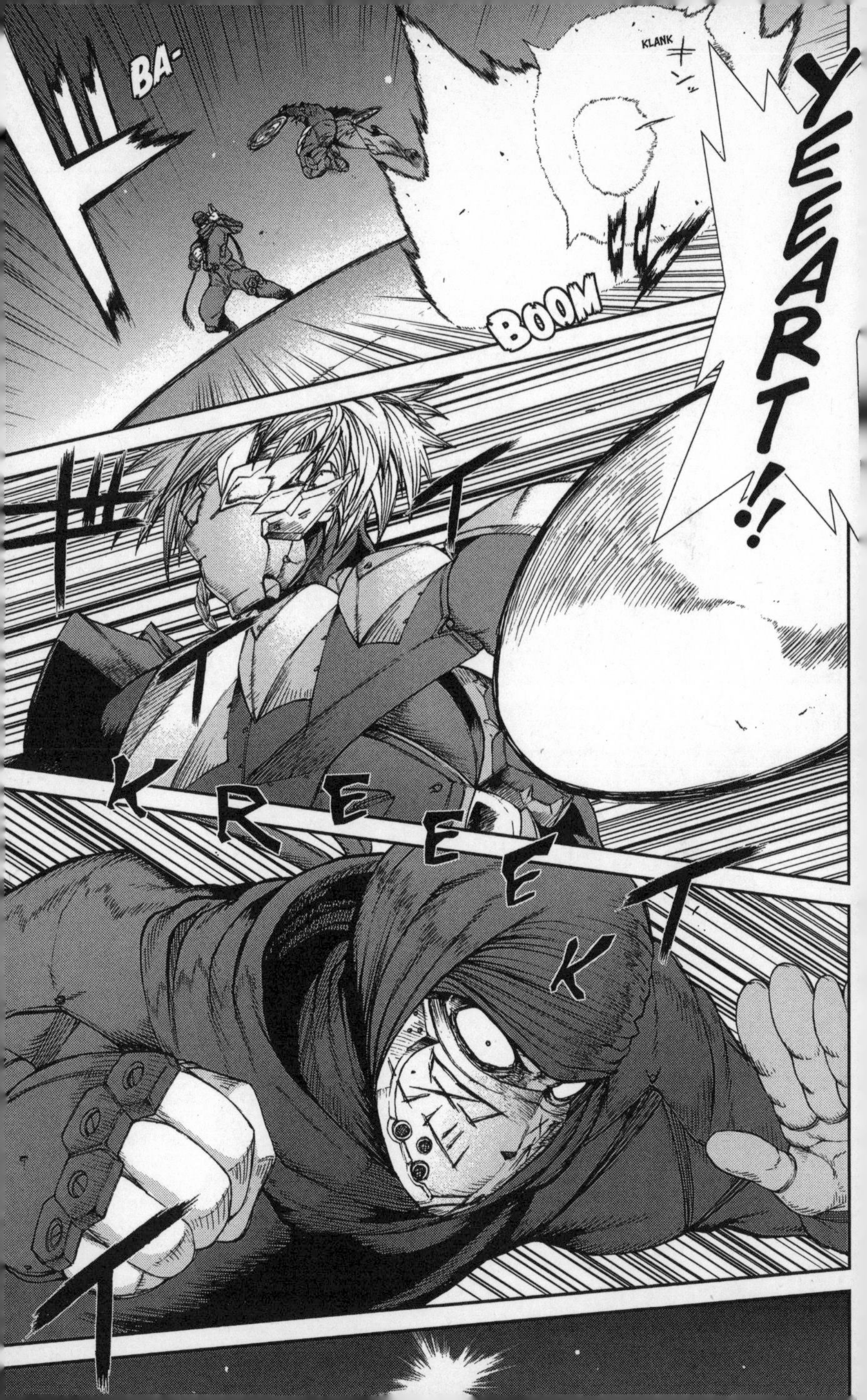
YEEARRT!!
KLANK
BOOM
BA-
KREEEKT

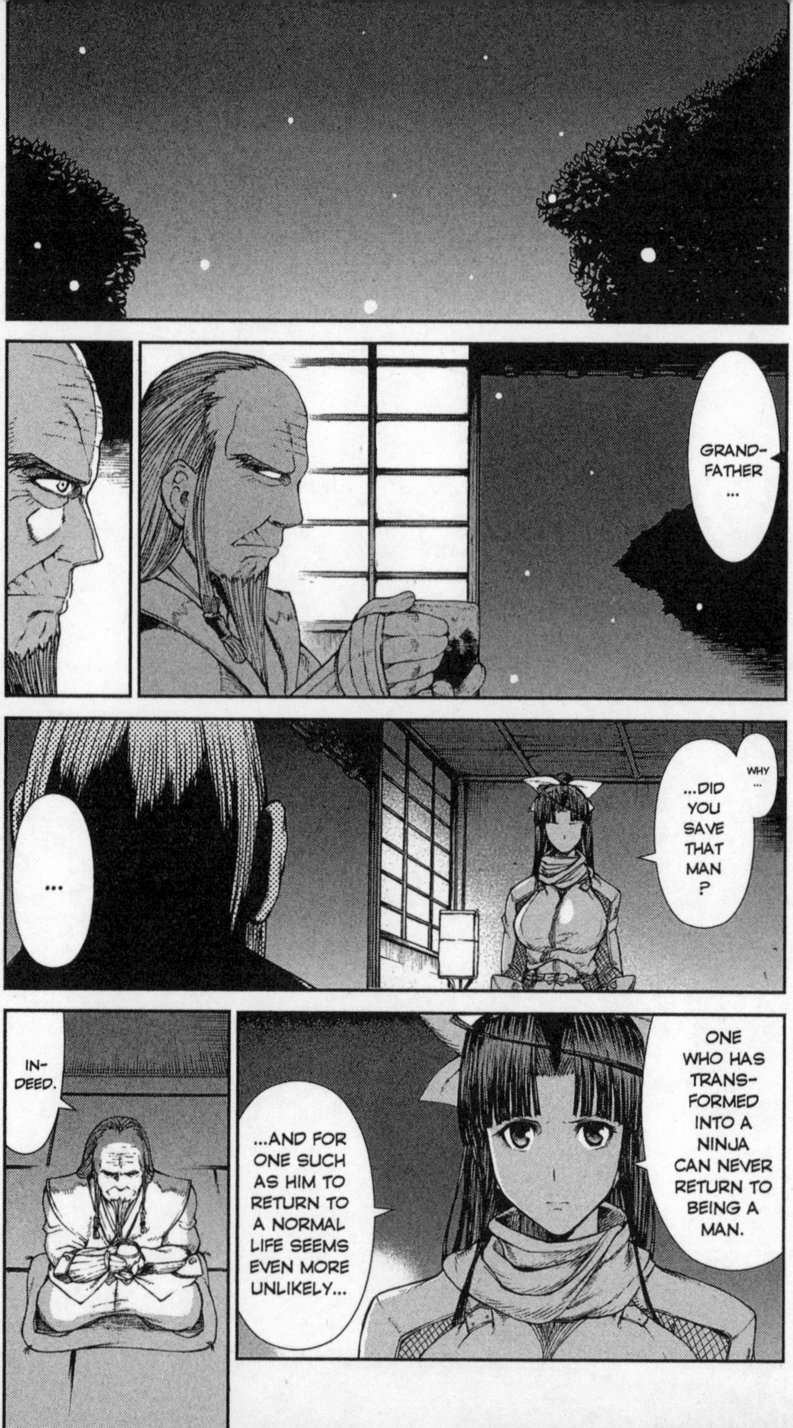
GRAND-FATHER ...
WHY ...
...DID YOU SAVE THAT MAN ?
...
ONE WHO HAS TRANS-FORMED INTO A NINJA CAN NEVER RETURN TO BEING A MAN.
...AND FOR ONE SUCH AS HIM TO RETURN TO A NORMAL LIFE SEEMS EVEN MORE UNLIKELY...
IN-DEED.

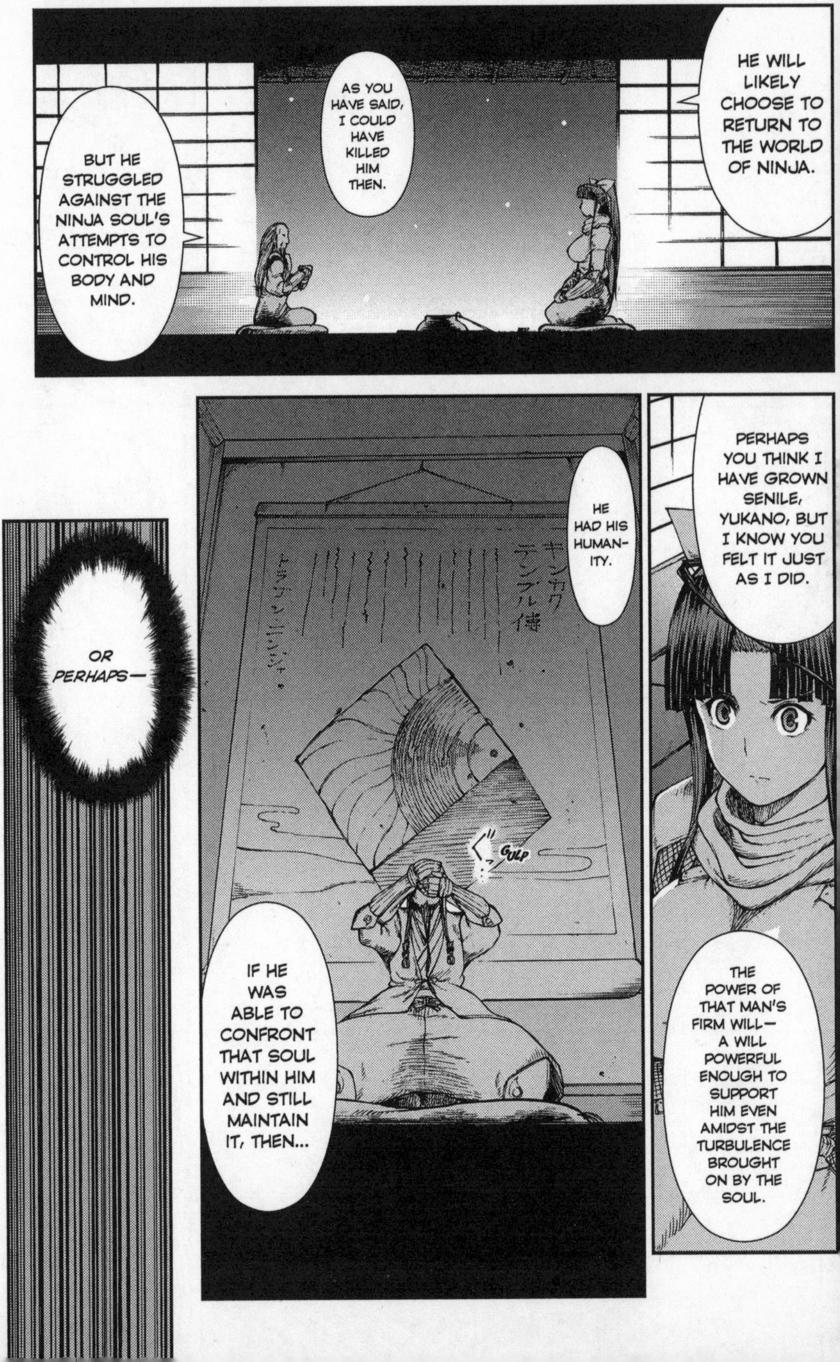
HE WILL LIKELY CHOOSE TO RETURN TO THE WORLD OF NINJA.
AS YOU HAVE SAID, I COULD HAVE KILLED HIM THEN.
BUT HE STRUGGLED AGAINST THE NINJA SOUL'S ATTEMPTS TO CONTROL HIS BODY AND MIND.
PERHAPS YOU THINK I HAVE GROWN SENILE, YUKANO, BUT I KNOW YOU FELT IT JUST AS I DID.
THE POWER OF THAT MAN'S FIRM WILL— A WILL POWERFUL ENOUGH TO SUPPORT HIM EVEN AMIDST THE TURBULENCE BROUGHT ON BY THE SOUL.
HE HAD HIS HUMAN-ITY.
GULP
IF HE WAS ABLE TO CONFRONT THAT SOUL WITHIN HIM AND STILL MAINTAIN IT, THEN...
OR PERHAPS—

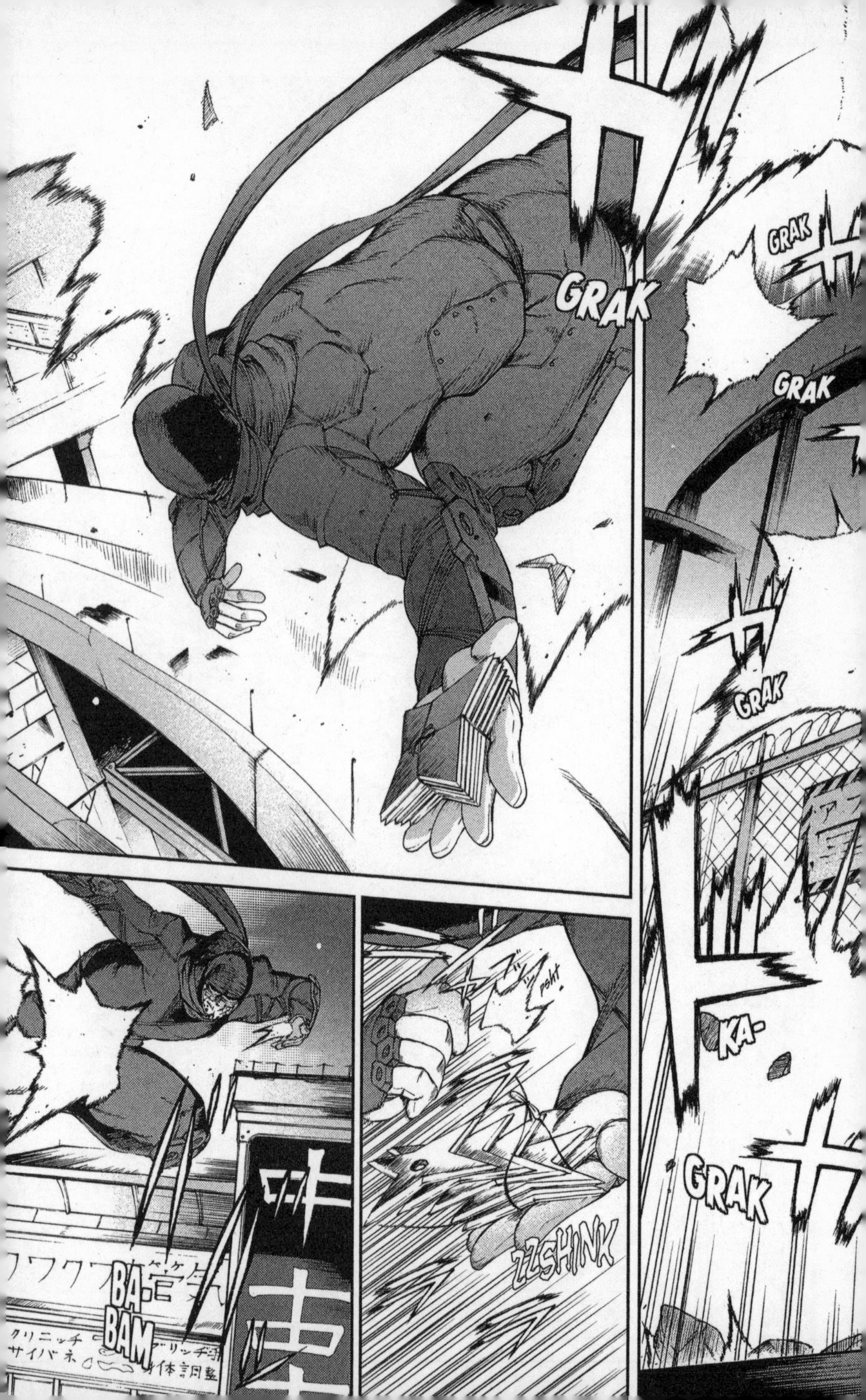
GRAK
GRAK
GRAK
KA-
GRAK
GRAK
psht
ZZSHINK
BA-
BAM

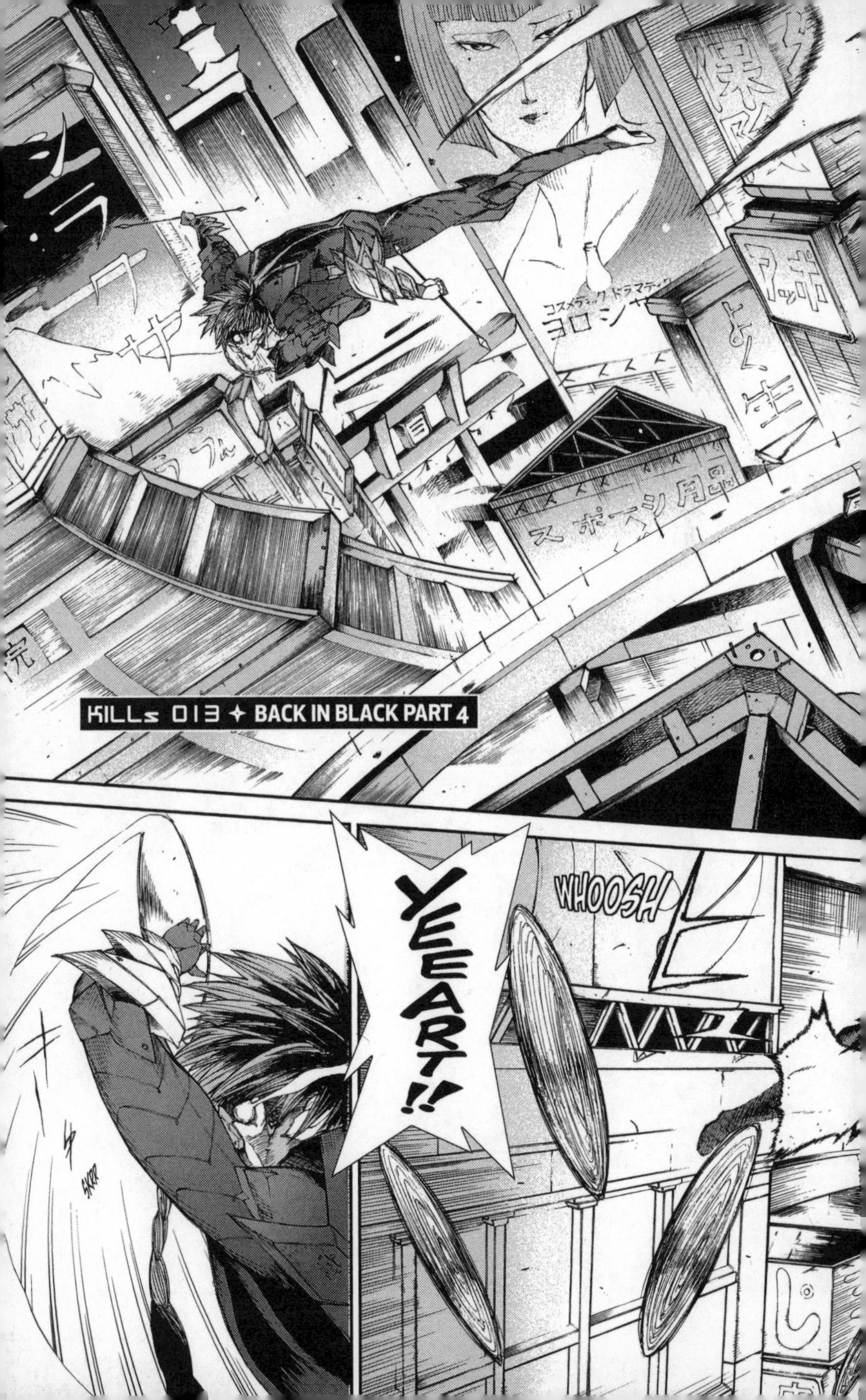
KILLs 013 ✦ BACK IN BLACK PART 4
WHOOSH
YEEART!!
GRRR

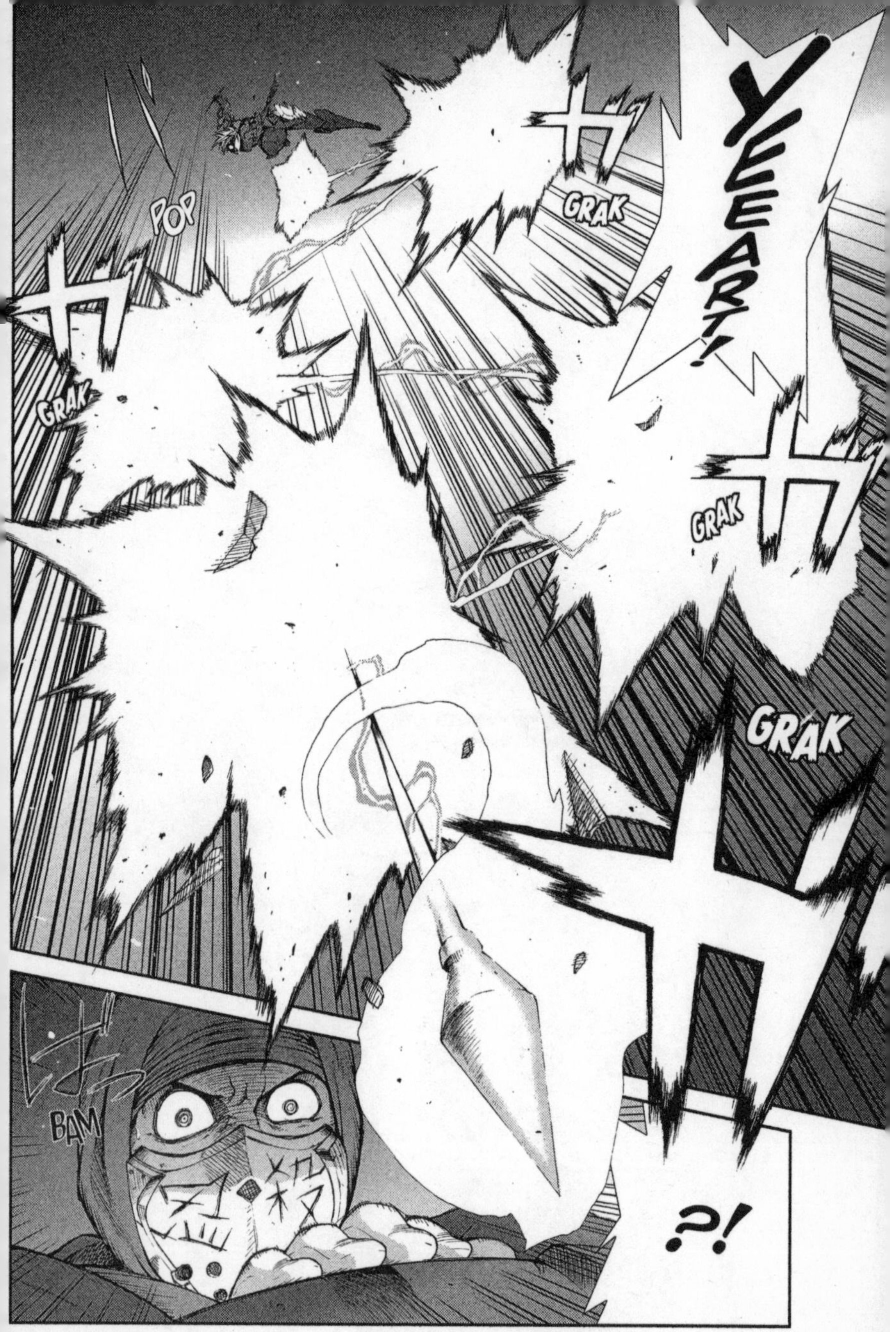
YEEART!
GRAK
POP
GRAK
GRAK
GRAK
?!
BAM

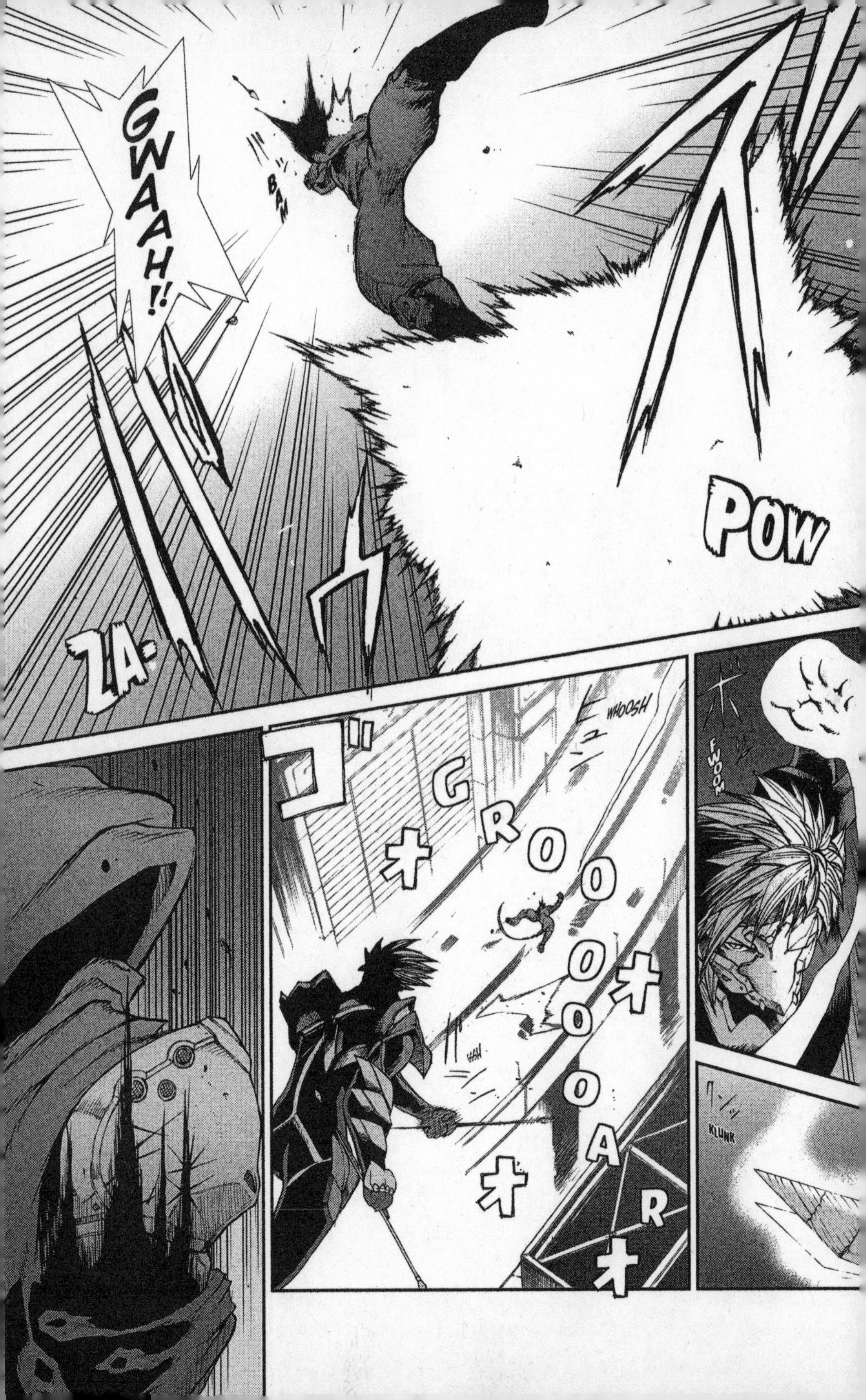

BAM
GWAAAH!!
POW
ZA-
FWOOM
KLUNK
WHOOSH
GROOOOOOAR

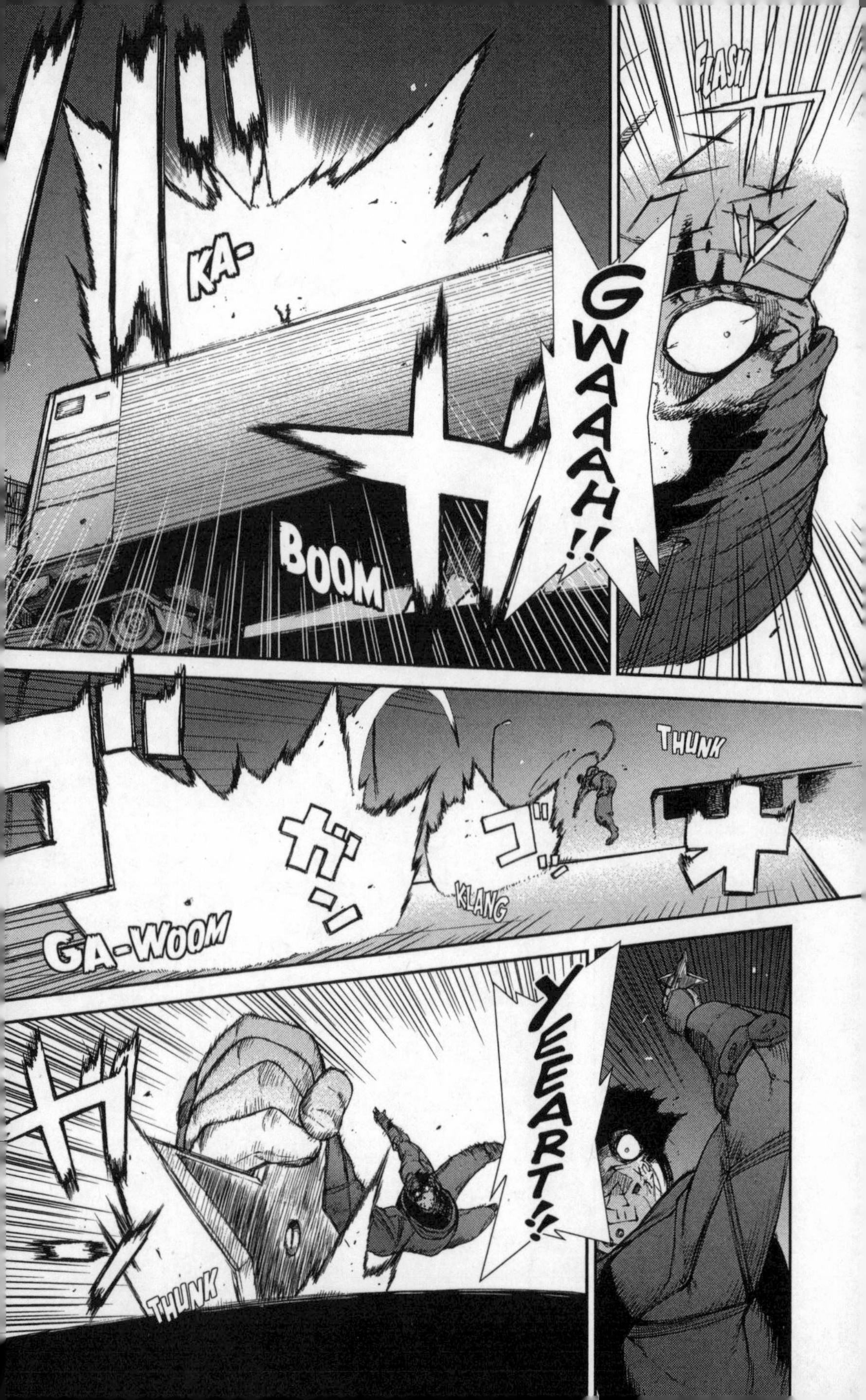
FLASH
GWAAAH!!
KA-
BOOM
THUNK
ゴッ
KLANG
ガーン
GA-WOOM
YEEEART!!
THUNK

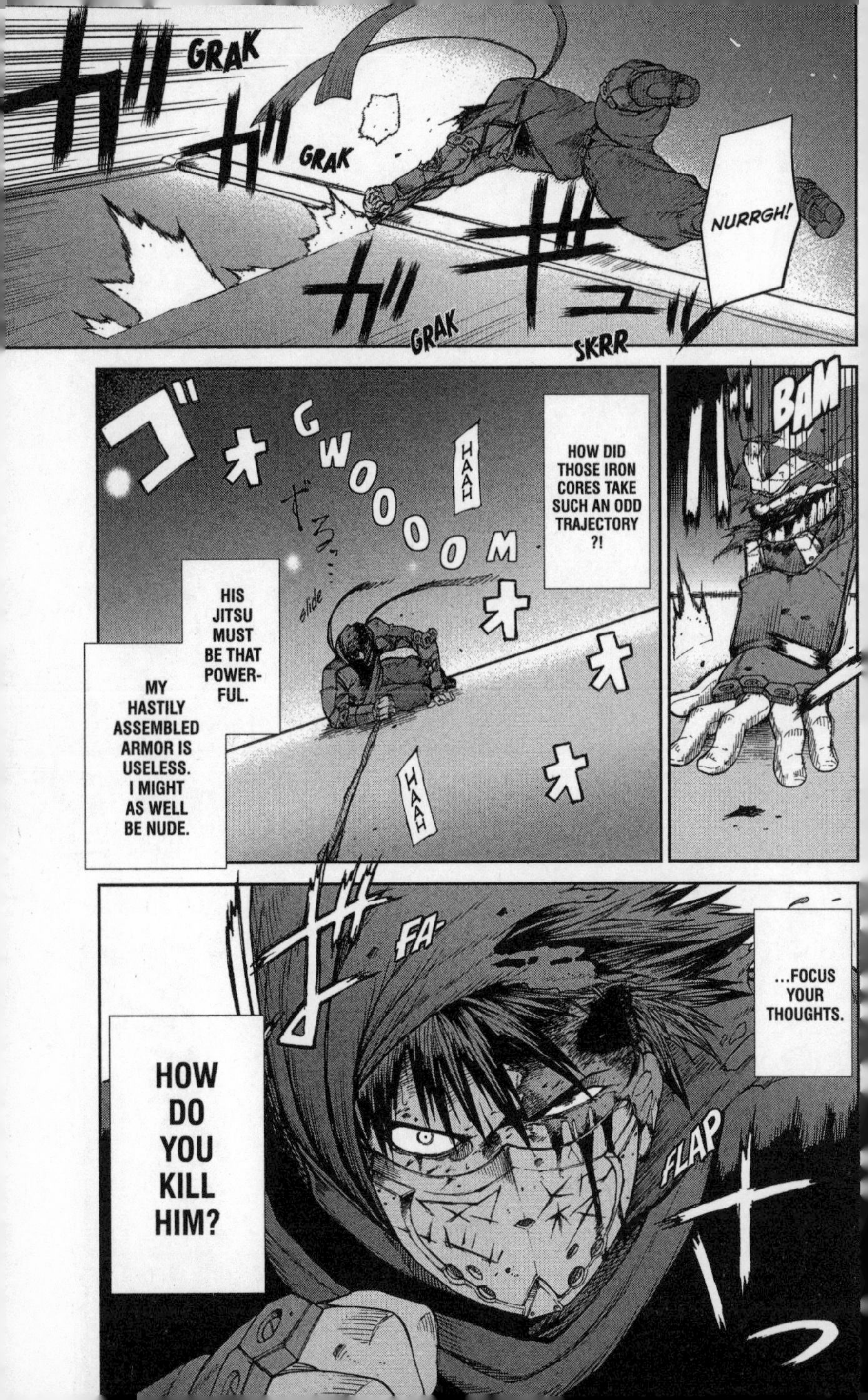
NURRGH!
GRAK
GRAK
SKRR
GRAK
BAM
HOW DID THOSE IRON CORES TAKE SUCH AN ODD TRAJECTORY?!
HAAH
GWOOOOOM
HAAH
HIS JITSU MUST BE THAT POWERFUL.
slide
MY HASTILY ASSEMBLED ARMOR IS USELESS. I MIGHT AS WELL BE NUDE.
...FOCUS YOUR THOUGHTS.
FA-
FLAP
HOW DO YOU KILL HIM?

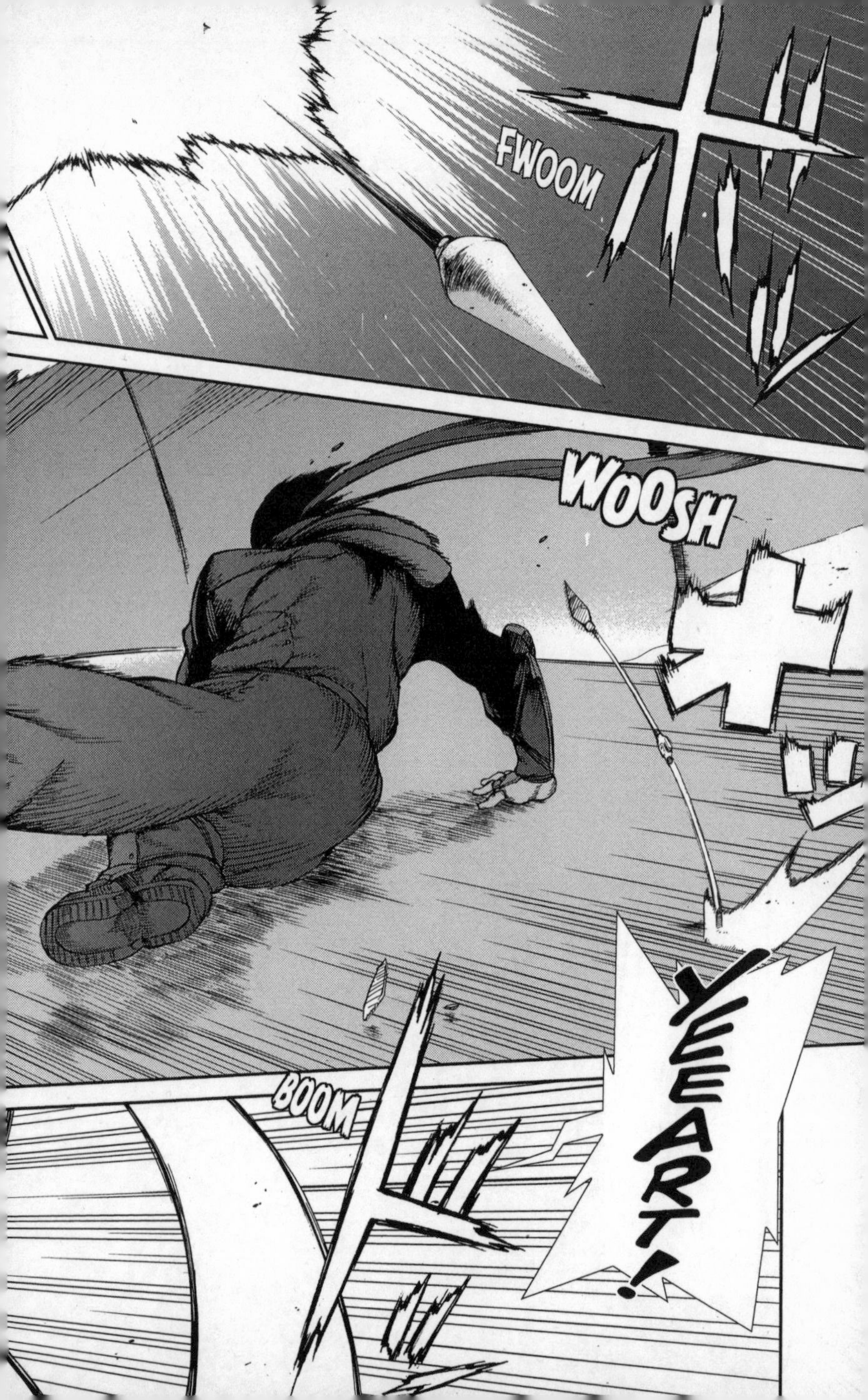
FWOOM
WOOSH
YEEART!
BOOM

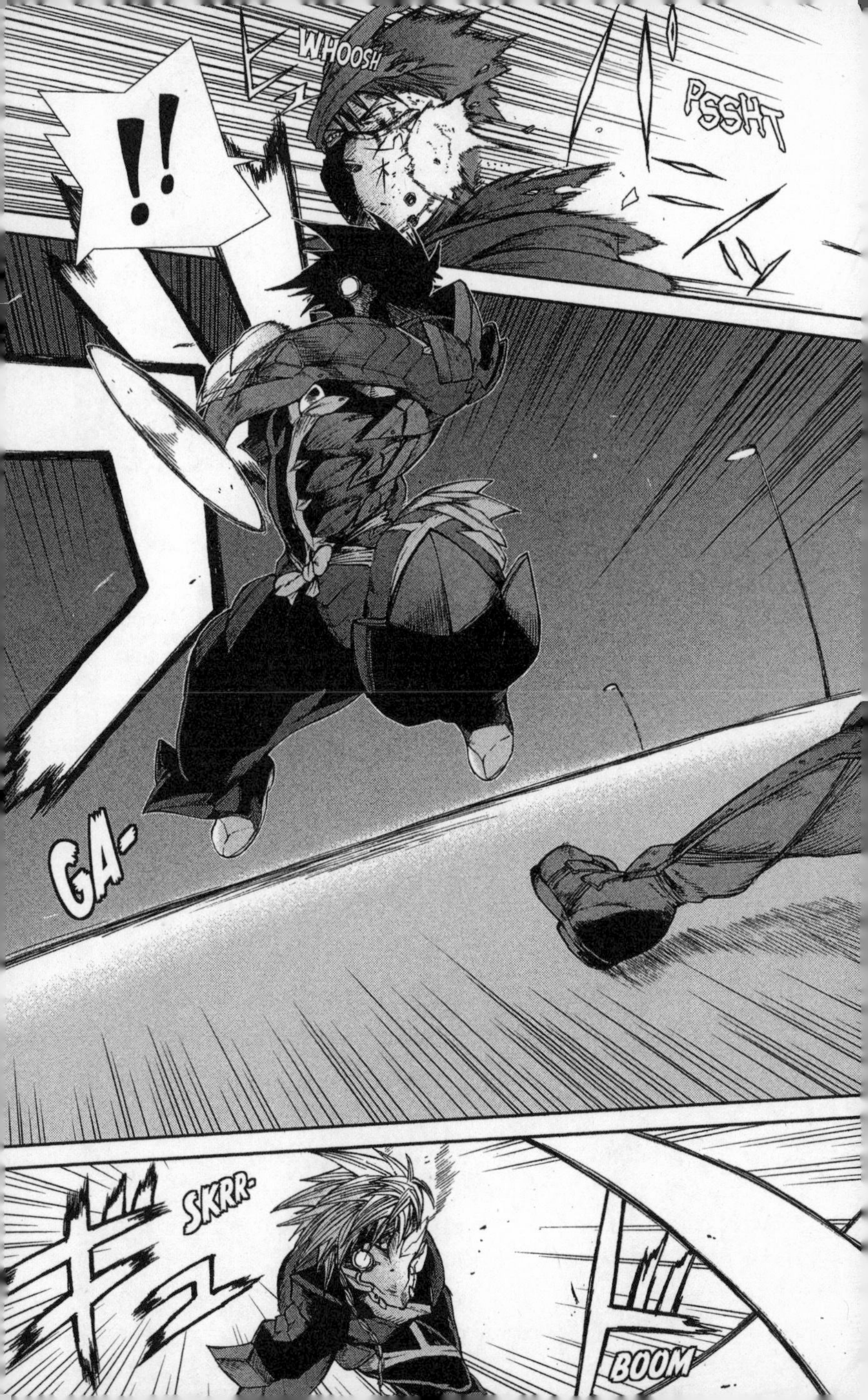
PSSHT
WHOOSH
!!
GA-
BOOM
SKRR-

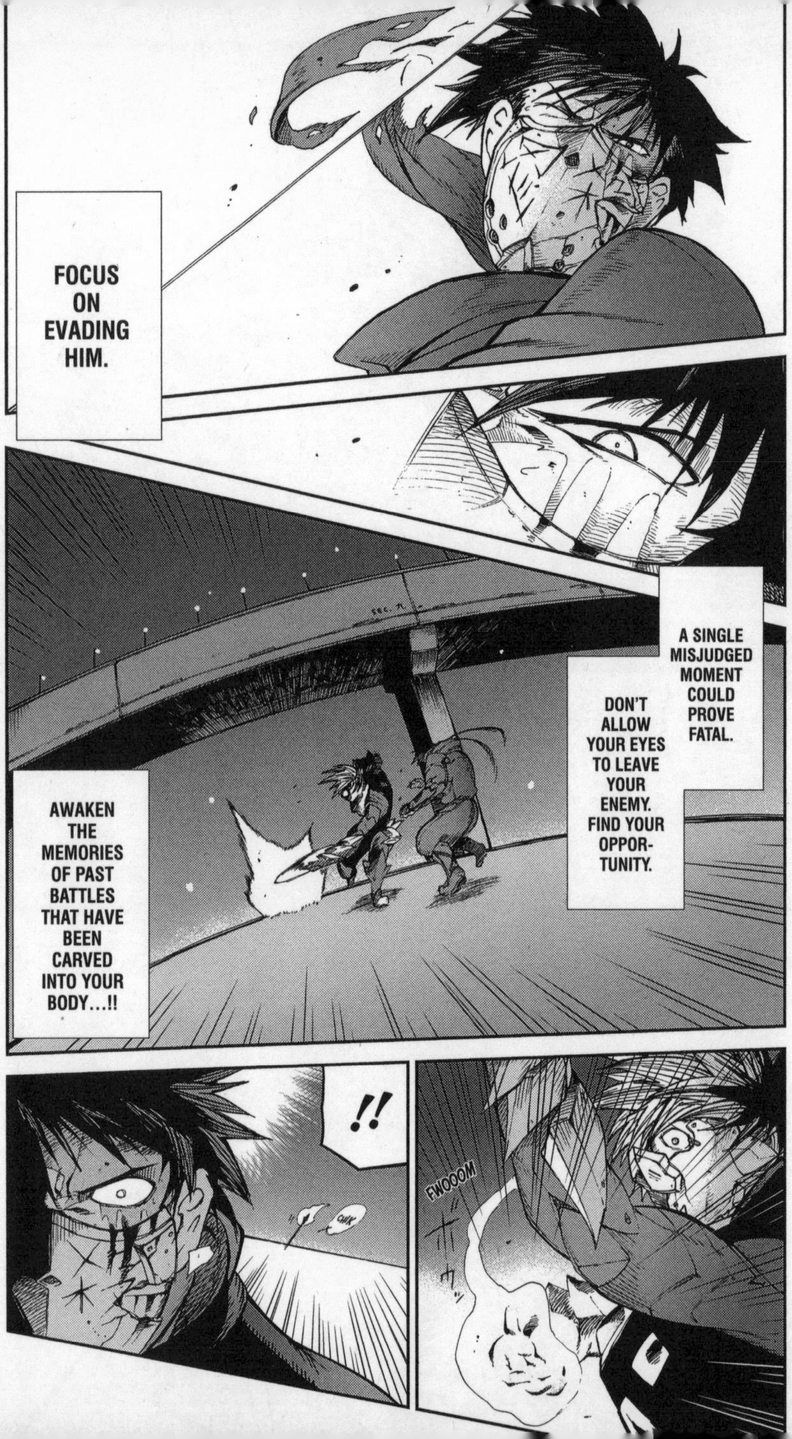

FOCUS ON EVADING HIM.
A SINGLE MISJUDGED MOMENT COULD PROVE FATAL.
DON'T ALLOW YOUR EYES TO LEAVE YOUR ENEMY. FIND YOUR OPPOR-TUNITY.
AWAKEN THE MEMORIES OF PAST BATTLES THAT HAVE BEEN CARVED INTO YOUR BODY...!!
FWOOOM
!!
CHK

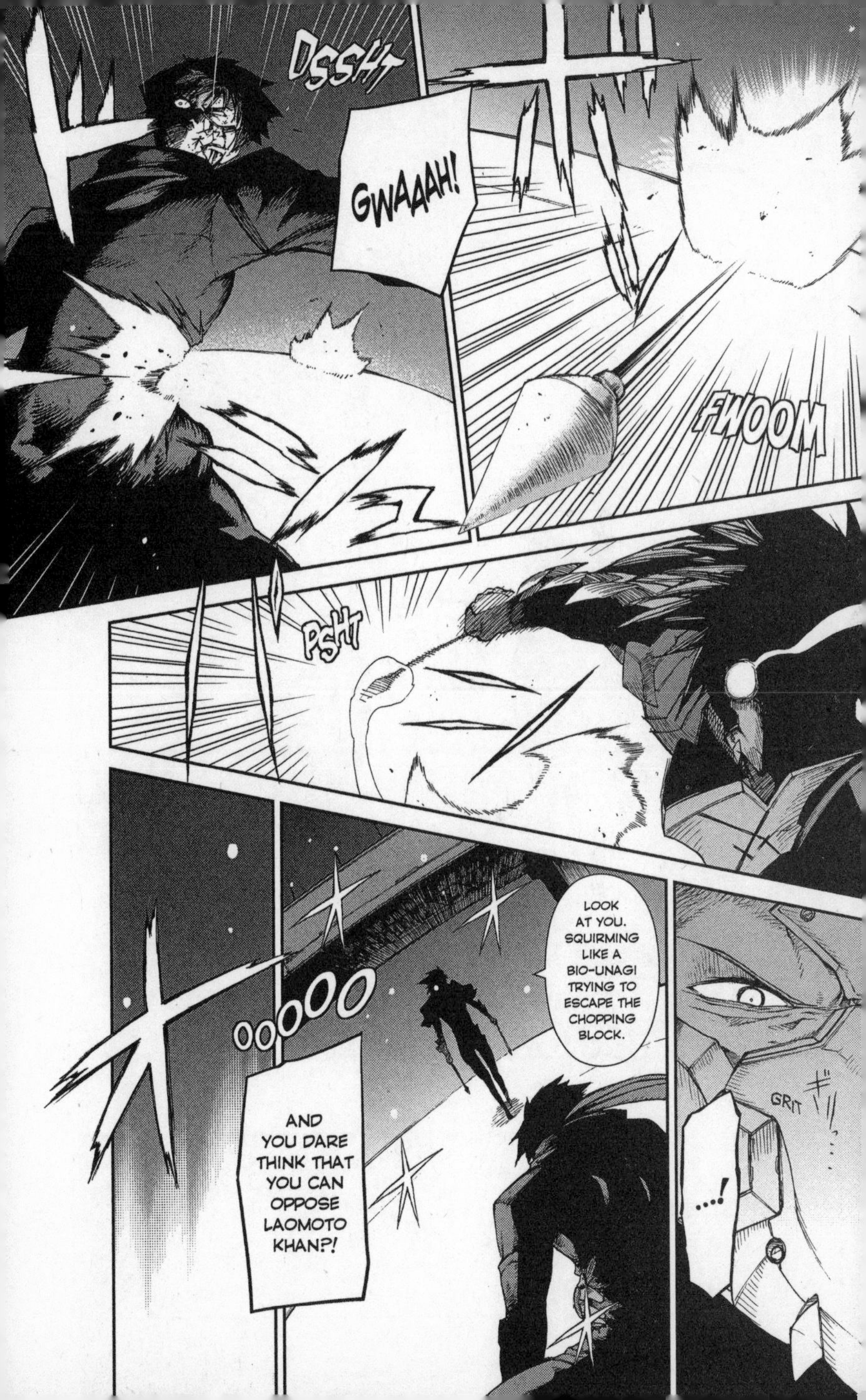
FWOOM
DSSHT
GWAAAH!
PSHT
LOOK AT YOU. SQUIRMING LIKE A BIO-UNAGI TRYING TO ESCAPE THE CHOPPING BLOCK.
GRIT
...!
OOOOO
AND YOU DARE THINK THAT YOU CAN OPPOSE LAOMOTO KHAN?!

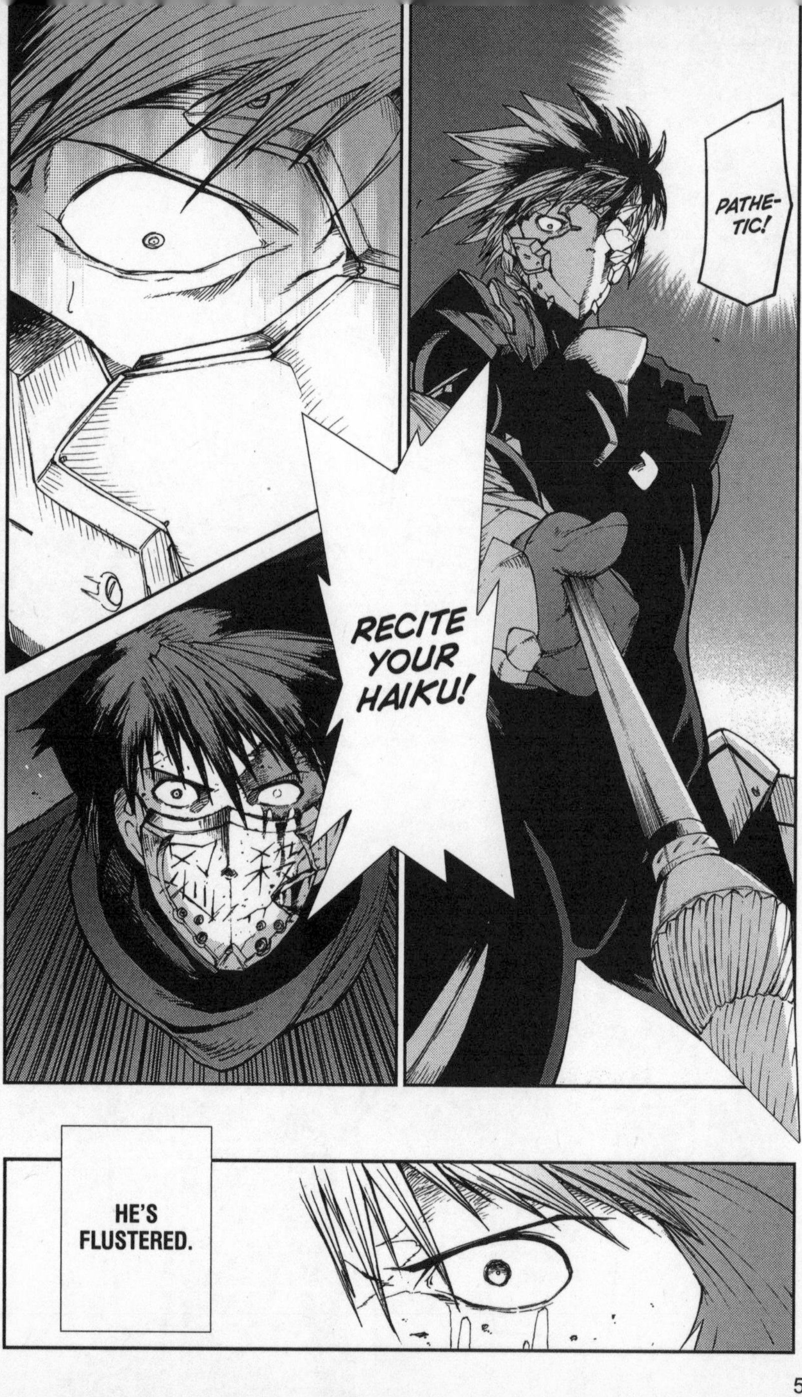
PATHE-
TIC!
RECITE YOUR HAIKU!
HE'S FLUSTERED.

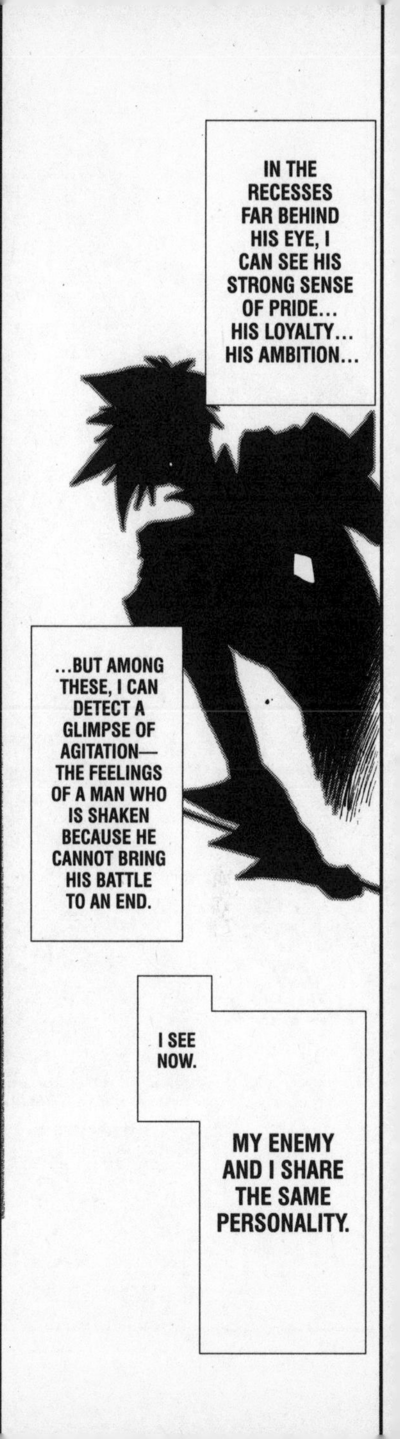
IN THE RECESSES FAR BEHIND HIS EYE, I CAN SEE HIS STRONG SENSE OF PRIDE... HIS LOYALTY... HIS AMBITION...
...BUT AMONG THESE, I CAN DETECT A GLIMPSE OF AGITATION— THE FEELINGS OF A MAN WHO IS SHAKEN BECAUSE HE CANNOT BRING HIS BATTLE TO AN END.
I SEE NOW.
MY ENEMY AND I SHARE THE SAME PERSONALITY.

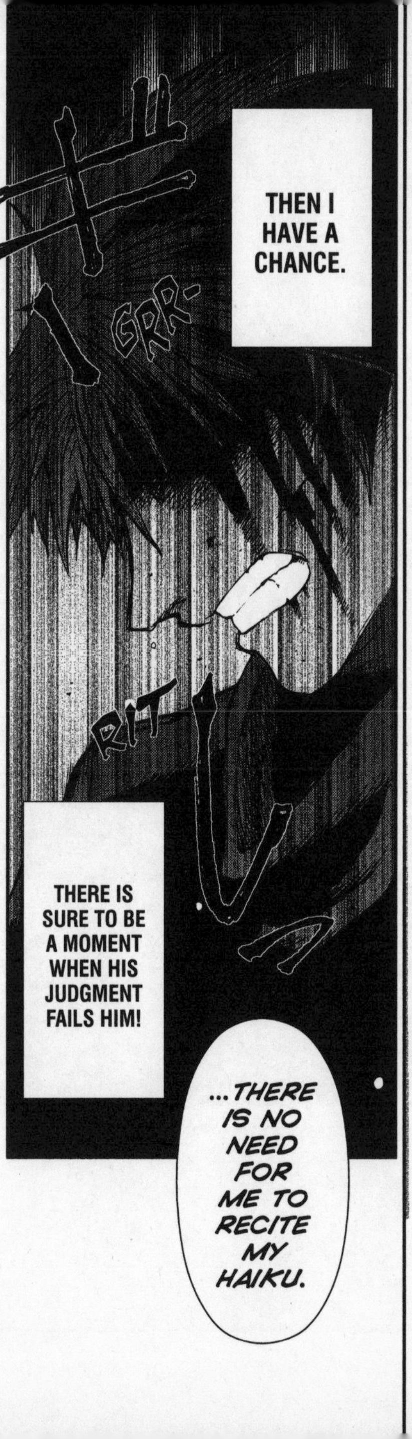
THEN I HAVE A CHANCE.
GRR-
RIT
THERE IS SURE TO BE A MOMENT WHEN HIS JUDGMENT FAILS HIM!
...THERE IS NO NEED FOR ME TO RECITE MY HAIKU.

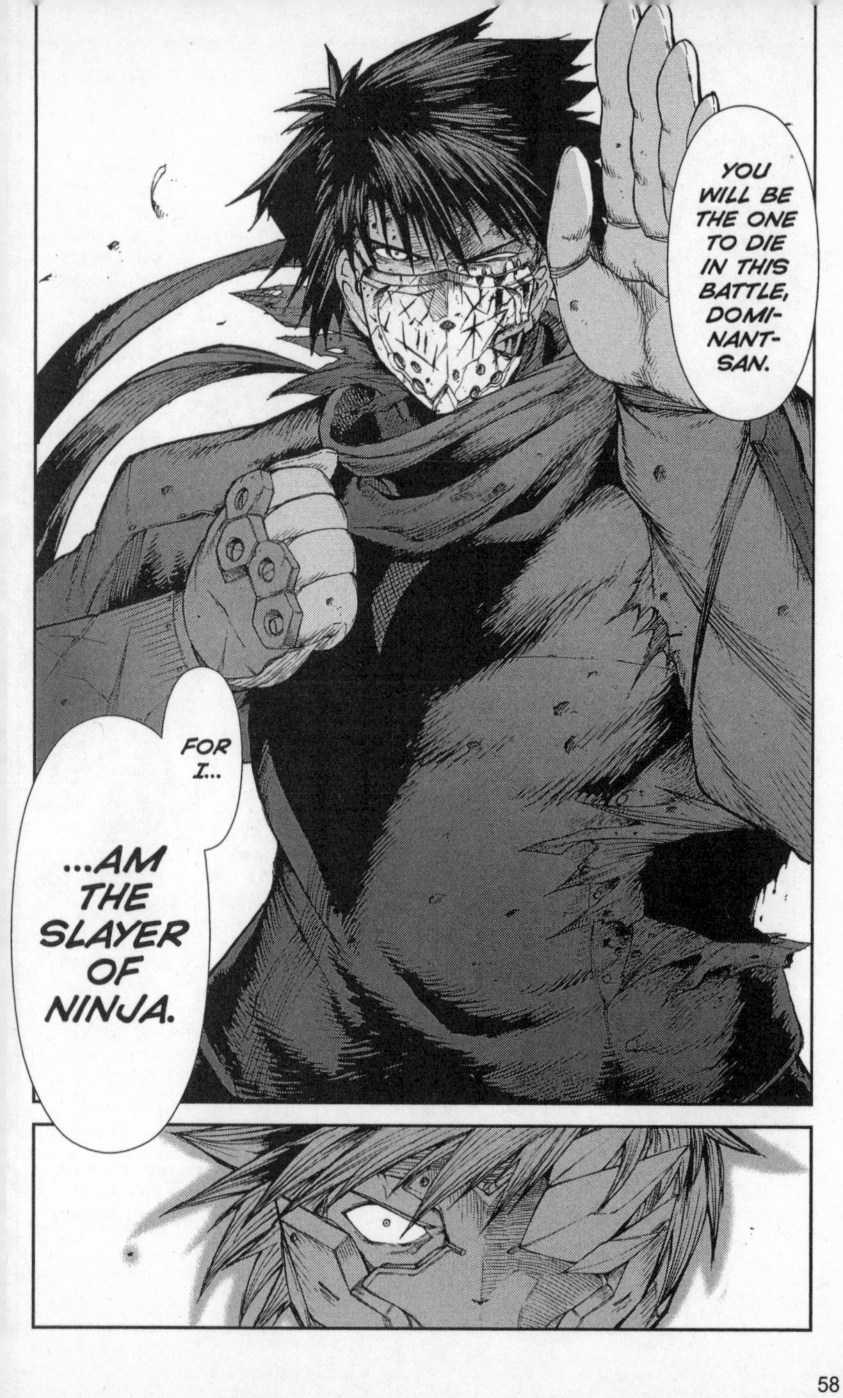
YOU WILL BE THE ONE TO DIE IN THIS BATTLE, DOMINANT-SAN.
FOR I...
...AM THE SLAYER OF NINJA.

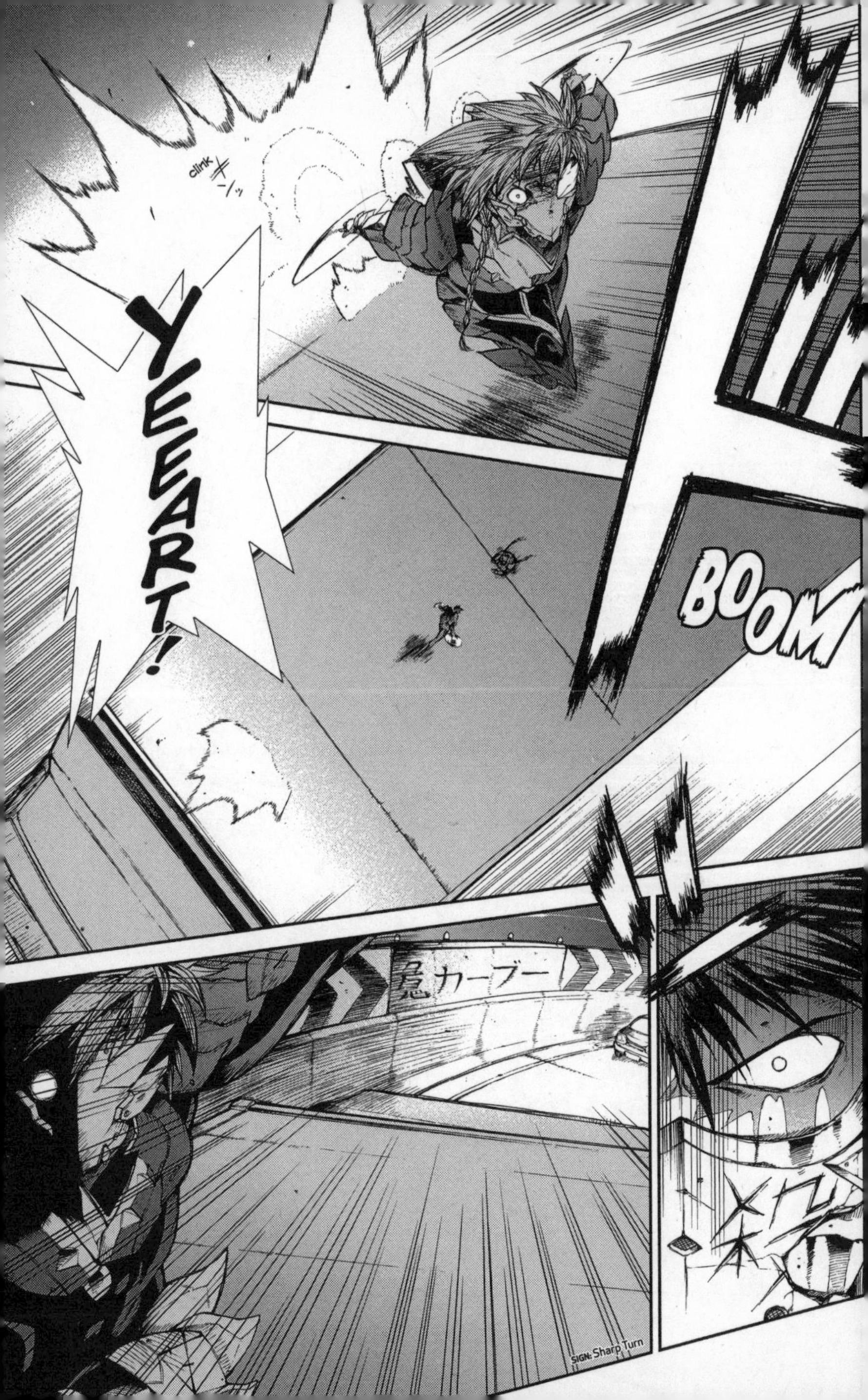
clink
YEEART!
BOOM
急カーブ
SIGN: Sharp Turn

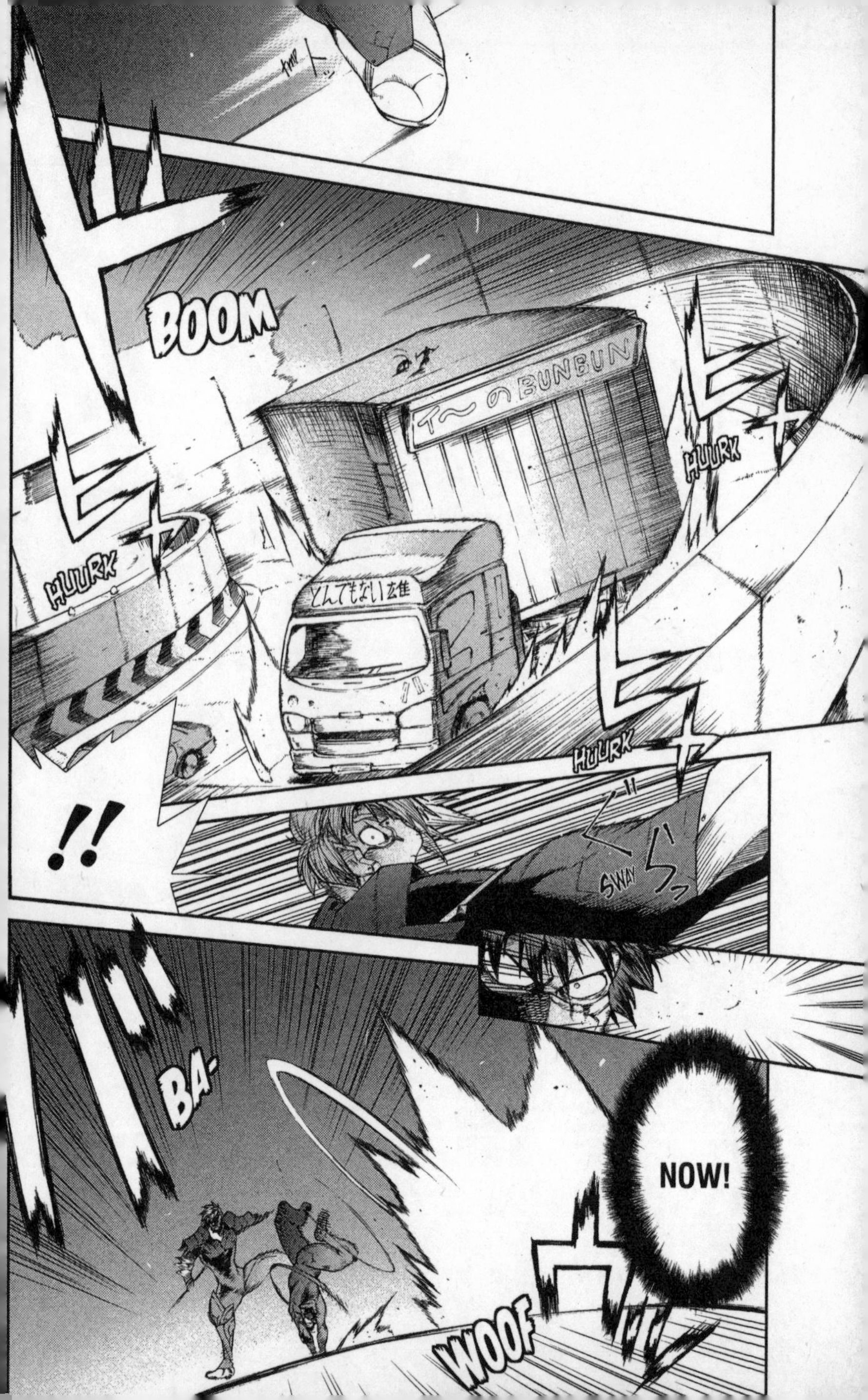
BOOM
HUURK
HUURK
HUURK
!!
SWAY
BA-
NOW!
WOOF

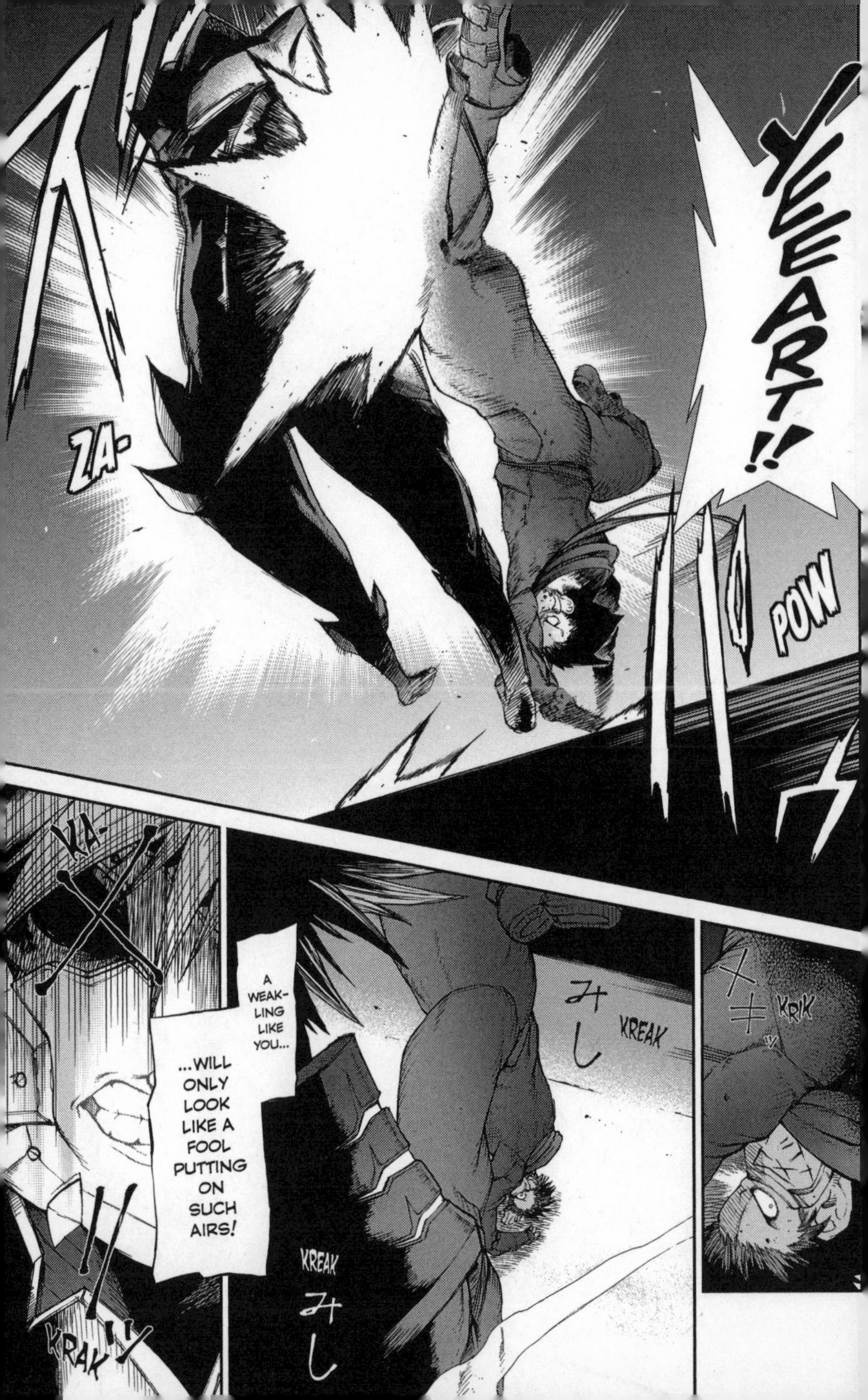
YEEART!!
POW
ZA-
メキッ
KRIK
みし
KREAK
A WEAK-LING LIKE YOU...
...WILL ONLY LOOK LIKE A FOOL PUTTING ON SUCH AIRS!
KREAK
みし
KA-
KRAK!!

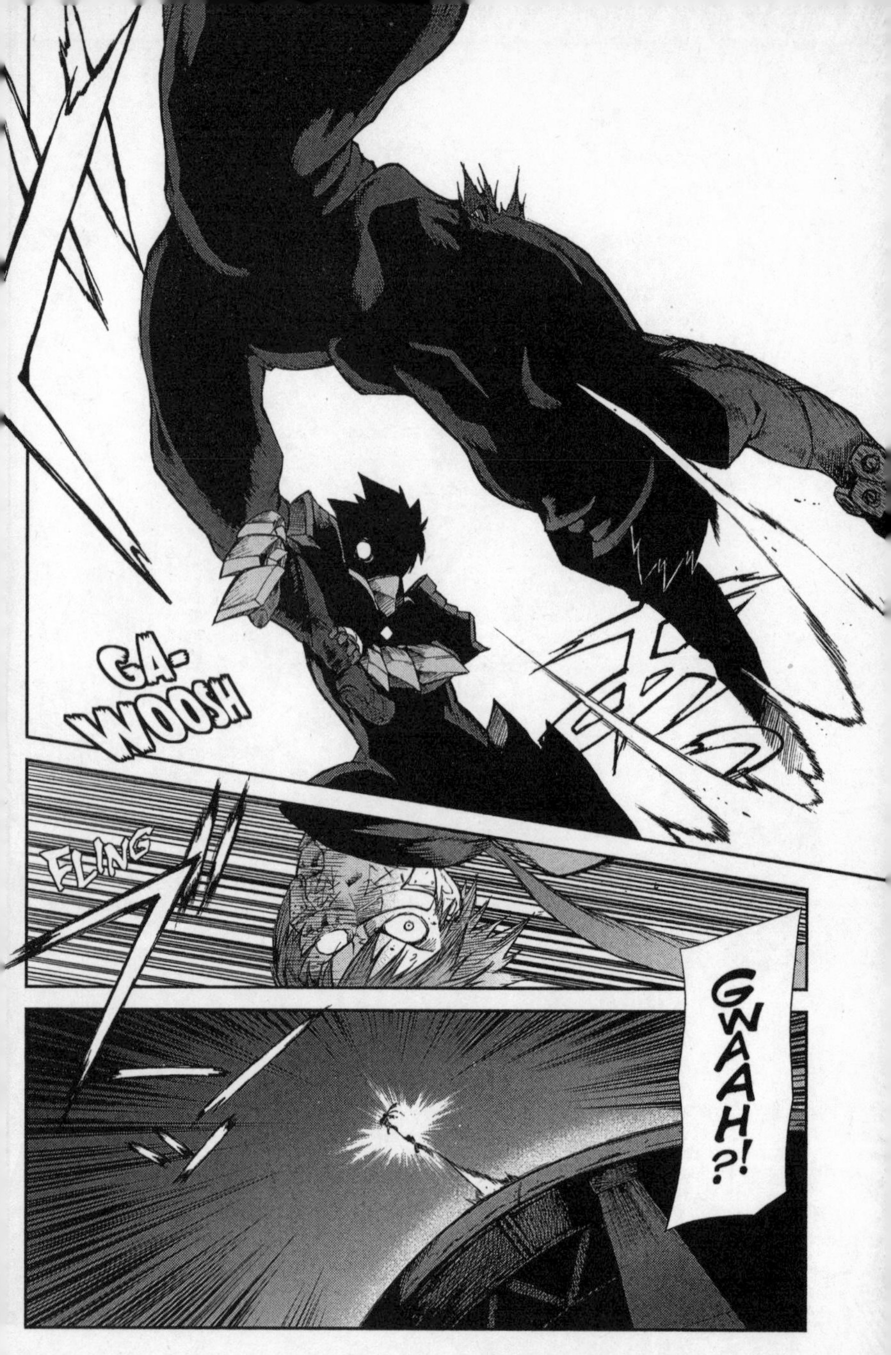
GA-WOOSH
FLING
GWAAH?!

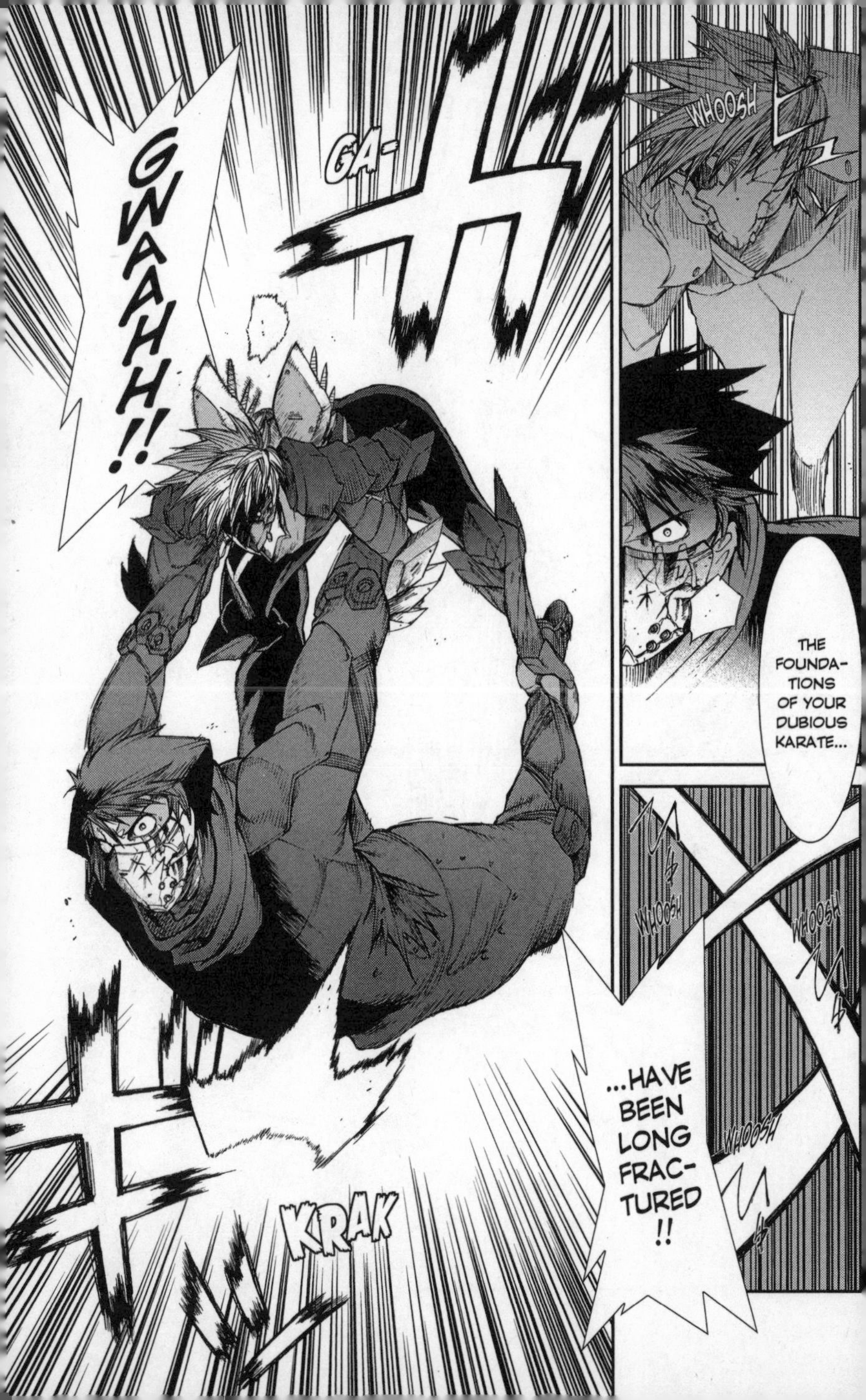
WHOOSH
THE FOUNDATIONS OF YOUR DUBIOUS KARATE...
WHOOSH
WHOOSH
WHOOSH
GA-
GWAAHHH!!
...HAVE BEEN LONG FRACTURED!!
KRAK

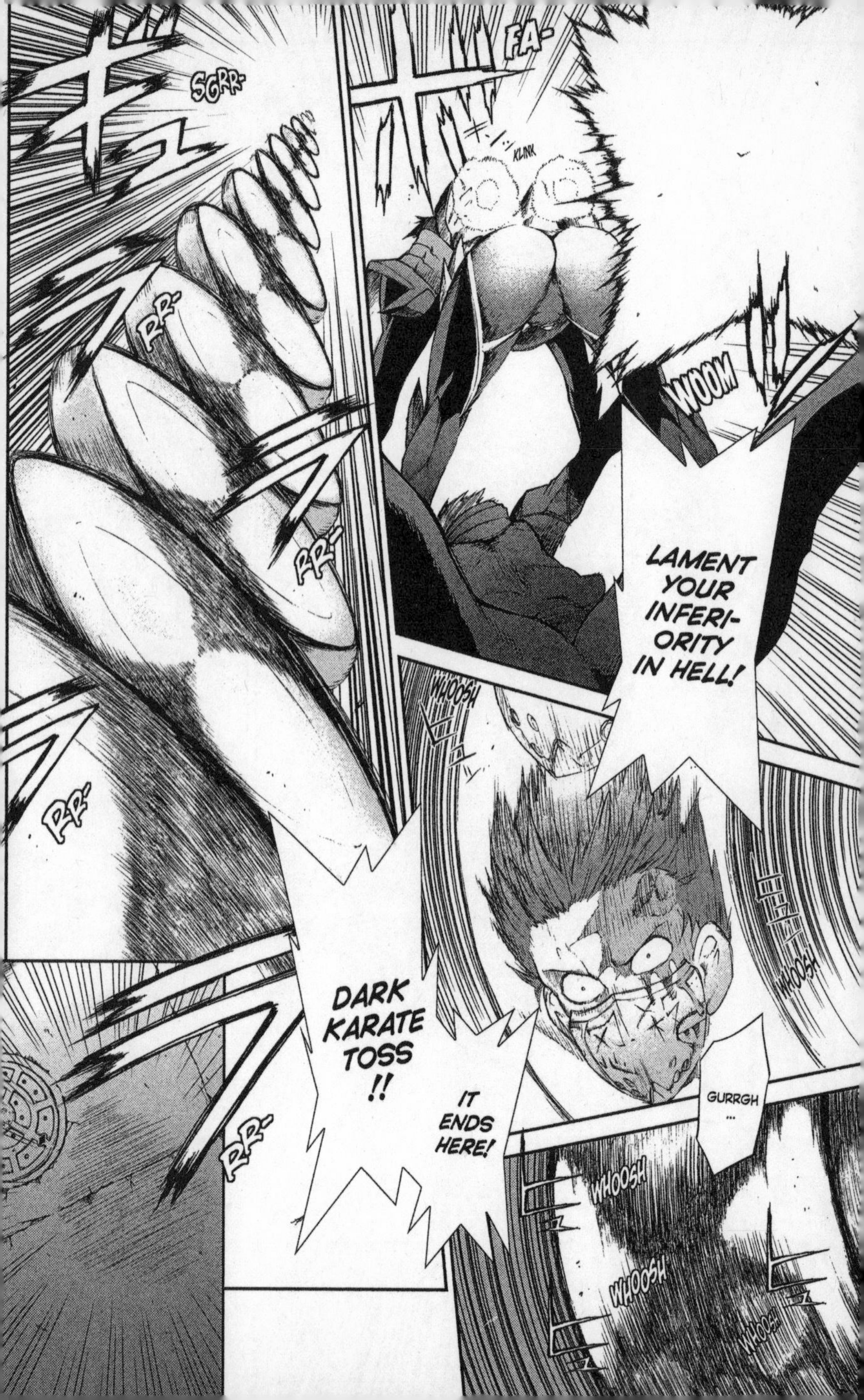
FA-
KLINK
WOOM
LAMENT YOUR INFERIORITY IN HELL!
SCRR-
RR-
RR-
RR-
WHOOSH
WHOOSH
GURRGH ...
IT ENDS HERE!
DARK KARATE TOSS !!
RR-
WHOOSH
WHOOSH
WHOOSH

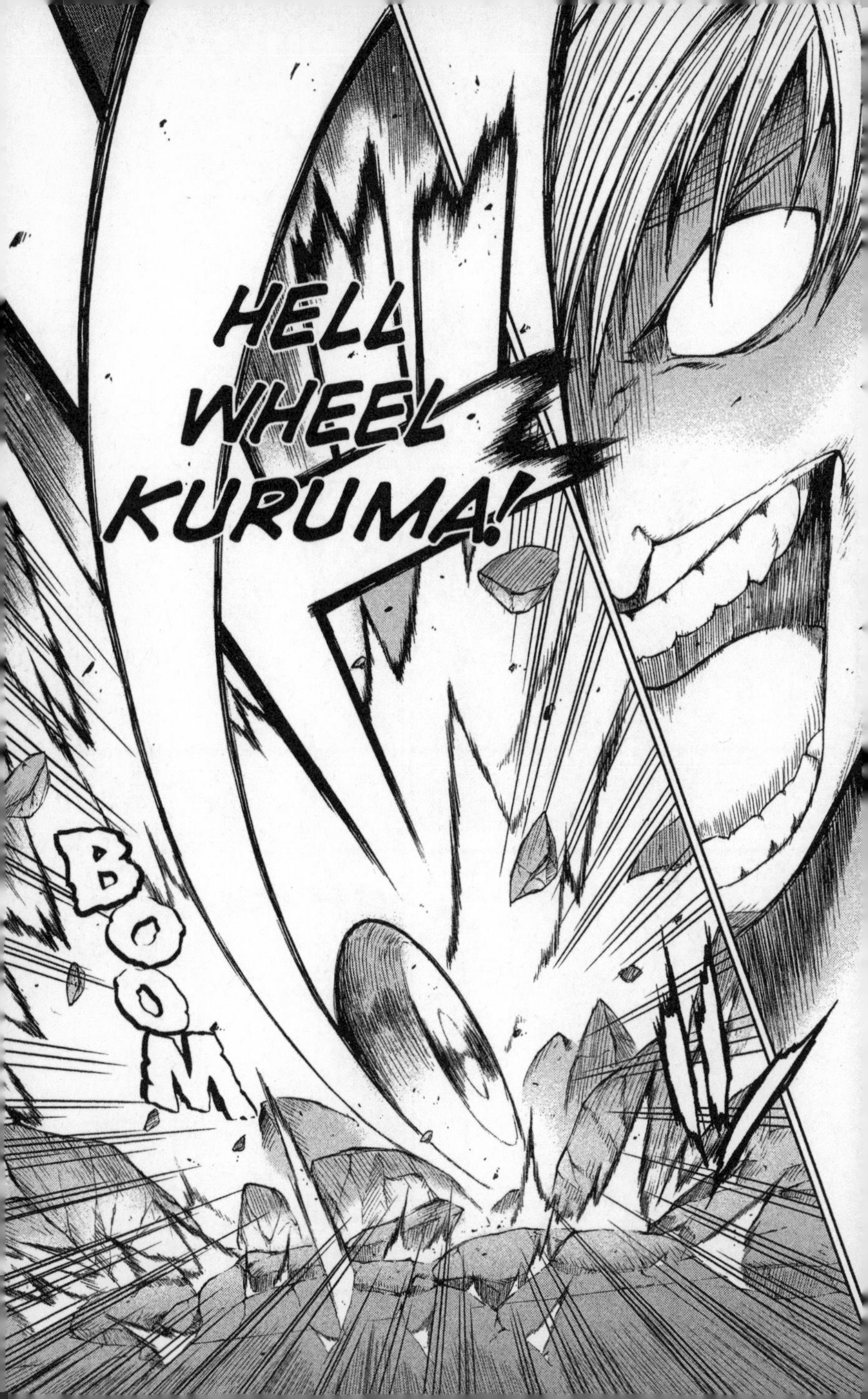
HELL WHEEL KURUMA!
BOOOM

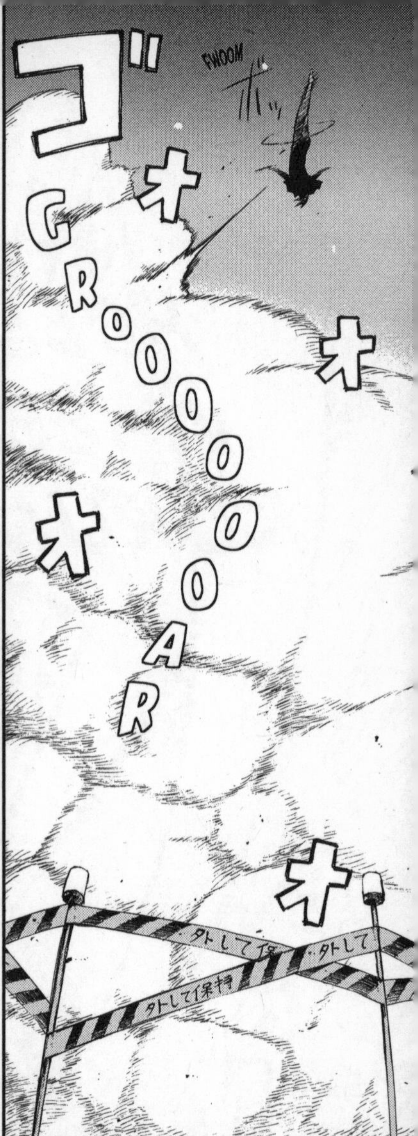
ゴオオオオ
GROOOOOOOOAR
FWOOM
ボッ
外して保持

POLICE TAPE: Get away and stay there/"Out keep"

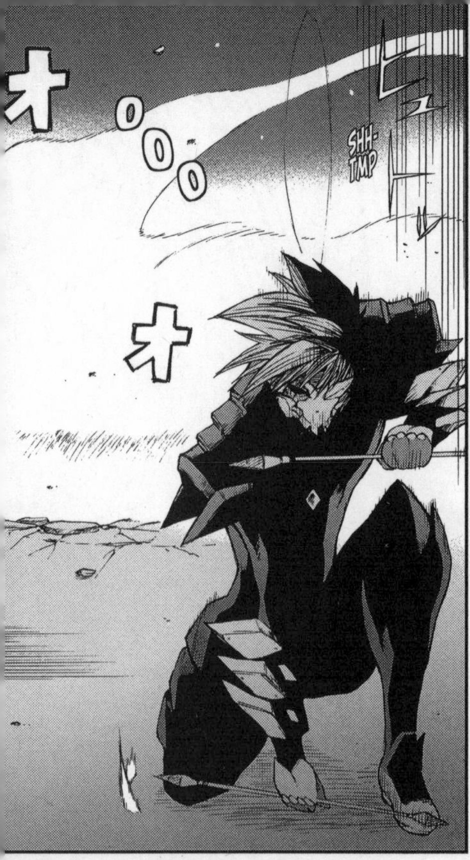
オOOO
オ
SHH-TMP

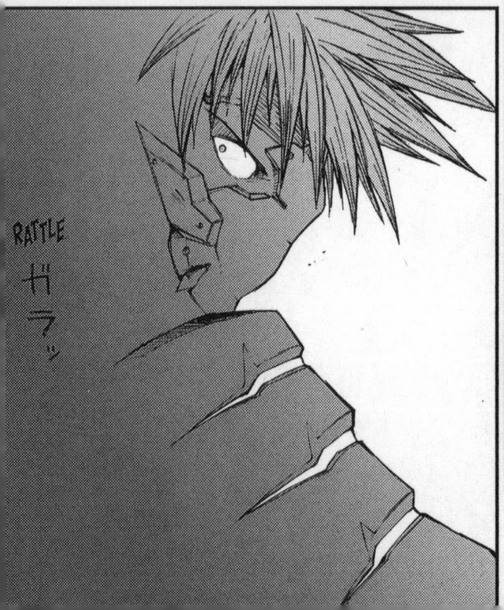
RATTLE
ガラッ

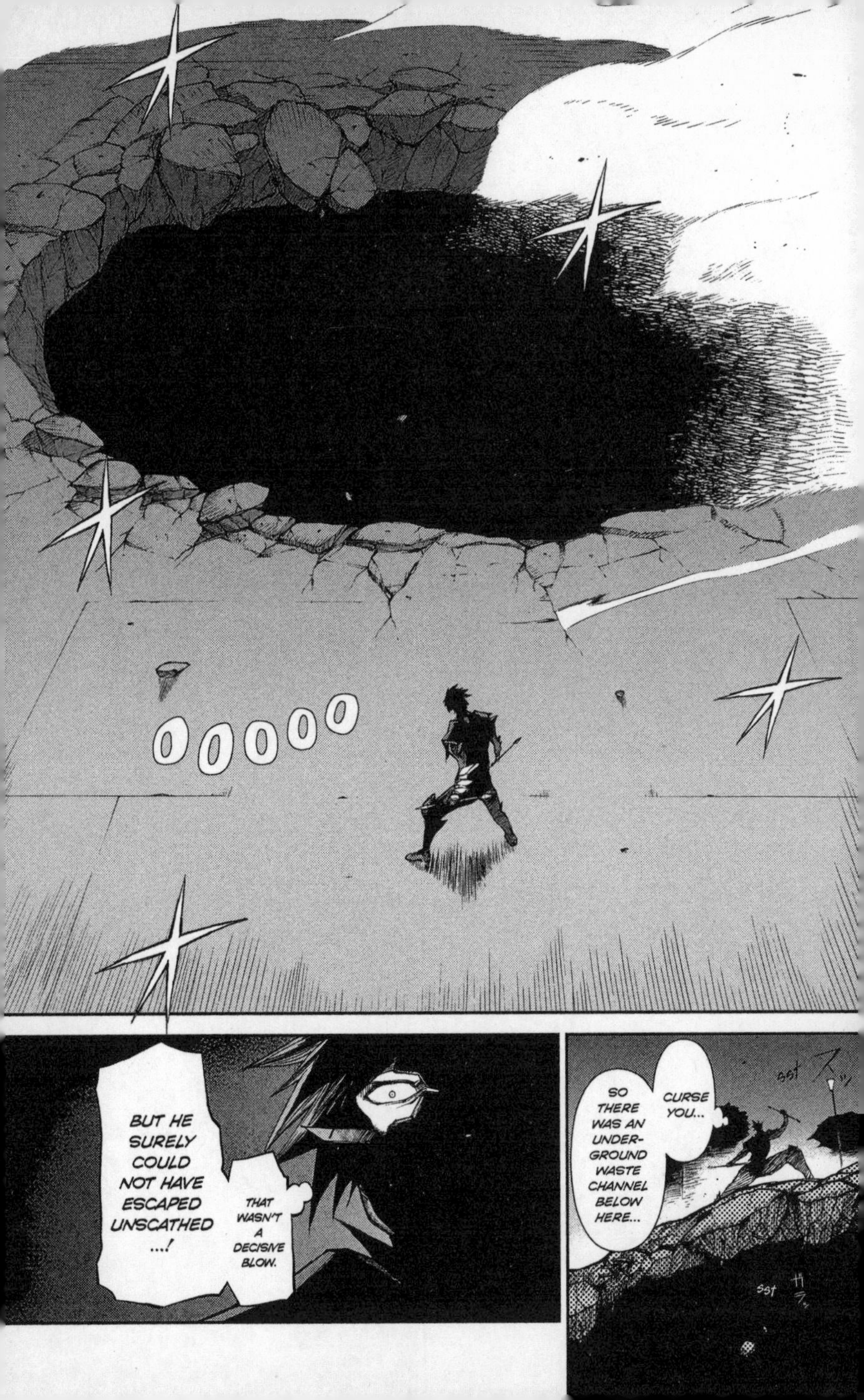
OOOOO
sst
CURSE YOU...
SO THERE WAS AN UNDER-GROUND WASTE CHANNEL BELOW HERE...
sst
THAT WASN'T A DECISIVE BLOW.
BUT HE SURELY COULD NOT HAVE ESCAPED UNSCATHED ...!

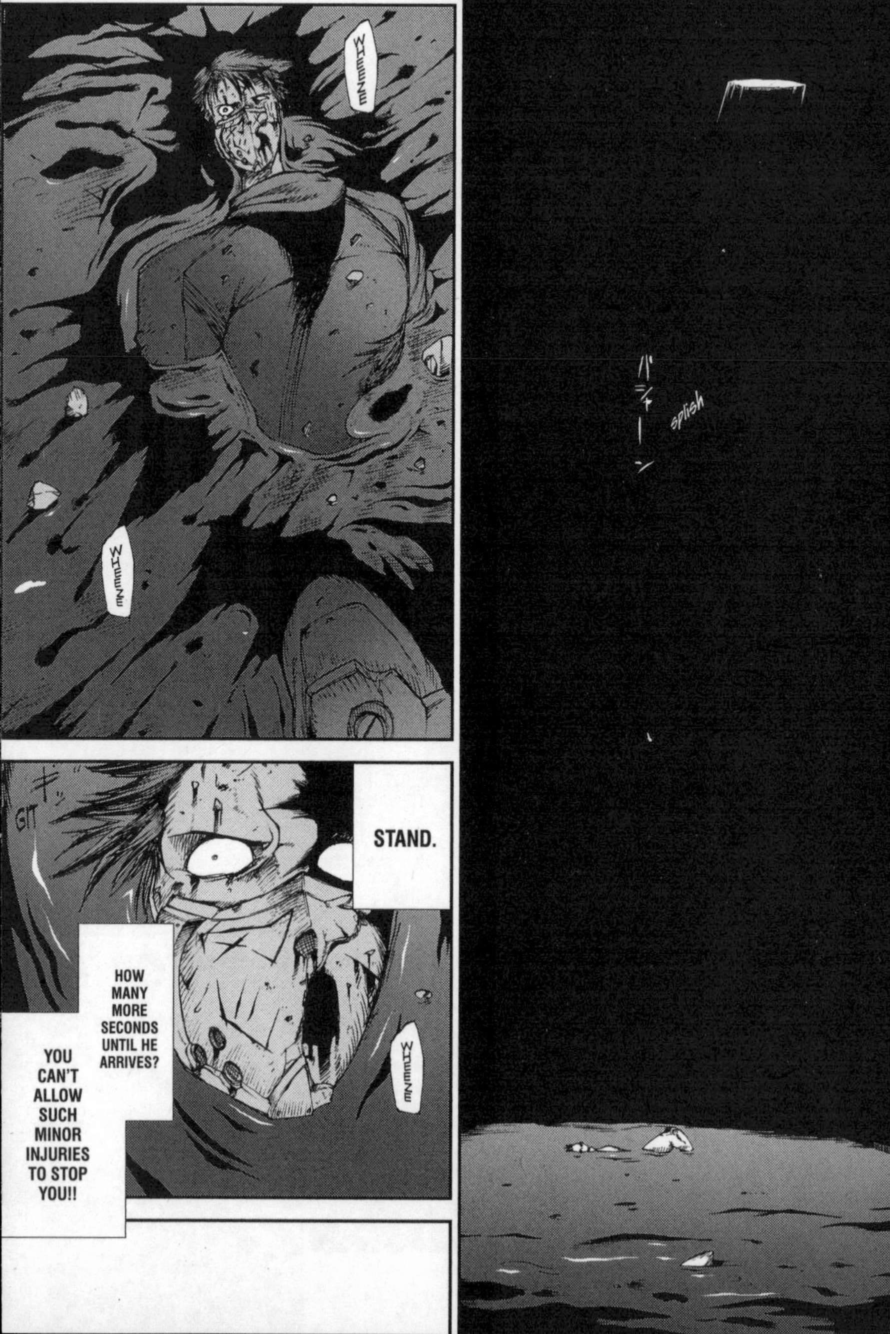
splish
WHEEZE
WHEEZE
GIT
STAND.
HOW MANY MORE SECONDS UNTIL HE ARRIVES?
YOU CAN'T ALLOW SUCH MINOR INJURIES TO STOP YOU!!
WHEEZE

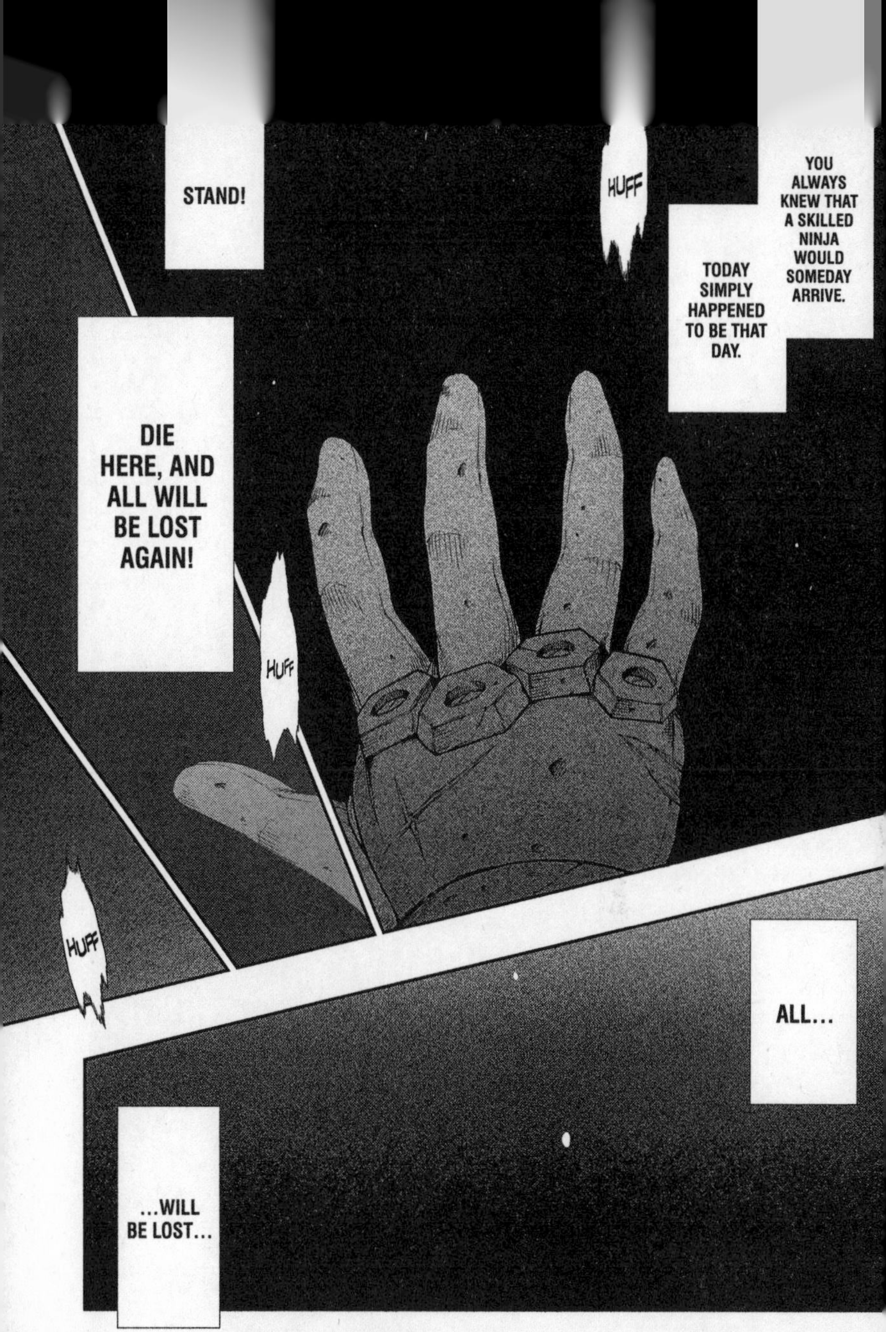
YOU ALWAYS KNEW THAT A SKILLED NINJA WOULD SOMEDAY ARRIVE.
TODAY SIMPLY HAPPENED TO BE THAT DAY.
HUFF
STAND!
DIE HERE, AND ALL WILL BE LOST AGAIN!
HUFF
HUFF
ALL...
...WILL BE LOST...

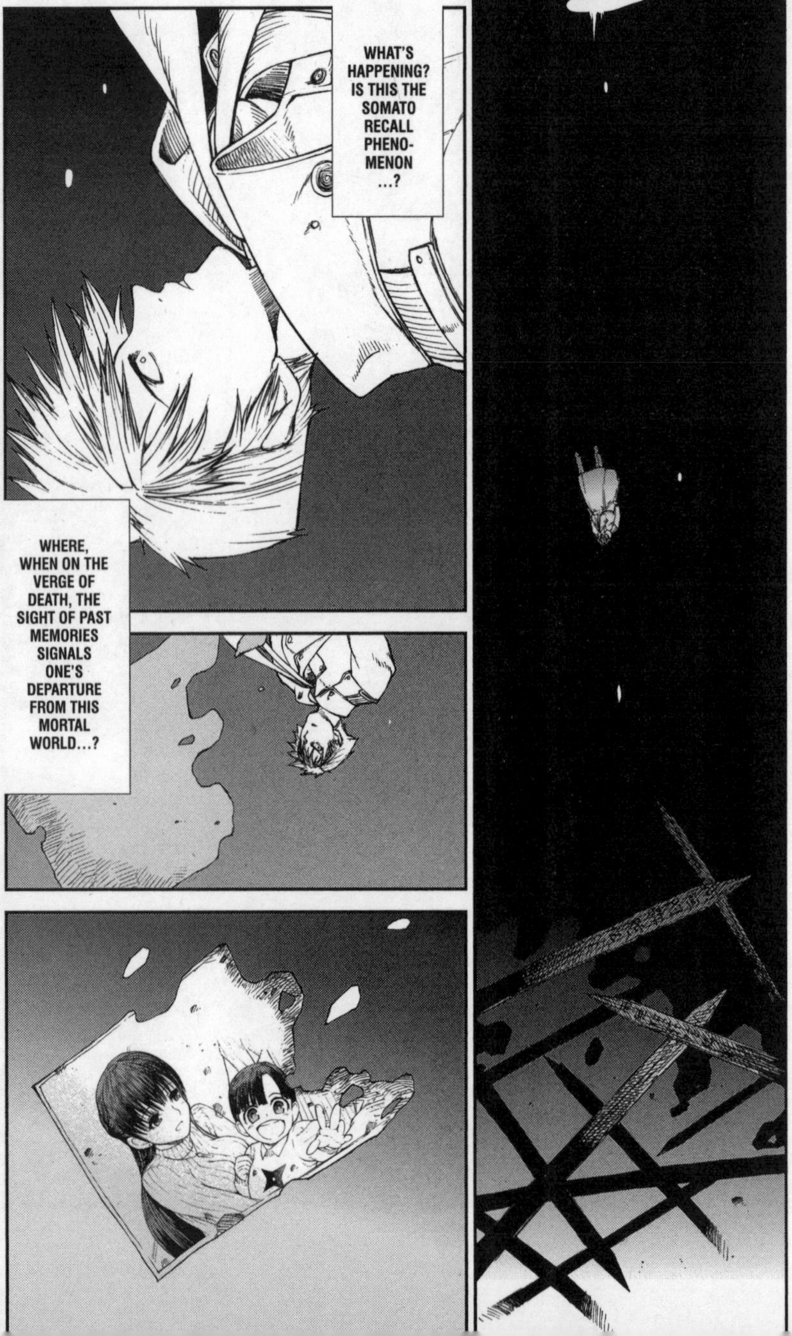
WHAT'S HAPPENING? IS THIS THE SOMATO RECALL PHENO-MENON ...?
WHERE, WHEN ON THE VERGE OF DEATH, THE SIGHT OF PAST MEMORIES SIGNALS ONE'S DEPARTURE FROM THIS MORTAL WORLD...?

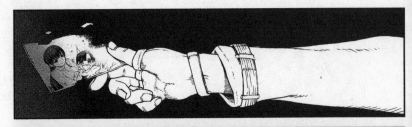

THAT'S RIGHT.

I DID NOT RETURN IN ORDER TO DIE HERE.

ANS-WER ME.

YOU, THE NINJA SOUL RESIDING WITH-IN MY BODY...

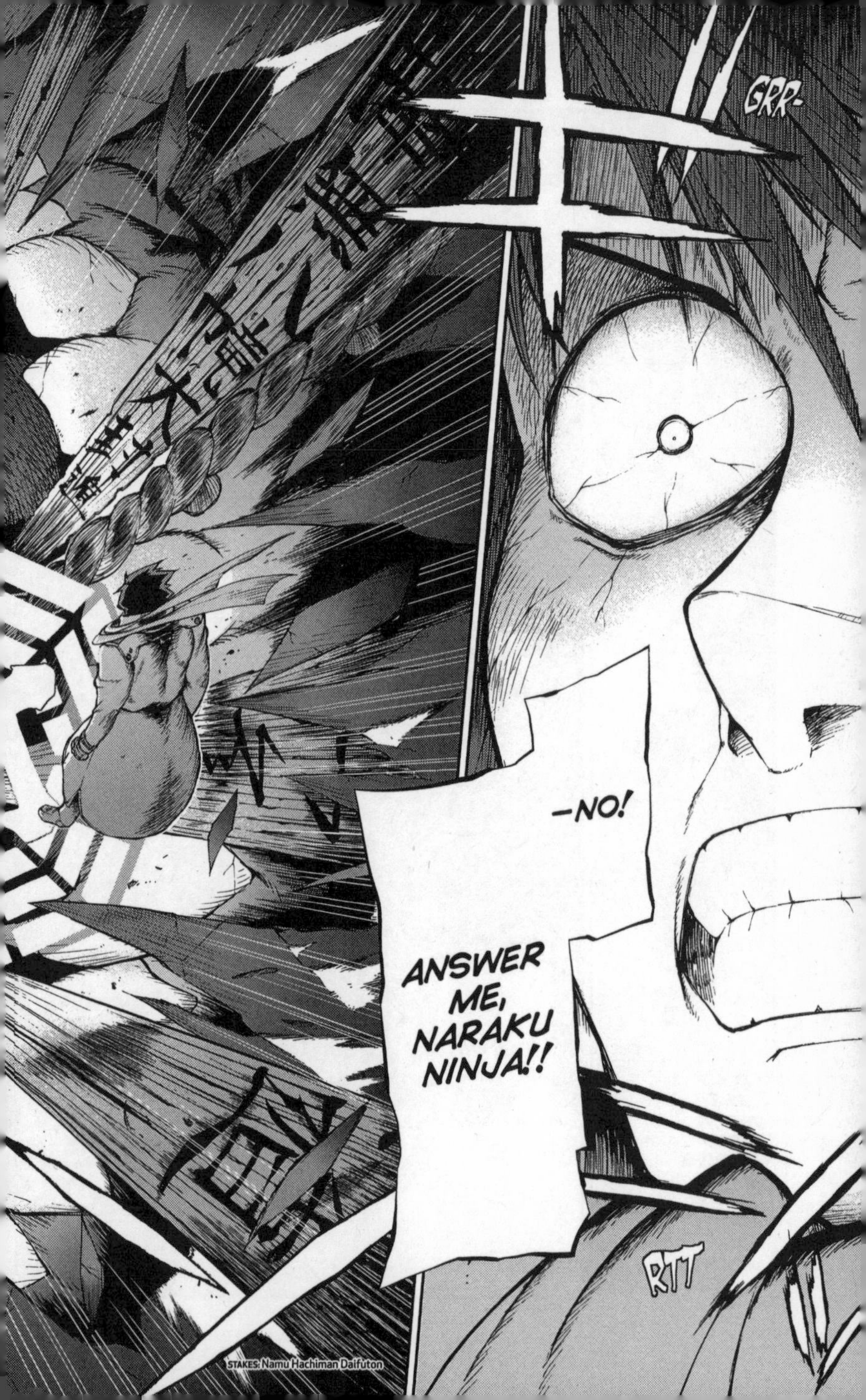
GRR-
–NO!
ANSWER ME, NARAKU NINJA!!
RTT
STAKES: Namu Hachiman Daifuton

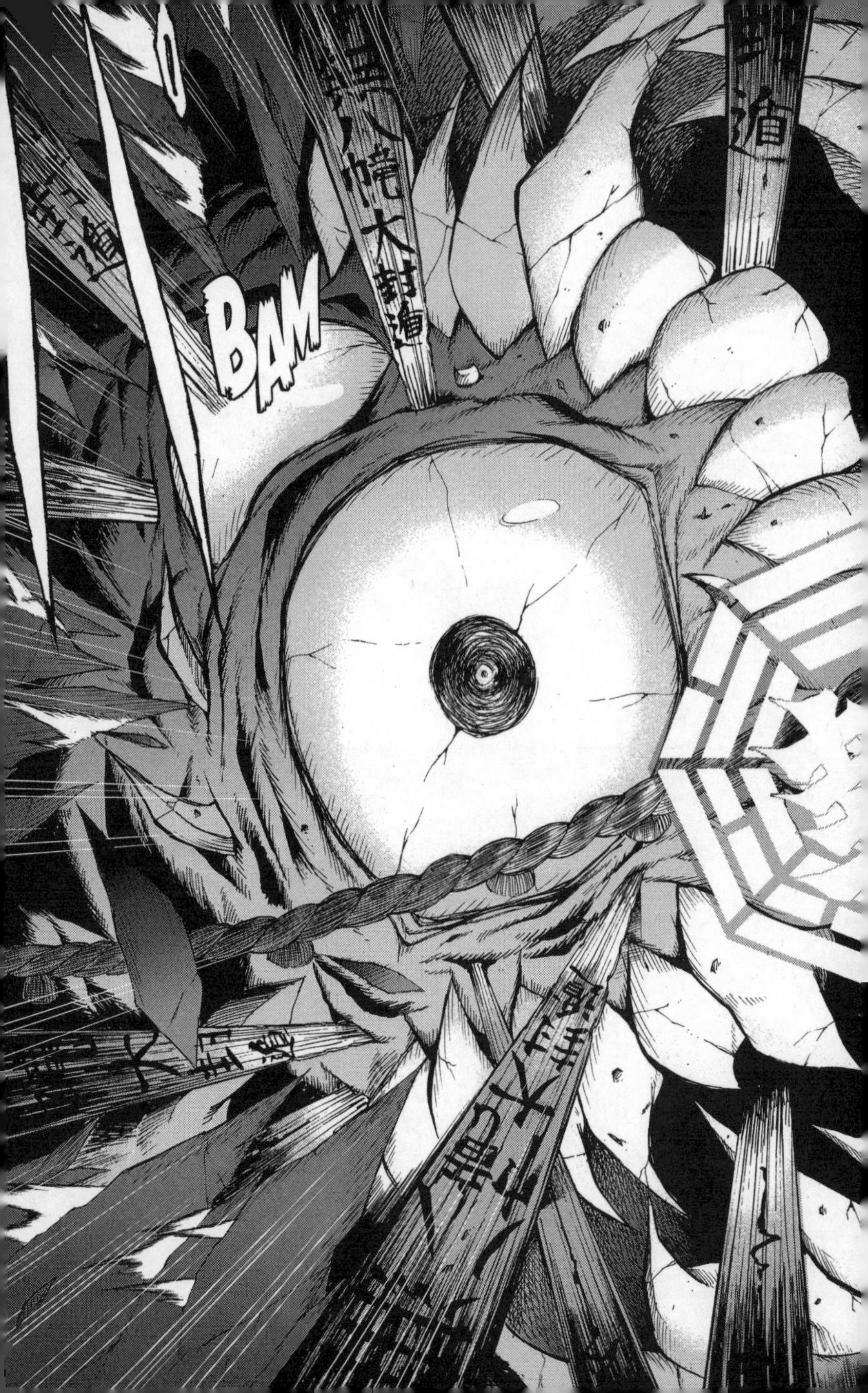
BAM

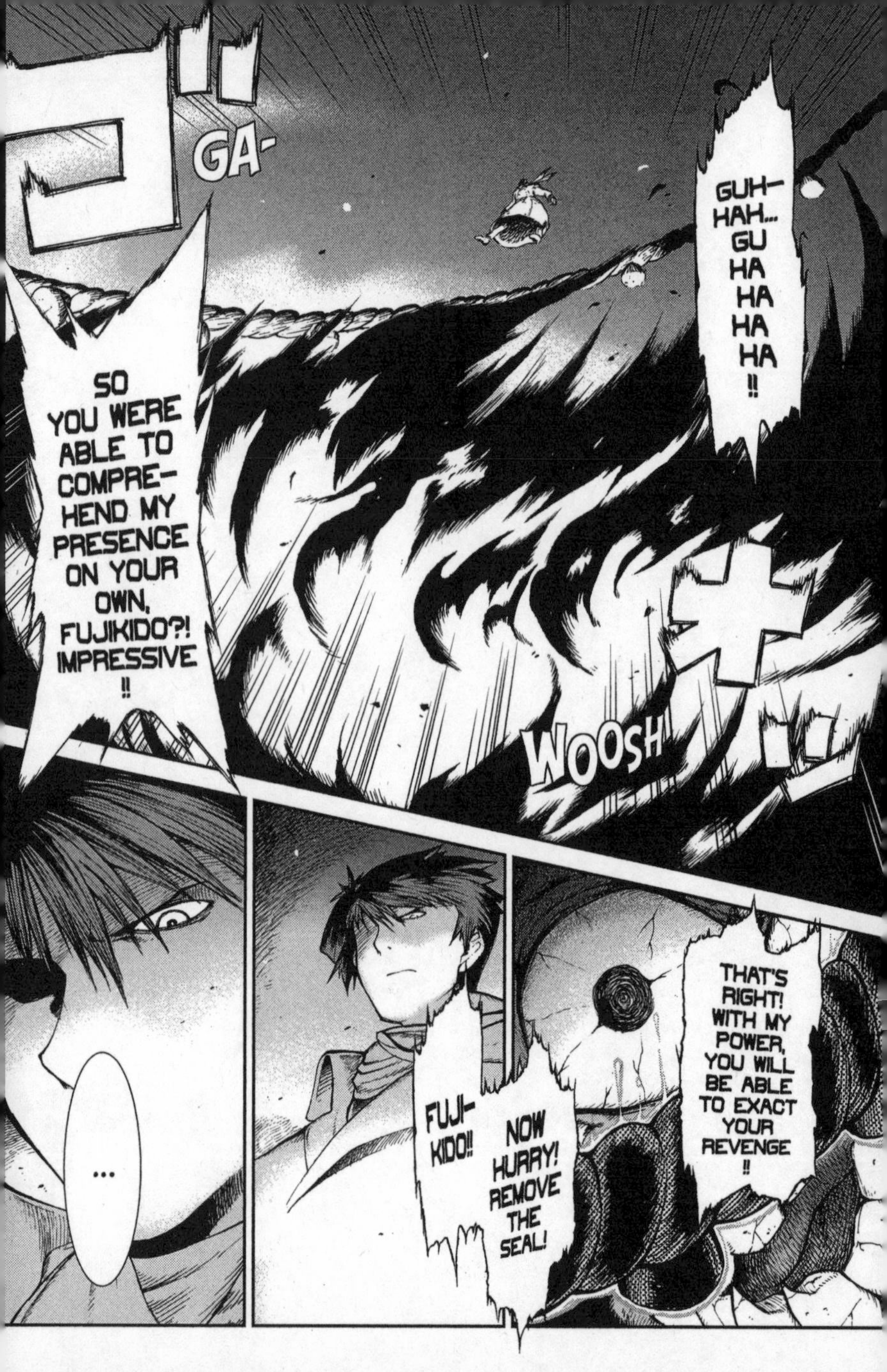
GUH-HAH... GU HA HA HA HA!!
GA-
SO YOU WERE ABLE TO COMPRE-HEND MY PRESENCE ON YOUR OWN, FUJIKIDO?! IMPRESSIVE!!
WOOSH
THAT'S RIGHT! WITH MY POWER, YOU WILL BE ABLE TO EXACT YOUR REVENGE!!
NOW HURRY! REMOVE THE SEAL!
FUJI-KIDO!!
...

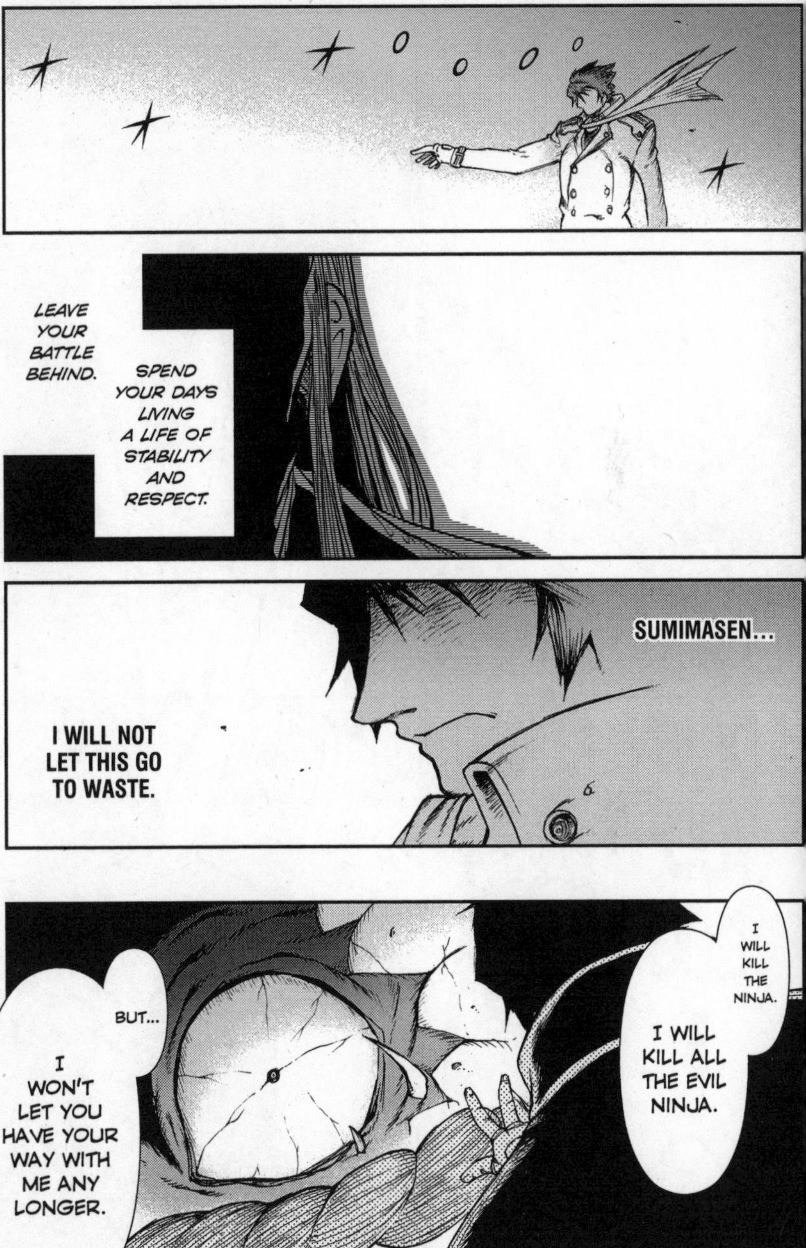

LEAVE YOUR BATTLE BEHIND.
SPEND YOUR DAYS LIVING A LIFE OF STABILITY AND RESPECT.
SUMIMASEN...
I WILL NOT LET THIS GO TO WASTE.
I WILL KILL THE NINJA.
I WILL KILL ALL THE EVIL NINJA.
BUT...
I WON'T LET YOU HAVE YOUR WAY WITH ME ANY LONGER.

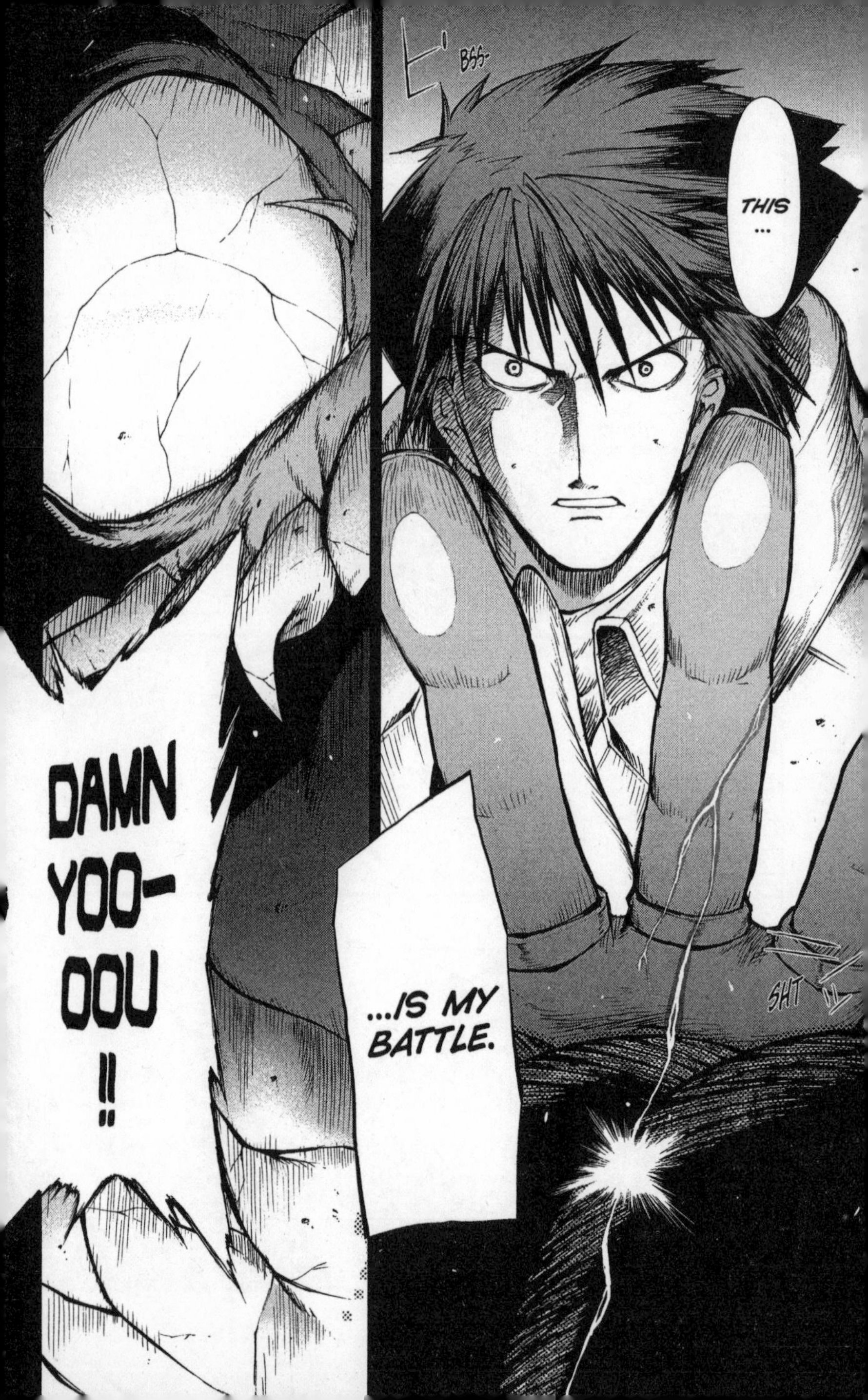
BSS-
THIS ...
...IS MY BATTLE.
SHT
DAMN YOO-OOU !!

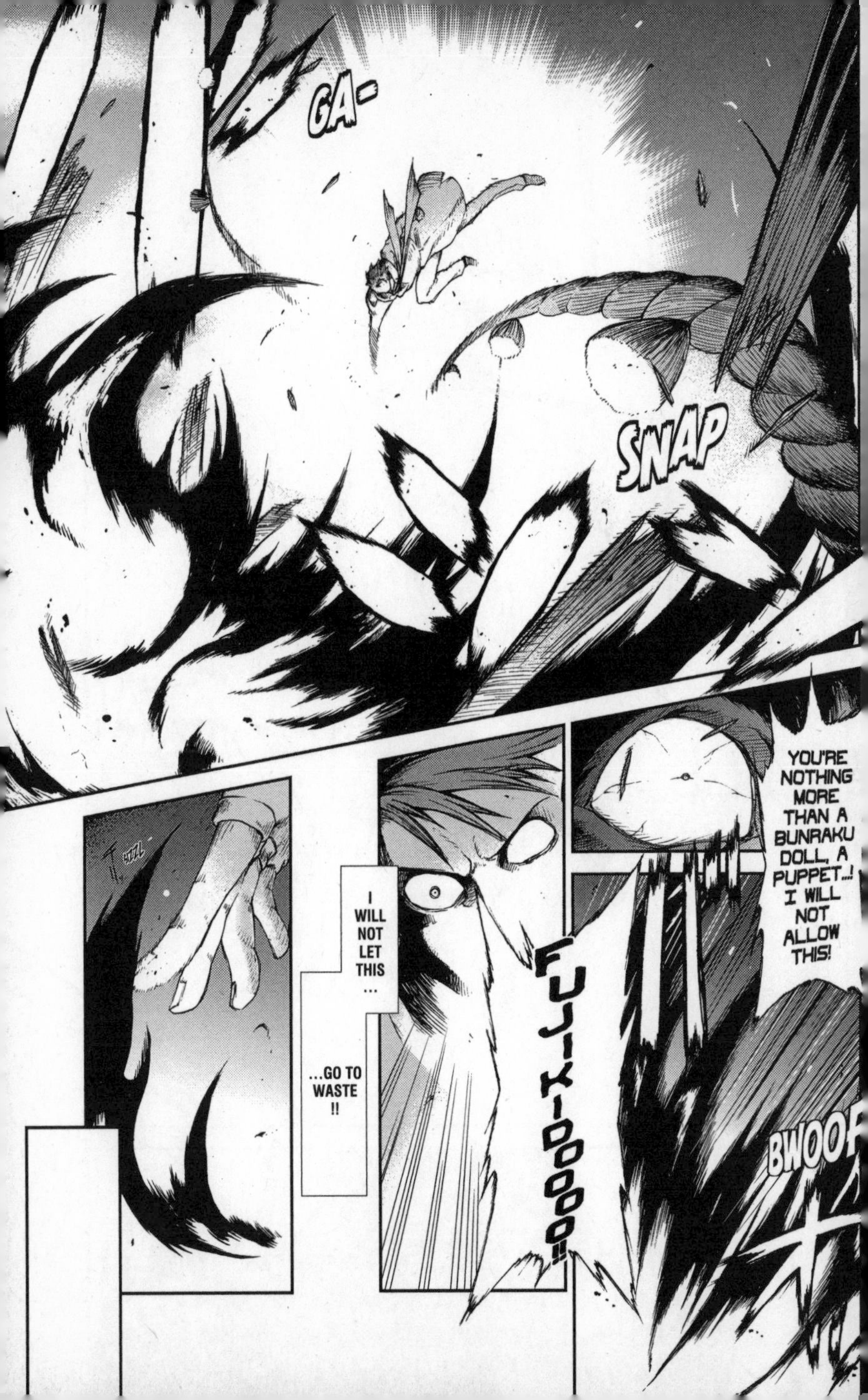
GA-
SNAP
YOU'RE NOTHING MORE THAN A BUNRAKU DOLL, A PUPPET...! I WILL NOT ALLOW THIS!
BWOOF
I WILL NOT LET THIS...
FUJIKIDOOOOO!!
...GO TO WASTE!!

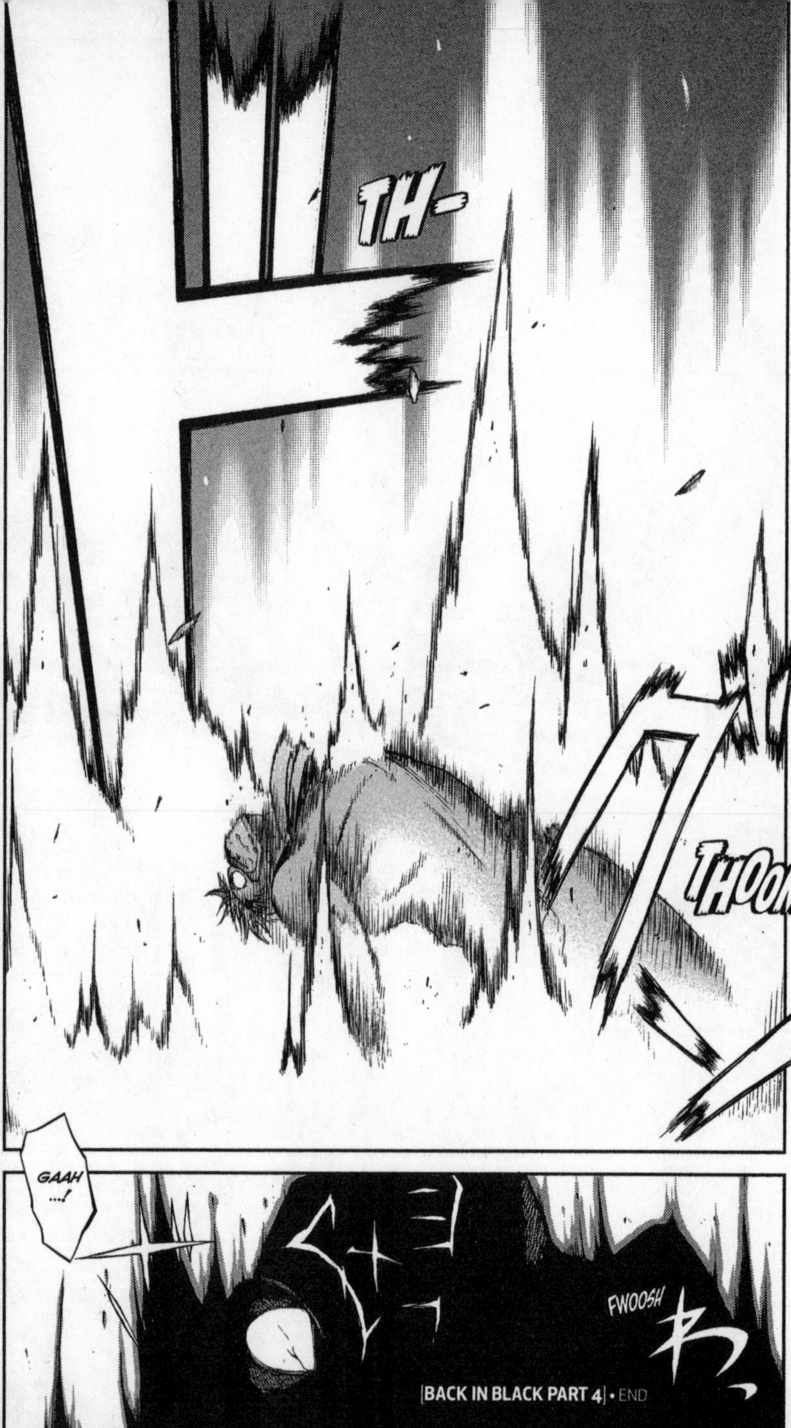
TH-
THOOM
GAAH ...!
FWOOSH

[BACK IN BLACK PART 4] • END

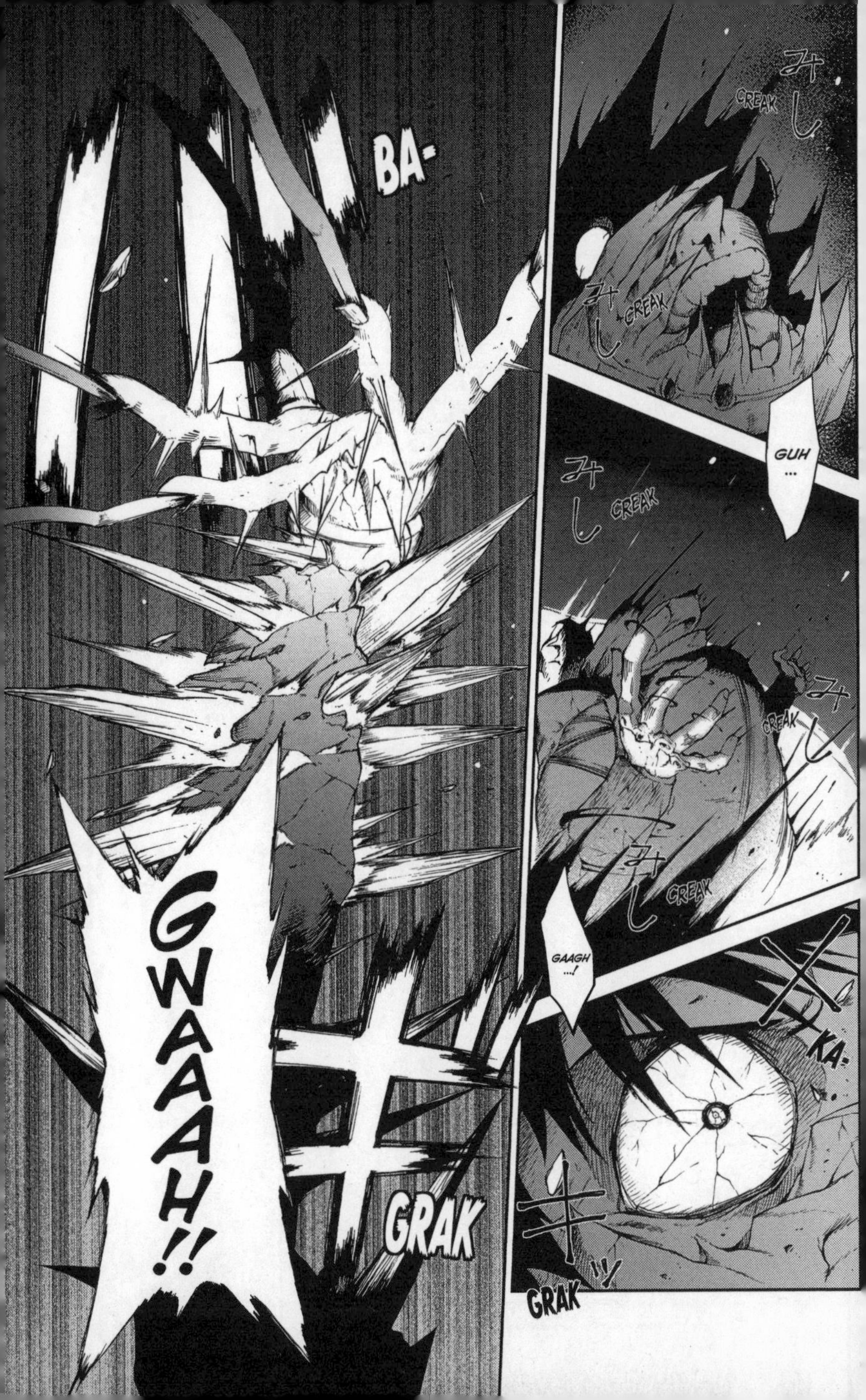
みし
CREAK
みし
CREAK
GUH ...
みし
CREAK
みし
CREAK
みし
CREAK
GAAGH ...!
KA-
GRAK
BA-
GWAAAH!!
GRAK

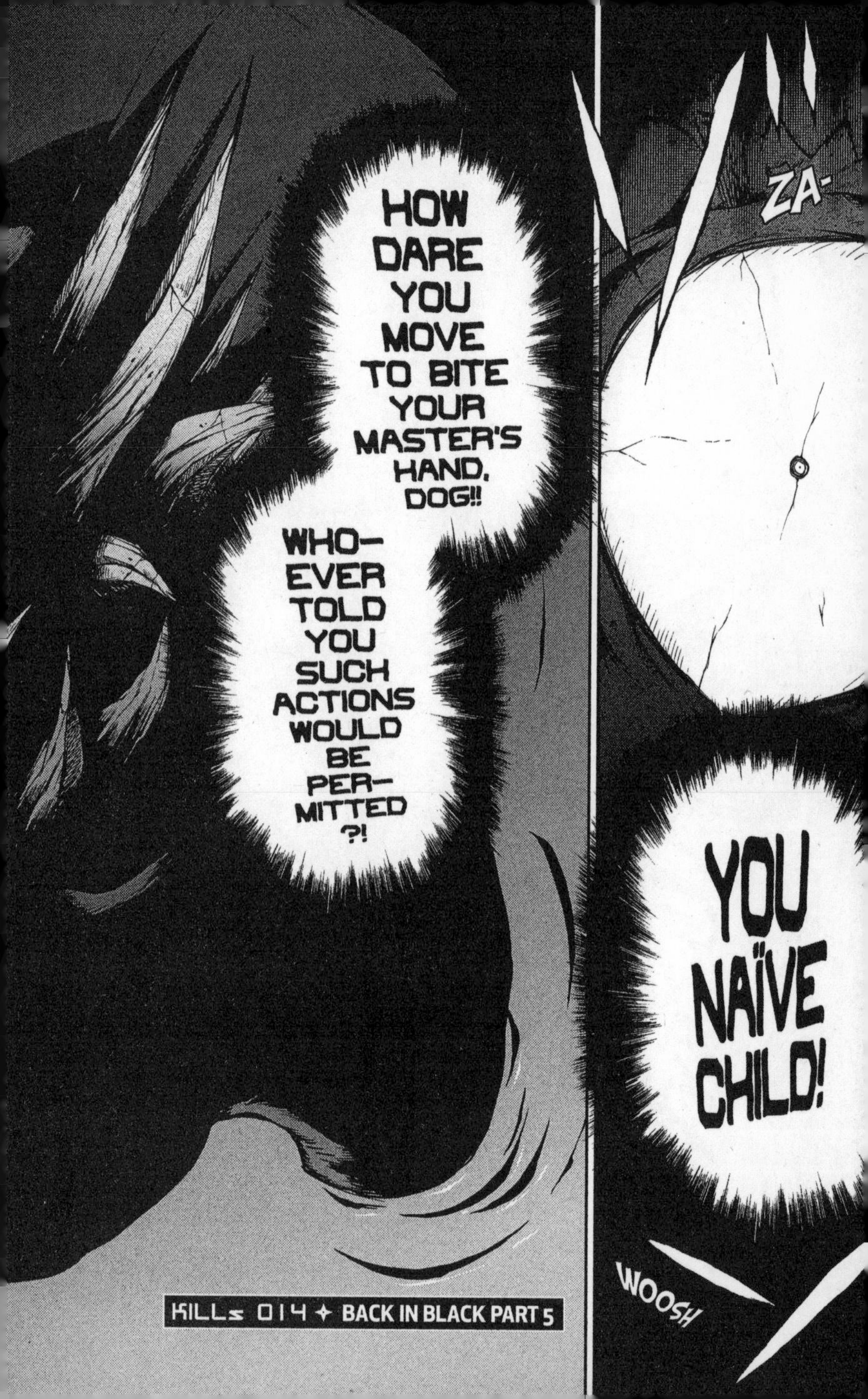
ZA-
YOU NAÏVE CHILD!
WOOSH
HOW DARE YOU MOVE TO BITE YOUR MASTER'S HAND, DOG!!
WHO-EVER TOLD YOU SUCH ACTIONS WOULD BE PER-MITTED ?!
KILLs 014 ✦ BACK IN BLACK PART 5

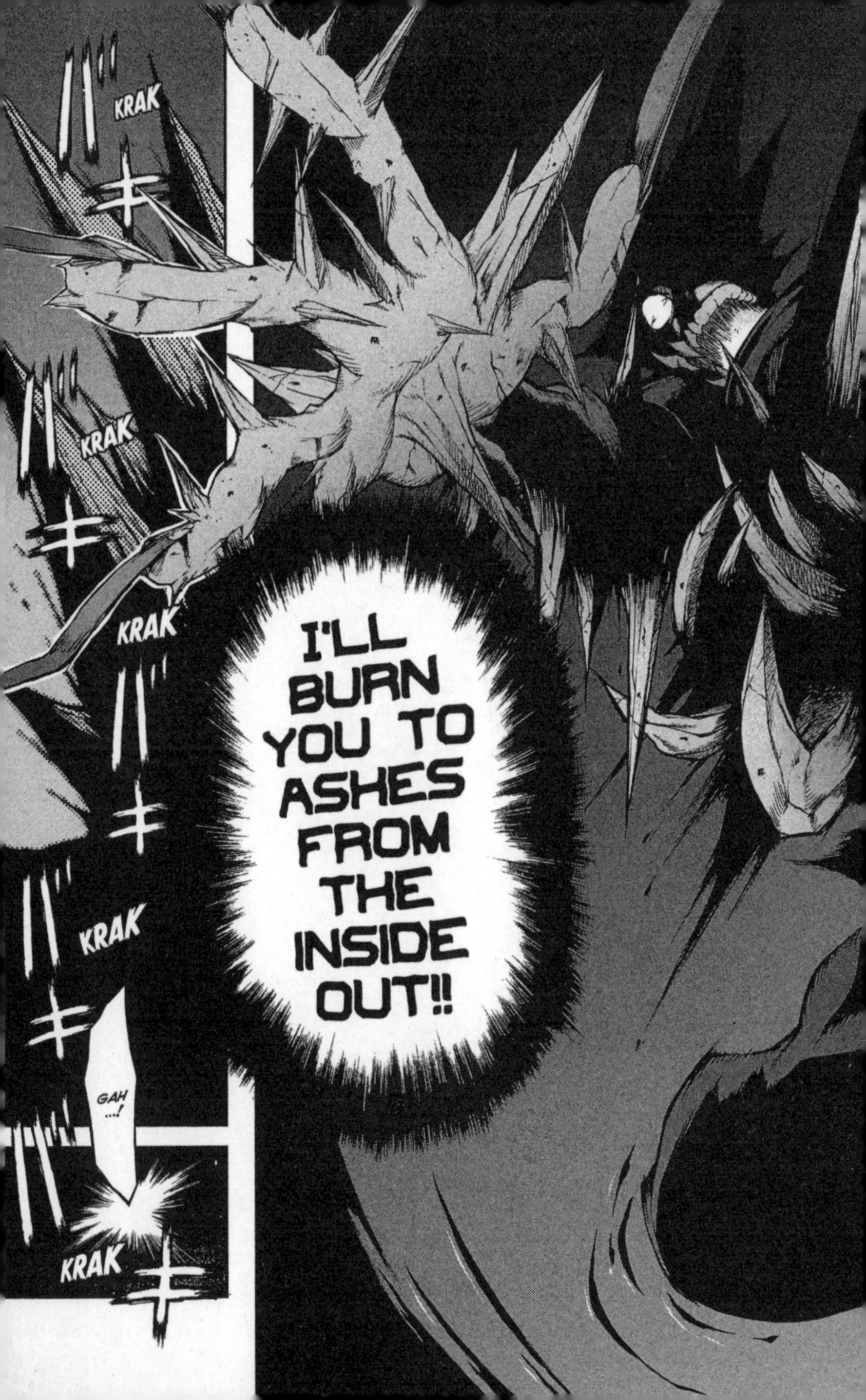
I'LL BURN YOU TO ASHES FROM THE INSIDE OUT!!
KRAK
KRAK
KRAK
KRAK
GAH...!
KRAK

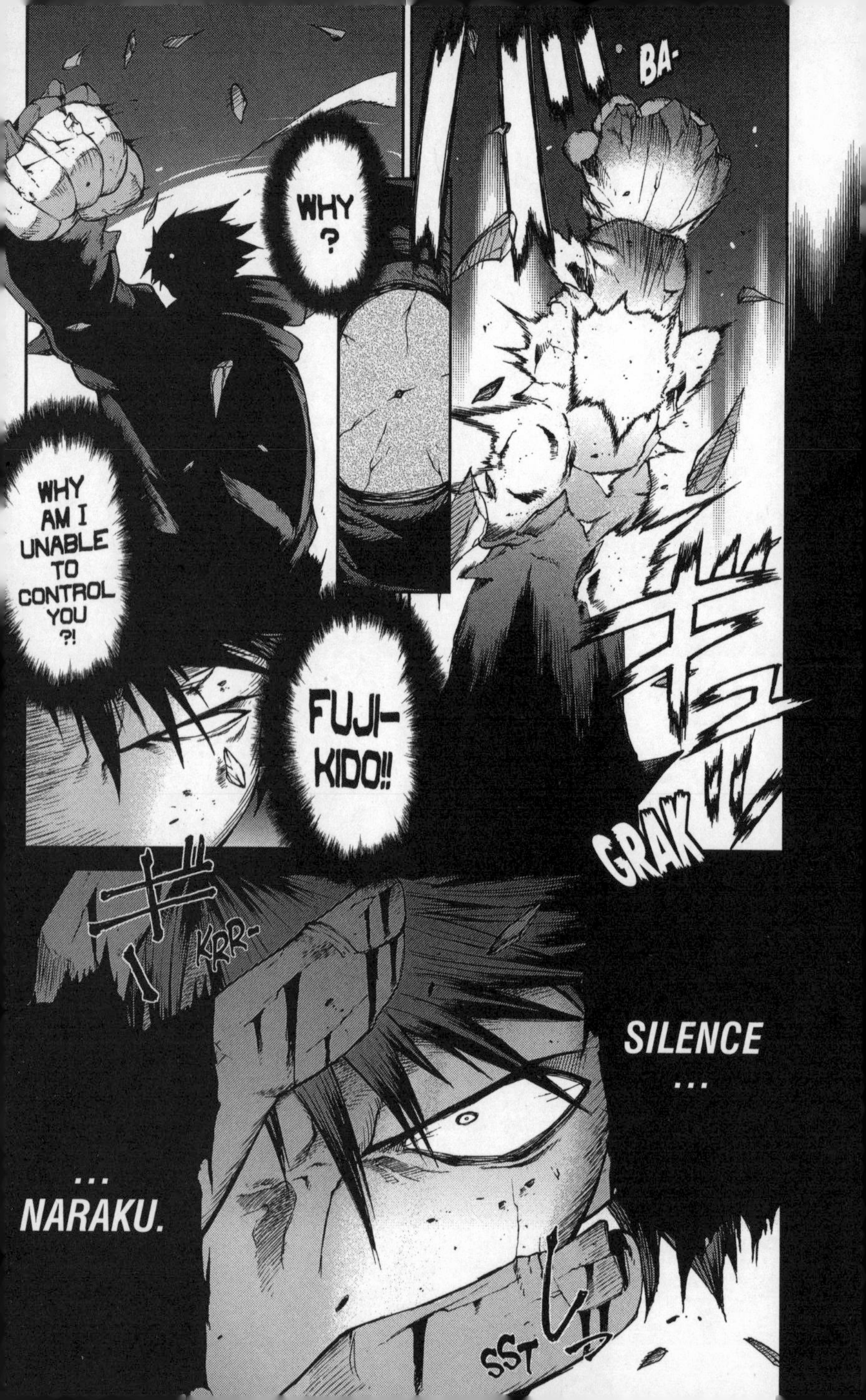
BA-
GRAK
WHY?
WHY AM I UNABLE TO CONTROL YOU?!
FUJI-KIDO!!
KRR-
SILENCE...
...NARAKU.
SST

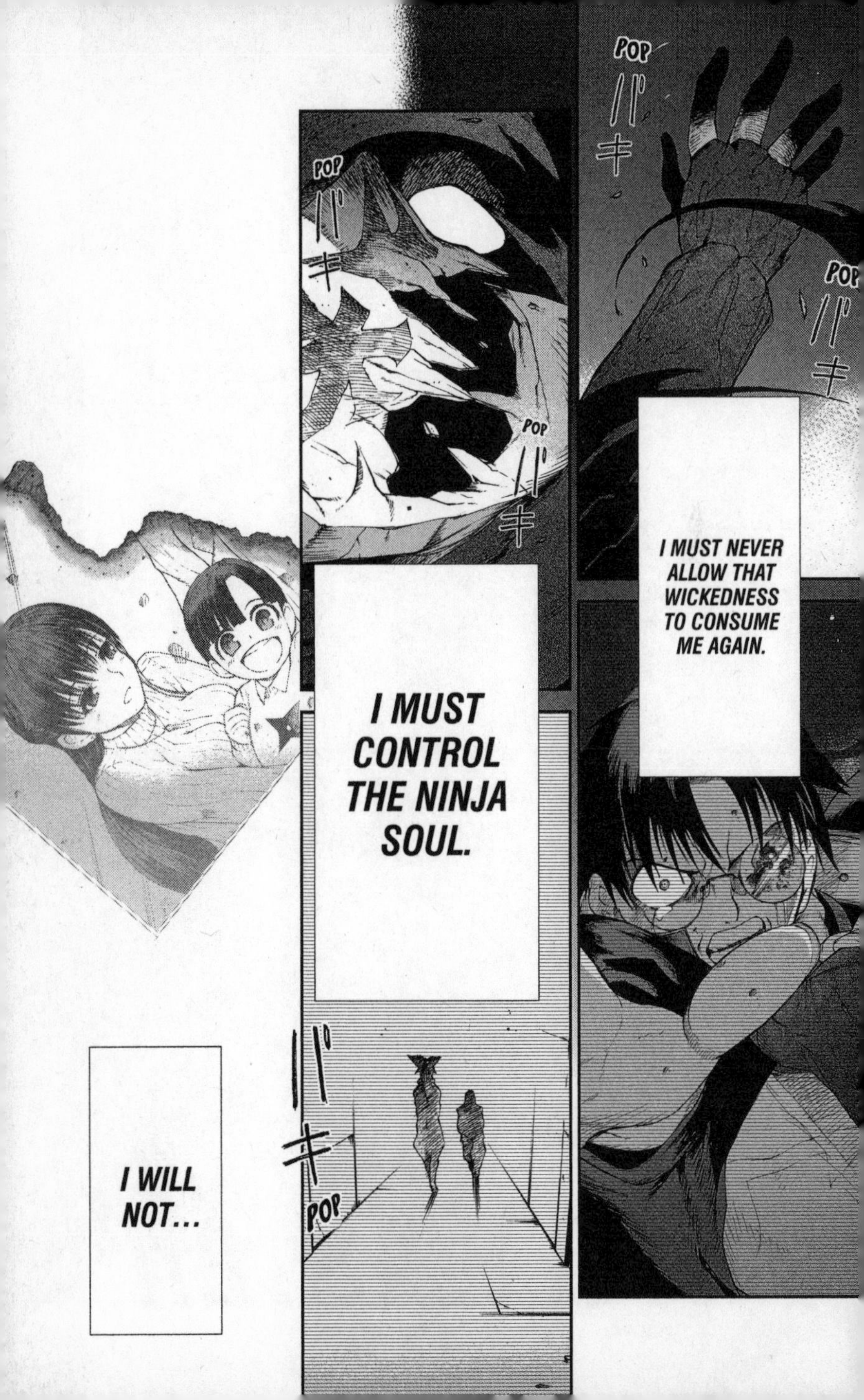
POP
パキ
POP
パキ
I MUST NEVER ALLOW THAT WICKEDNESS TO CONSUME ME AGAIN.
POP
パキ
POP
パキ
I MUST CONTROL THE NINJA SOUL.
パキ
POP
I WILL NOT...

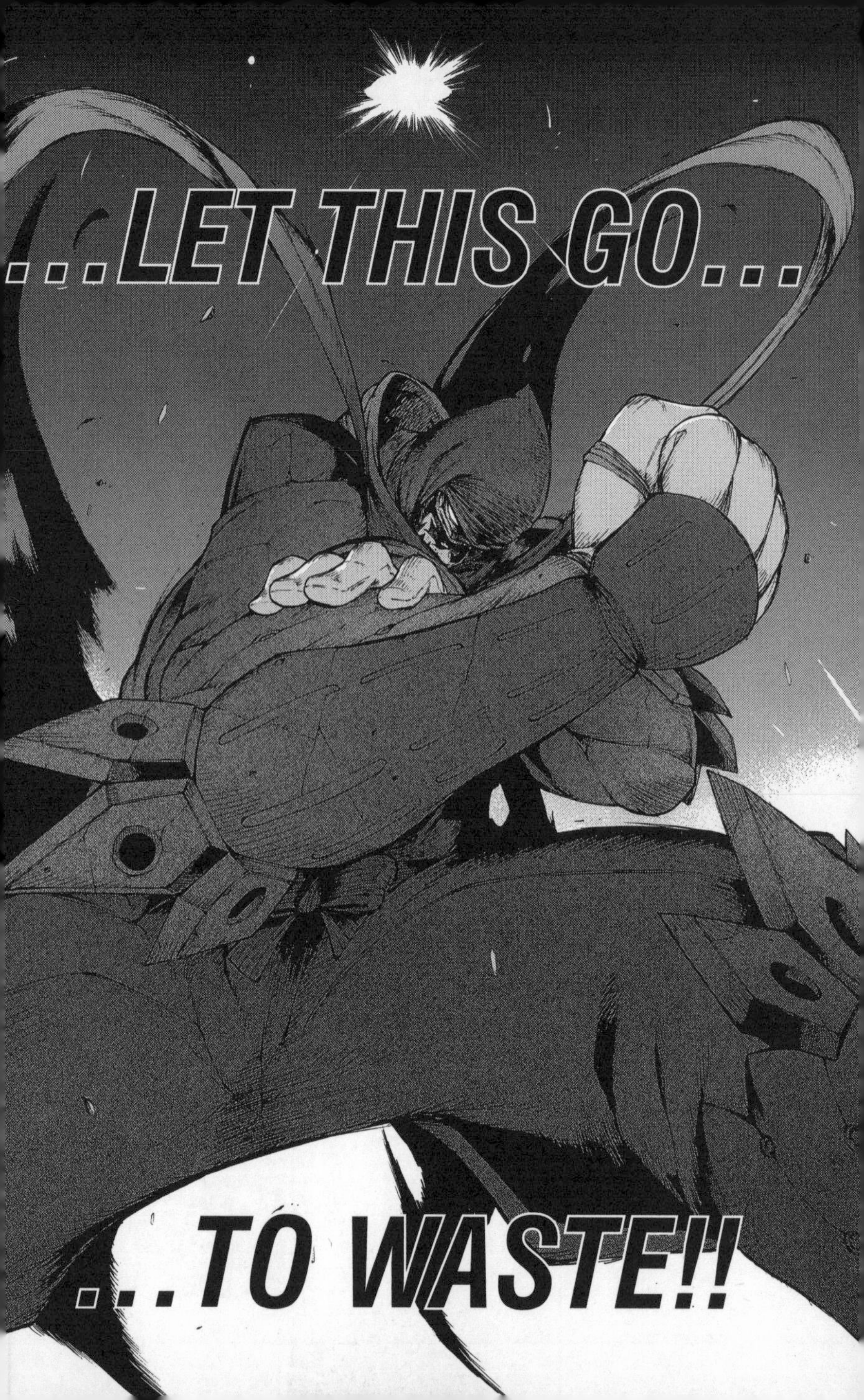
...LET THIS GO...
...TO WASTE!!

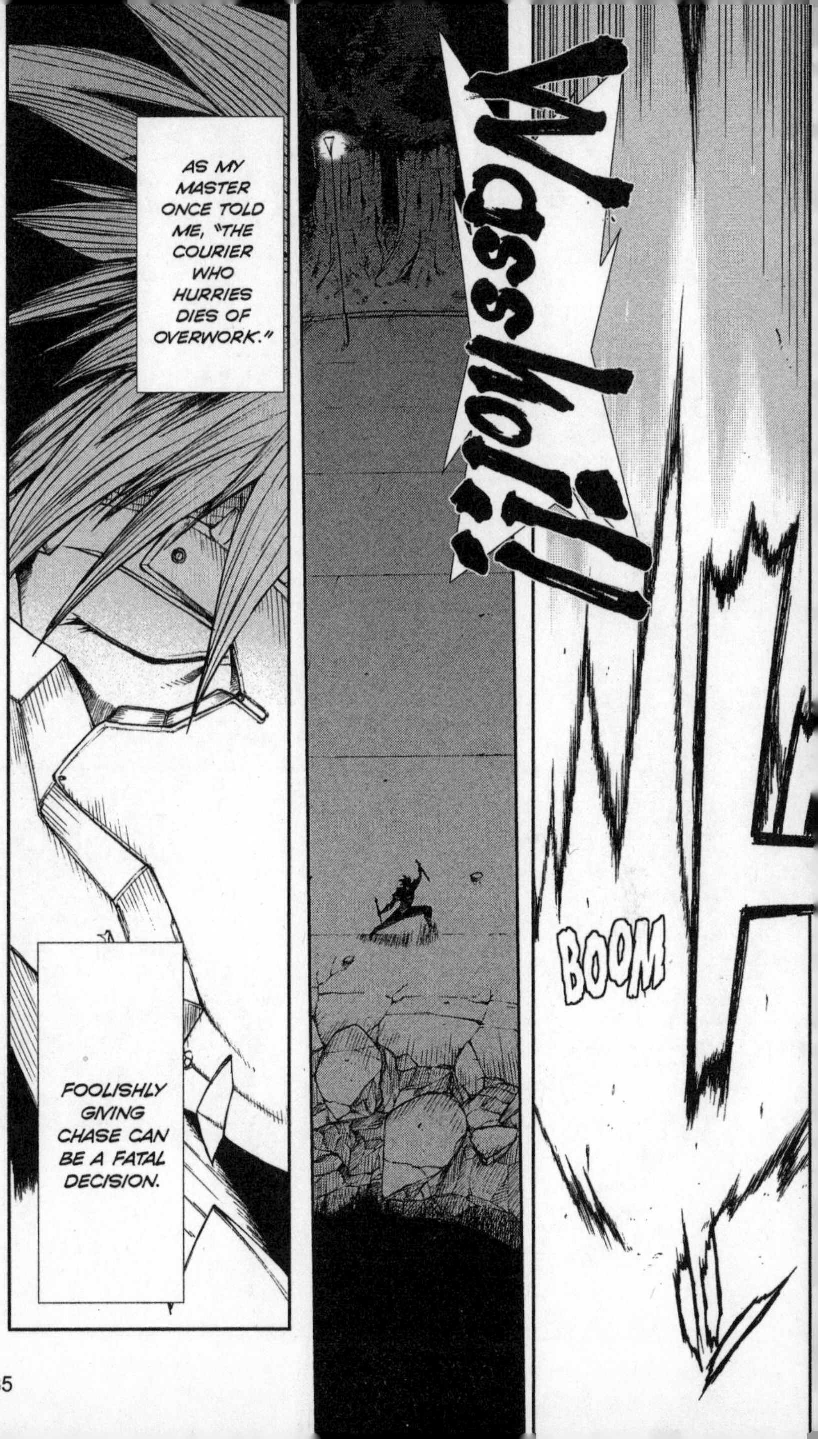
Wasshoi!!
BOOM
AS MY MASTER ONCE TOLD ME, "THE COURIER WHO HURRIES DIES OF OVERWORK."
FOOLISHLY GIVING CHASE CAN BE A FATAL DECISION.

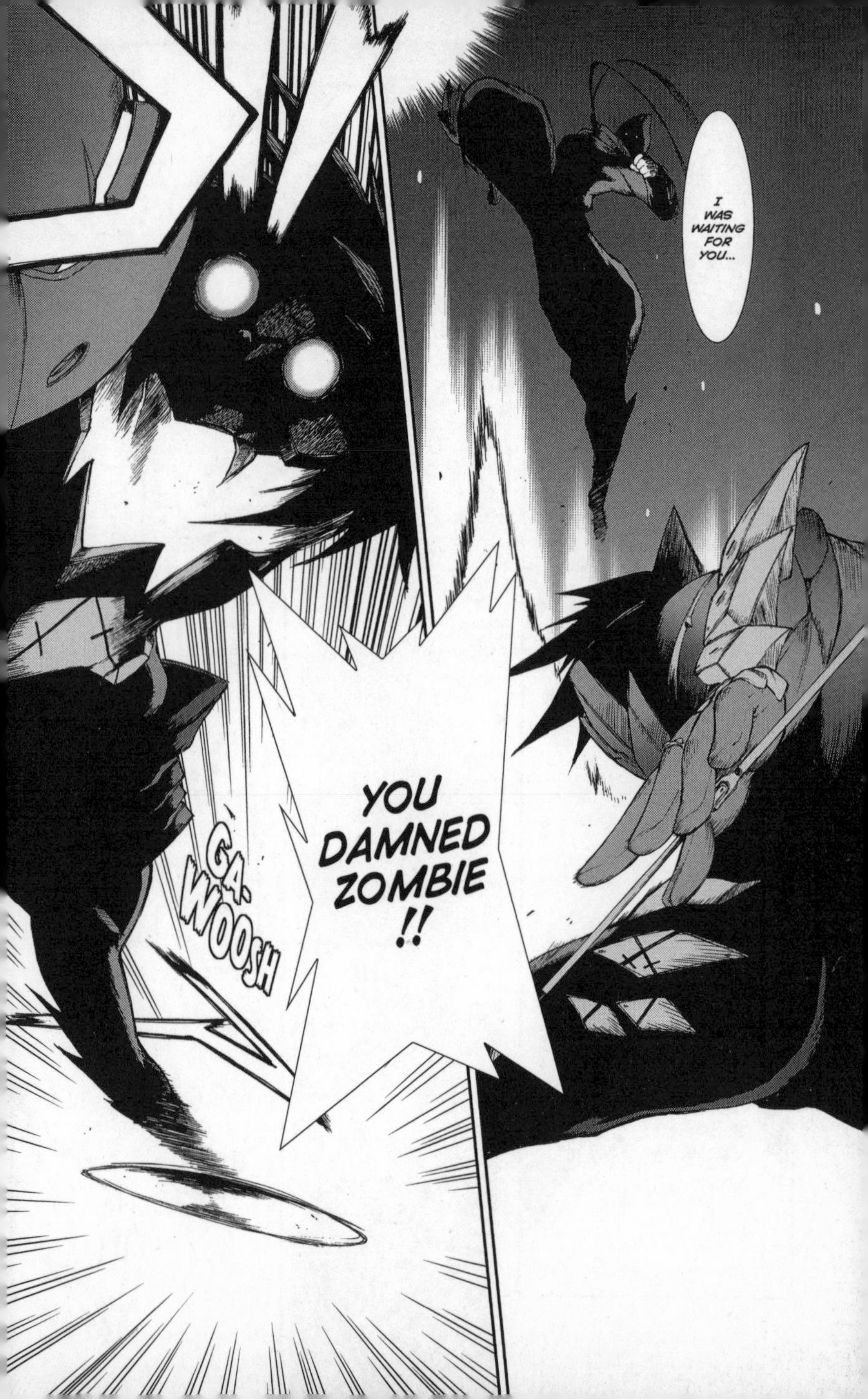
I WAS WAITING FOR YOU...
YOU DAMNED ZOMBIE !!
GA-WOOSH

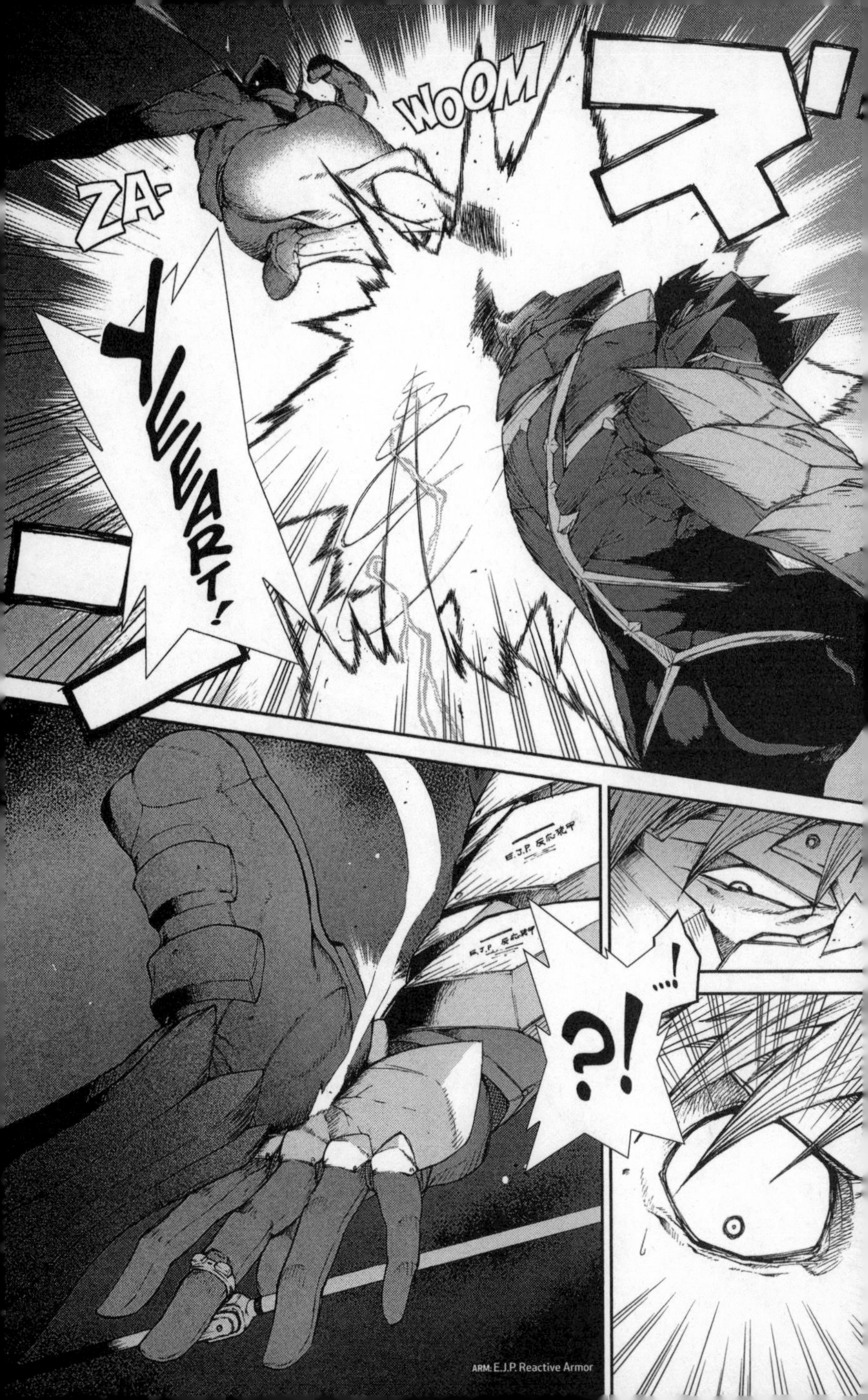
WOOM
ZA-
...!
?!
ARM: E.J.P. Reactive Armor

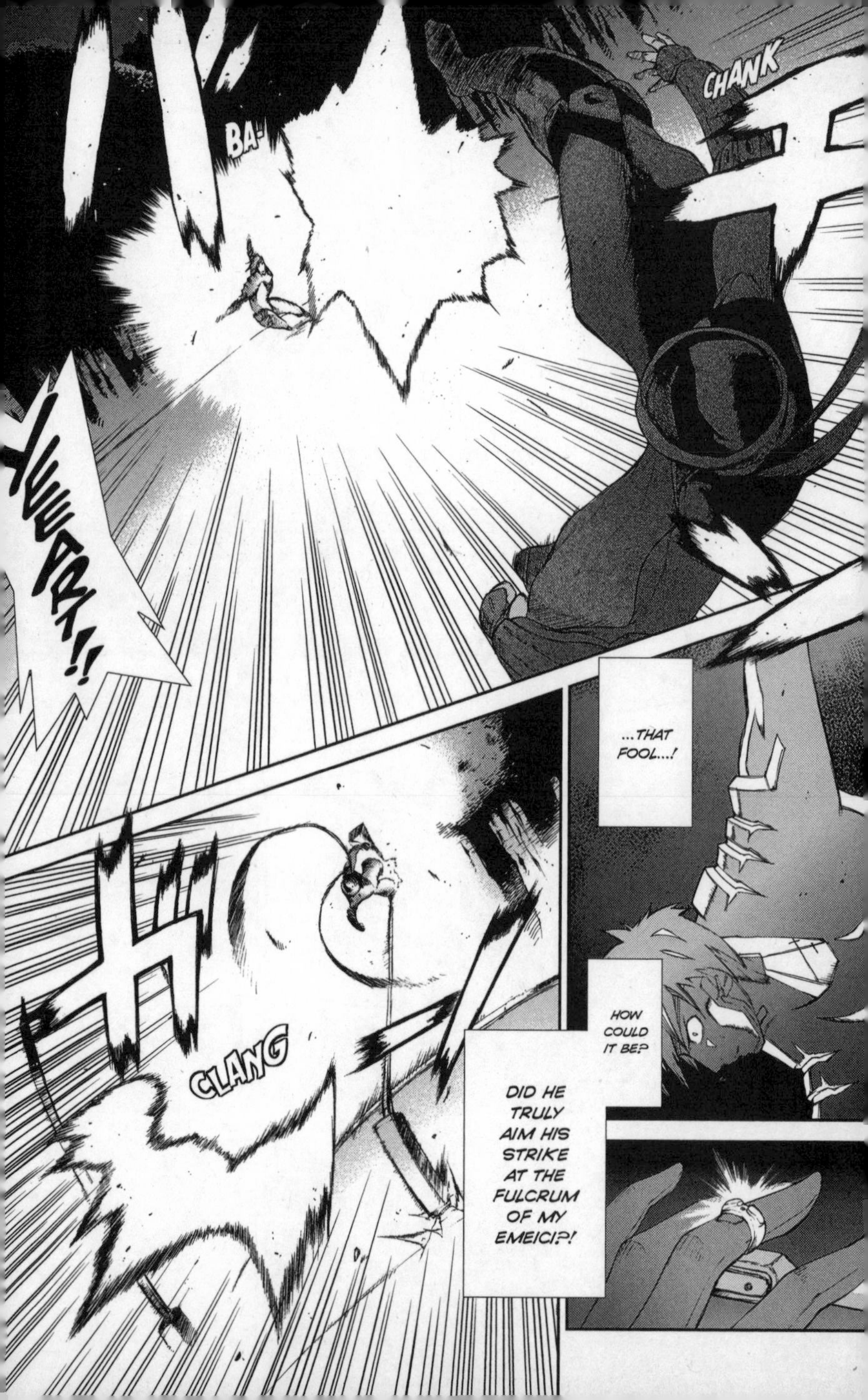
CHANK
BA-
YUEARK!!
...THAT FOOL...!
HOW COULD IT BE?
DID HE TRULY AIM HIS STRIKE AT THE FULCRUM OF MY EMEICI?!
CLANG

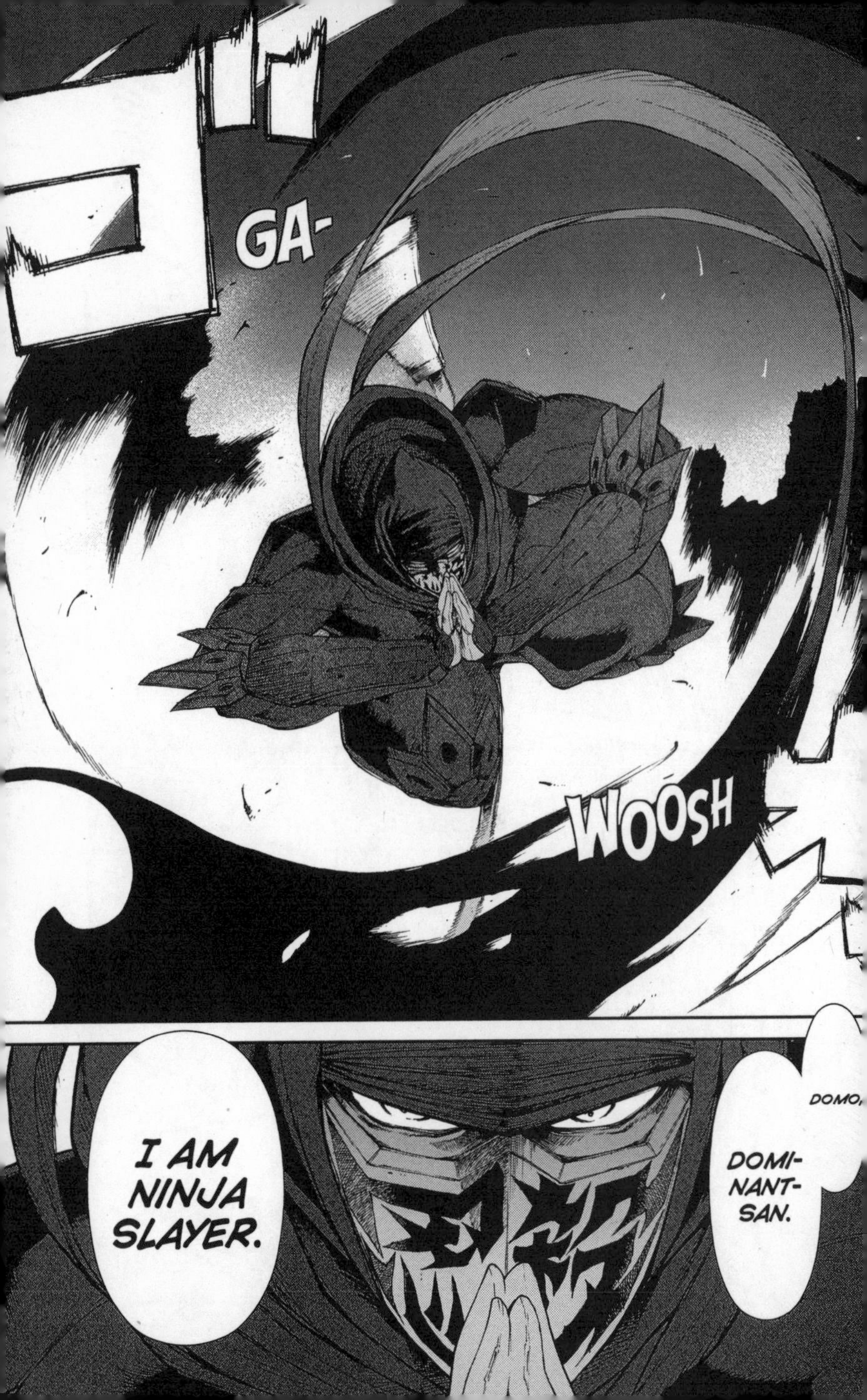
GA-
WOOSH
DOMO,
DOMI-NANT-SAN.
I AM NINJA SLAYER.

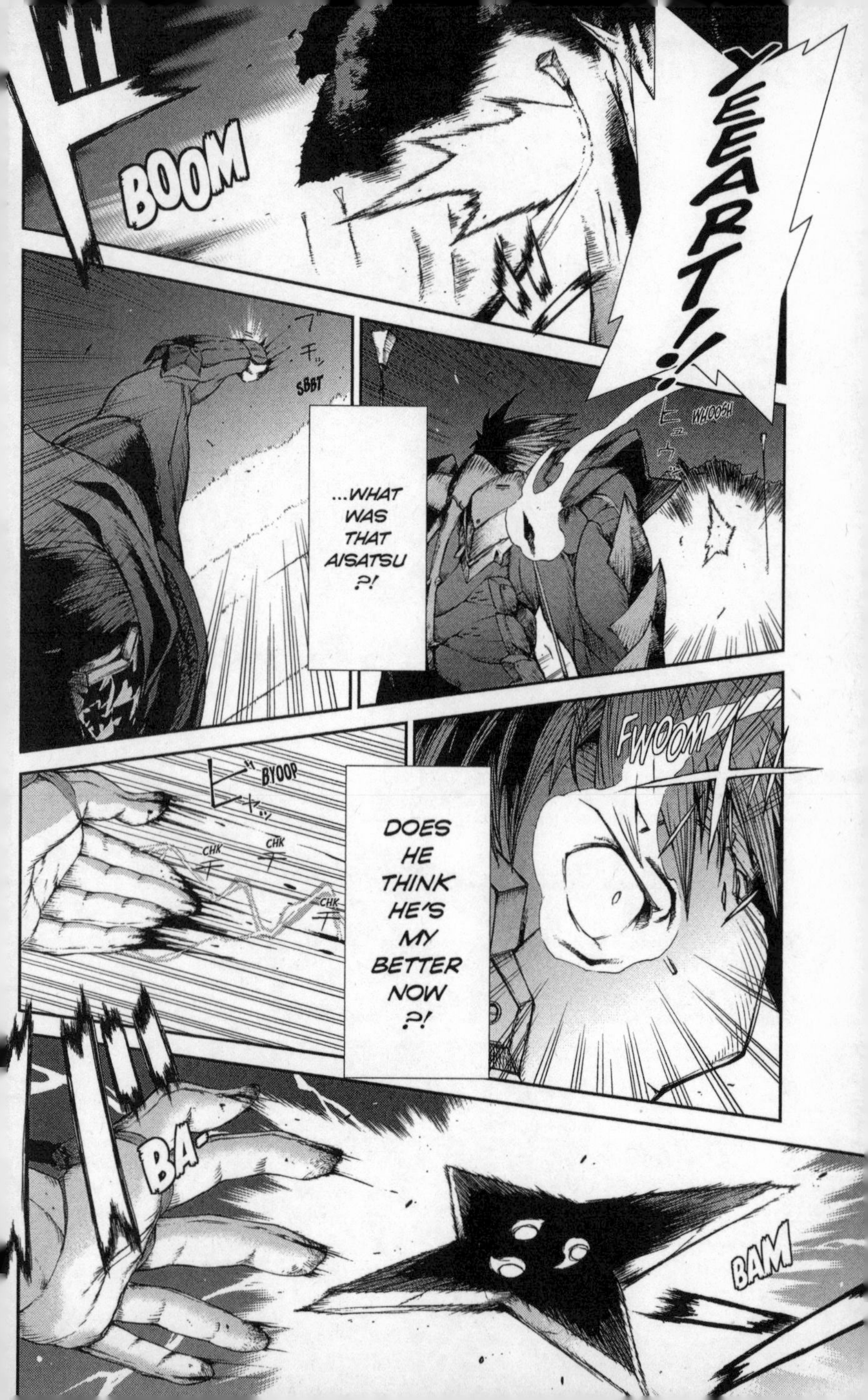
YEEARRT!!
BOOM
WHOOSH
...WHAT WAS THAT AISATSU?!
SBBT
FWOOM
DOES HE THINK HE'S MY BETTER NOW?!
BYOOP
CHK
CHK
CHK
BA-
BAM

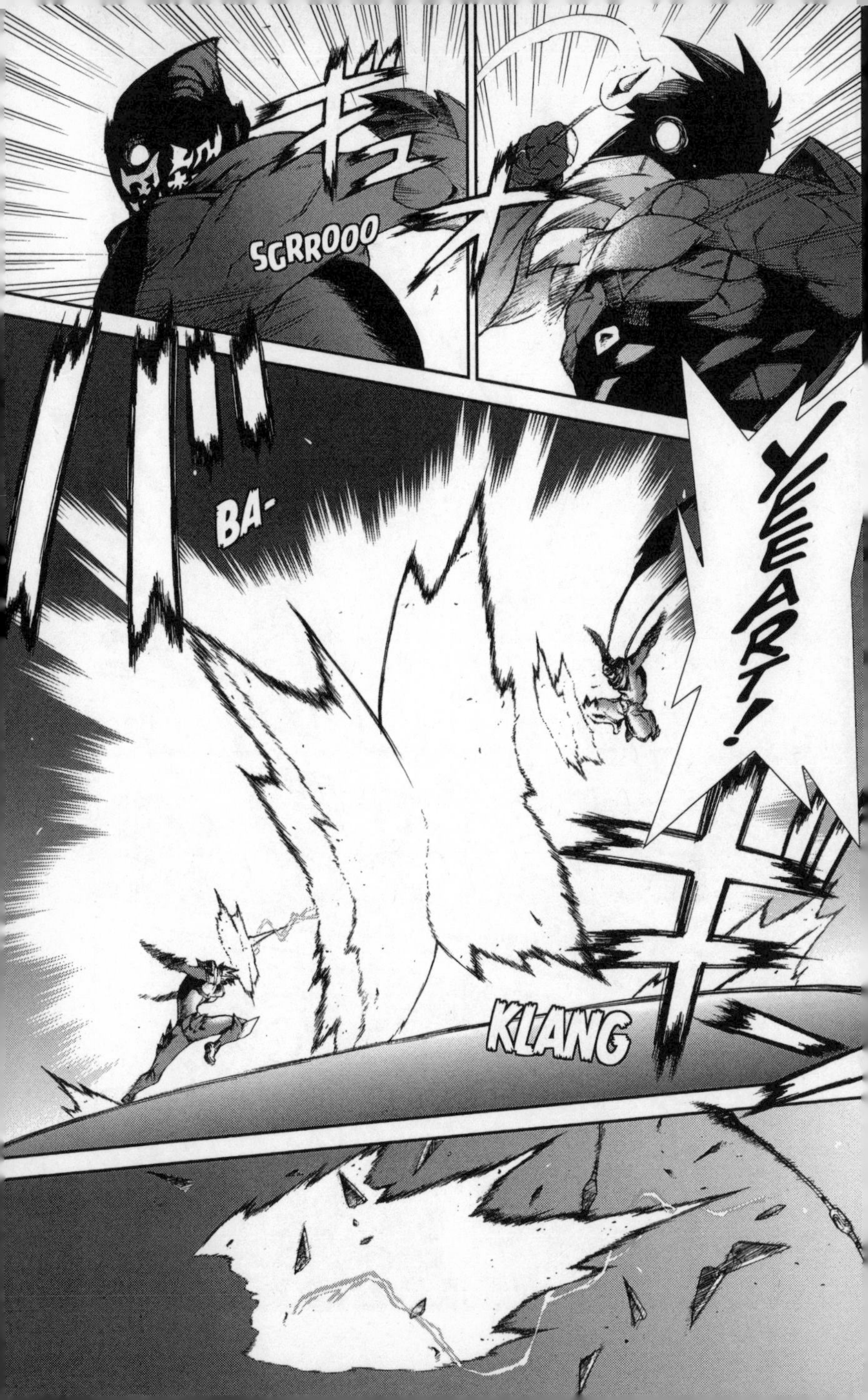
SGRROOO
YEEART!
BA-
KLANG

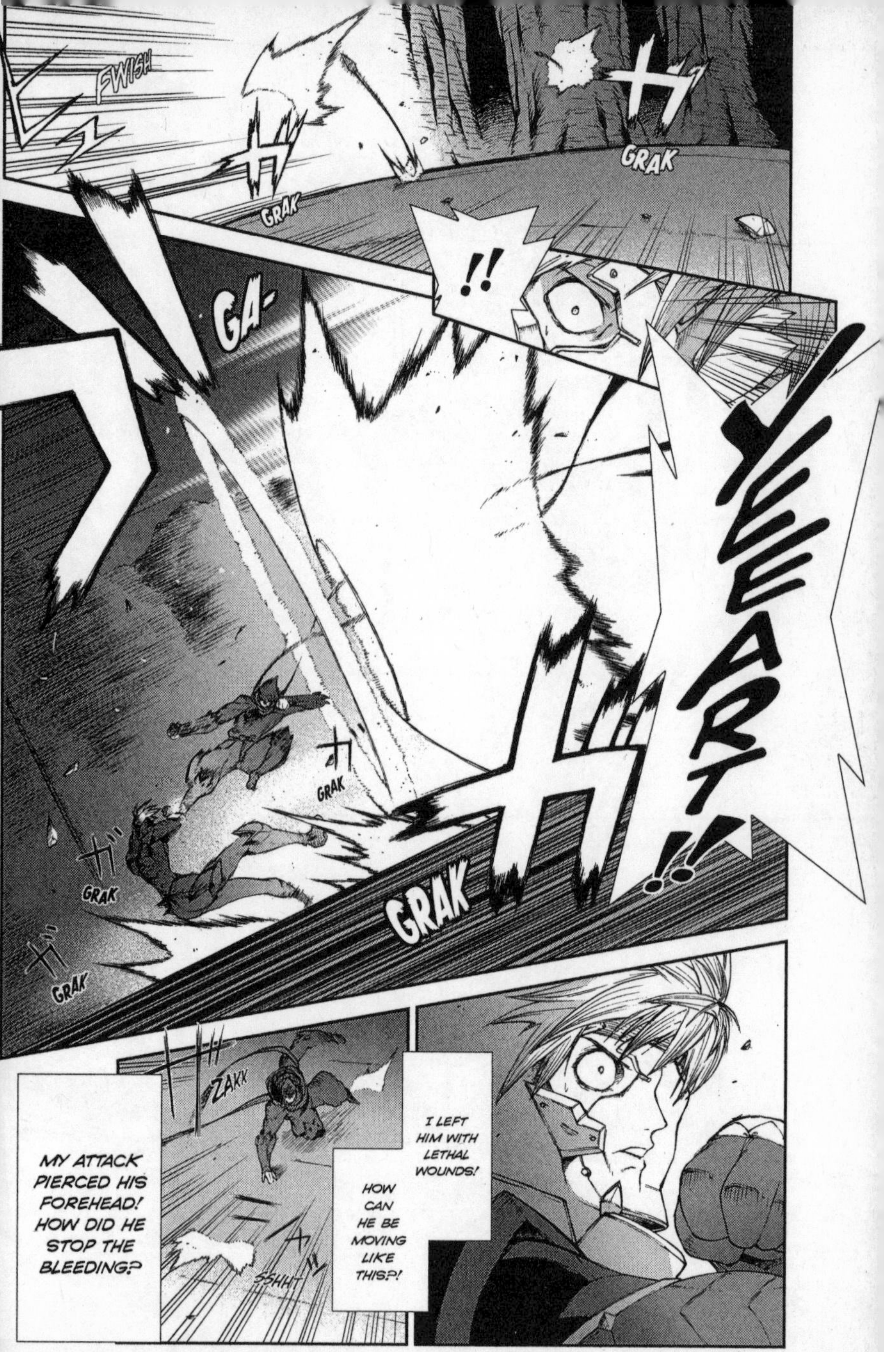
GRAK
FWISH
GRAK
!!
YEEEART!!
GA-
GRAK
GRAK
GRAK
GRAK
I LEFT HIM WITH LETHAL WOUNDS!
HOW CAN HE BE MOVING LIKE THIS?!
ZAKK
MY ATTACK PIERCED HIS FOREHEAD! HOW DID HE STOP THE BLEEDING?
SSHHT

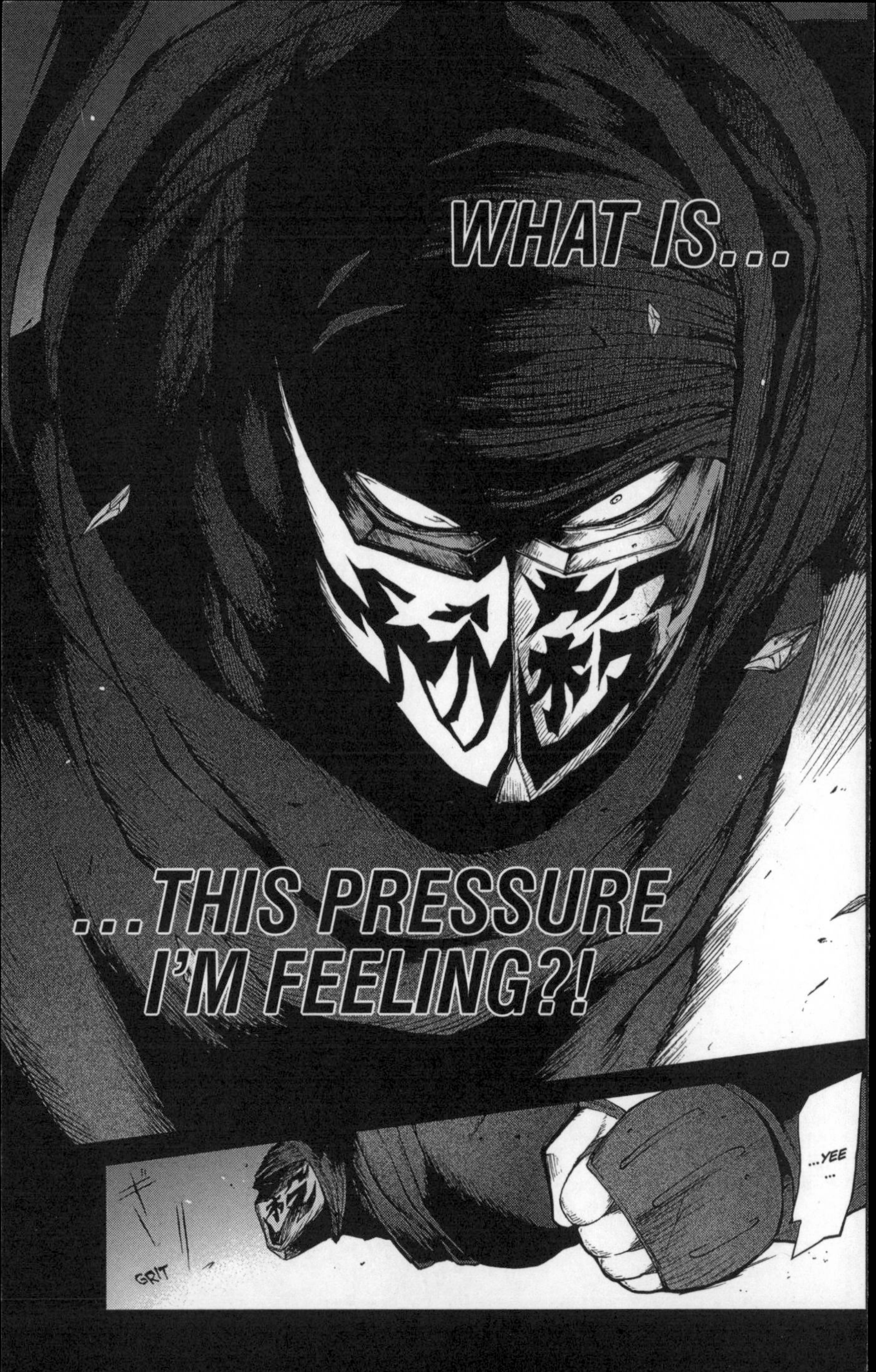
WHAT IS...
...THIS PRESSURE I'M FEELING?!
...YEE ...
GRIT

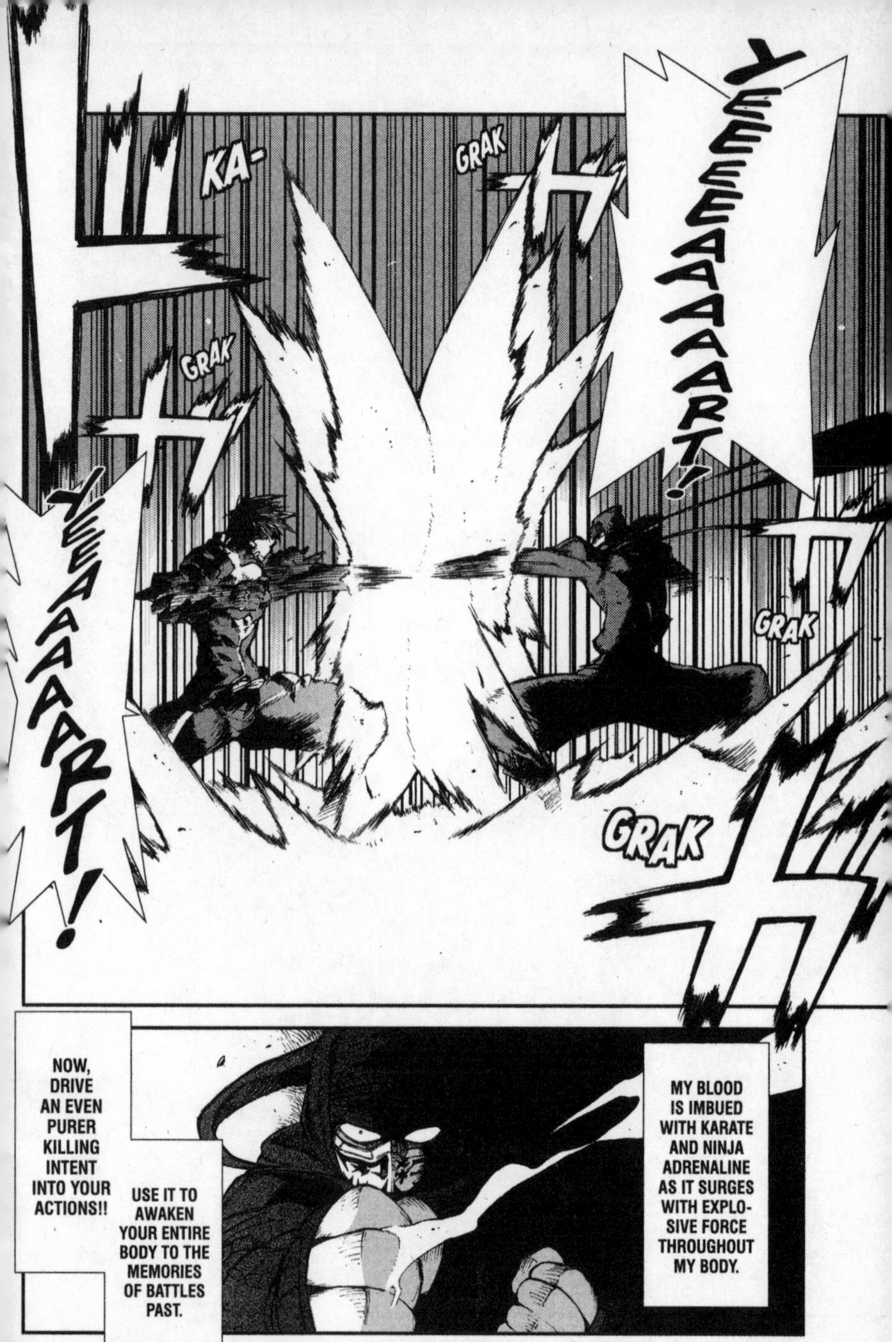
YEEEEAAAAART!
GRAK
KA-
GRAK
YEEEAAAAART!
GRAK
GRAK
MY BLOOD IS IMBUED WITH KARATE AND NINJA ADRENALINE AS IT SURGES WITH EXPLOSIVE FORCE THROUGHOUT MY BODY.
USE IT TO AWAKEN YOUR ENTIRE BODY TO THE MEMORIES OF BATTLES PAST.
NOW, DRIVE AN EVEN PURER KILLING INTENT INTO YOUR ACTIONS!!

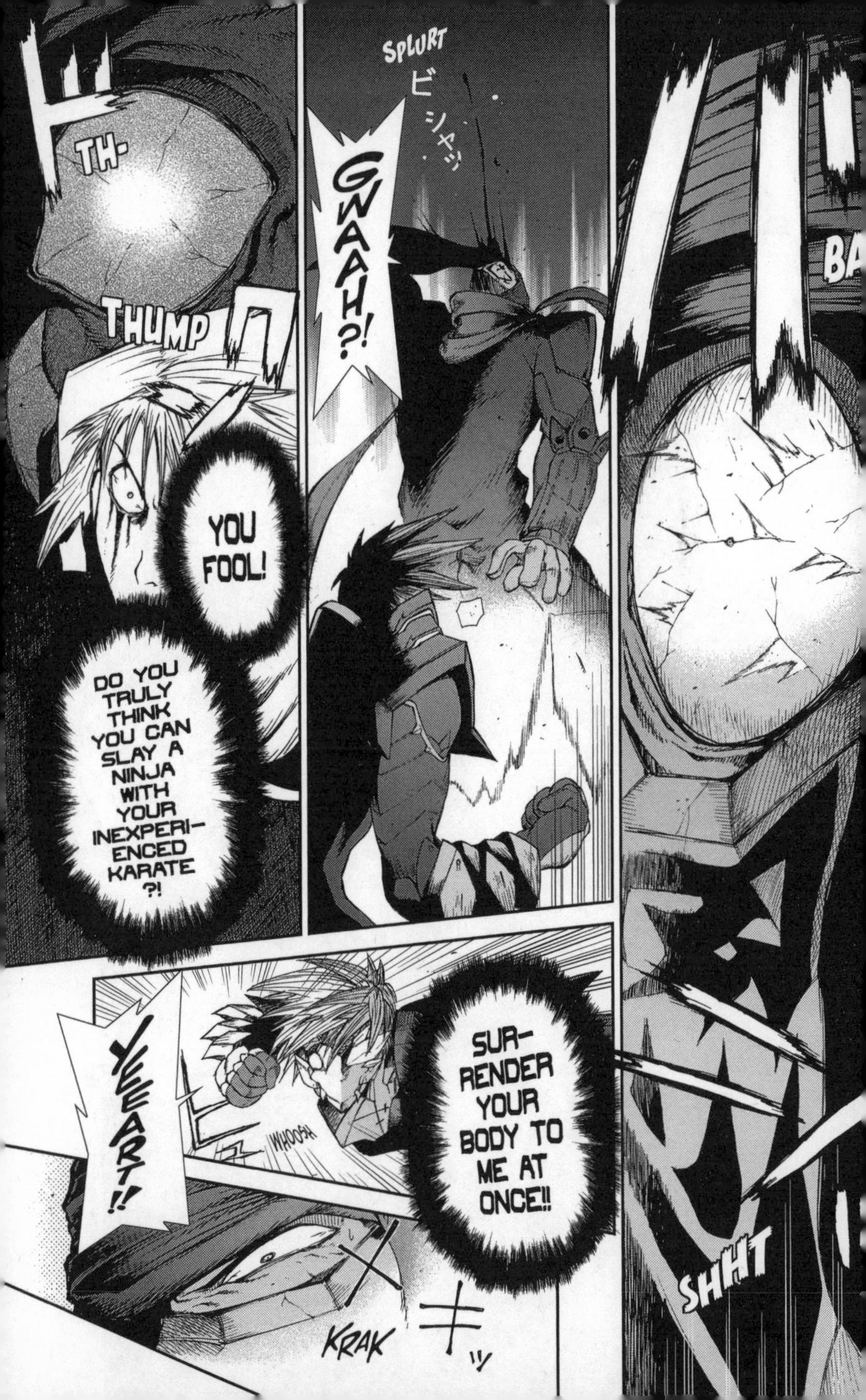
BA
SHHT
SPLURT
ビシャッ
GWAAH?!
TH-
THUMP
YOU FOOL!
DO YOU TRULY THINK YOU CAN SLAY A NINJA WITH YOUR INEXPERI-ENCED KARATE?!
SUR-RENDER YOUR BODY TO ME AT ONCE!!
YEEART!!
WHOOSH
KRAK
キッ

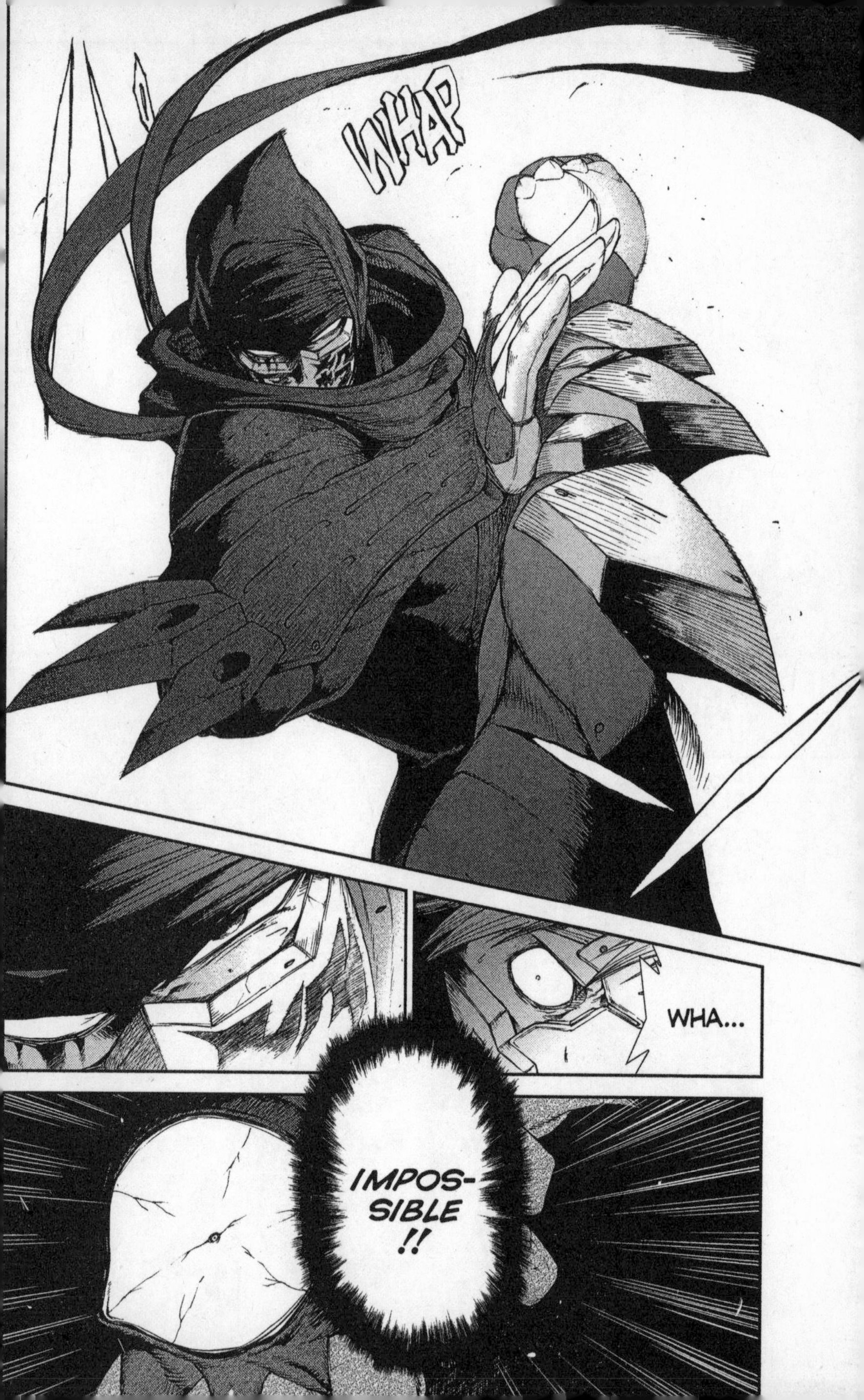
WHAP
WHA...
IMPOSSIBLE!!

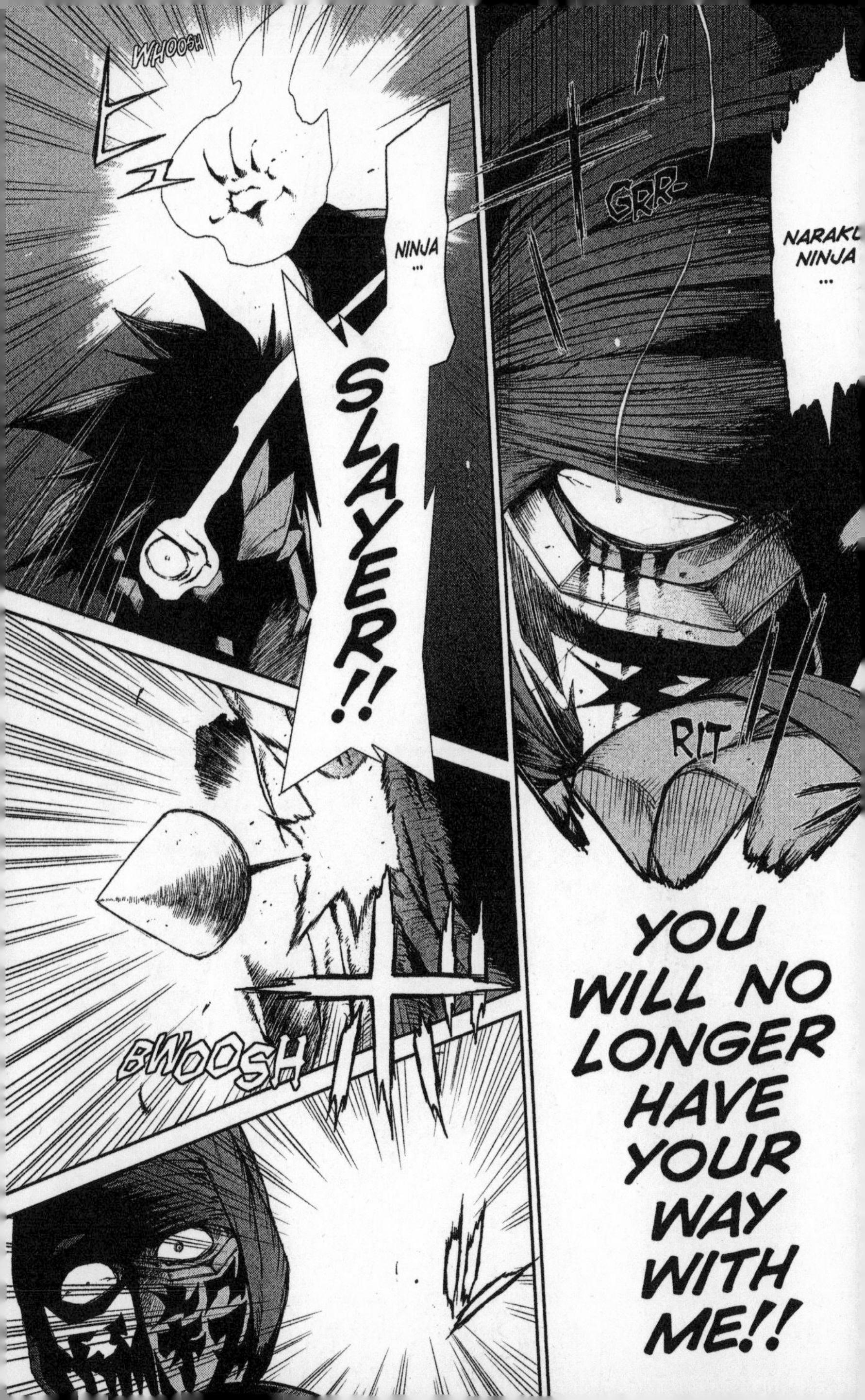
GRR-
NARAKU NINJA ...
RIT
YOU WILL NO LONGER HAVE YOUR WAY WITH ME!!
WHOOSH
NINJA ...
SLAYER!!
BWOOSH

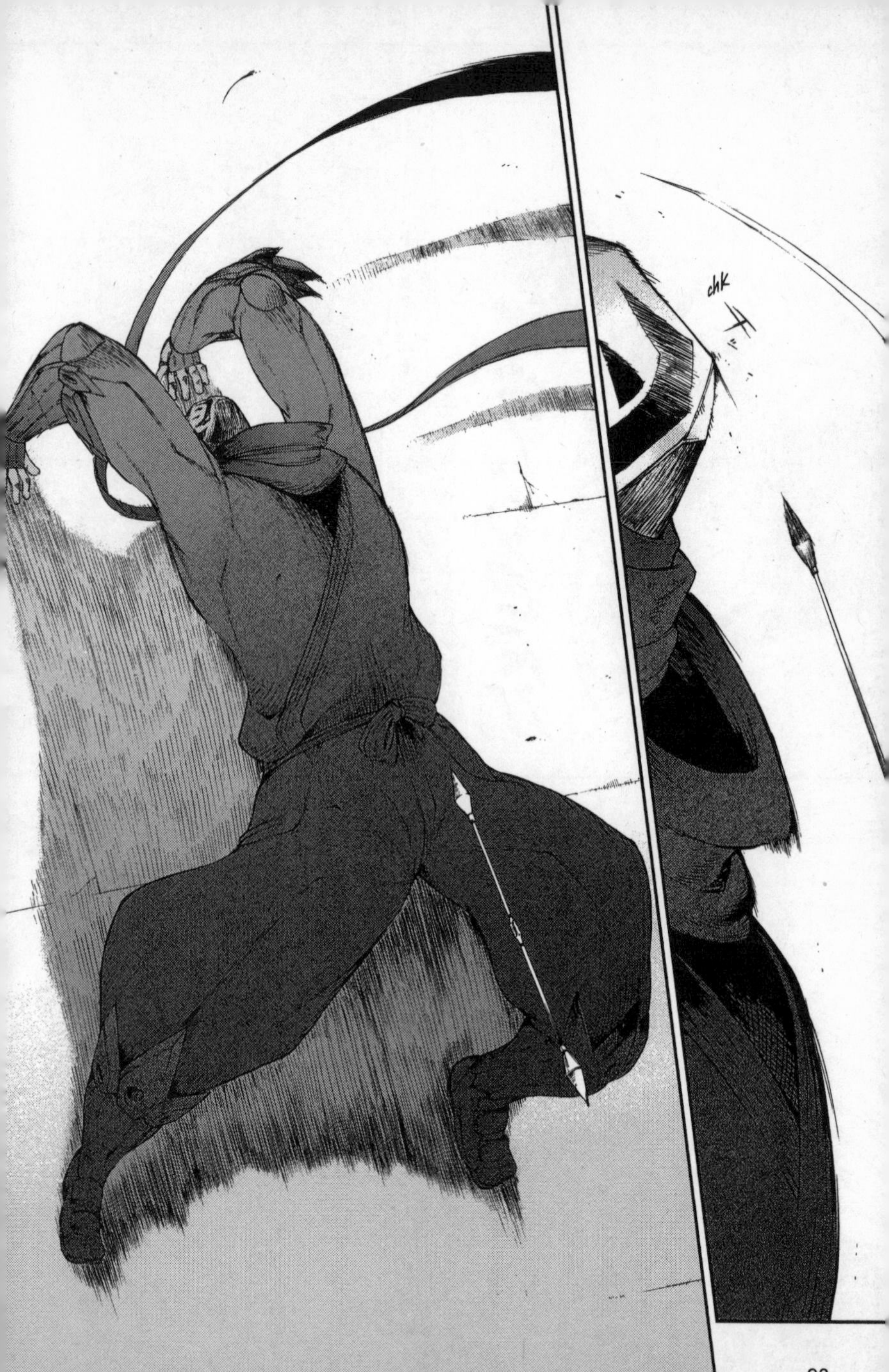
chk

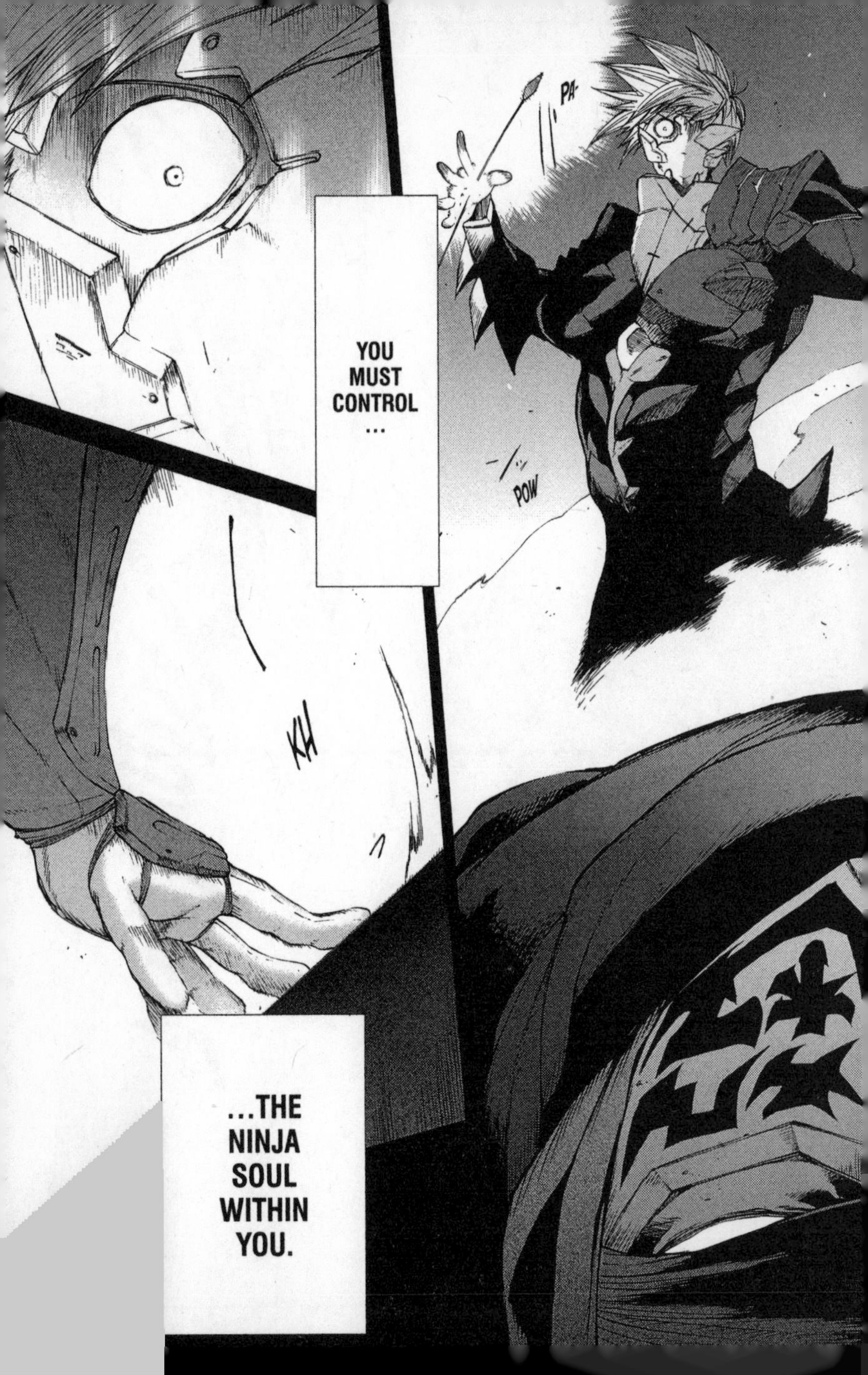
PA-
POW
YOU MUST CONTROL ...
KH
...THE NINJA SOUL WITHIN YOU.

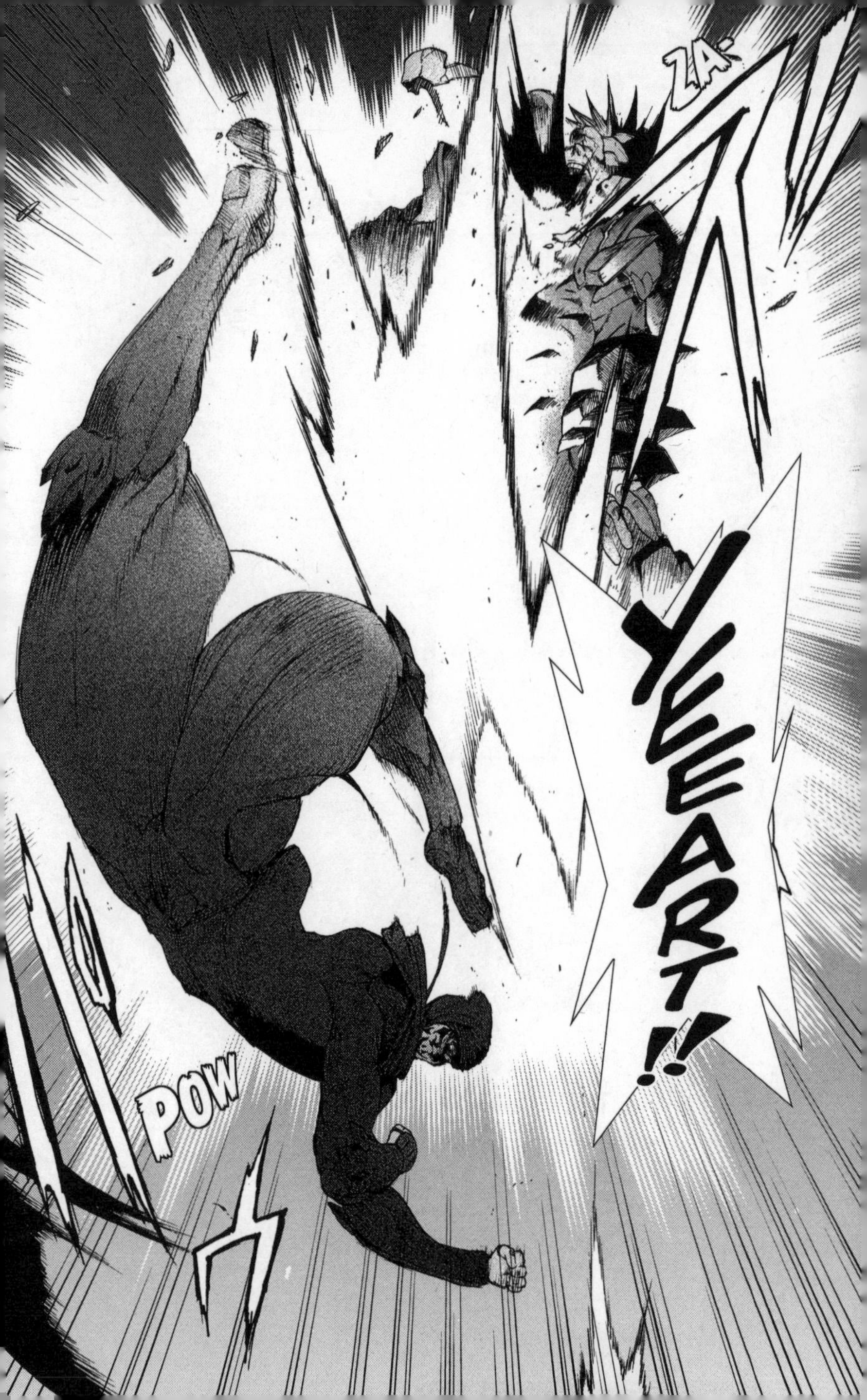
ZA
YEEART!!
POW

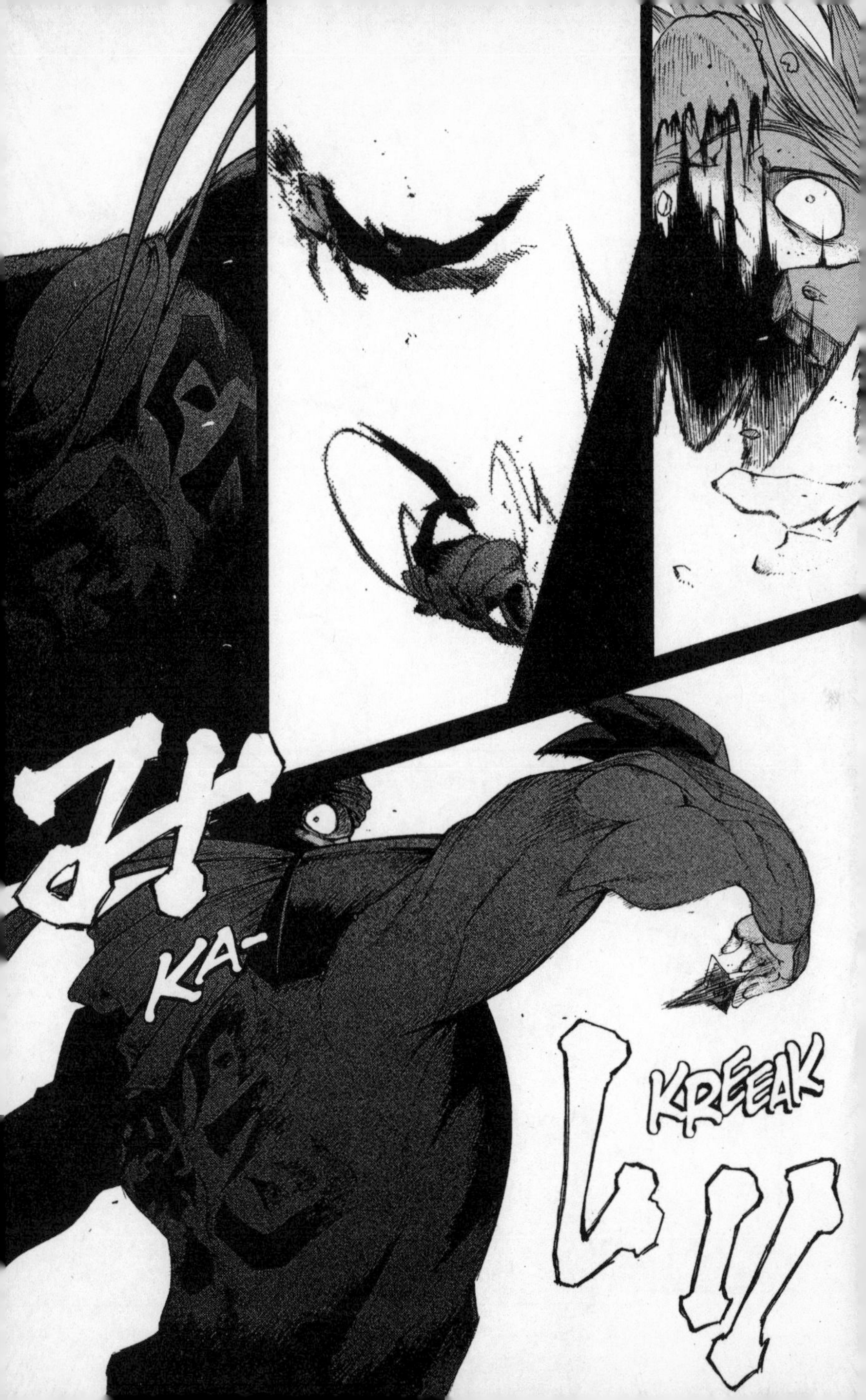
KREEAK
KA-

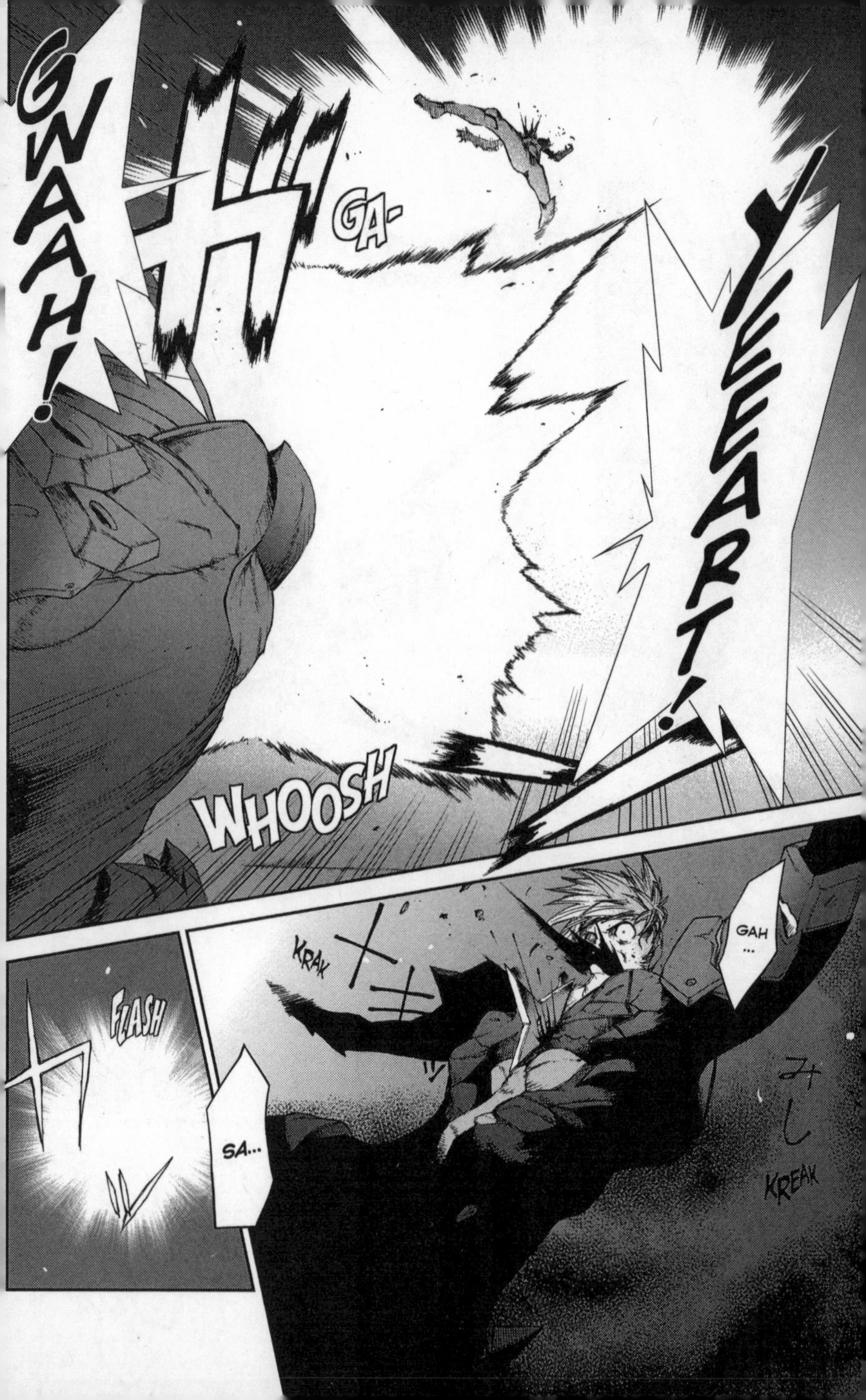
YEEEART!
GA-
GWAAH!
WHOOSH
GAH...
KRAK
みし
KREAK
SA...
FLASH

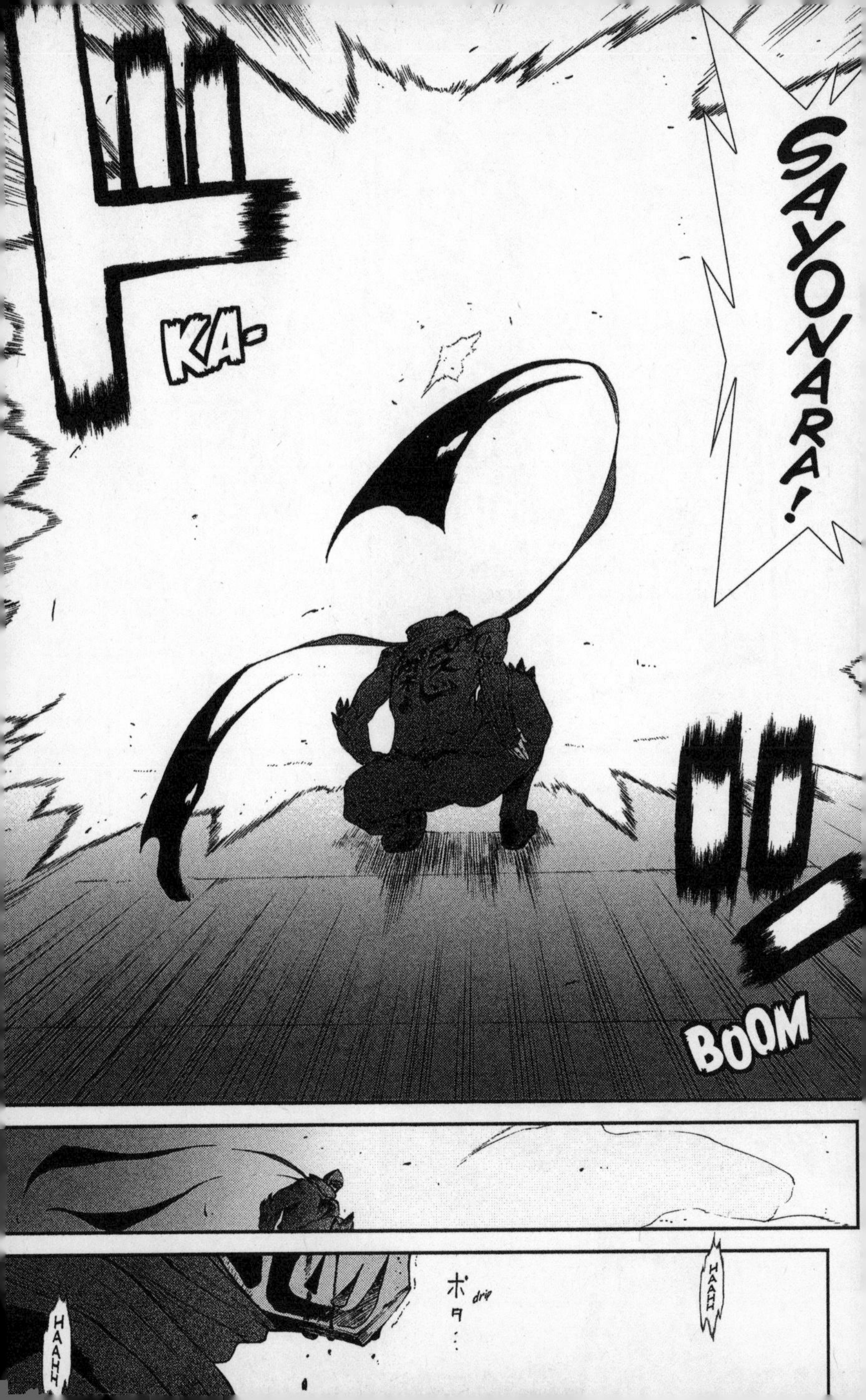
SAYONARA!
KA-
BOOM
HAAHH
ポタ
drip
HAAHH

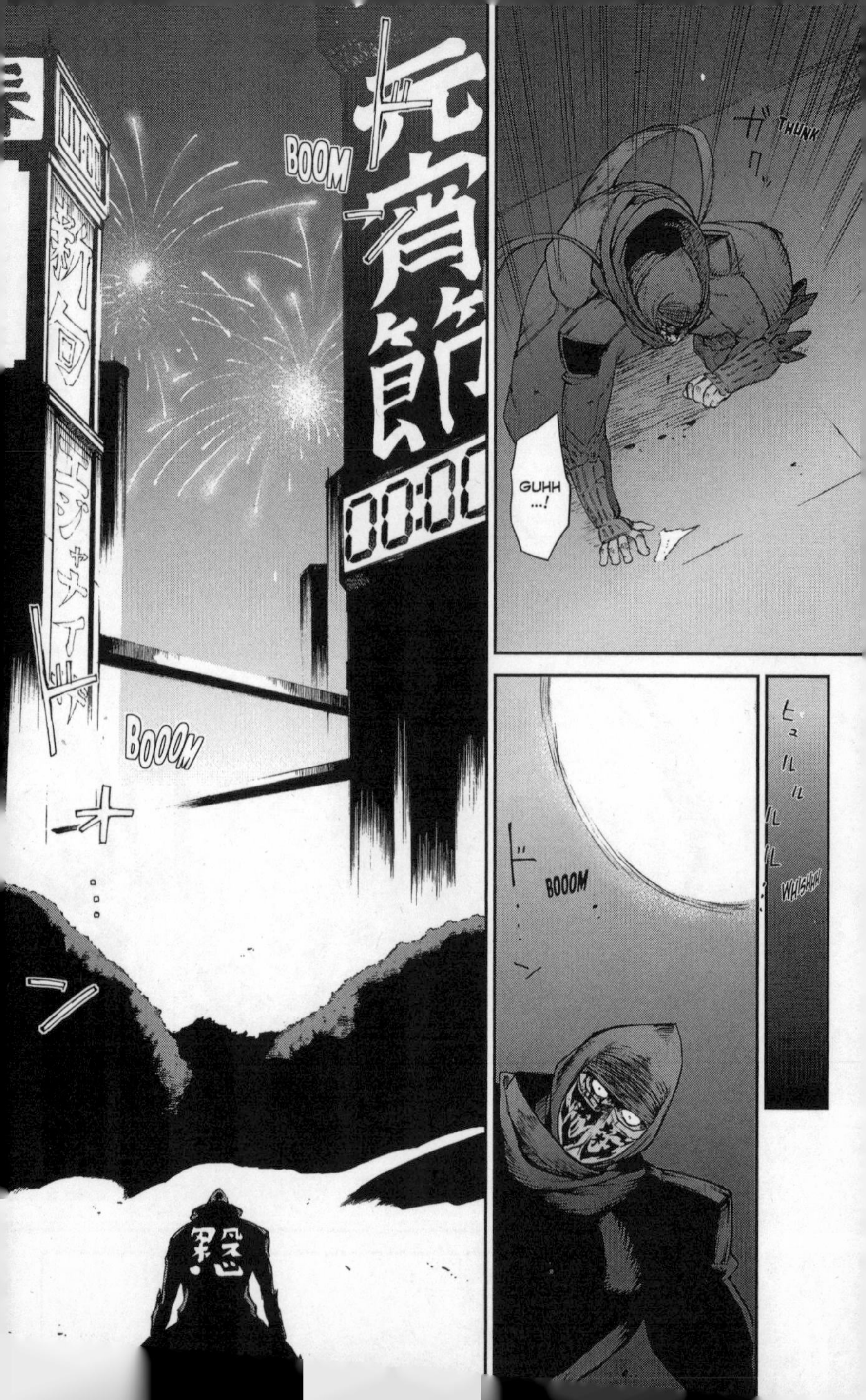

THUNK
GUHH ...!
WHSHH
BOOOM
元宵節
00:00
BOOM
BOOOM

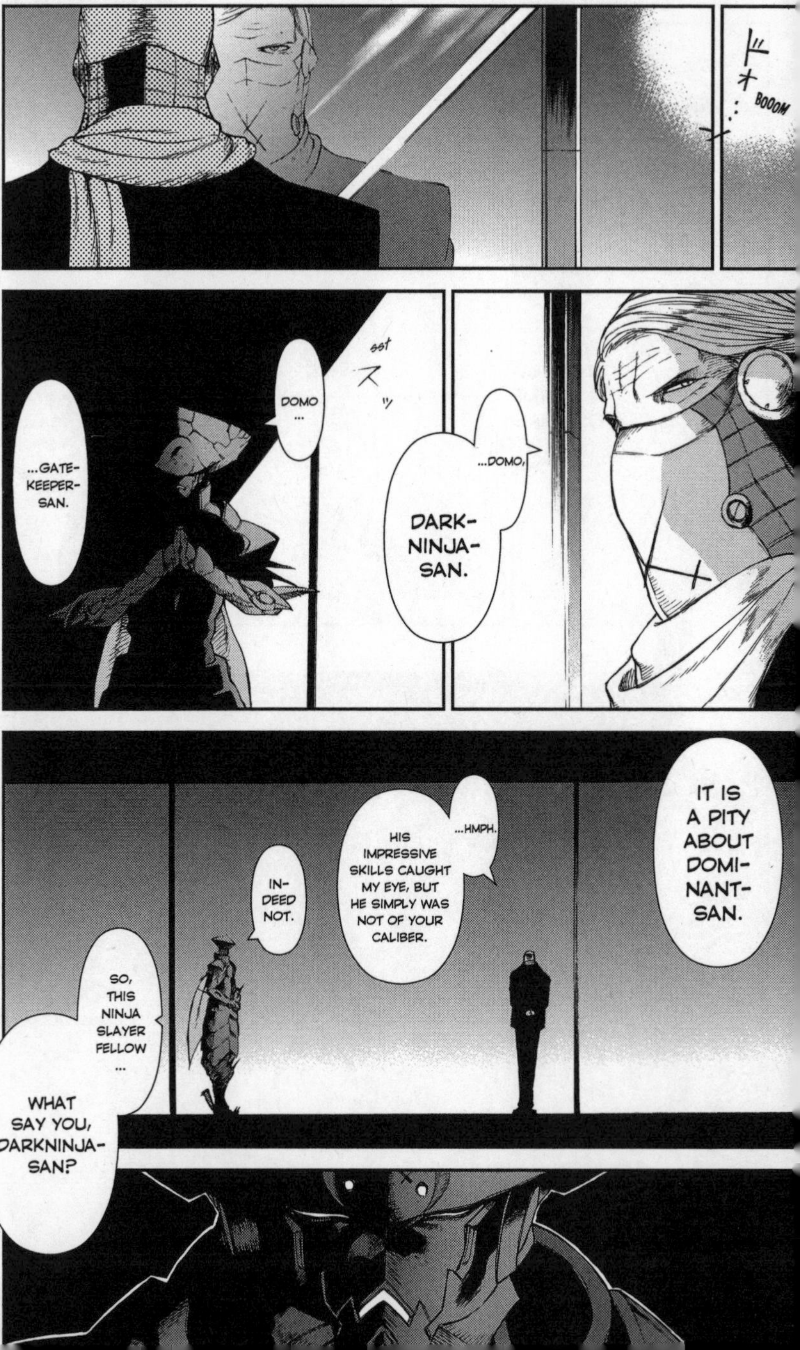
ドオ…
BOOOM
...DOMO,
DARK-NINJA-SAN.
sst
スッ
DOMO ...
...GATE-KEEPER-SAN.
IT IS A PITY ABOUT DOMI-NANT-SAN.
...HMPH.
HIS IMPRESSIVE SKILLS CAUGHT MY EYE, BUT HE SIMPLY WAS NOT OF YOUR CALIBER.
IN-DEED NOT.
SO, THIS NINJA SLAYER FELLOW ...
WHAT SAY YOU, DARKNINJA-SAN?

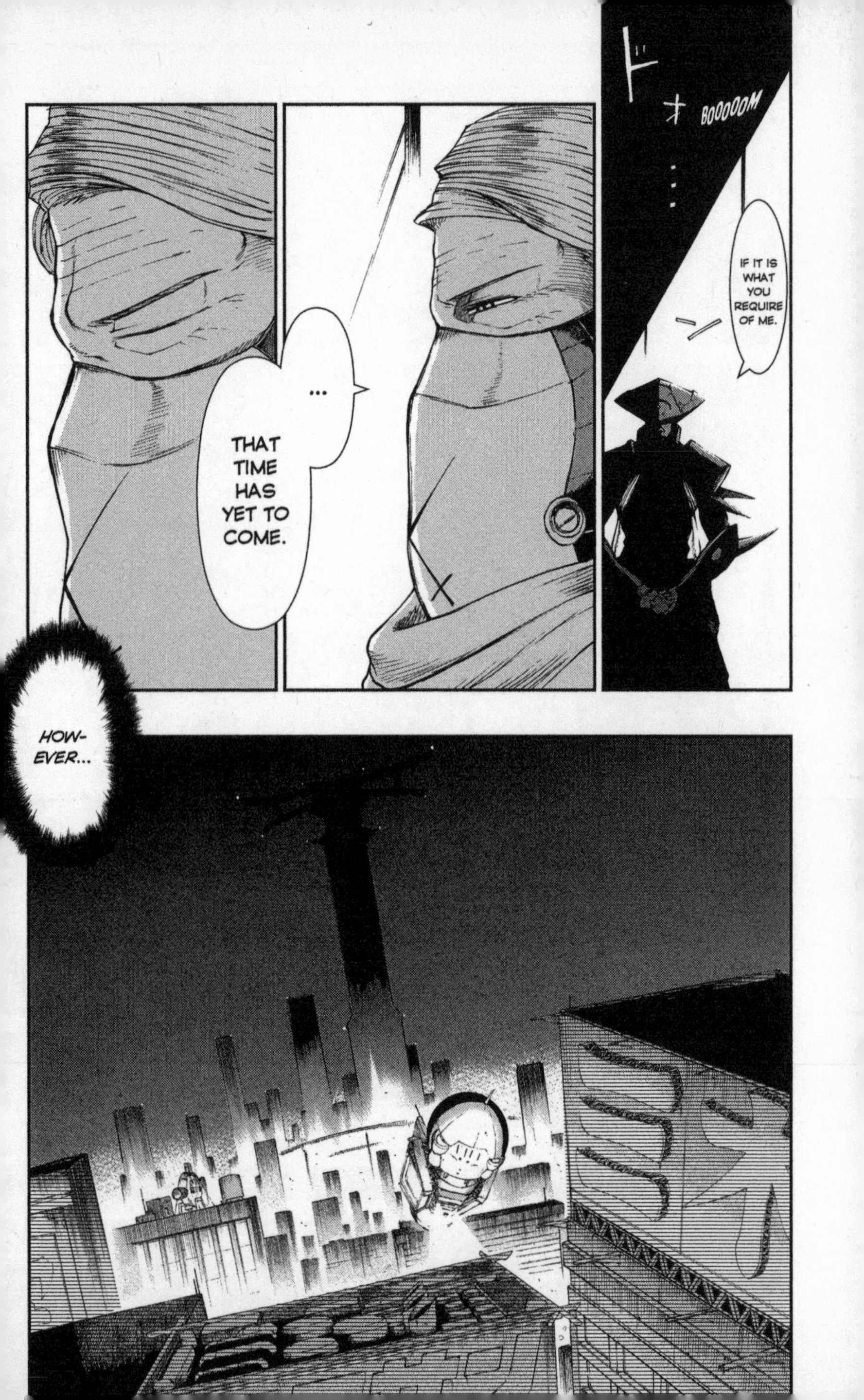
ドォ
BOOOOOM
...
IF IT IS WHAT YOU REQUIRE OF ME.
... THAT TIME HAS YET TO COME.
HOW-EVER...

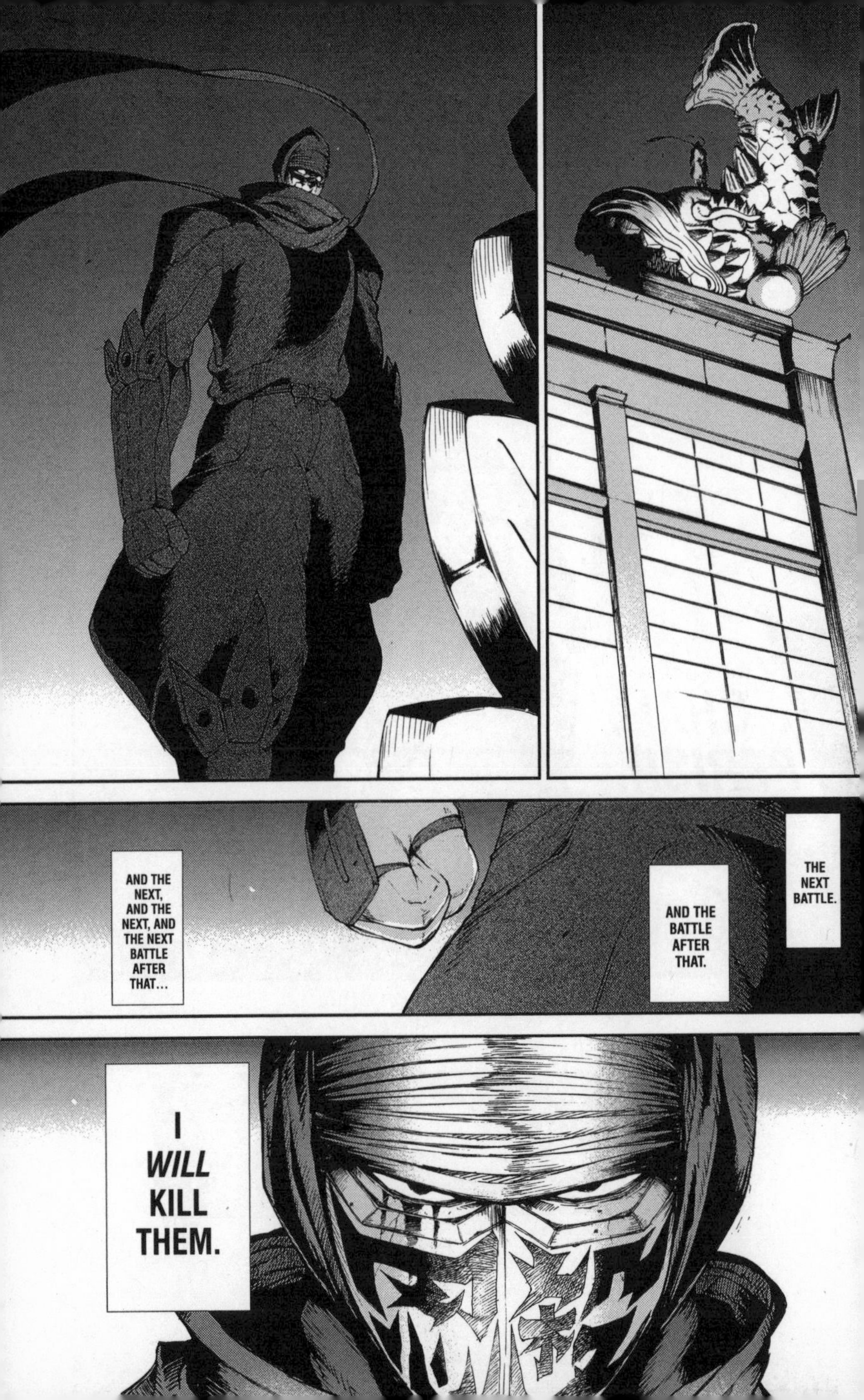
THE NEXT BATTLE.
AND THE BATTLE AFTER THAT.
AND THE NEXT, AND THE NEXT, AND THE NEXT BATTLE AFTER THAT…
I *WILL* KILL THEM.

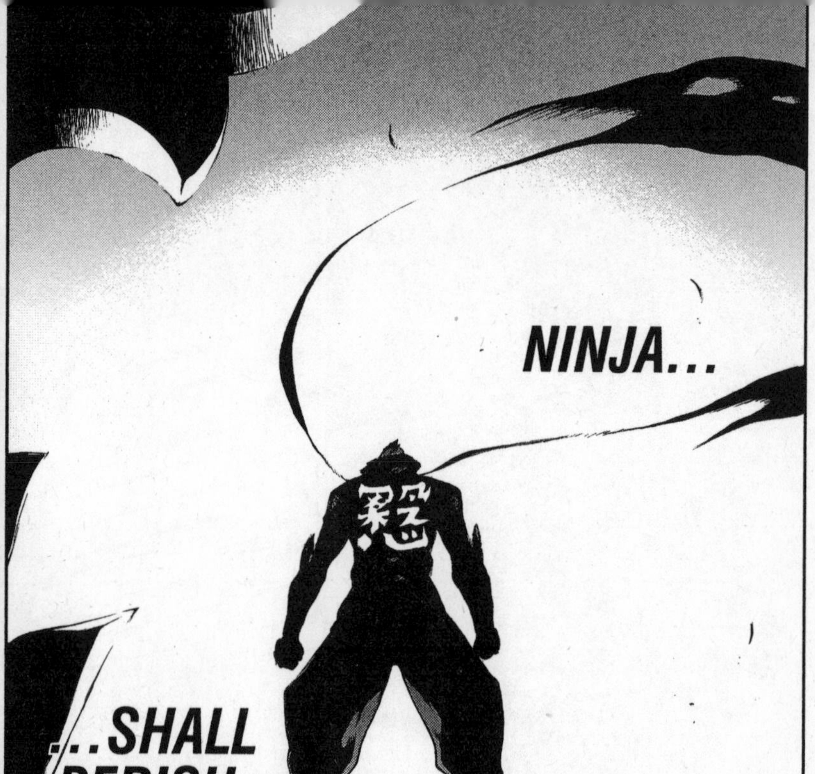
NINJA...
...SHALL PERISH.

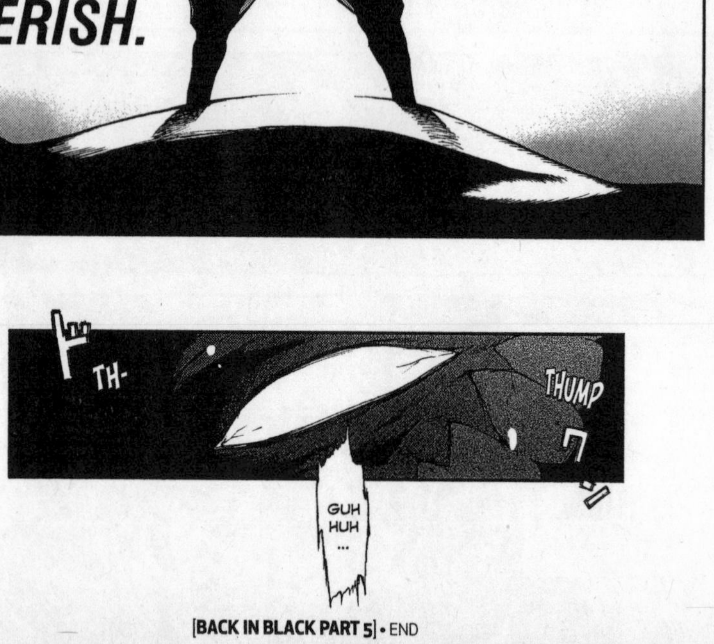
TH-
THUMP
GUH HUH ...

[BACK IN BLACK PART 5] • END

NINJA SLAYER KILLs!!

NINJA SLAYER
KILLs!!

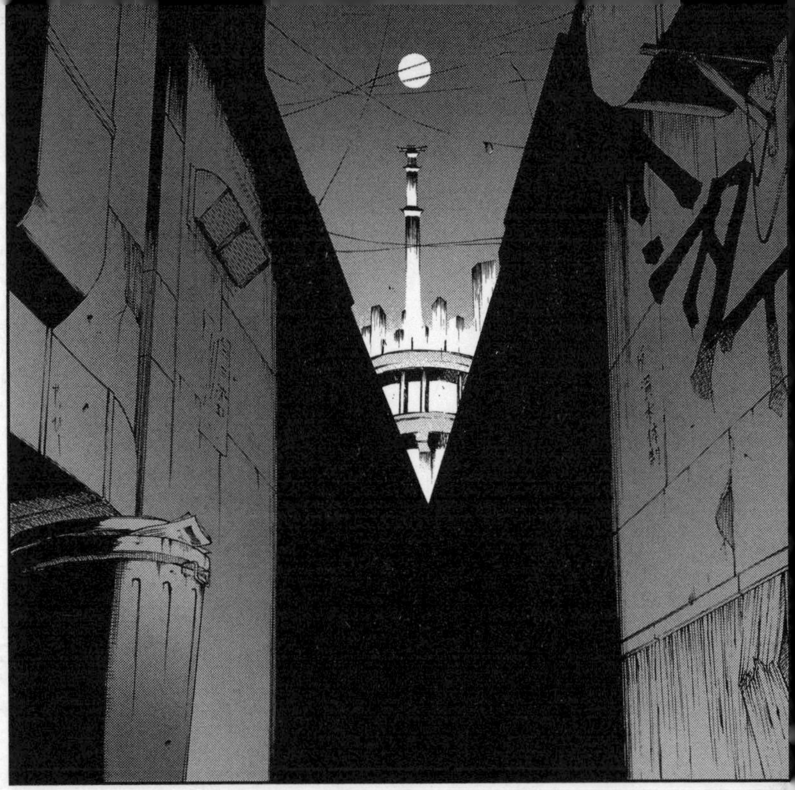

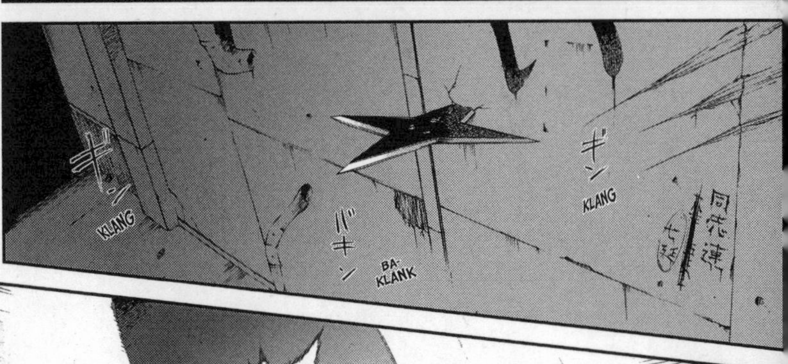
ギン
KLANG
バキン
BA-KLANK
ギーン
KLANG

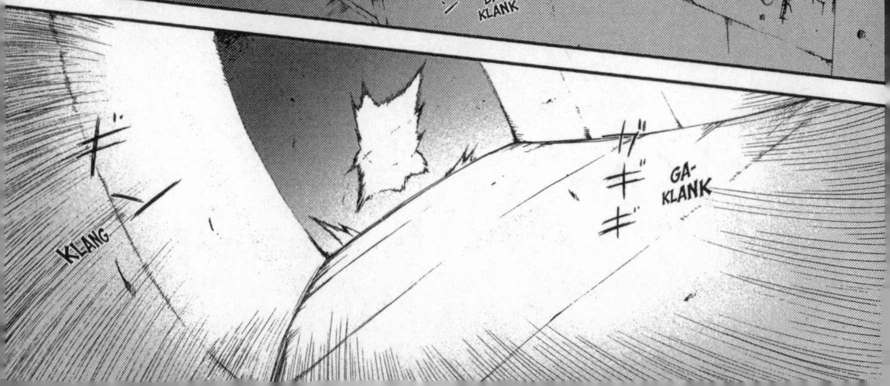
ガギギ
GA-KLANK
ギーン
KLANG

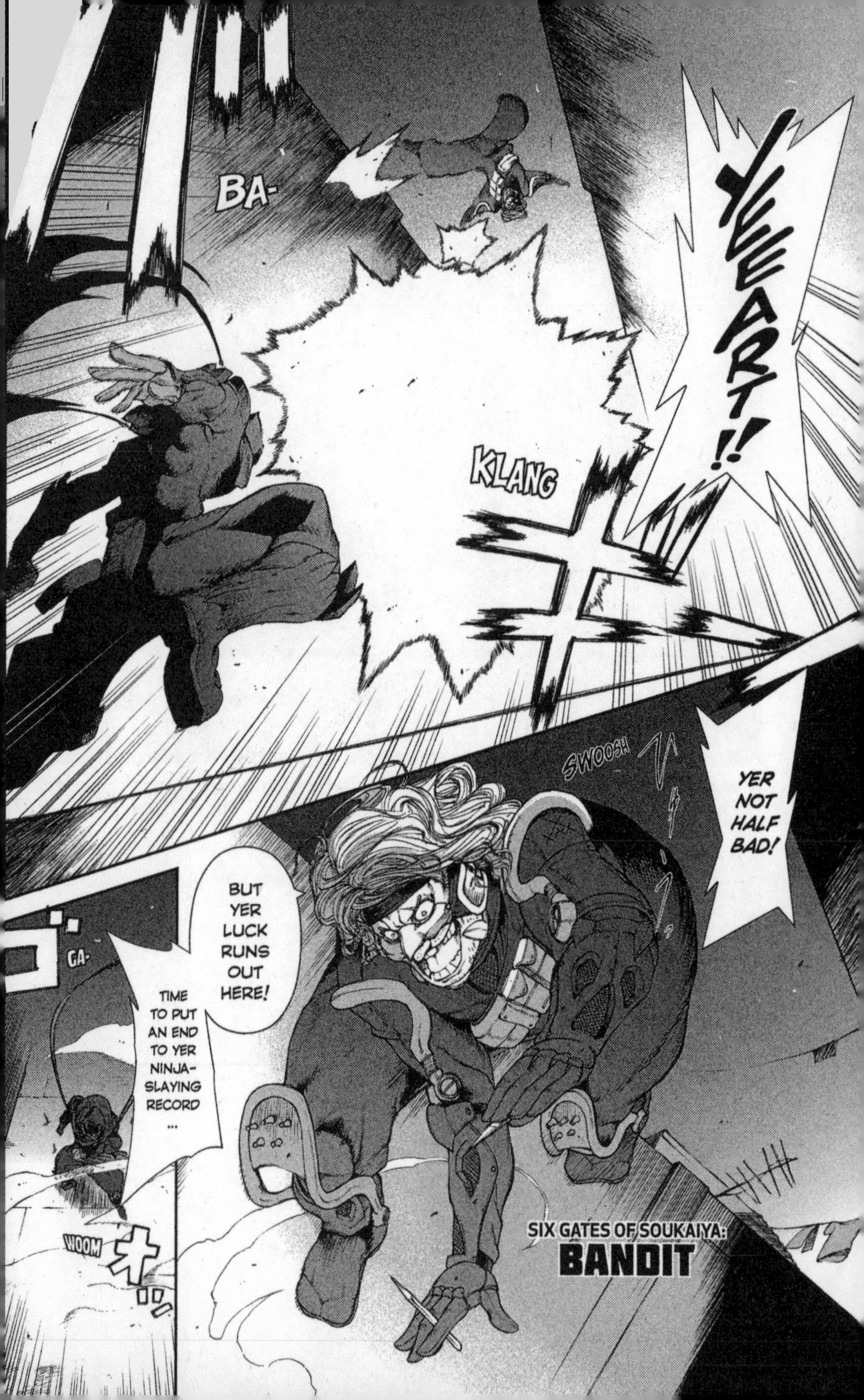
YEEEART!!
BA-
KLANG
SWOOSH
YER NOT HALF BAD!
BUT YER LUCK RUNS OUT HERE!
GA-
TIME TO PUT AN END TO YER NINJA-SLAYING RECORD ...
WOOM
SIX GATES OF SOUKAIYA:
BANDIT

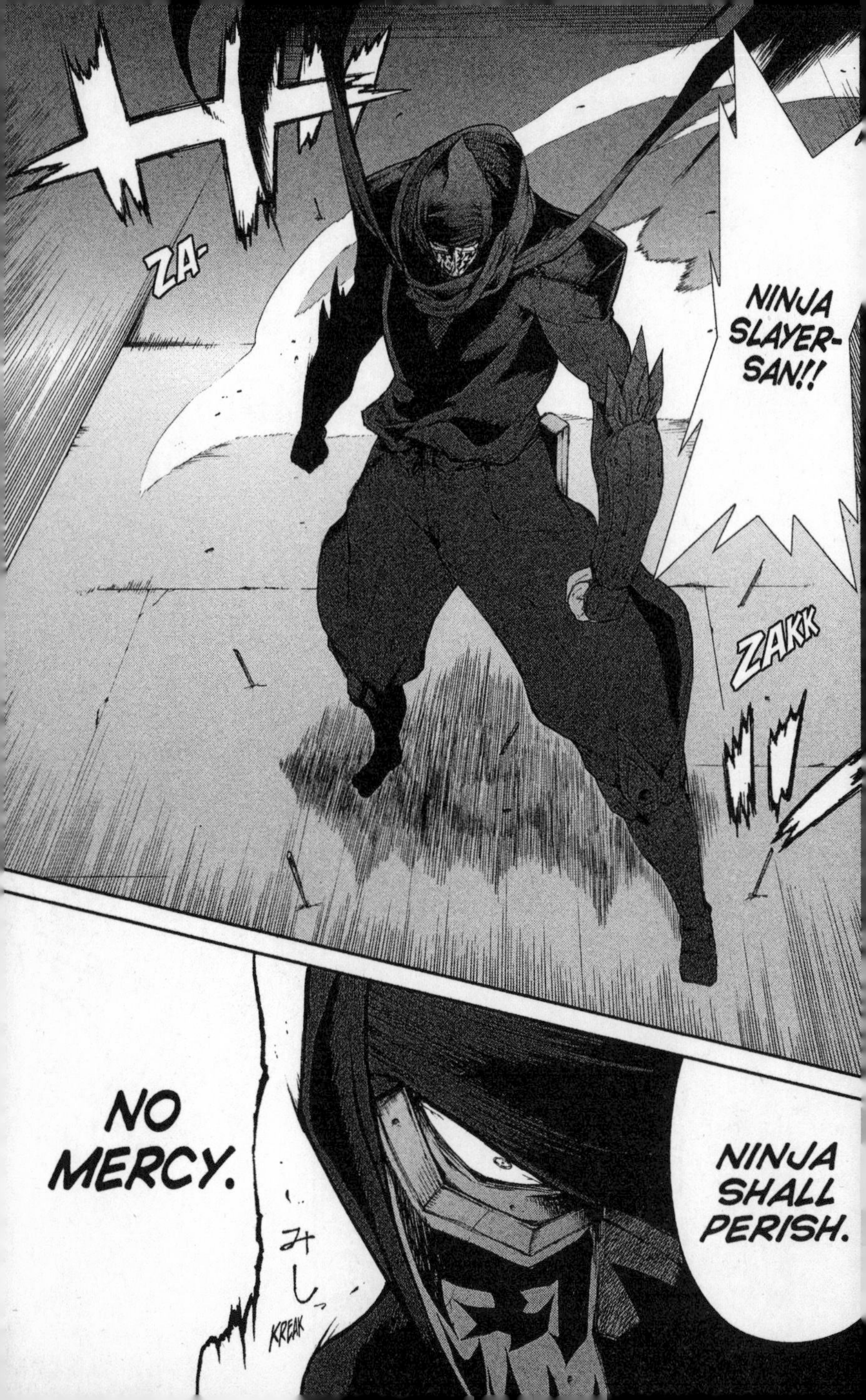
NINJA SLAYER-SAN!!
ZA-
ZAKK
NINJA SHALL PERISH.
みしっ
KREAK
NO MERCY.

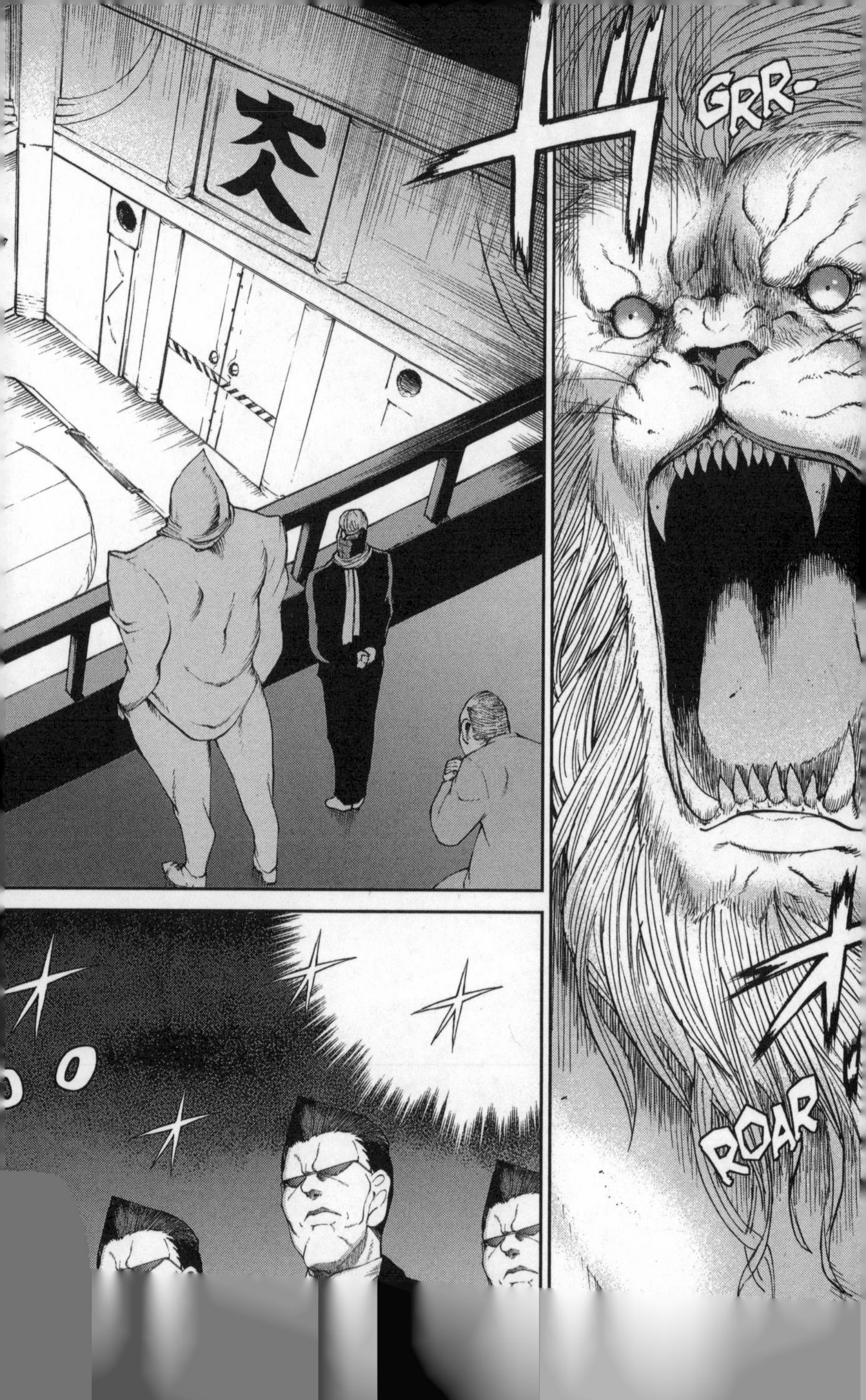
GRR-
ROAR

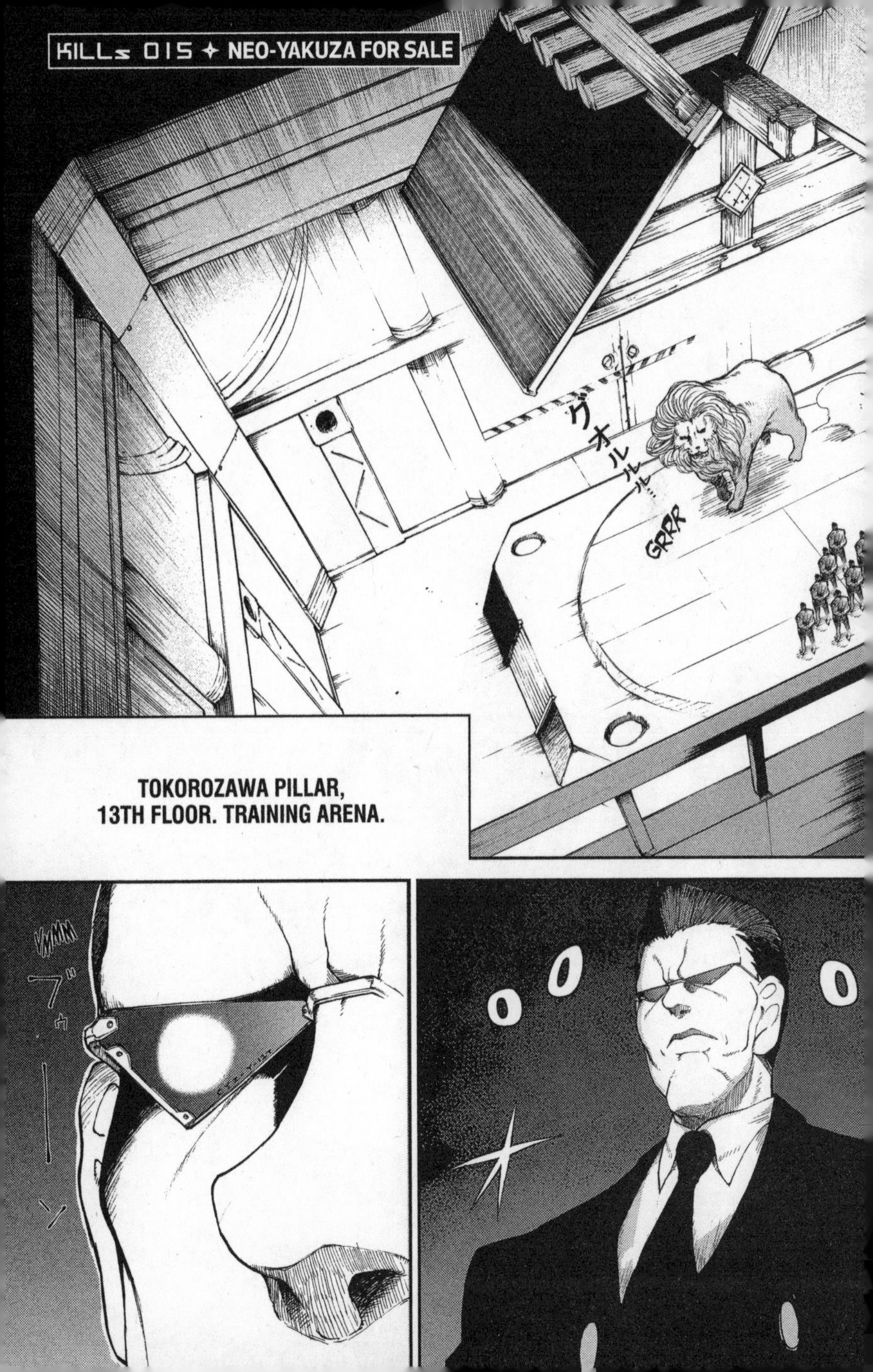
KILLs 015 ✦ NEO-YAKUZA FOR SALE
グオルルル…
GRRR
TOKOROZAWA PILLAR, 13TH FLOOR. TRAINING ARENA.
VMMM
ヴゥーーン

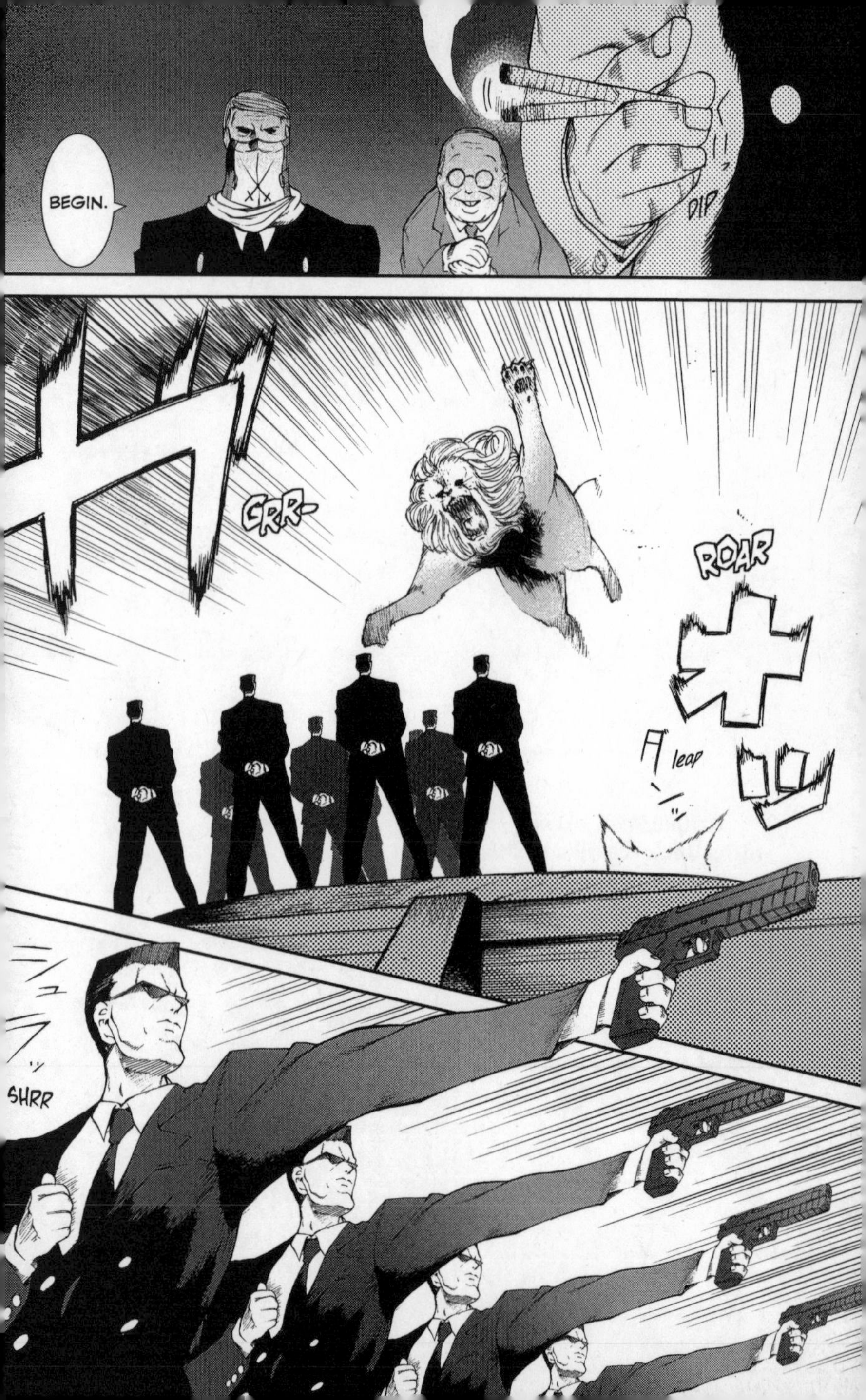
DIP
BEGIN.
GRR-
ROAR
leap
SHRR

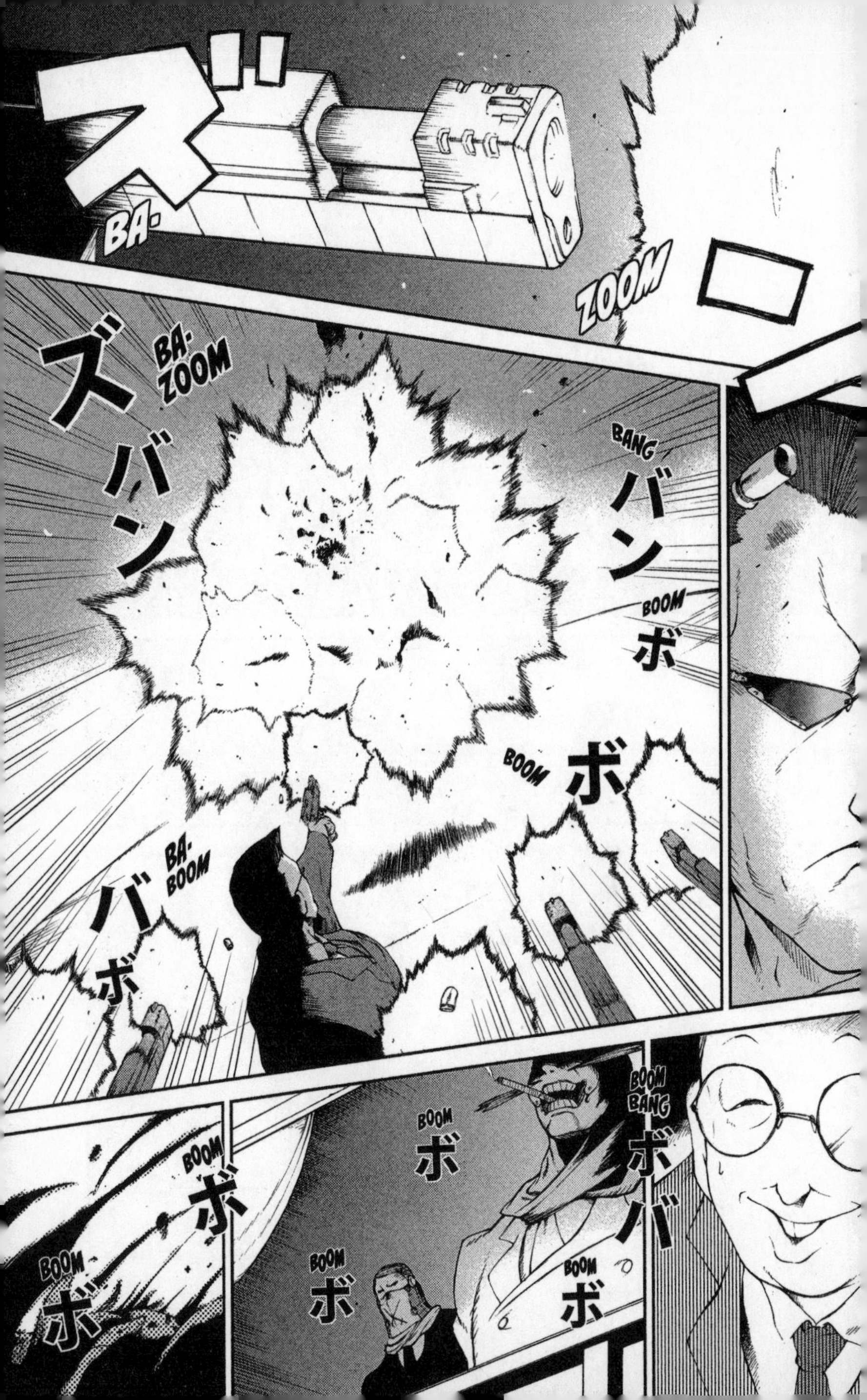
ズ
BA-
ZOOM
BANG
バン
BOOM
ボ
BOOM
ボ
ズバン
BA-
ZOOM
BA-
BOOM
バボ
BOOM
BANG
ボバ
BOOM
ボ
BOOM
ボ
BOOM
ボ
BOOM
ボ
BOOM
ボ

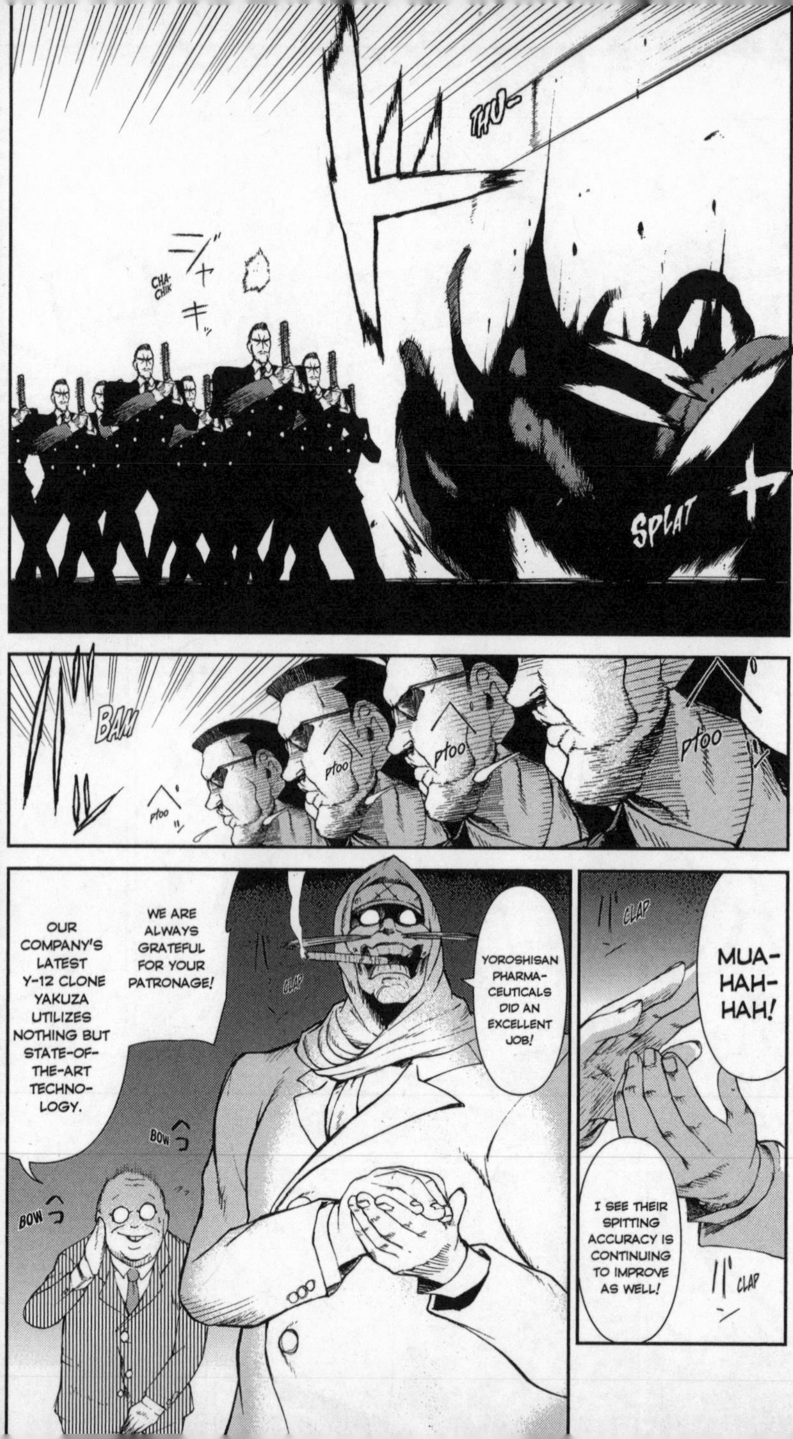
THU-
ジャキッ
CHA-CHIK
SPLAT
BAM
ptoo
ptoo
ptoo
ptoo
CLAP
MUA-HAH-HAH!
I SEE THEIR SPITTING ACCURACY IS CONTINUING TO IMPROVE AS WELL!
CLAP
YOROSHISAN PHARMACEUTICALS DID AN EXCELLENT JOB!
CLAP
WE ARE ALWAYS GRATEFUL FOR YOUR PATRONAGE!
OUR COMPANY'S LATEST Y-12 CLONE YAKUZA UTILIZES NOTHING BUT STATE-OF-THE-ART TECHNOLOGY.
BOW
BOW

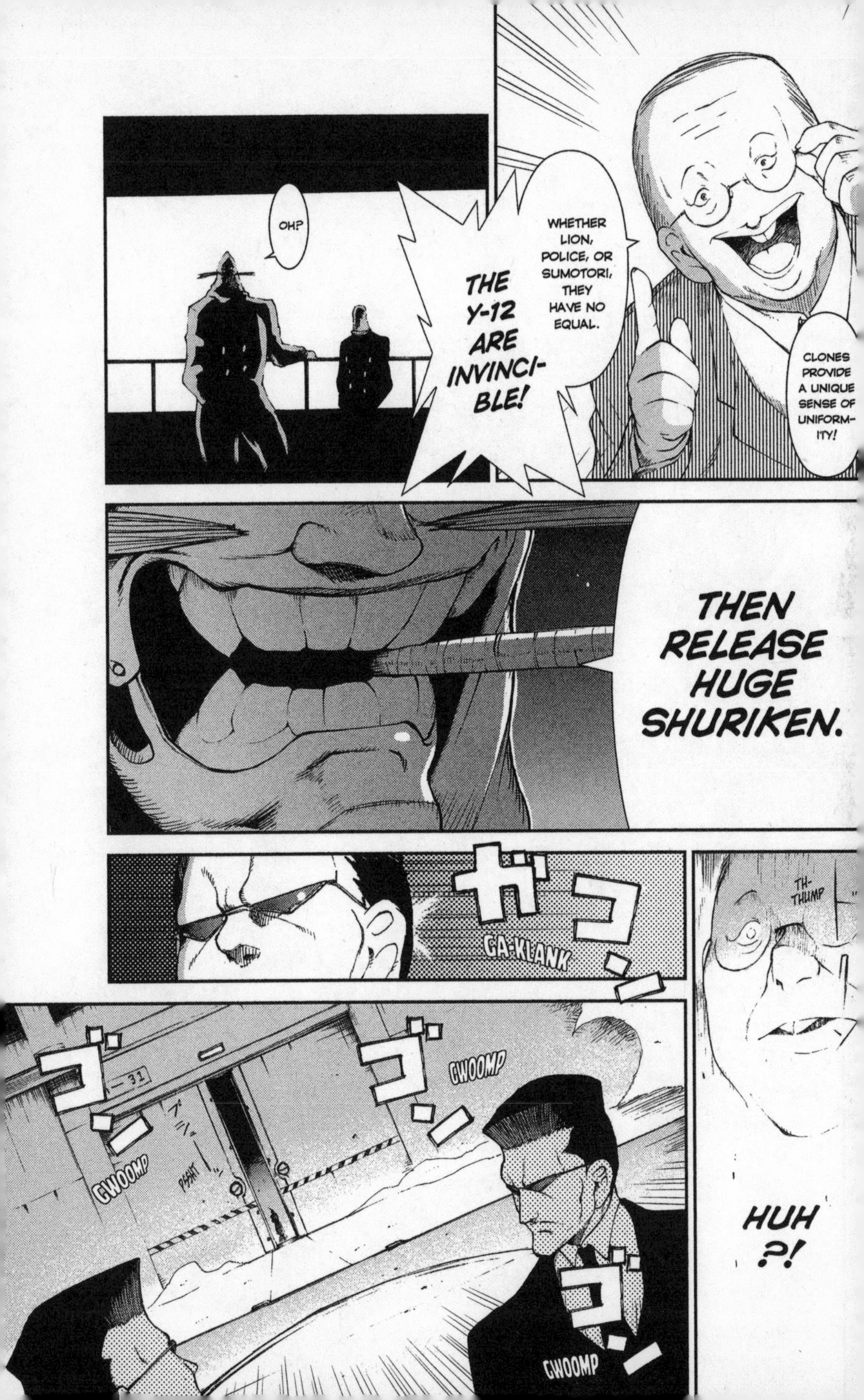
CLONES PROVIDE A UNIQUE SENSE OF UNIFORMITY!
WHETHER LION, POLICE, OR SUMOTORI, THEY HAVE NO EQUAL.
THE Y-12 ARE INVINCIBLE!
OH?
THEN RELEASE HUGE SHURIKEN.
TH-THUMP
HUH ?!
CA-KLANK
GWOOMP
PSSHT
GWOOMP
GWOOMP

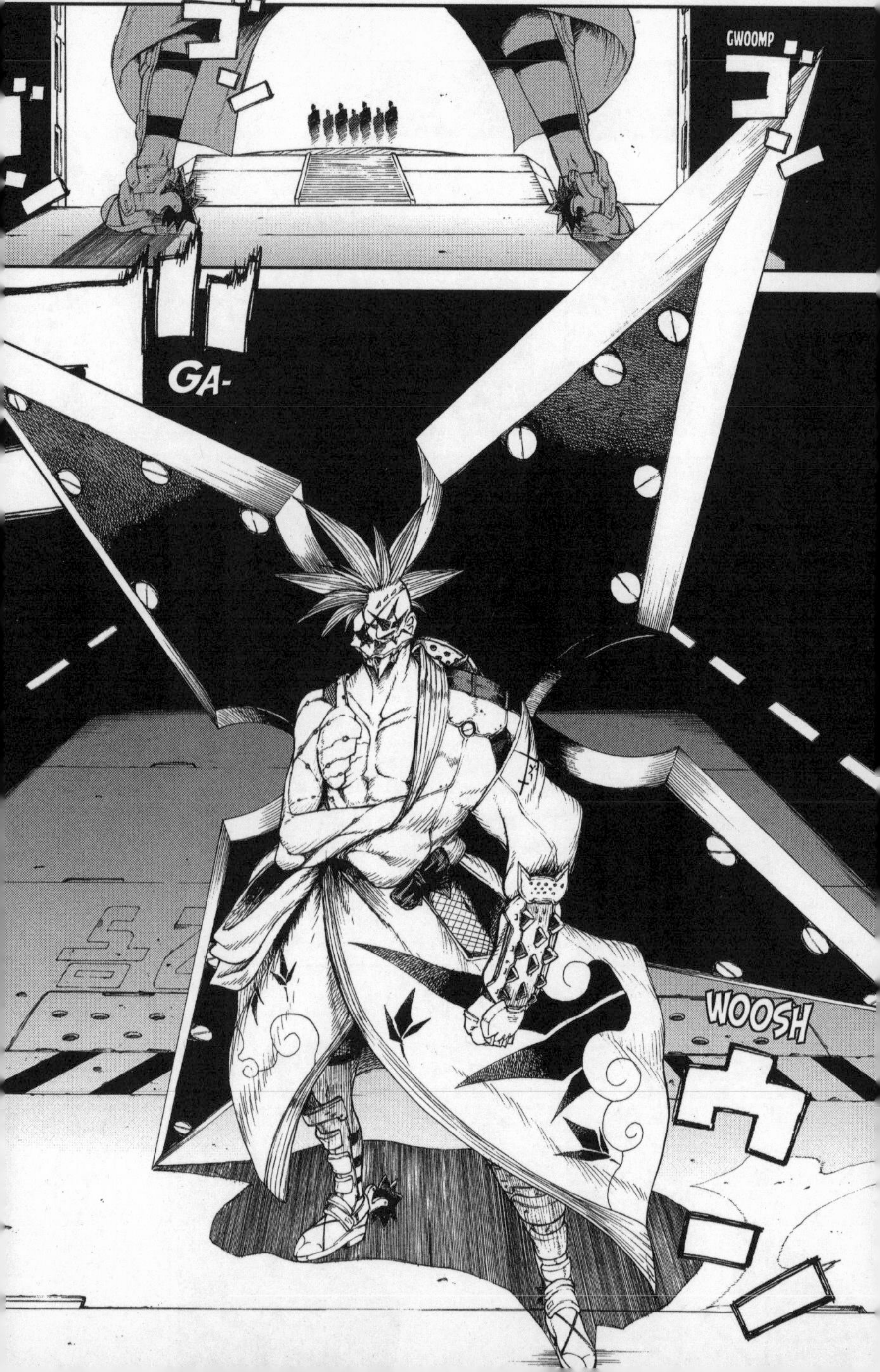
GWOOMP
GWOOMP
GA-
WOOSH

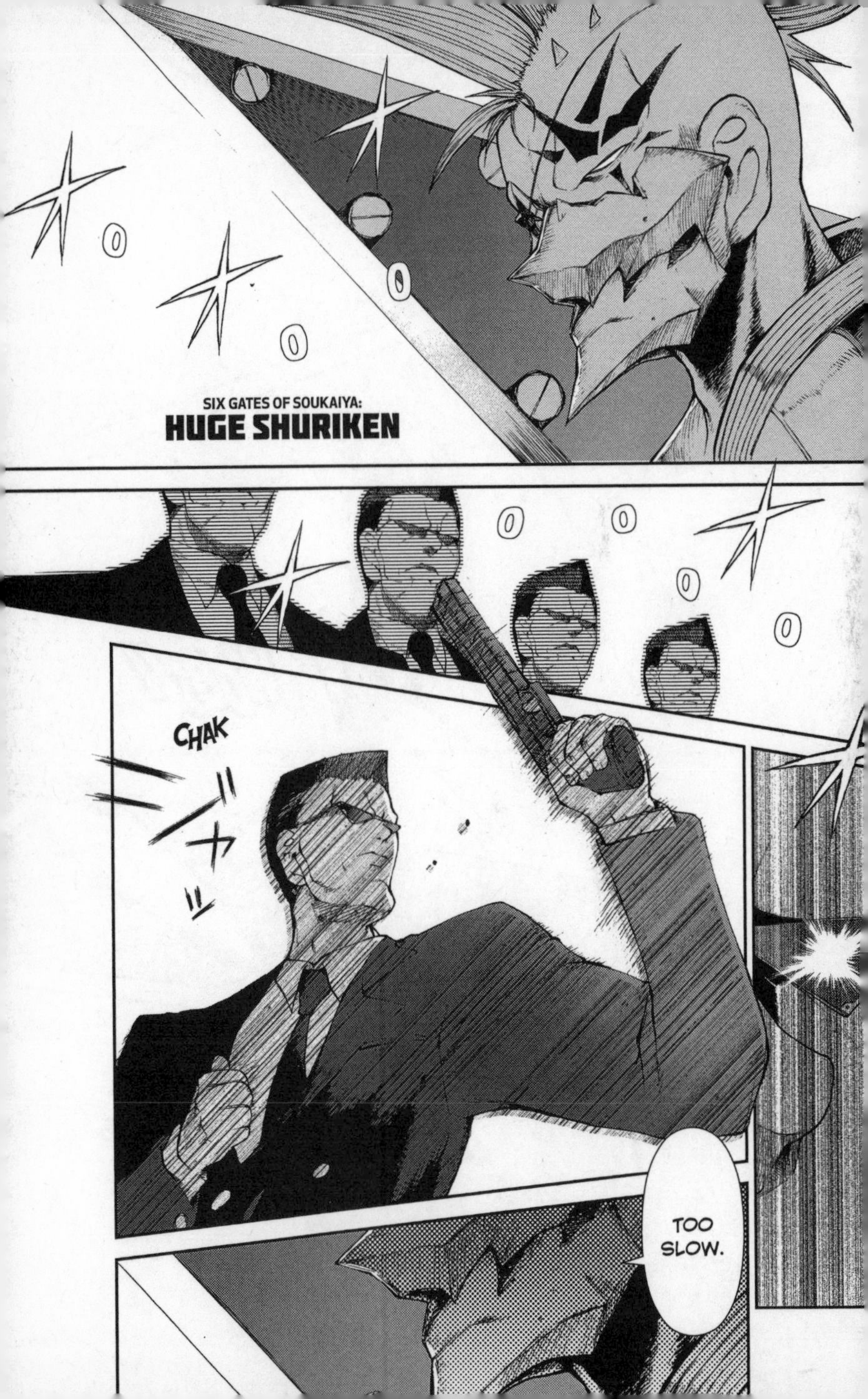
SIX GATES OF SOUKAIYA:
HUGE SHURIKEN
CHAK
TOO SLOW.

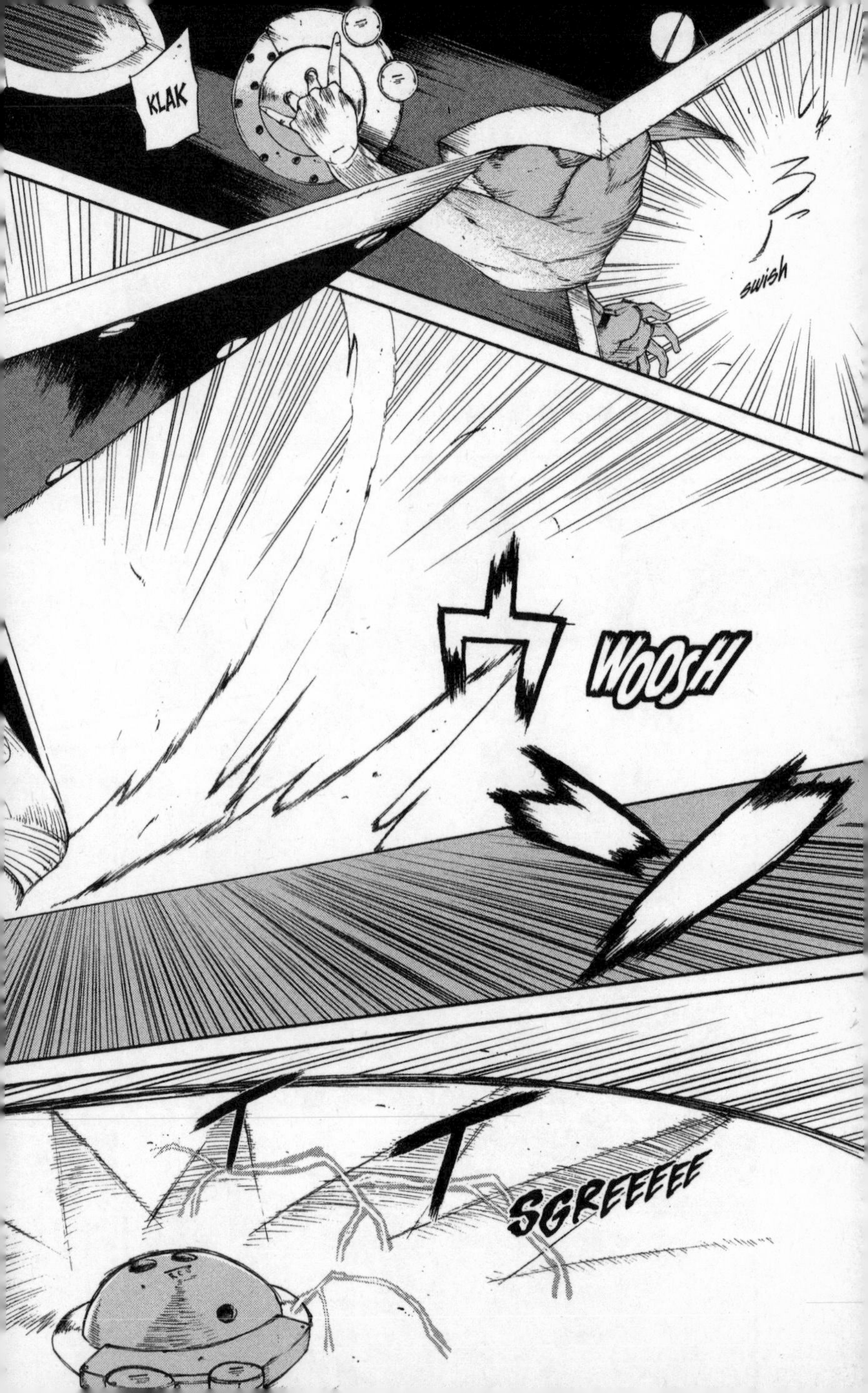
KLAK
swish
WOOSH
SGREEEEE

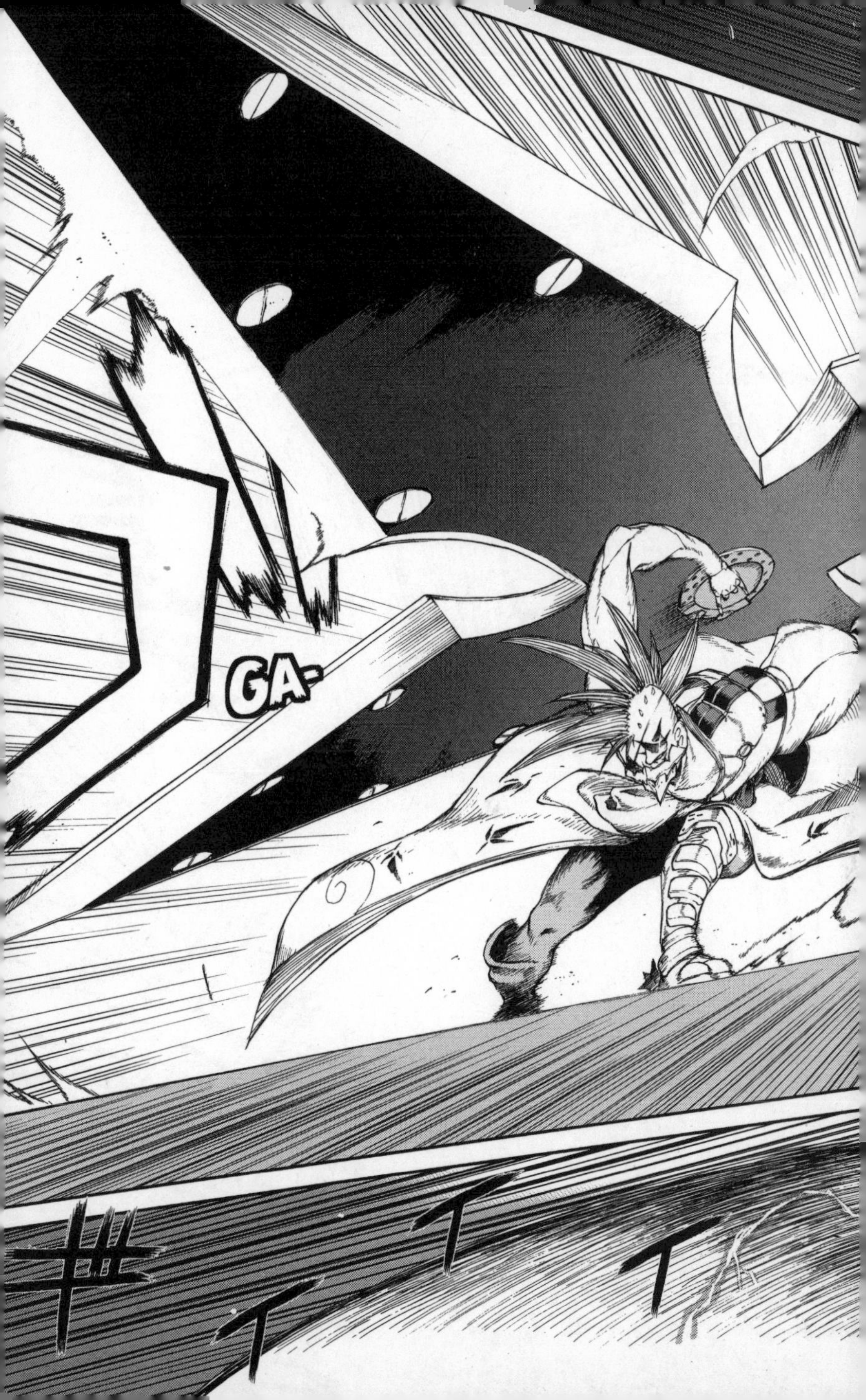
GA-

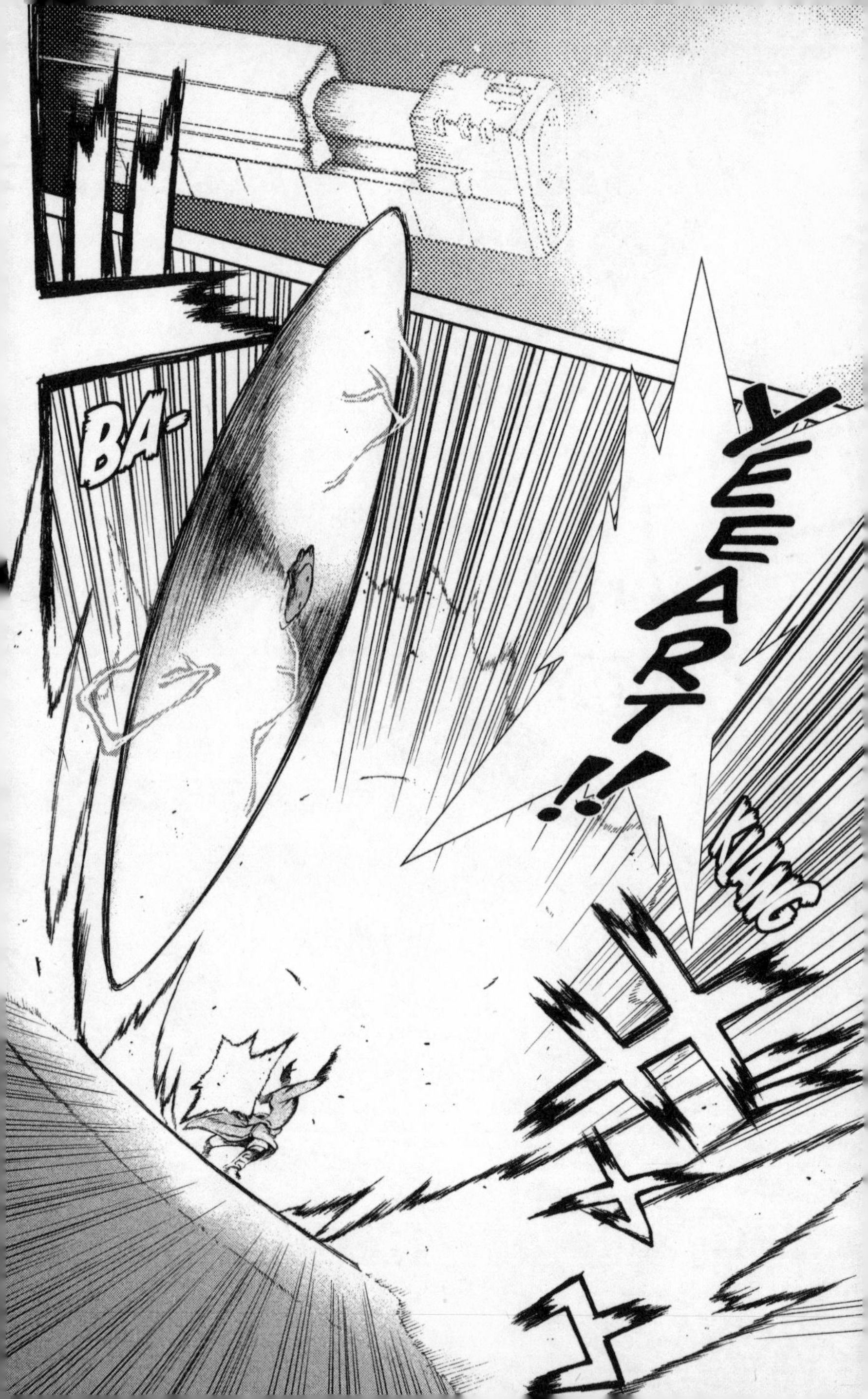
YEEART!!
BA-
KRANG

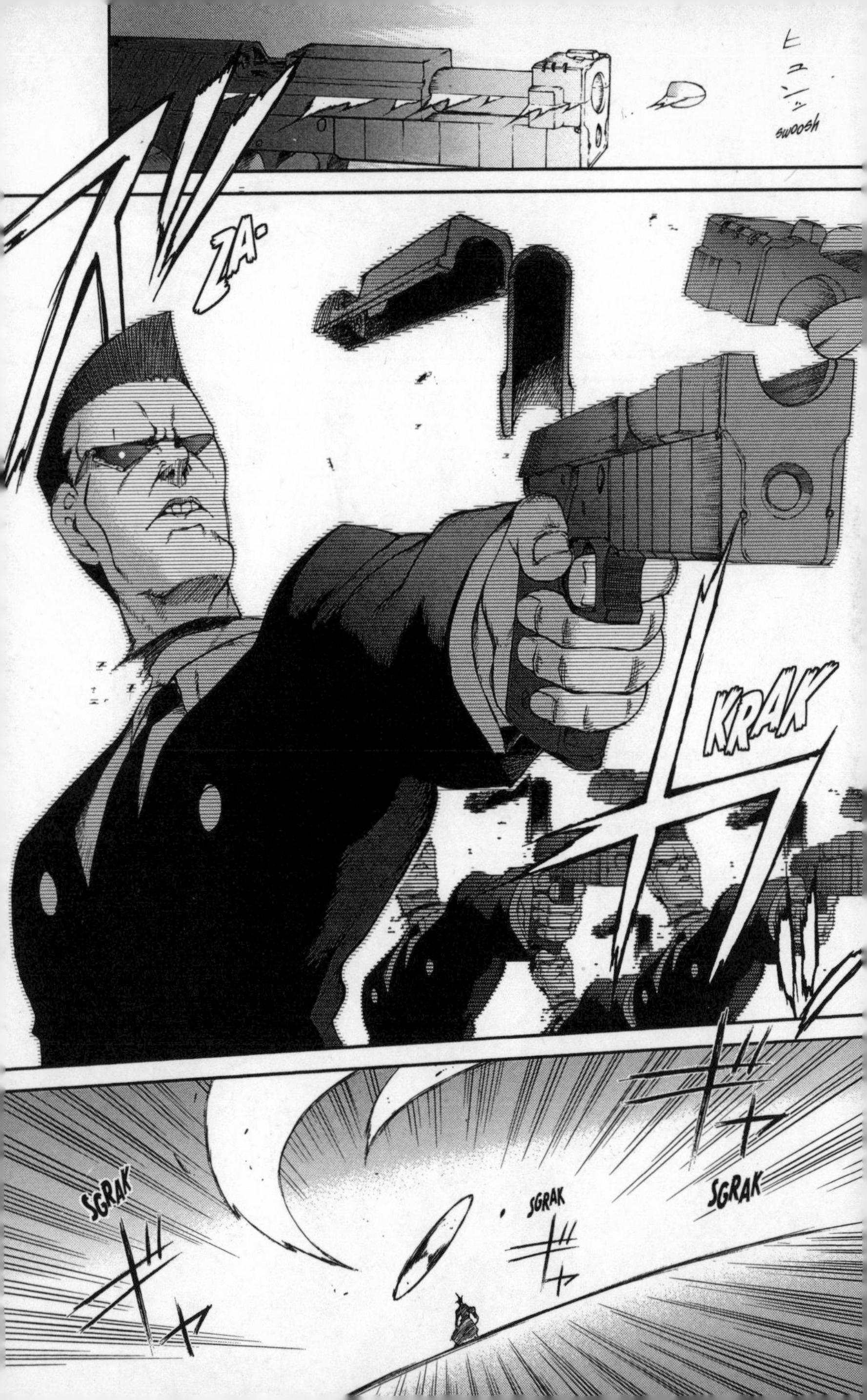
ヒュンッ
swoosh
ZA-
KRAK
SGRAK
SGRAK
SGRAK

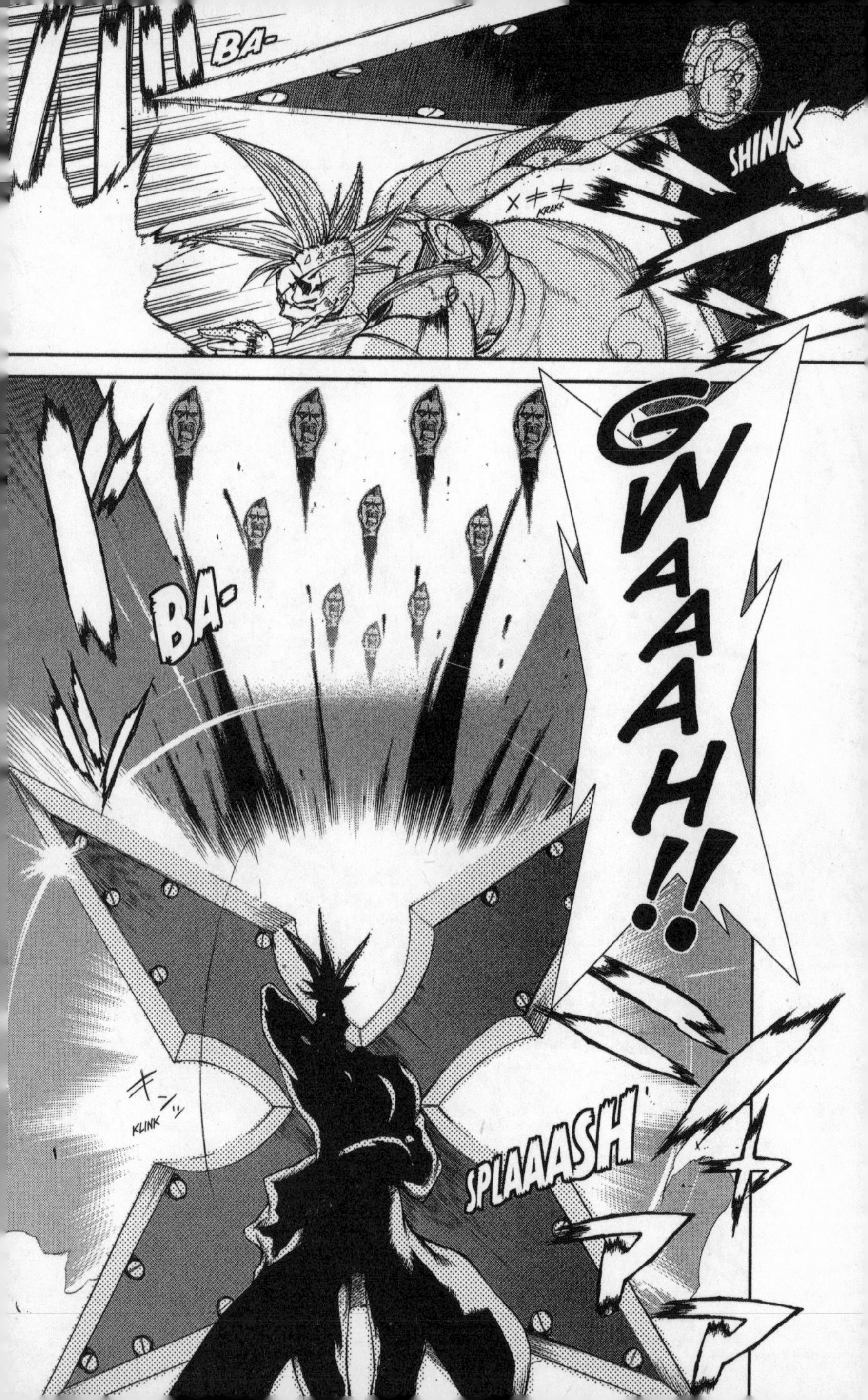
SHINK
KRAKK
BA-
GWAAAH!!
BA-
SPLAAASH
KLINK

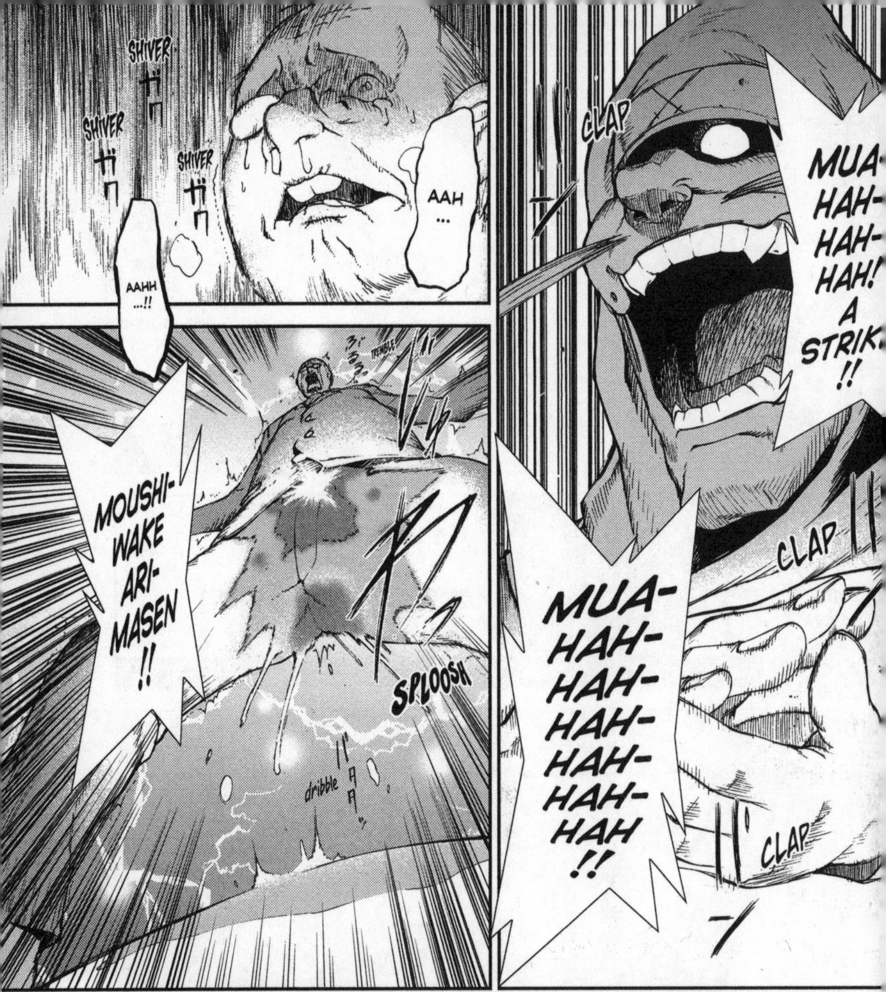
CLAP
MUA HAH-HAH-HAH! A STRIK...!!
MUA-HAH-HAH-HAH-HAH-HAH-HAH!!
CLAP
CLAP
SHIVER
SHIVER
SHIVER
AAH ...
AAHH ...!!
MOUSHIWAKE ARI-MASEN!!
TREMBLE
SPLOOSH
dribble

*MOUSHIWAKE ARIMASEN = MY DEEPEST APOLOGIES

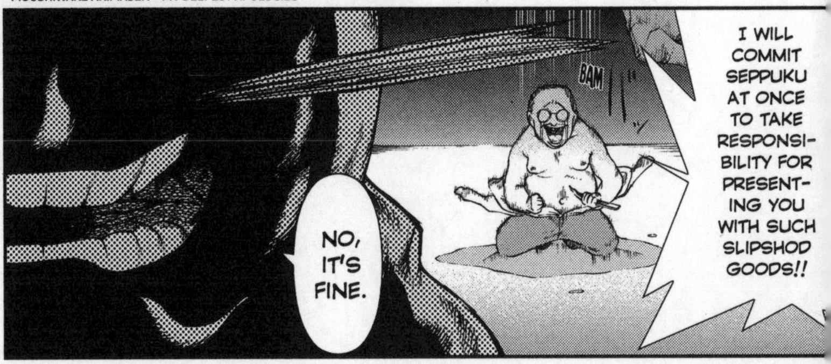
I WILL COMMIT SEPPUKU AT ONCE TO TAKE RESPONSIBILITY FOR PRESENTING YOU WITH SUCH SLIPSHOD GOODS!!
BAM
NO, IT'S FINE.

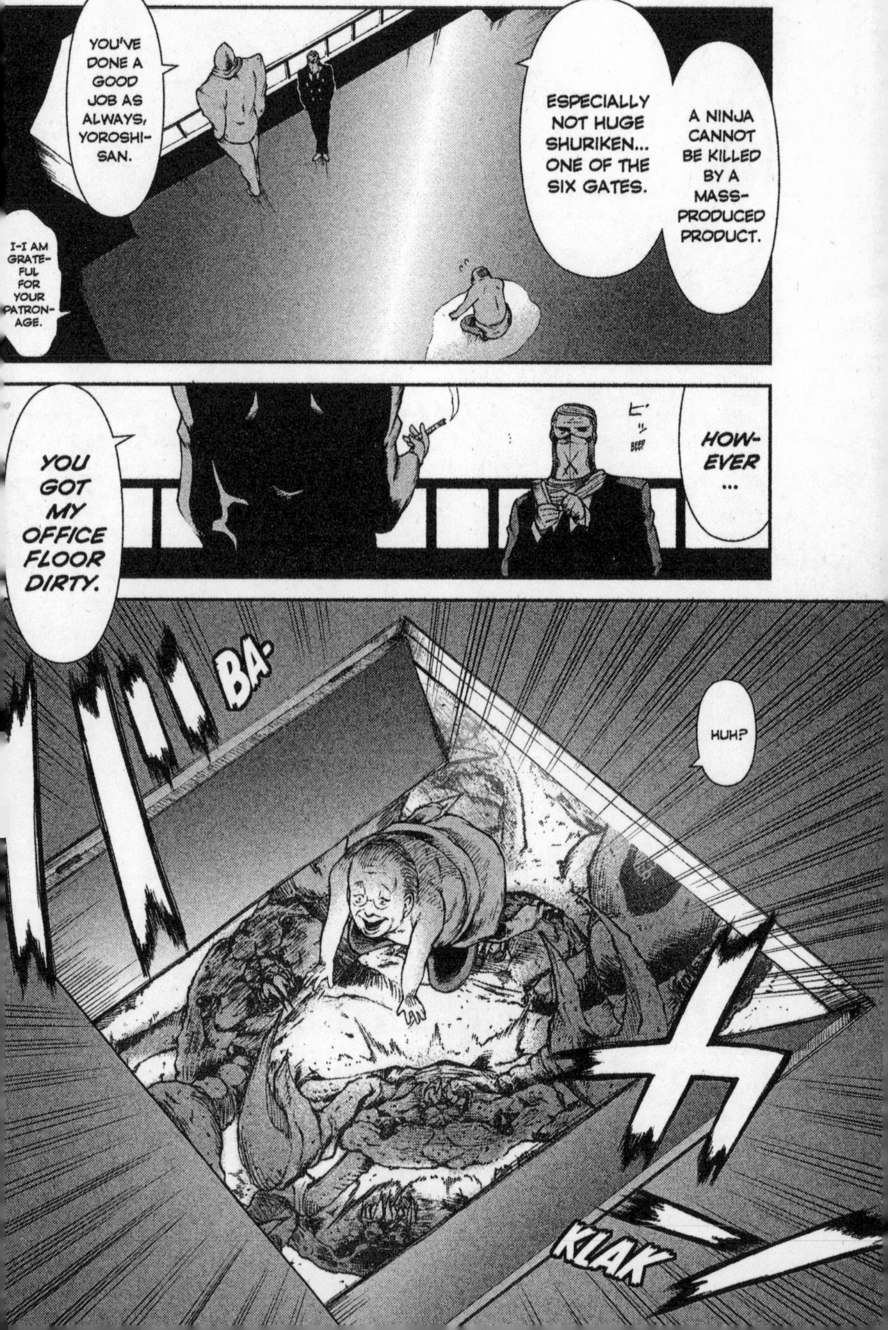
A NINJA CANNOT BE KILLED BY A MASS-PRODUCED PRODUCT.
ESPECIALLY NOT HUGE SHURIKEN... ONE OF THE SIX GATES.
YOU'VE DONE A GOOD JOB AS ALWAYS, YOROSHI-SAN.
I-I AM GRATE-FUL FOR YOUR PATRON-AGE.
HOW-EVER...
BEEP
YOU GOT MY OFFICE FLOOR DIRTY.
HUH?
BA-
KLAK

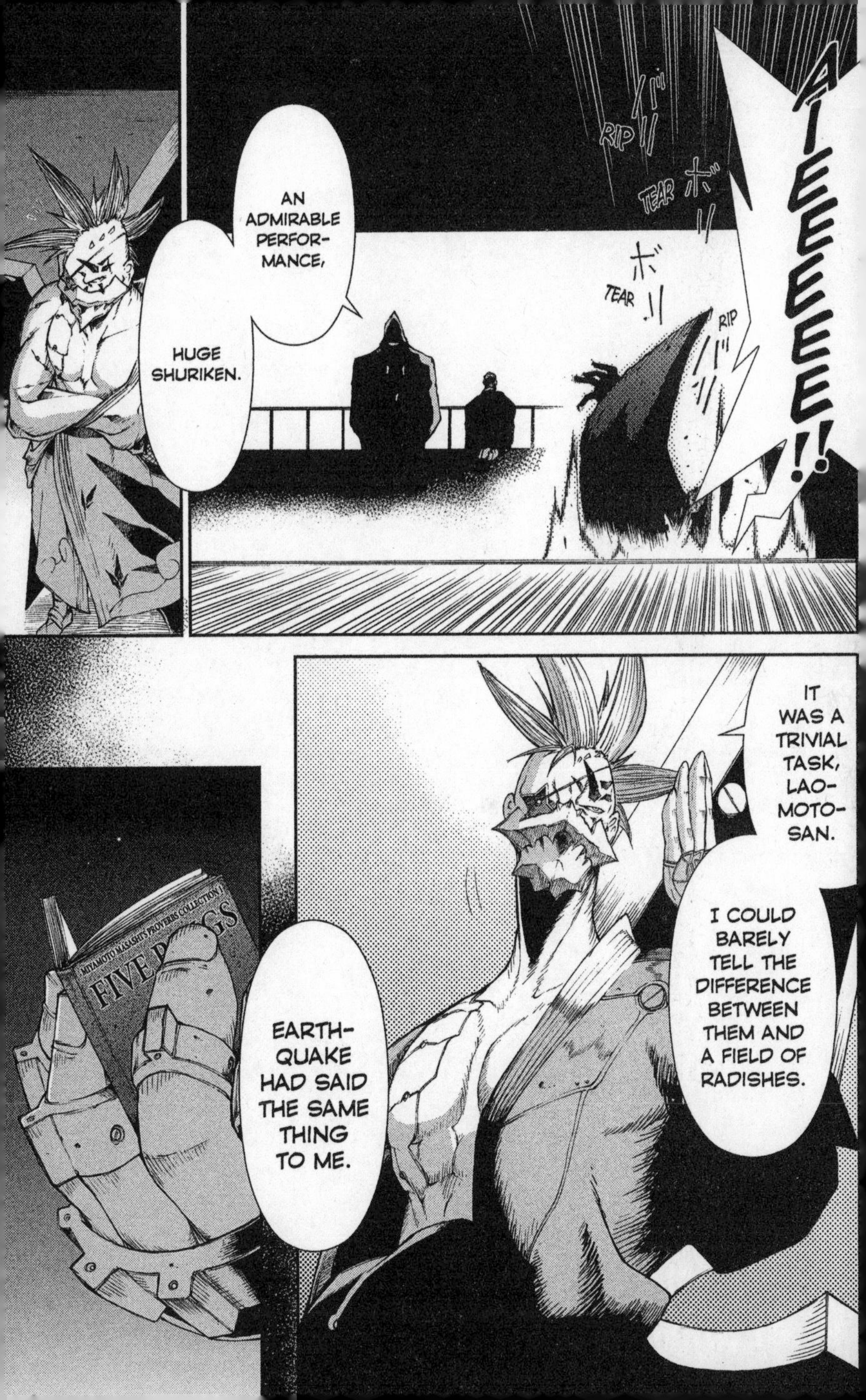
AIEEEEEEE!!
RIP
TEAR
TEAR
RIP
AN ADMIRABLE PERFORMANCE,
HUGE SHURIKEN.
IT WAS A TRIVIAL TASK, LAO-MOTO-SAN.
I COULD BARELY TELL THE DIFFERENCE BETWEEN THEM AND A FIELD OF RADISHES.
MIYAMOTO MASASHI'S PROVERBS COLLECTION 1
EARTH-QUAKE HAD SAID THE SAME THING TO ME.

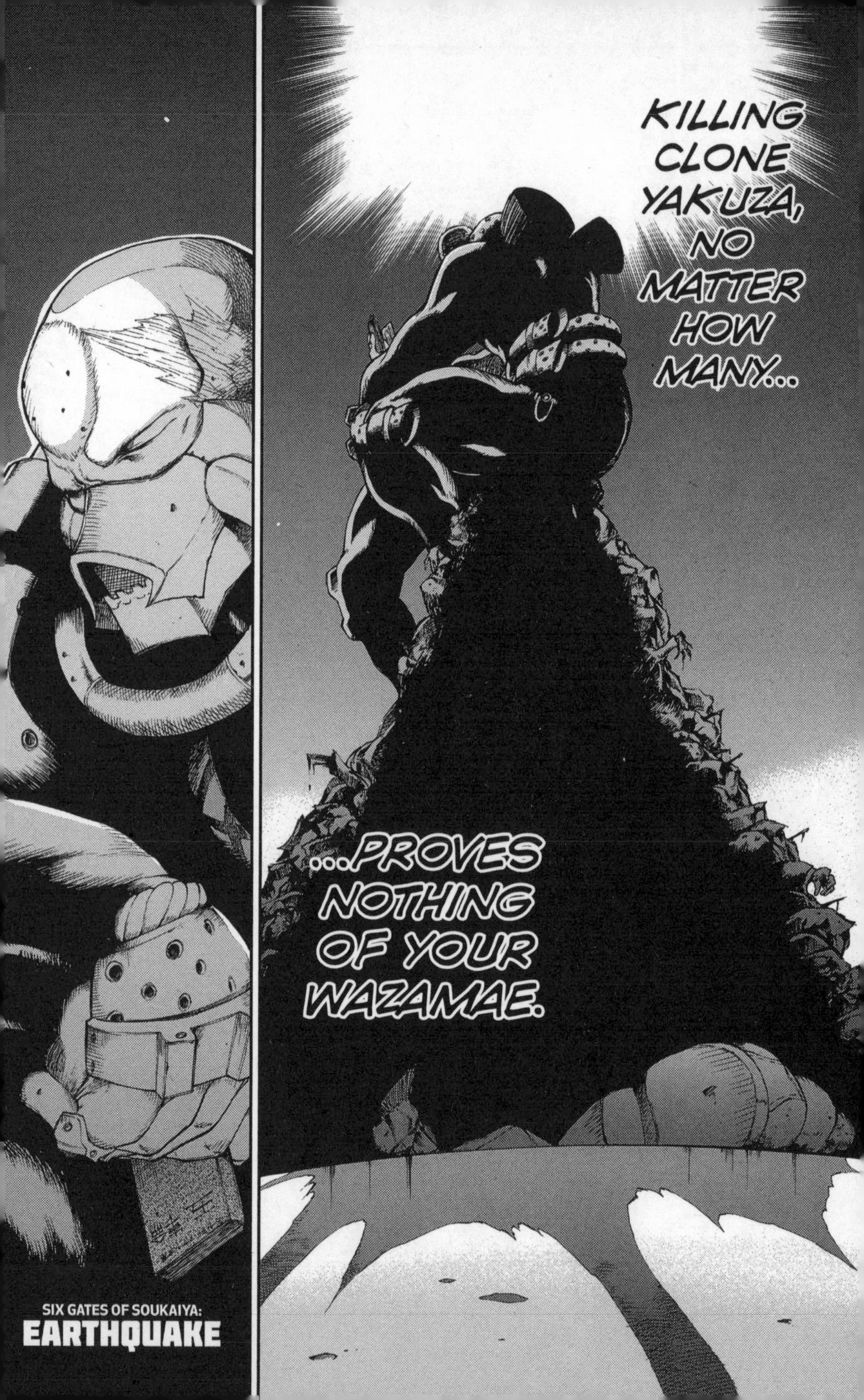
KILLING CLONE YAKUZA, NO MATTER HOW MANY...
...PROVES NOTHING OF YOUR WAZAMAE.
SIX GATES OF SOUKAIYA:
EARTHQUAKE

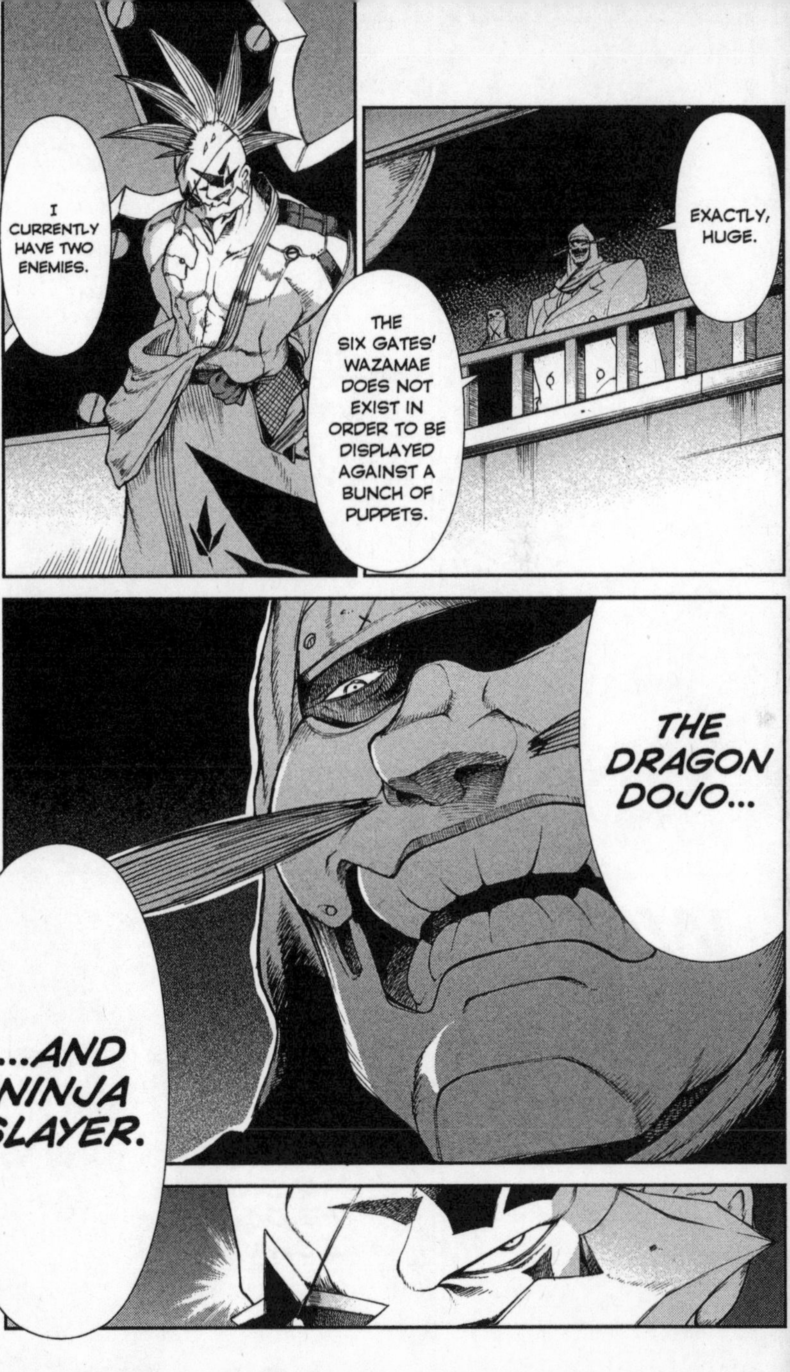
EXACTLY, HUGE.
THE SIX GATES' WAZAMAE DOES NOT EXIST IN ORDER TO BE DISPLAYED AGAINST A BUNCH OF PUPPETS.
I CURRENTLY HAVE TWO ENEMIES.
THE DRAGON DOJO...
...AND NINJA SLAYER.

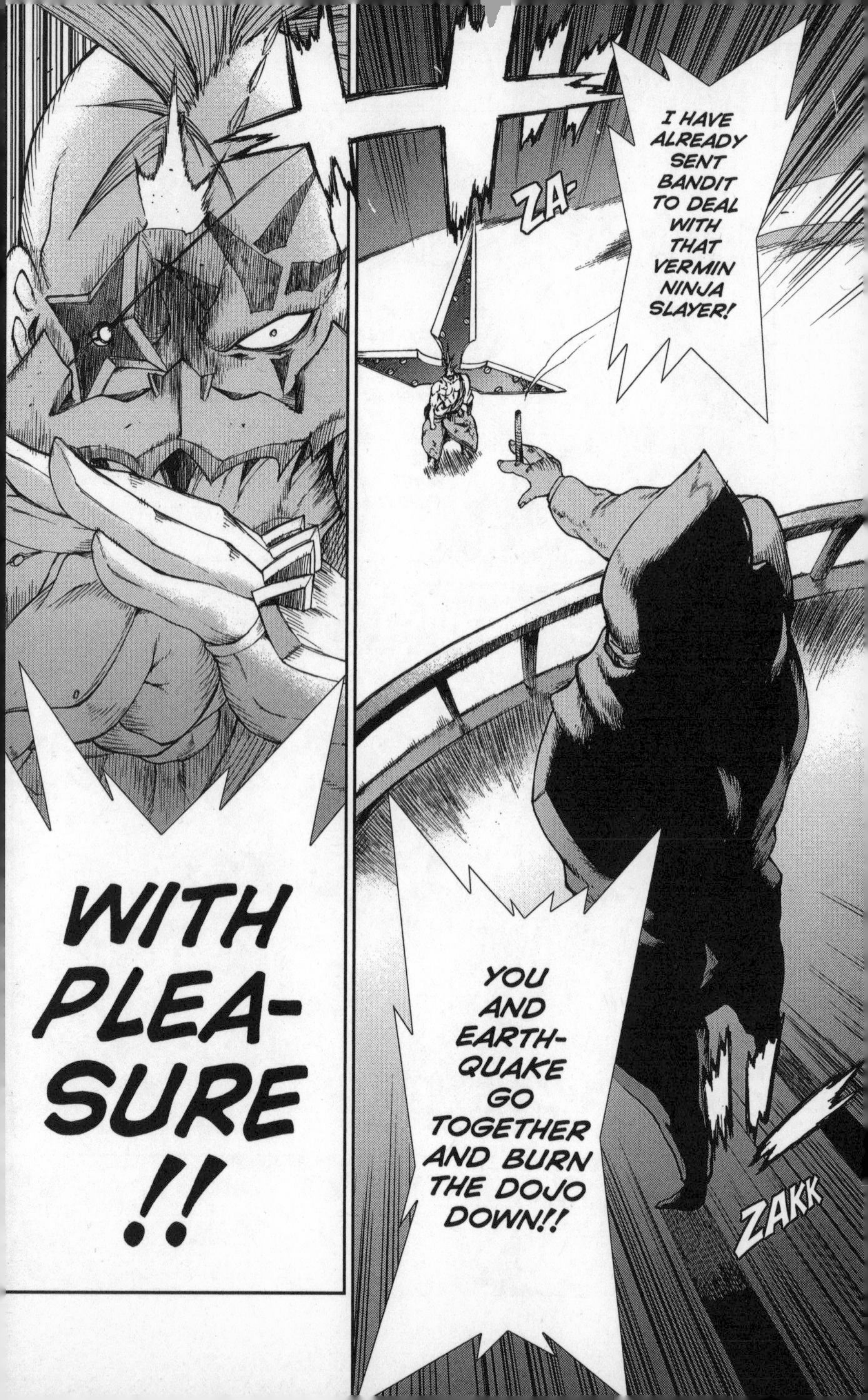
I HAVE ALREADY SENT BANDIT TO DEAL WITH THAT VERMIN NINJA SLAYER!
ZA-
YOU AND EARTH-QUAKE GO TOGETHER AND BURN THE DOJO DOWN!!
ZAKK
WITH PLEA-SURE!!

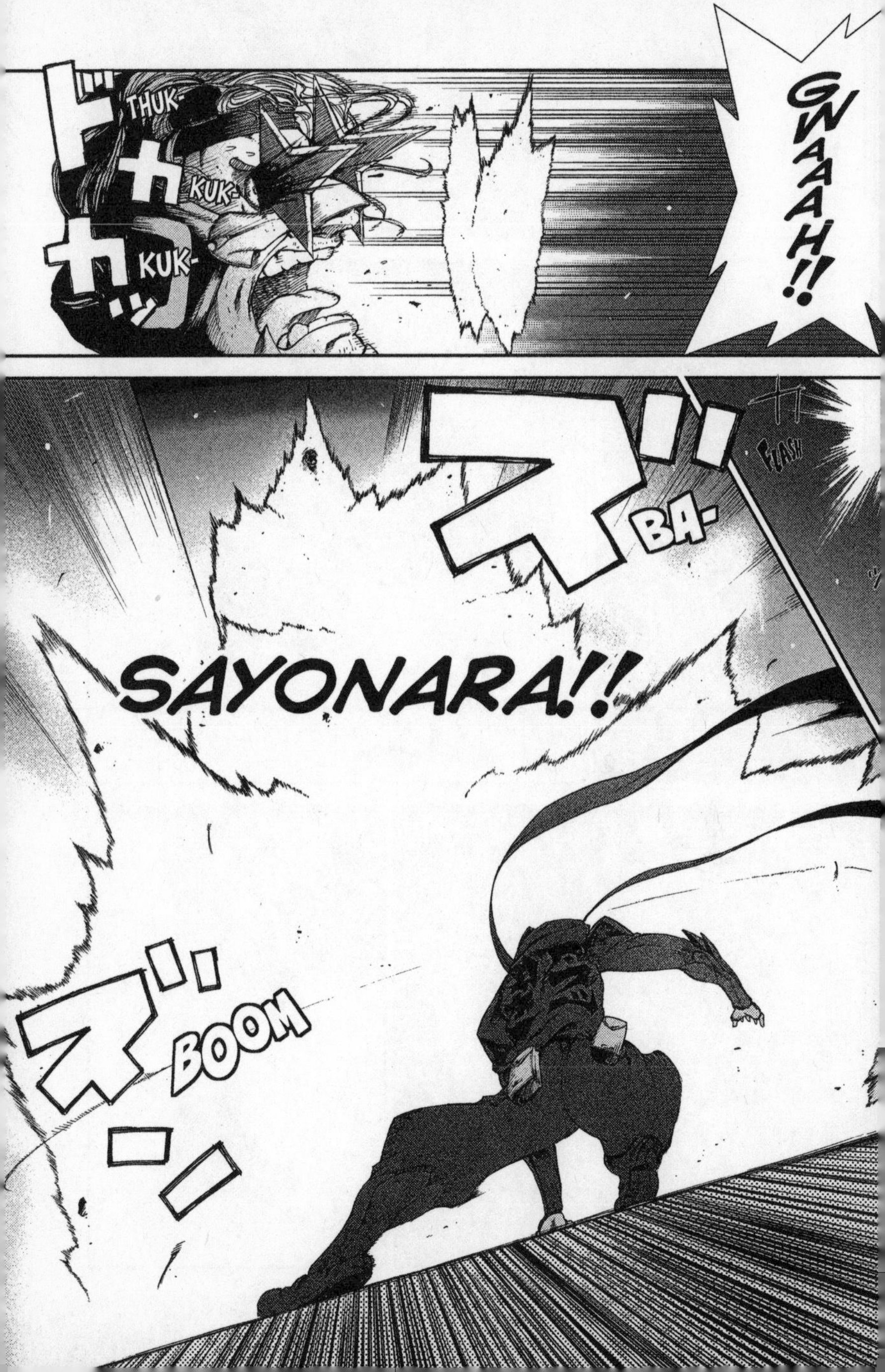
GWAAAH!!
ドカカッ
THUK-
KUK-
KUK-
FLASH
BA-
SAYONARA!!
BOOM

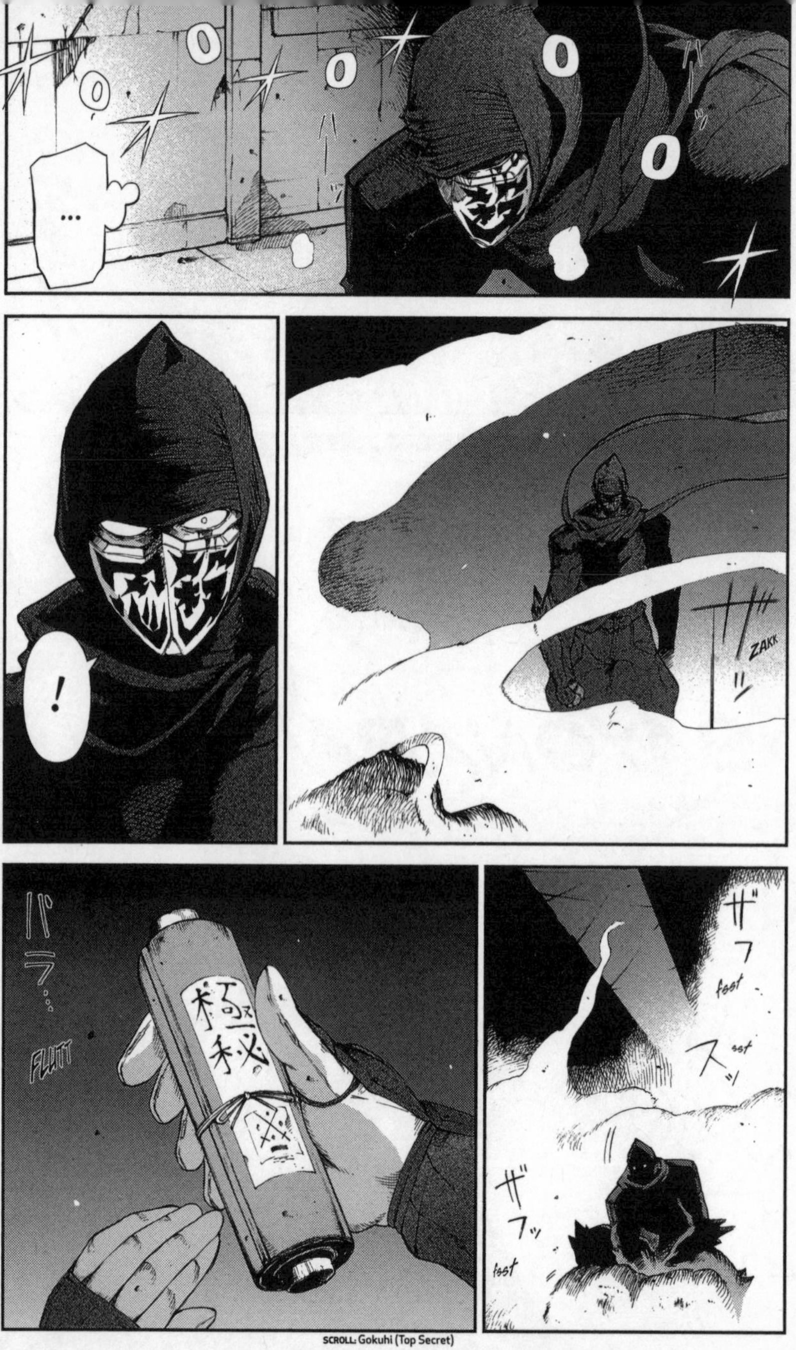
O O O O O
...
ZAKK
!
fsst
sst
fsst
FLUTT

SCROLL: Gokuhi (Top Secret)

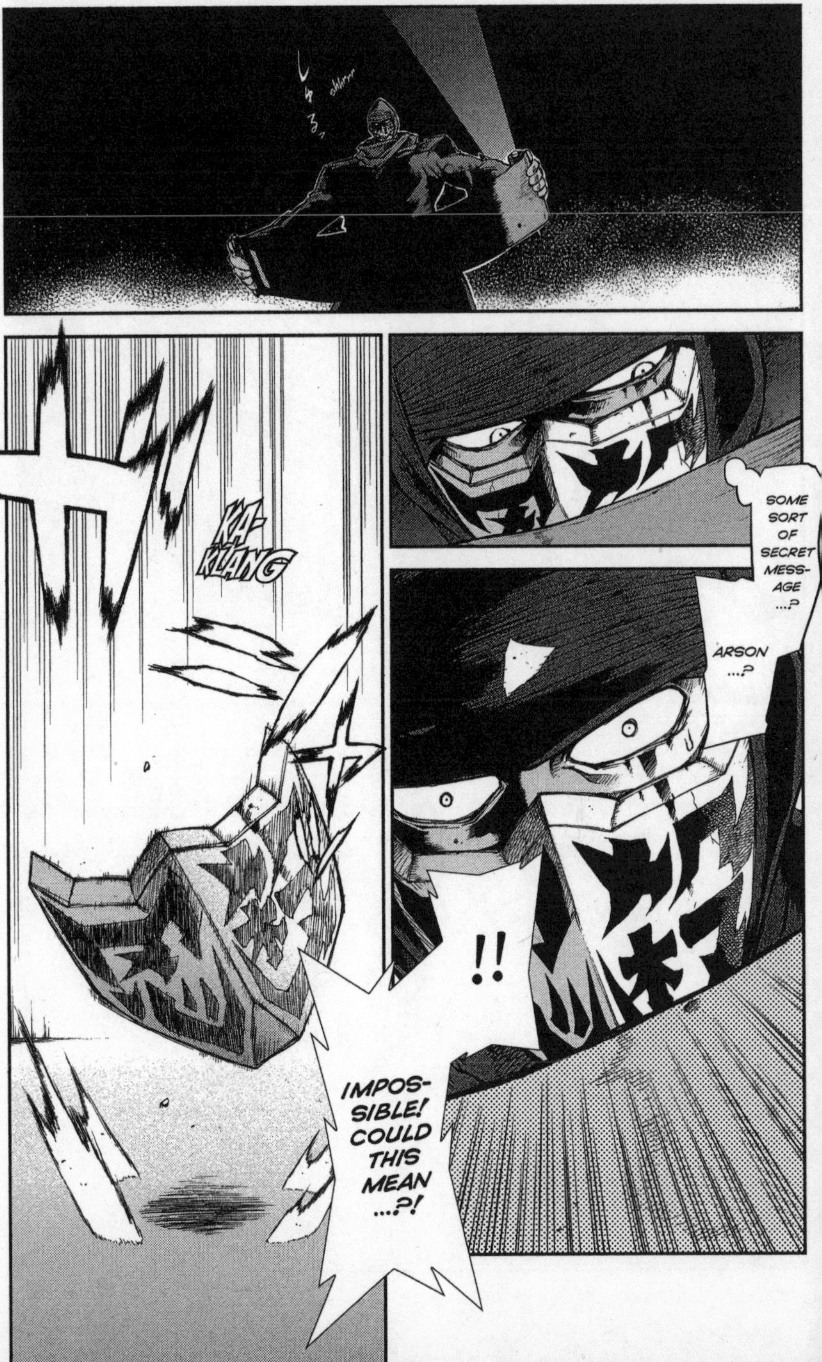
しゅる
shhrrr
SOME SORT OF SECRET MESSAGE ...?
ARSON ...?
!!
IMPOSSIBLE! COULD THIS MEAN ...?!
KA-KLANG

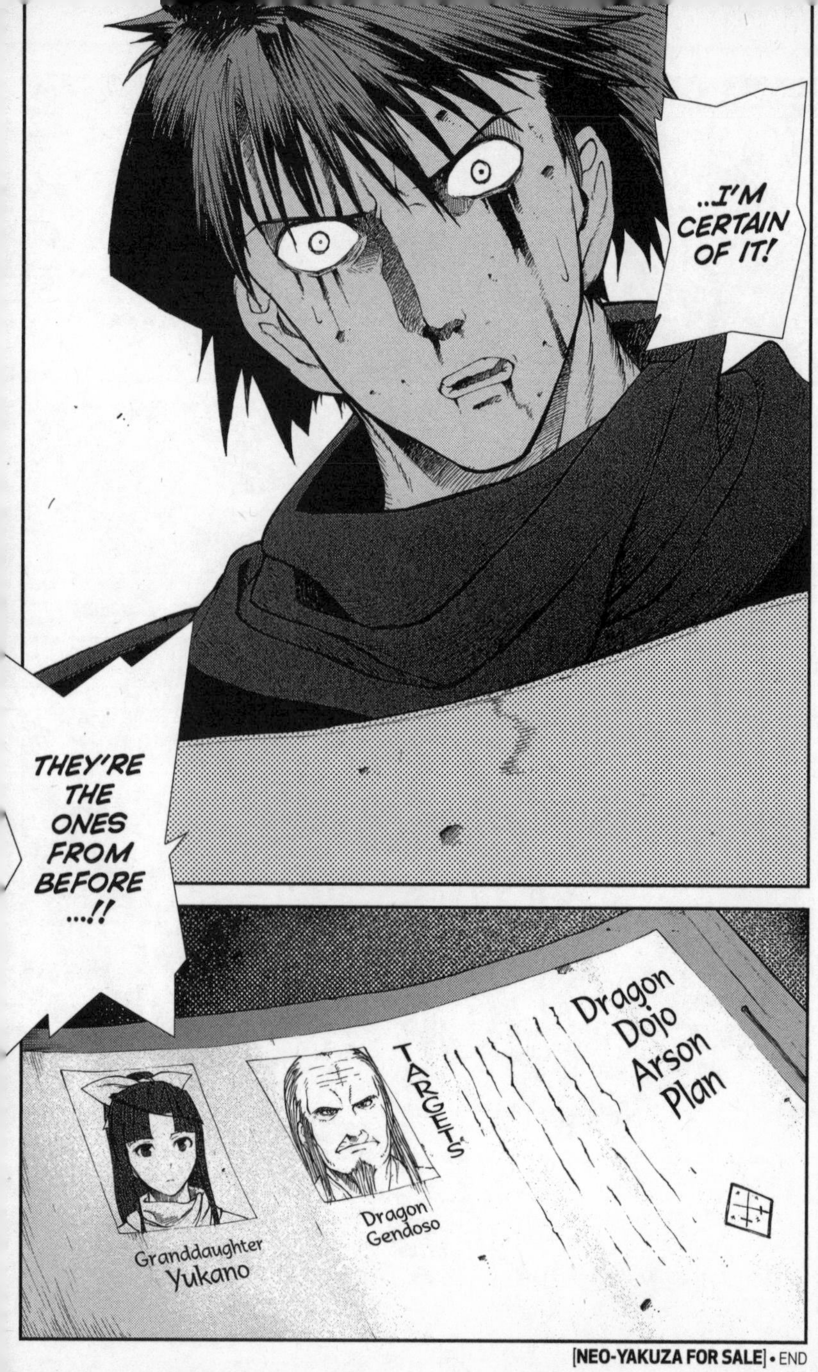
...I'M CERTAIN OF IT!
THEY'RE THE ONES FROM BEFORE ...!!
Dragon Dojo Arson Plan
TARGETS
Dragon Gendoso
Granddaughter Yukano

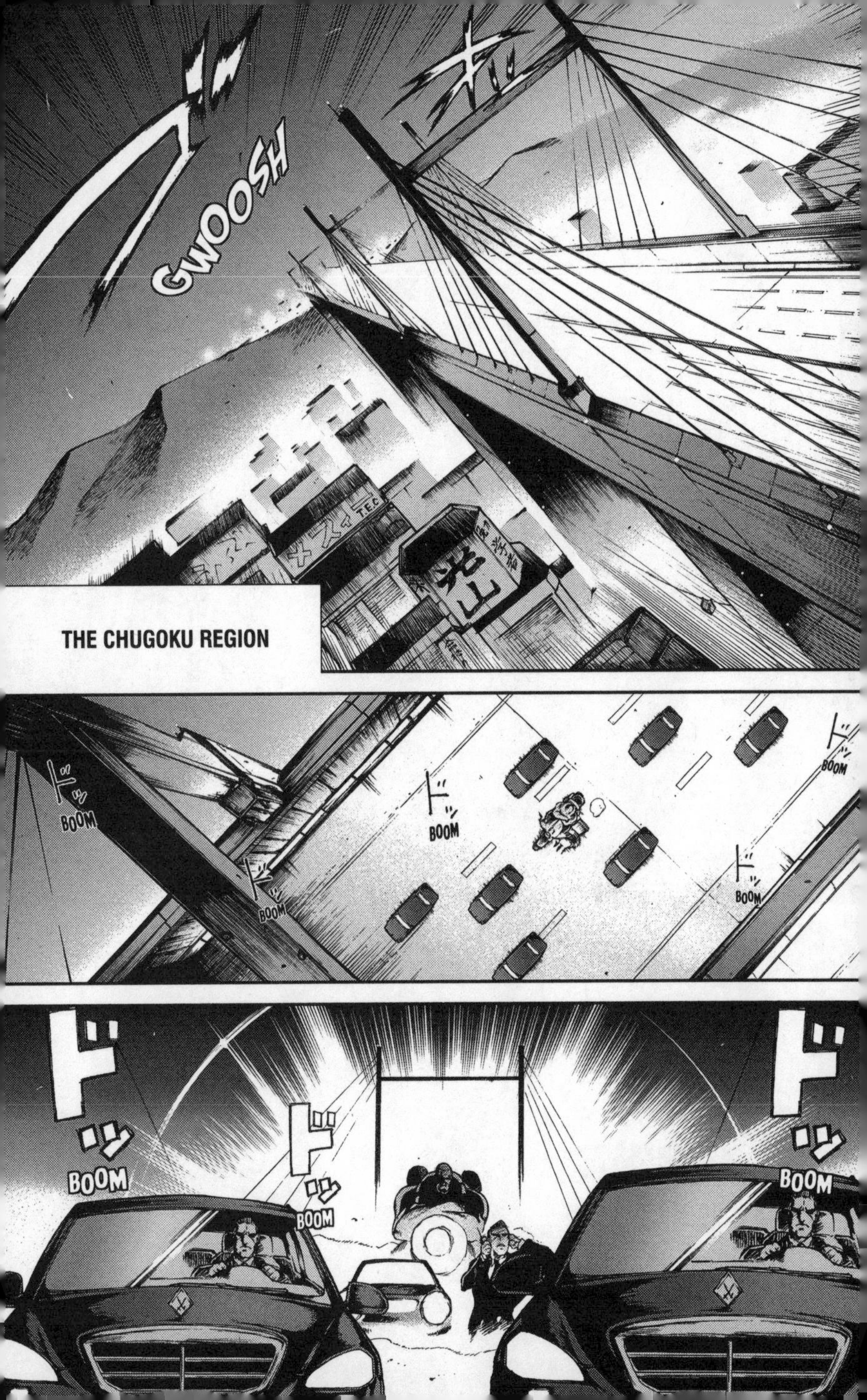
GWOOSH
THE CHUGOKU REGION
BOOM
BOOM
BOOM
BOOM
BOOM
BOOM
BOOM
BOOM

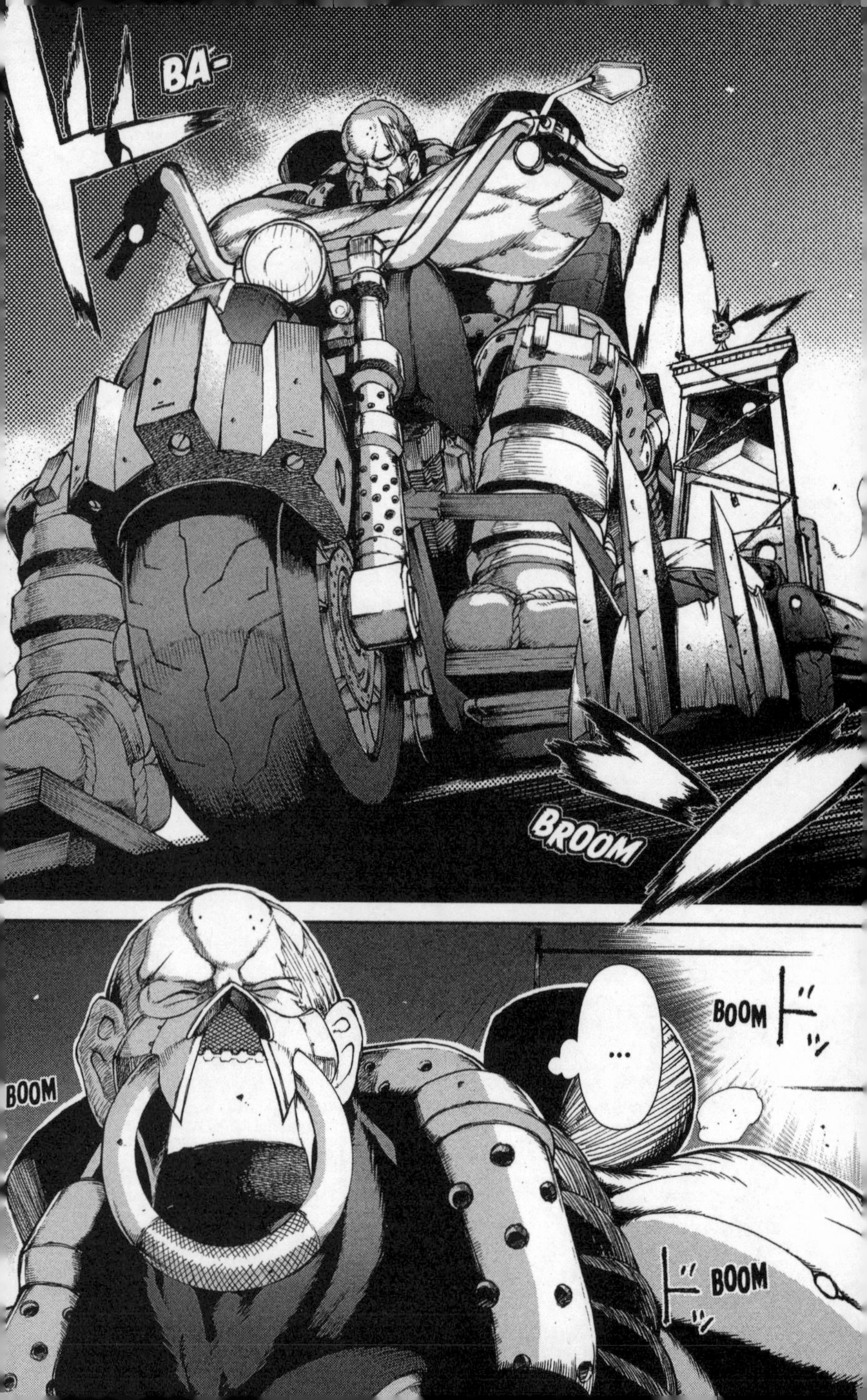
BA-
BROOM
BOOM ドッ
...
BOOM
ドッ BOOM

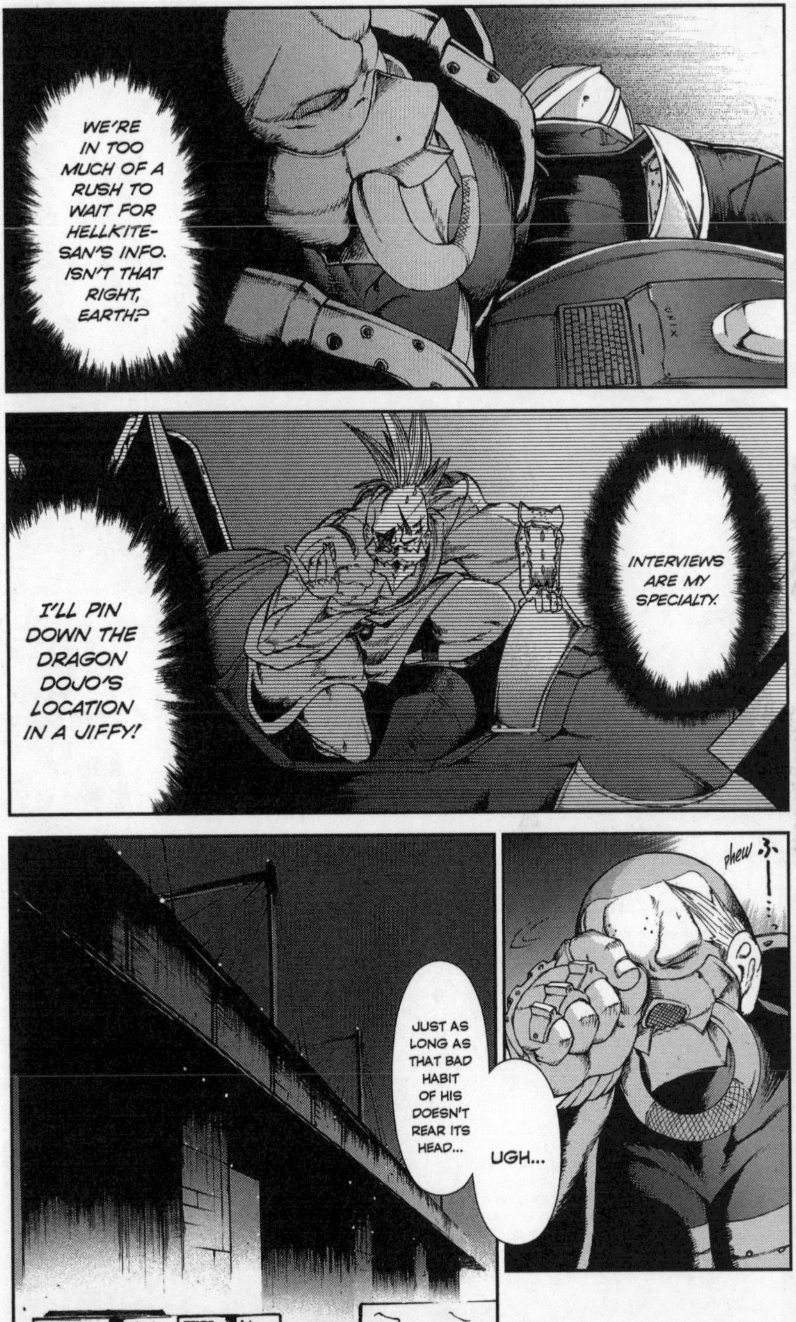
WE'RE IN TOO MUCH OF A RUSH TO WAIT FOR HELLKITE-SAN'S INFO. ISN'T THAT RIGHT, EARTH?
INTERVIEWS ARE MY SPECIALTY.
I'LL PIN DOWN THE DRAGON DOJO'S LOCATION IN A JIFFY!
phew ふー
JUST AS LONG AS THAT BAD HABIT OF HIS DOESN'T REAR ITS HEAD...
UGH...

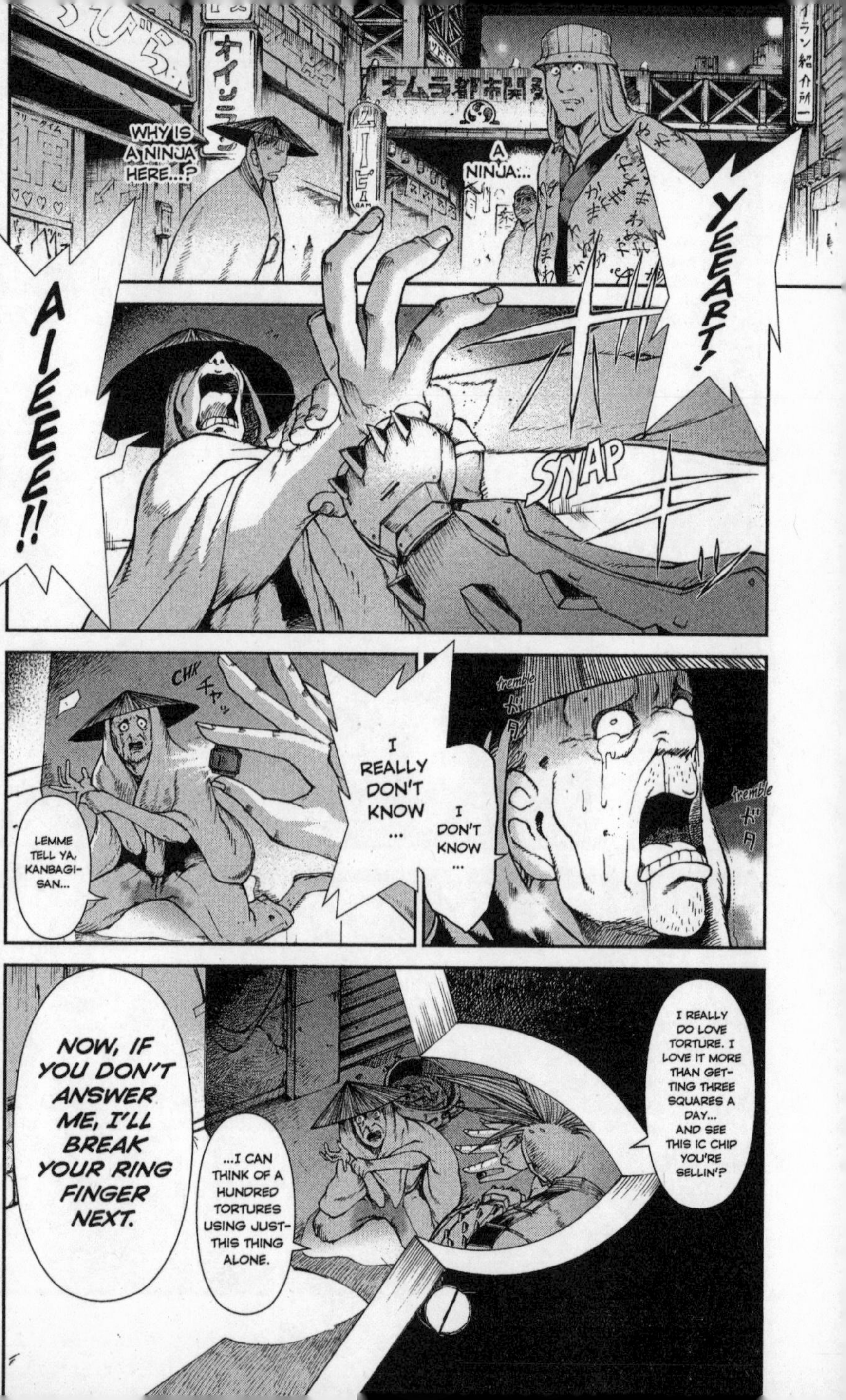
YEEEART!
A NINJA...
WHY IS A NINJA HERE...?
SNAP
AIEEEE!!
tremble
tremble
I DON'T KNOW...
I REALLY DON'T KNOW...
CHK
LEMME TELL YA, KANBAGI-SAN...
I REALLY DO LOVE TORTURE. I LOVE IT MORE THAN GETTING THREE SQUARES A DAY... AND SEE THIS IC CHIP YOU'RE SELLIN'?
...I CAN THINK OF A HUNDRED TORTURES USING JUST THIS THING ALONE.
NOW, IF YOU DON'T ANSWER ME, I'LL BREAK YOUR RING FINGER NEXT.

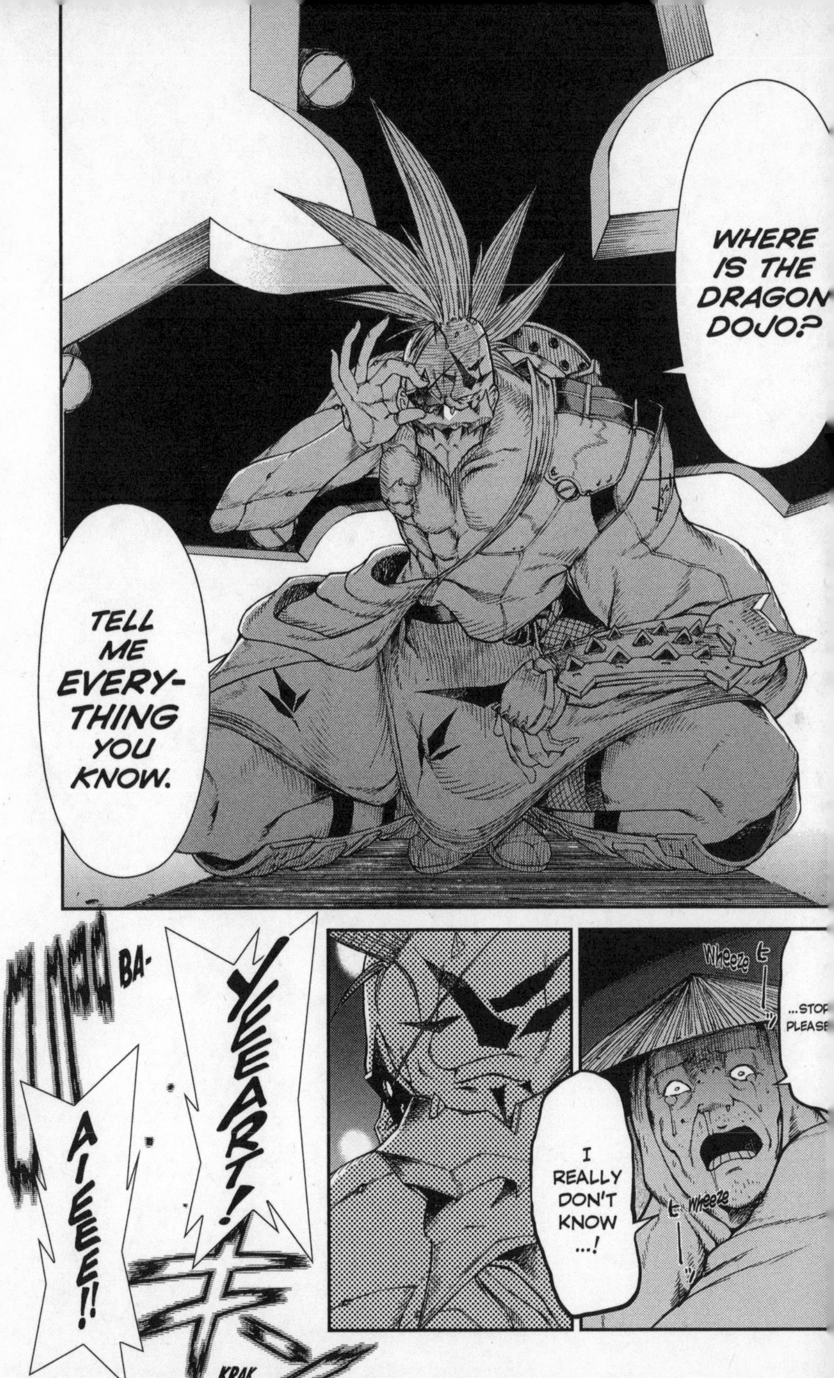
WHERE IS THE DRAGON DOJO?
TELL ME EVERYTHING YOU KNOW.
Wheeze
...STOP PLEASE
I REALLY DON'T KNOW ...!
Wheeze
BA-
YEEART!!
AIEEE!!
KRAK

KILLs 016 ✦ SURPRISED DOJO PART 1

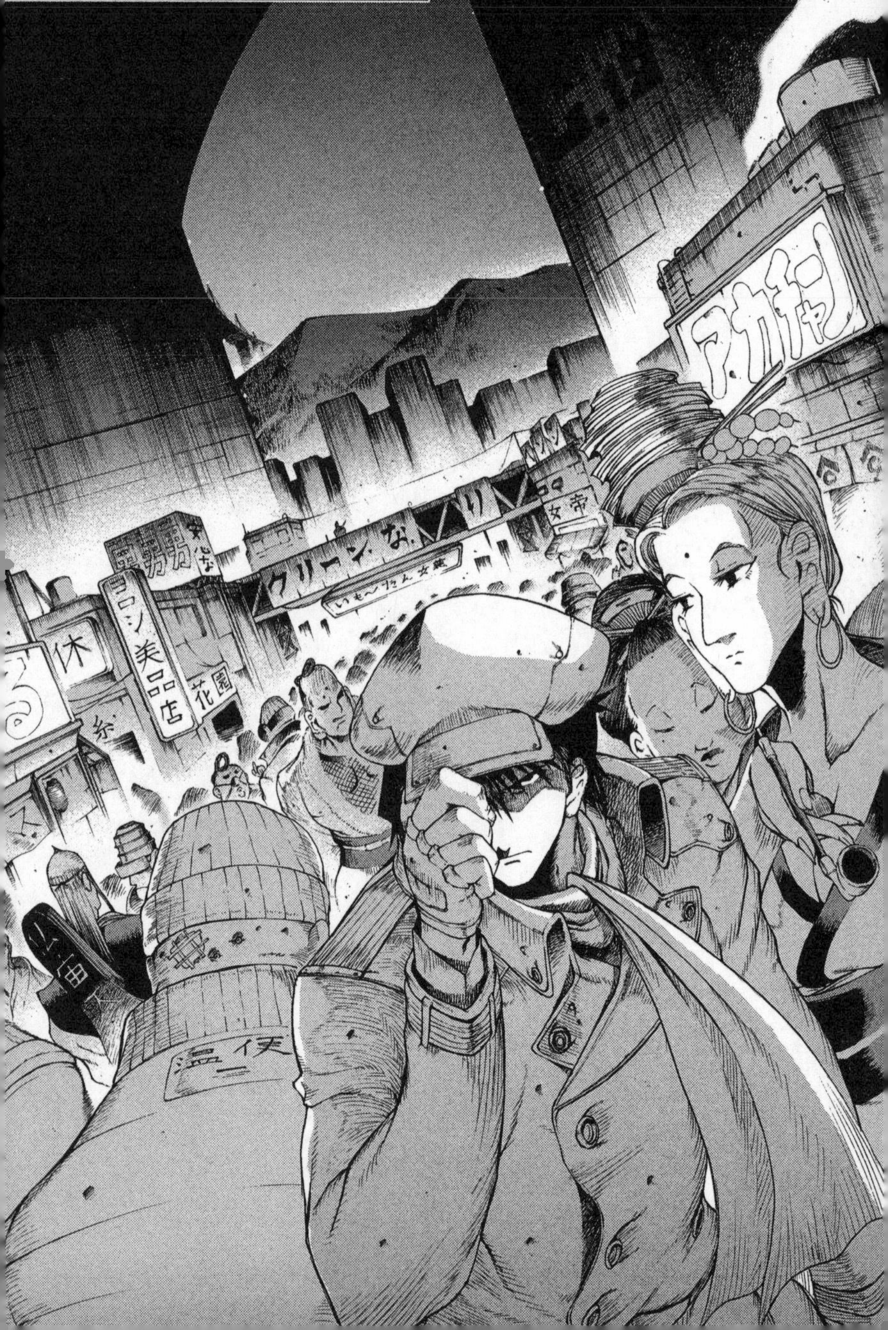
花園
休
女帝

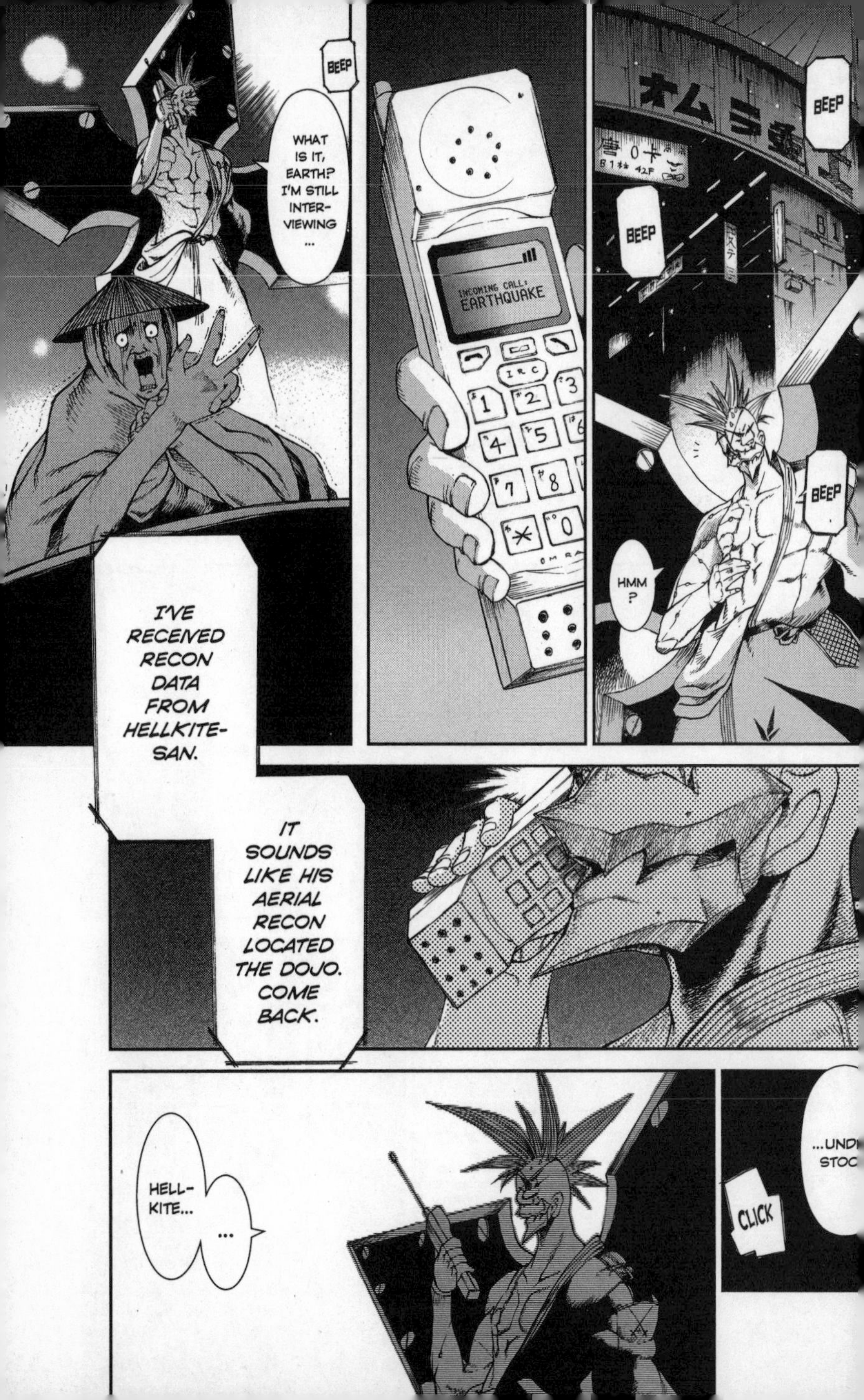
BEEP
BEEP
BEEP
HMM?
INCOMING CALL: EARTHQUAKE
BEEP
WHAT IS IT, EARTH? I'M STILL INTER-VIEWING...
I'VE RECEIVED RECON DATA FROM HELLKITE-SAN.
IT SOUNDS LIKE HIS AERIAL RECON LOCATED THE DOJO. COME BACK.
...UND STOC
CLICK
HELL-KITE...
...

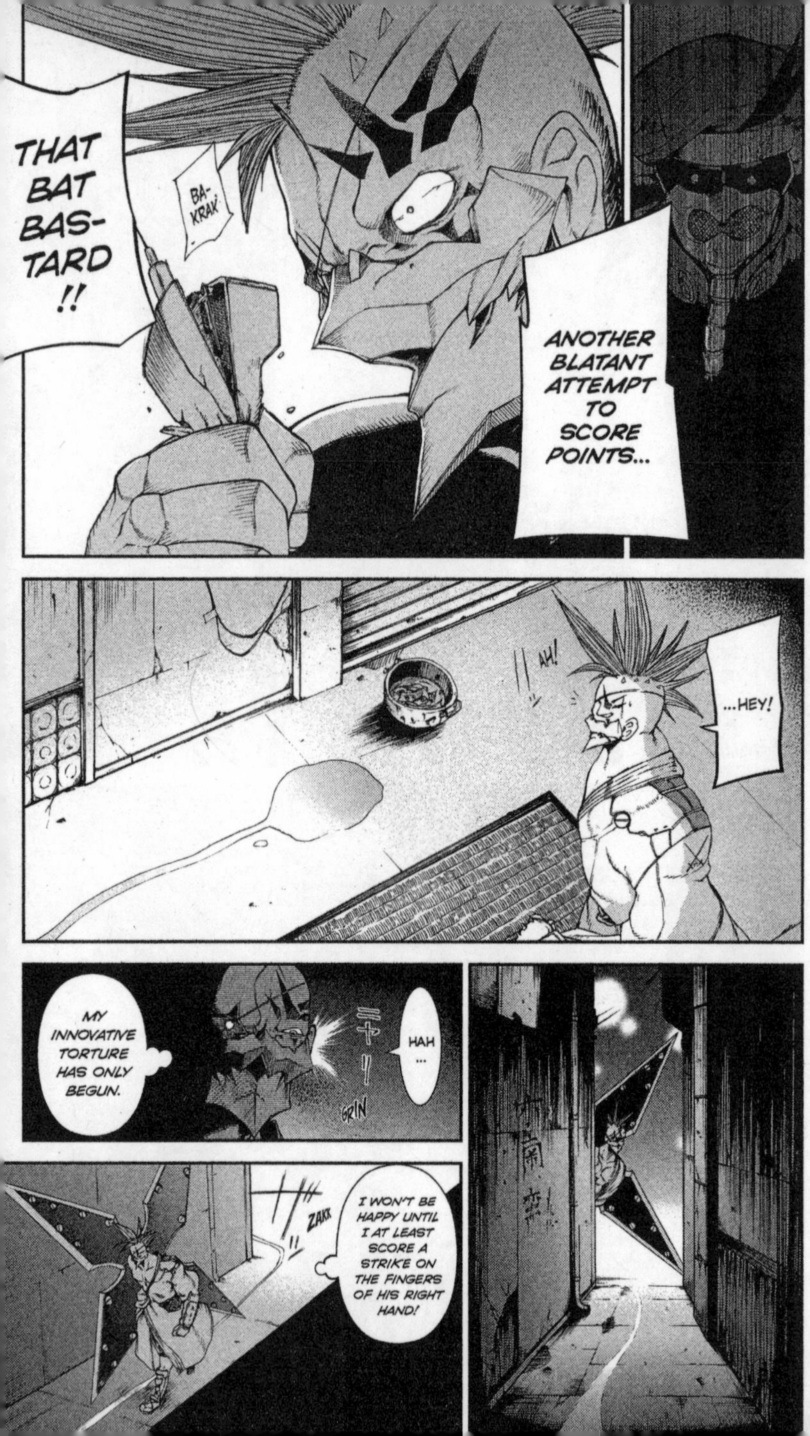
ANOTHER BLATANT ATTEMPT TO SCORE POINTS...
BA-KRAX
THAT BAT BAS-TARD !!
...HEY!
AH!
HAH ...
ニヤリ
GRIN
MY INNOVATIVE TORTURE HAS ONLY BEGUN.
I WON'T BE HAPPY UNTIL I AT LEAST SCORE A STRIKE ON THE FINGERS OF HIS RIGHT HAND!
ZAKK

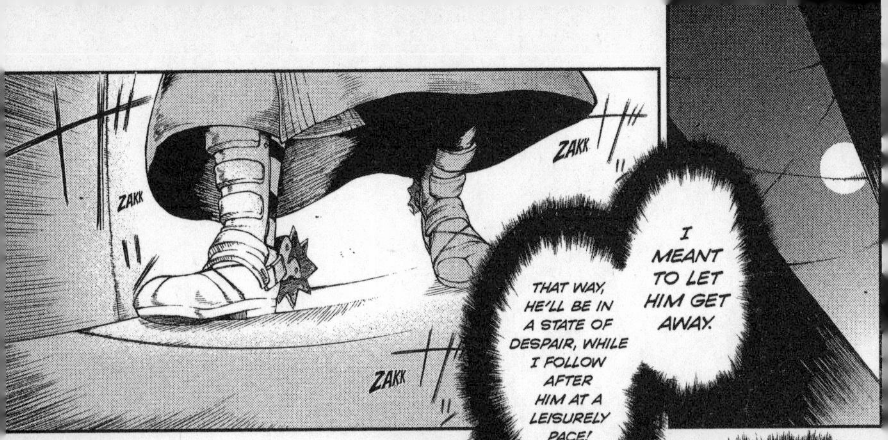
ZAKK
ZAKK
ZAKK
I MEANT TO LET HIM GET AWAY.
THAT WAY, HE'LL BE IN A STATE OF DESPAIR, WHILE I FOLLOW AFTER HIM AT A LEISURELY PACE!
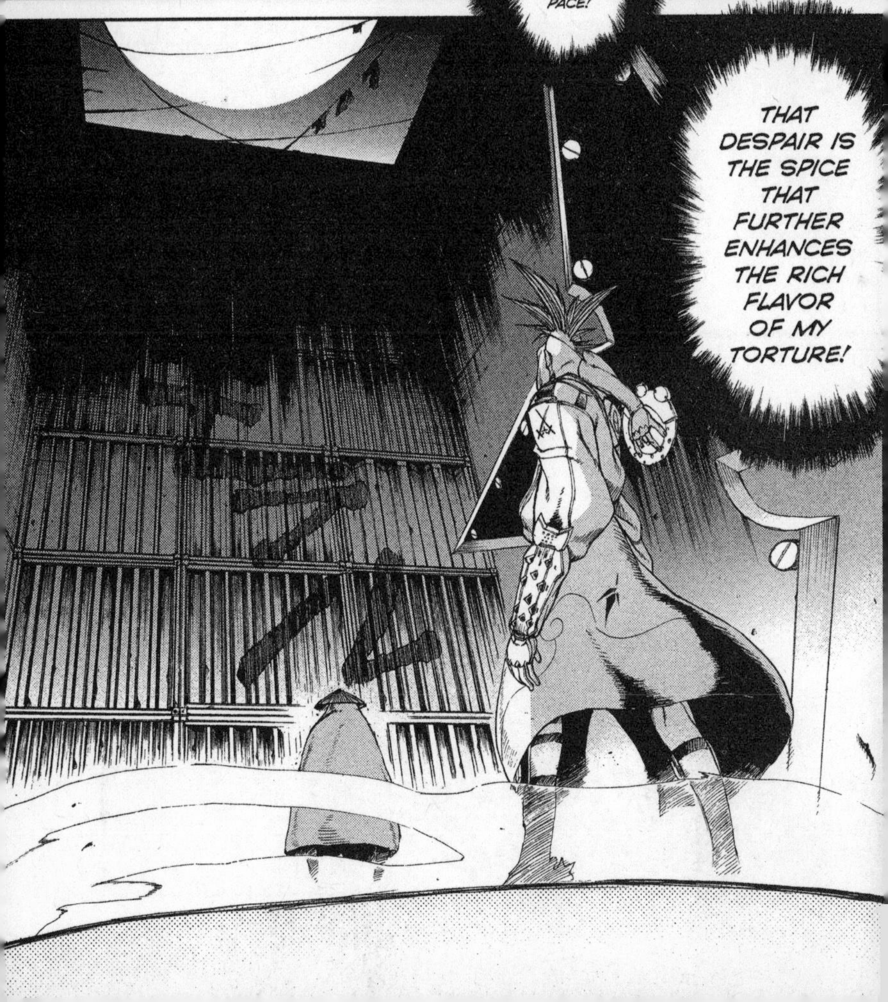
THAT DESPAIR IS THE SPICE THAT FURTHER ENHANCES THE RICH FLAVOR OF MY TORTURE!

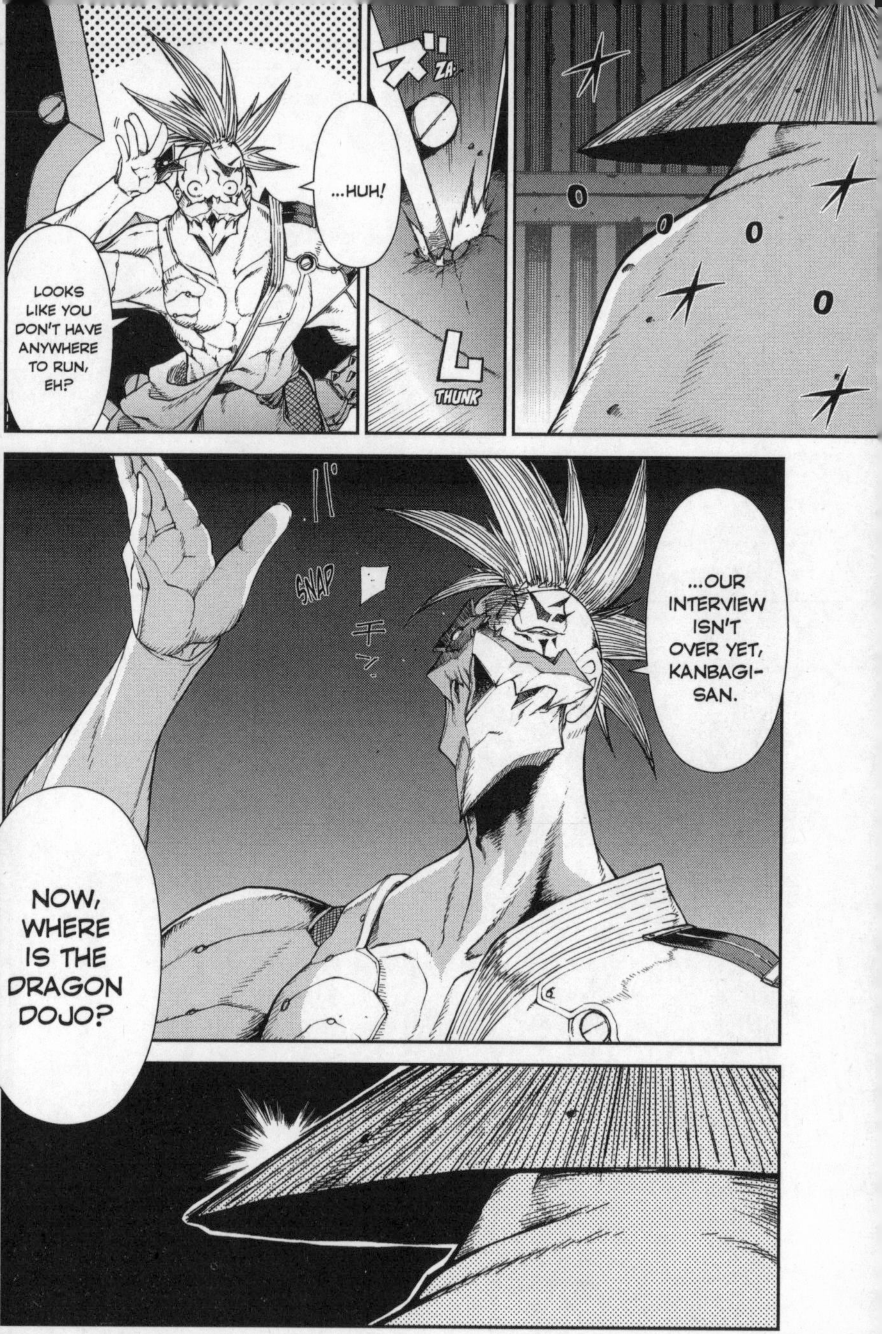
ZA
...HUH!
THUNK
LOOKS LIKE YOU DON'T HAVE ANYWHERE TO RUN, EH?
SNAP
...OUR INTERVIEW ISN'T OVER YET, KANBAGI-SAN.
NOW, WHERE IS THE DRAGON DOJO?

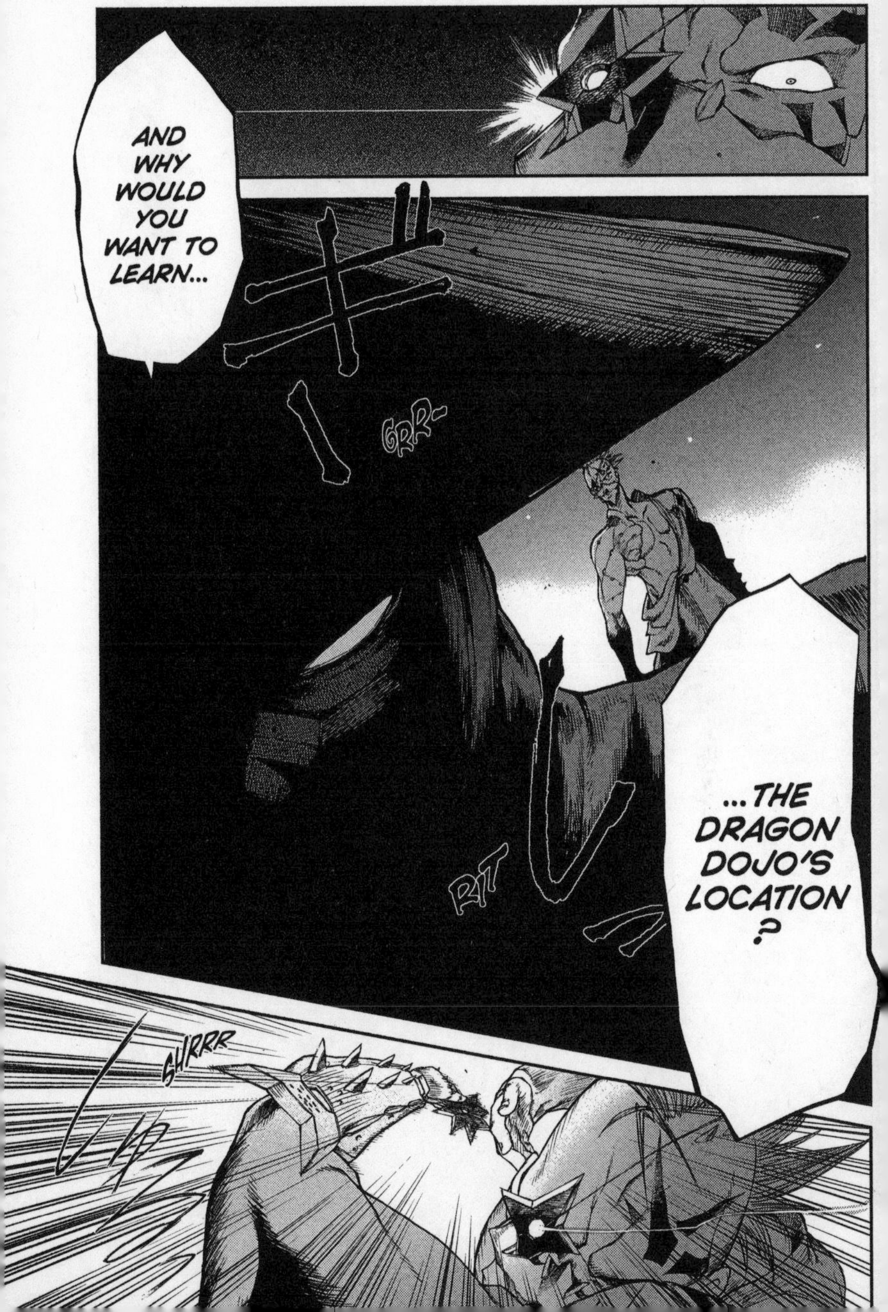
AND WHY WOULD YOU WANT TO LEARN...
GRR-
RIT
...THE DRAGON DOJO'S LOCATION?
SHRRR

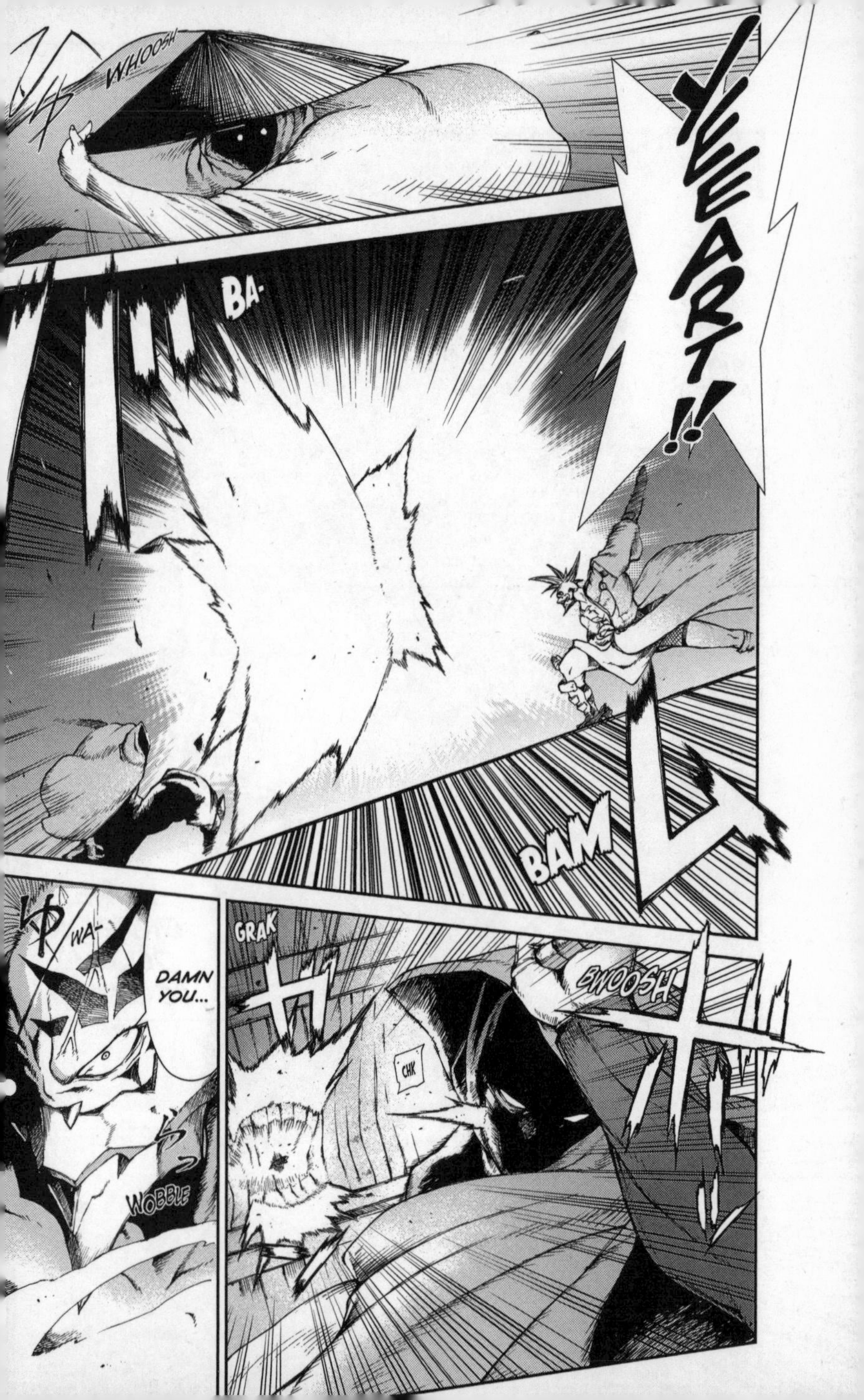

WHOOSH
YEEEART!!
BA-
BAM
BWOOSH
GRAK
CHK
WA-
DAMN YOU...
WOBBLE

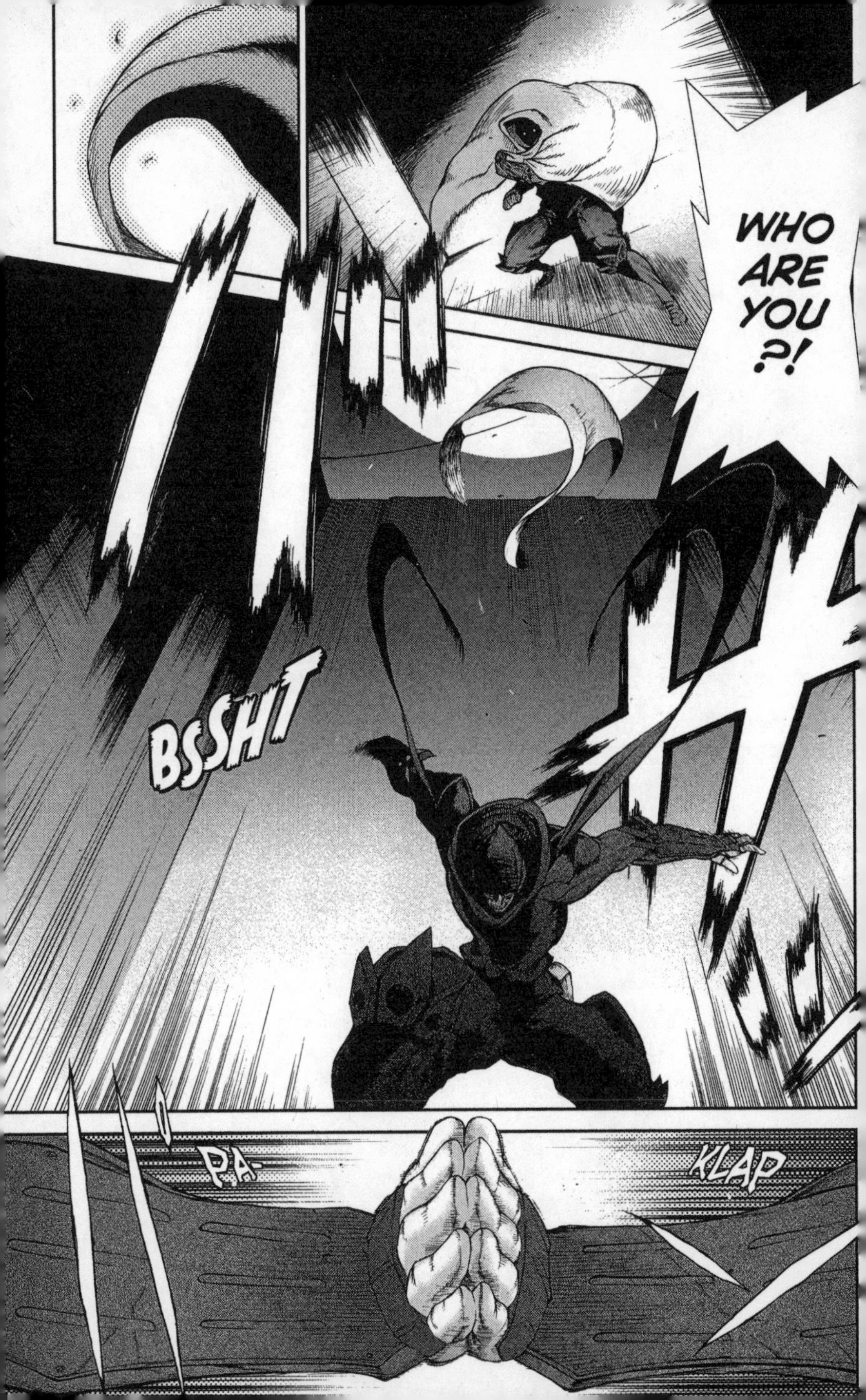
WHO ARE YOU ?!
BSSHT
KLAP
PA-

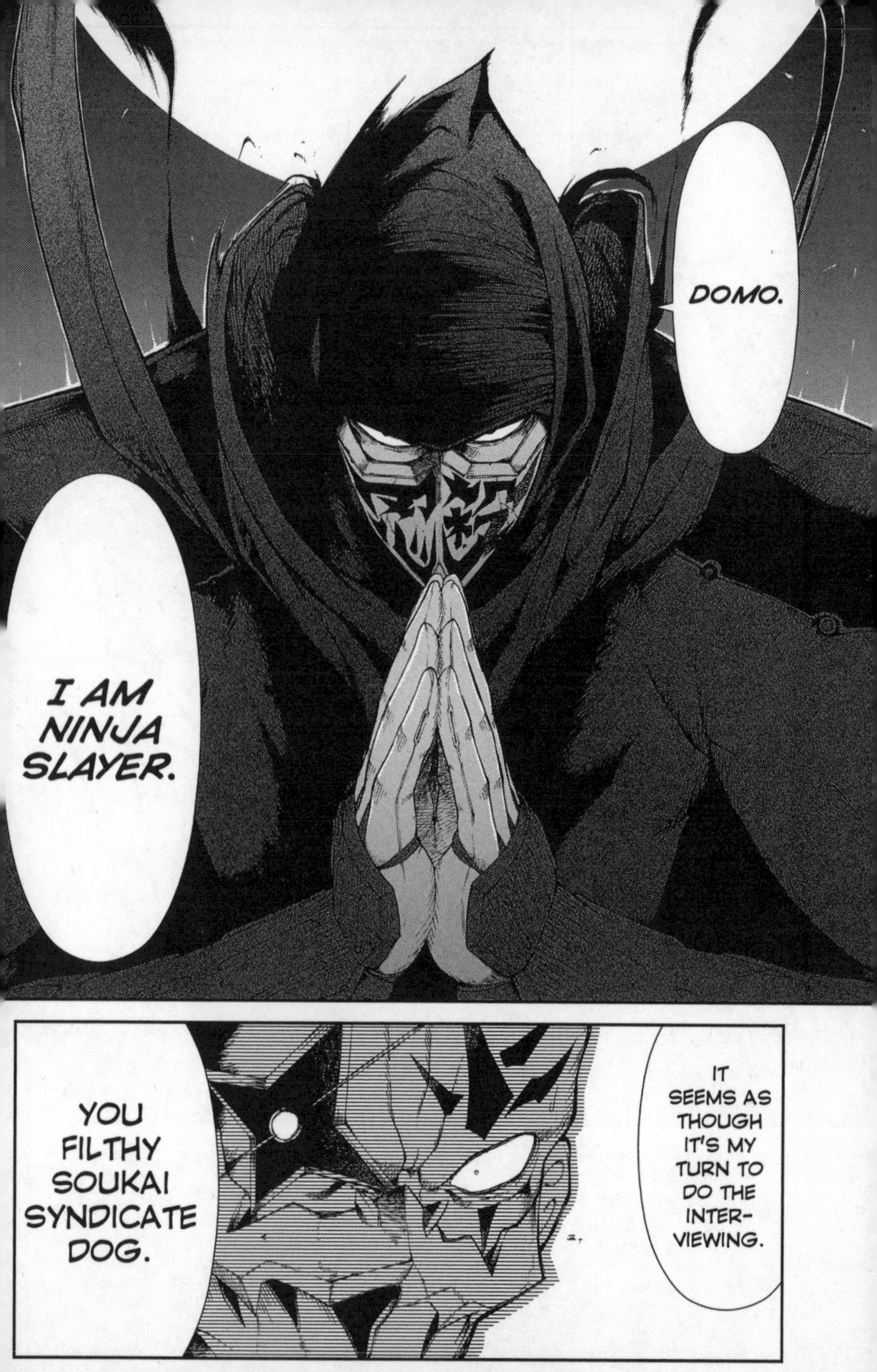
DOMO.
I AM NINJA SLAYER.
IT SEEMS AS THOUGH IT'S MY TURN TO DO THE INTER-VIEWING.
YOU FILTHY SOUKAI SYNDICATE DOG.

...HE'S TAKING TOO LONG.

BOOM

CLICK

BOOM

BOOM

WHAT ARE YOU DOING, HUGE?

STILL TORTUR-ING?

ARE YOU TRYING TO TEST MY PATIENCE?!

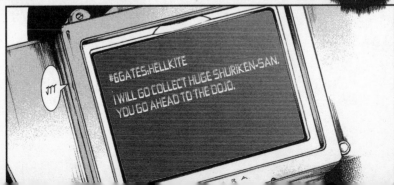

JTT

#6GATES:HELLKITE
I WILL GO COLLECT HUGE SHURIKEN-SAN.
YOU GO AHEAD TO THE DOJO.

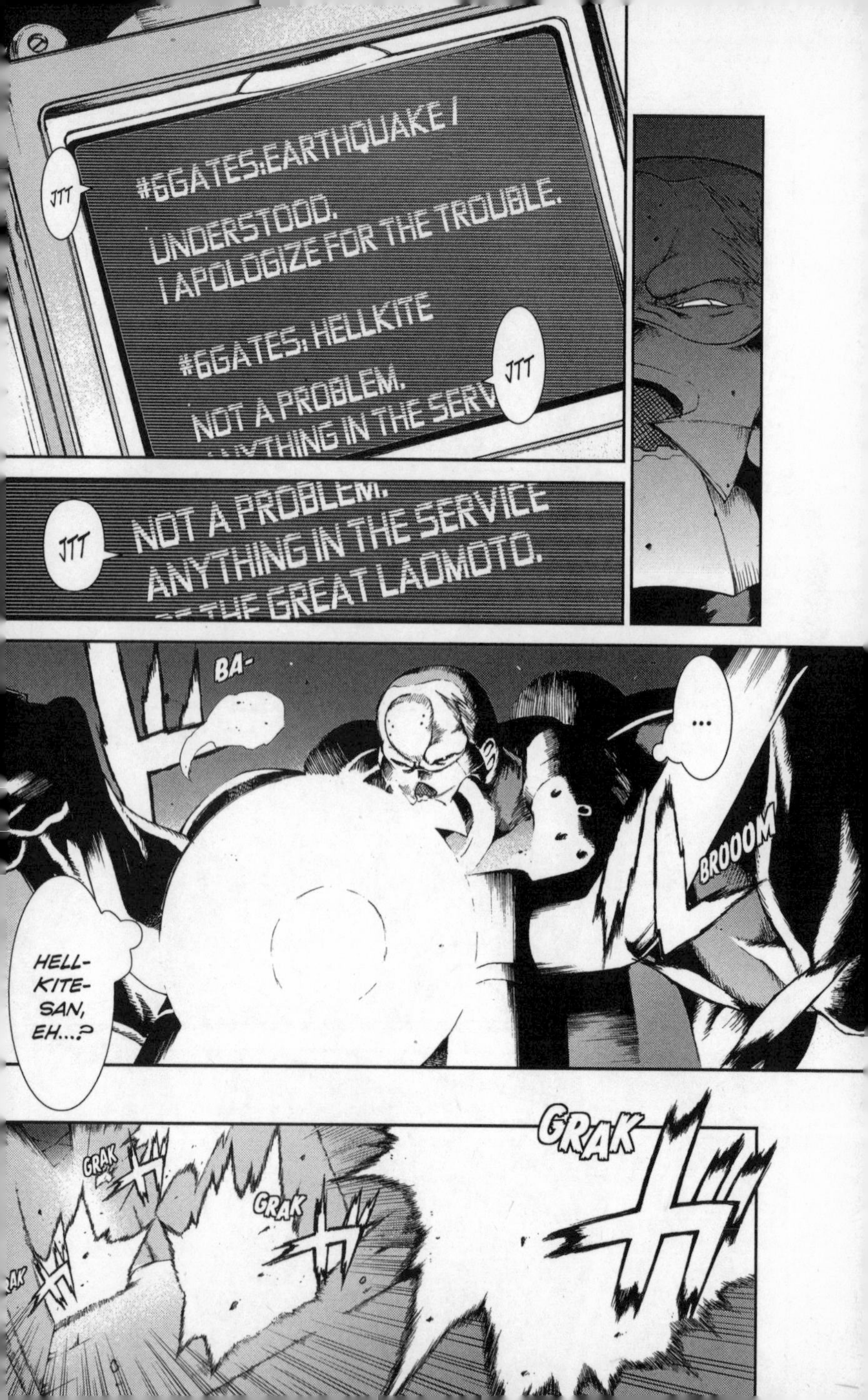
JTT
#6GATES:EARTHQUAKE /
UNDERSTOOD.
I APOLOGIZE FOR THE TROUBLE.
#6GATES: HELLKITE
JTT
NOT A PROBLEM.
ANYTHING IN THE SERV
JTT
NOT A PROBLEM.
ANYTHING IN THE SERVICE
GREAT LAOMOTO.
...
BA-
BROOOM
HELL-KITE-SAN, EH...?
GRAK
GRAK
GRAK

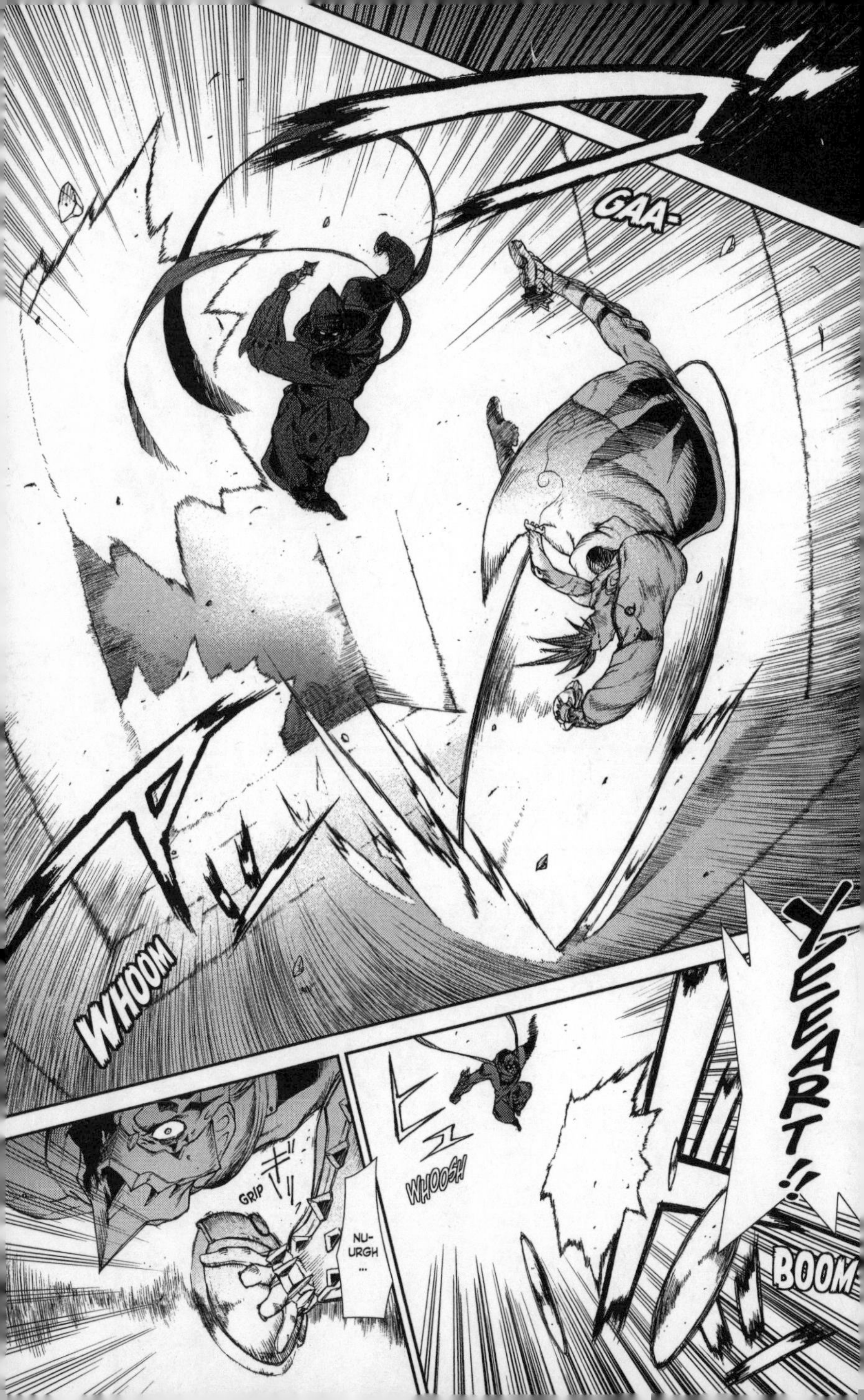
GAA-
WHOOM
YEEART!!
BOOM
WHOOSH
NU-
URGH
...
GRIP

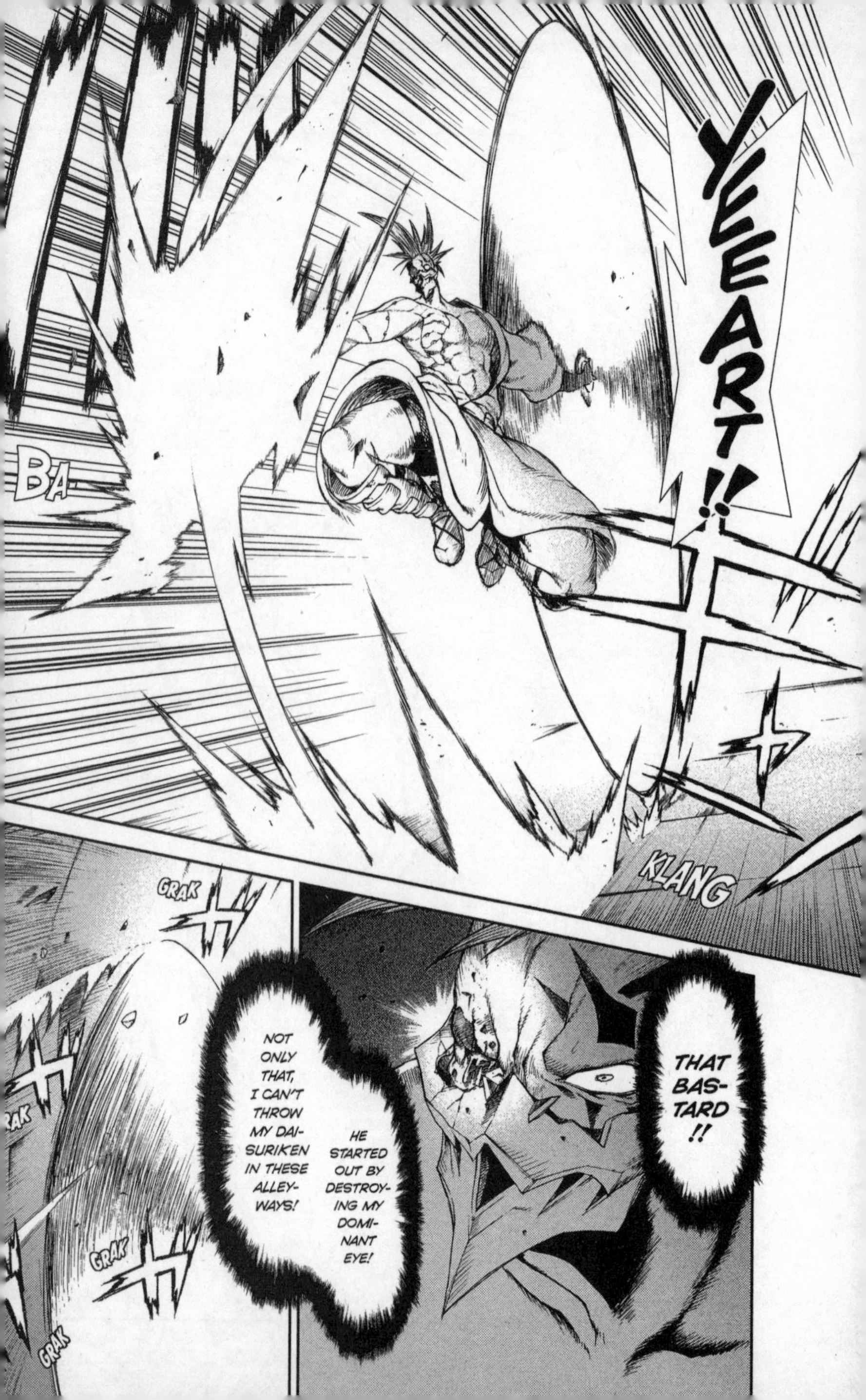
YEEART!!
BA
KLANG
THAT BAS-TARD!!
HE STARTED OUT BY DESTROY-ING MY DOMI-NANT EYE!
NOT ONLY THAT, I CAN'T THROW MY DAI-SURIKEN IN THESE ALLEY-WAYS!
GRAK
GRAK
GRAK

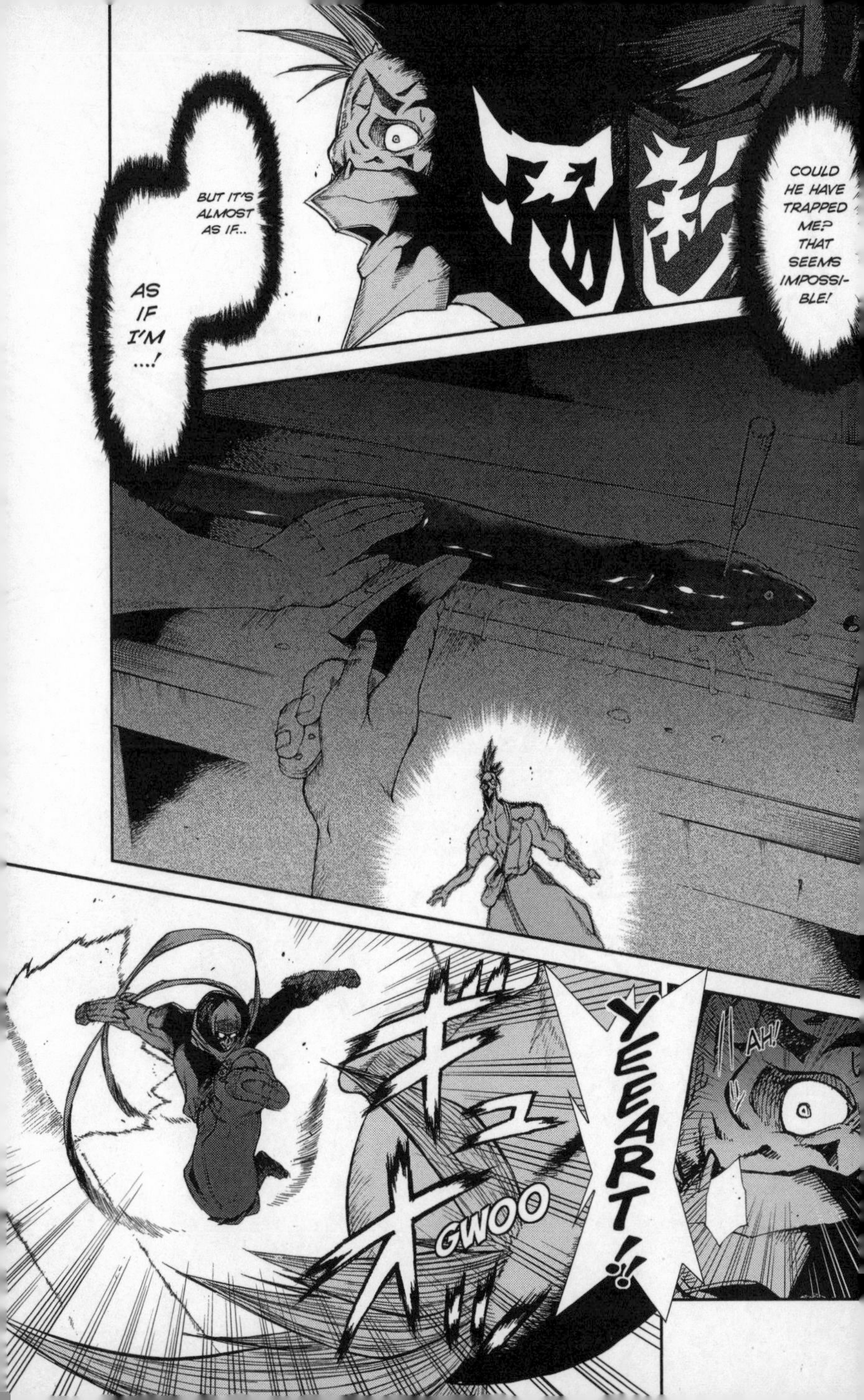
COULD HE HAVE TRAPPED ME? THAT SEEMS IMPOSSIBLE!
BUT IT'S ALMOST AS IF...
AS IF I'M ...!
AH!
YEEEART!!
GWOO

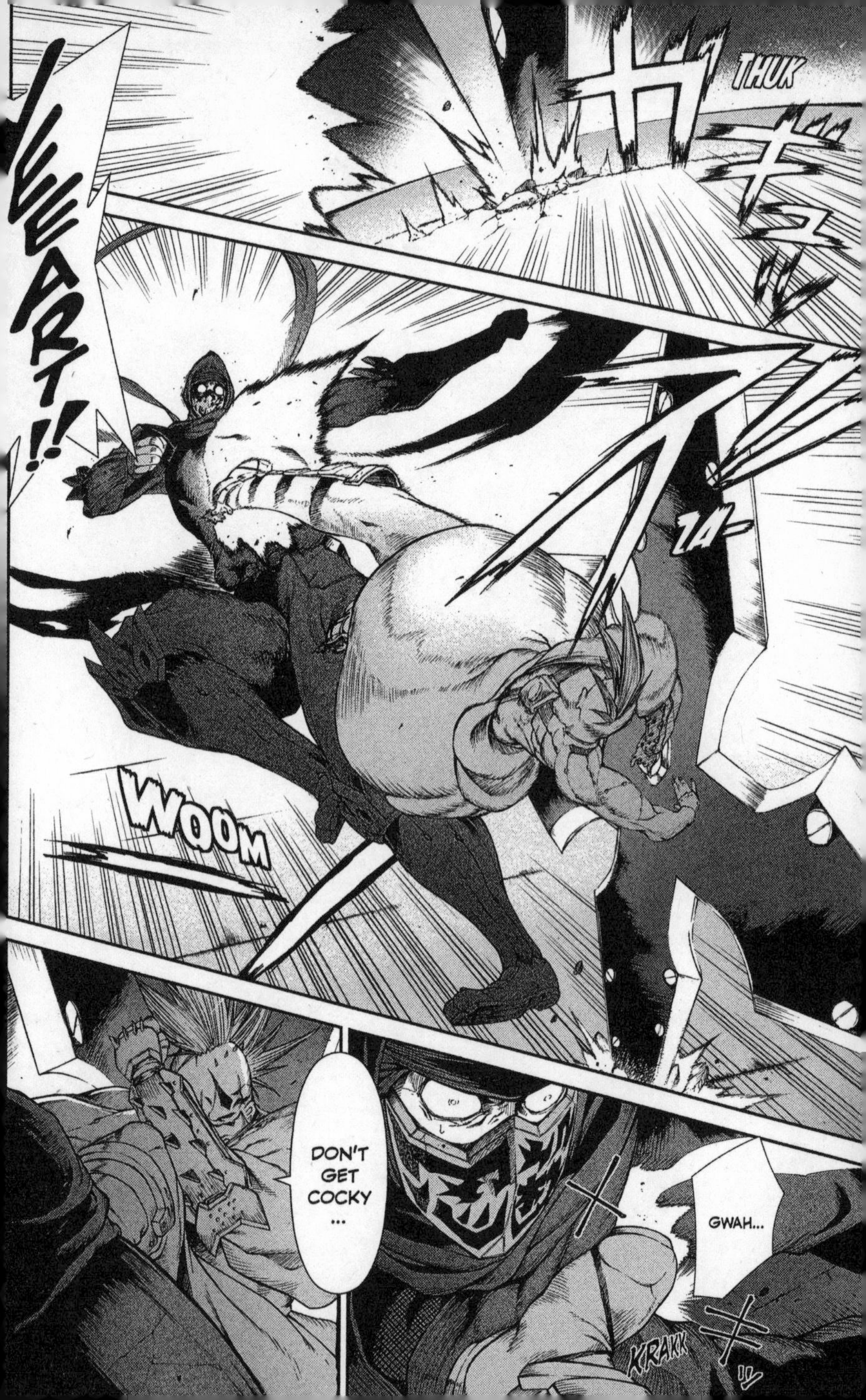
THUK
HEEART!!
WOOM
GWAH...
DON'T GET COCKY ...
KRAKK

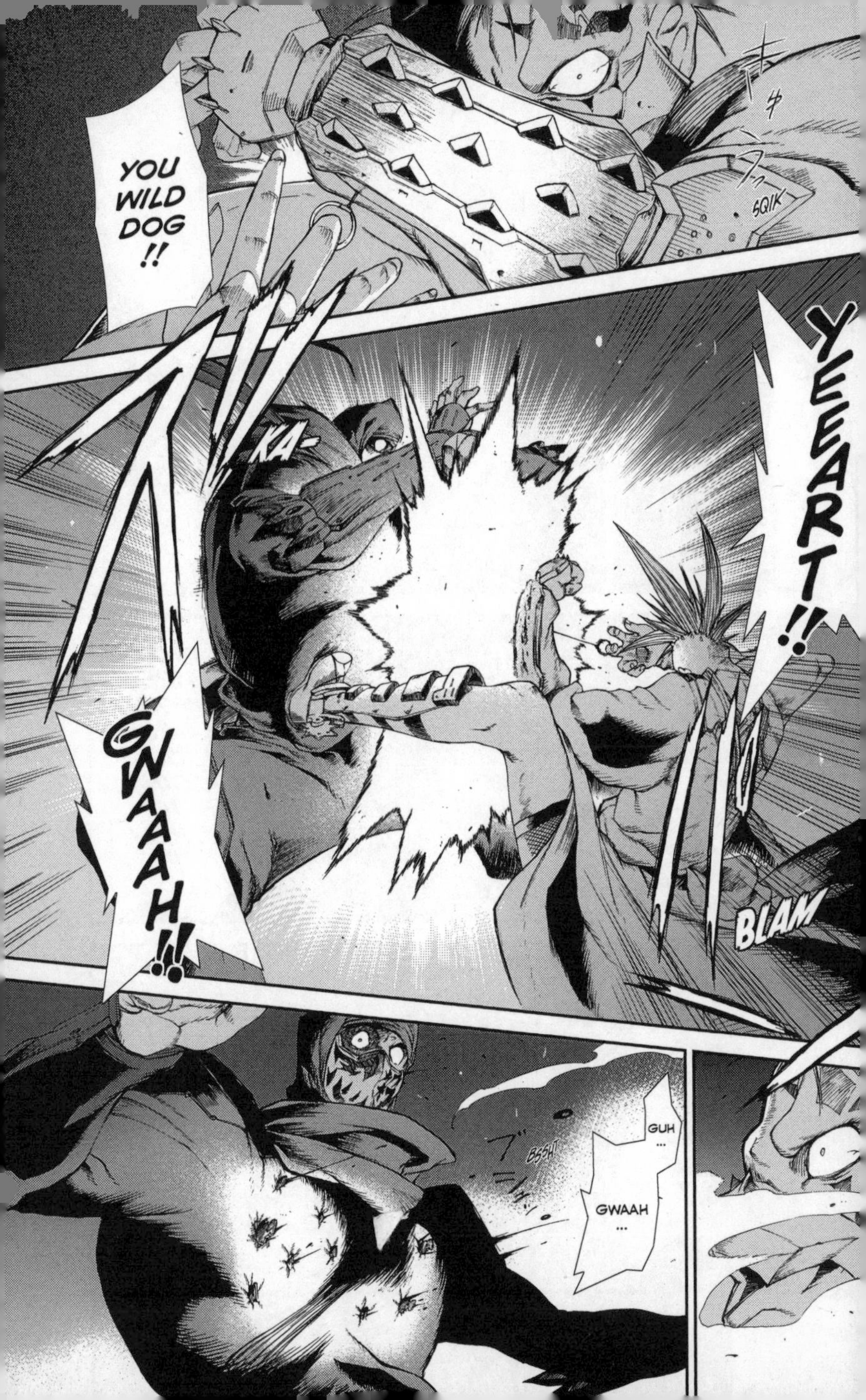
SQIK
YOU WILD DOG!!
YEEART!!
BLAM
KA-
GWAAAH!!
GUH...
BSSHT
GWAAH...

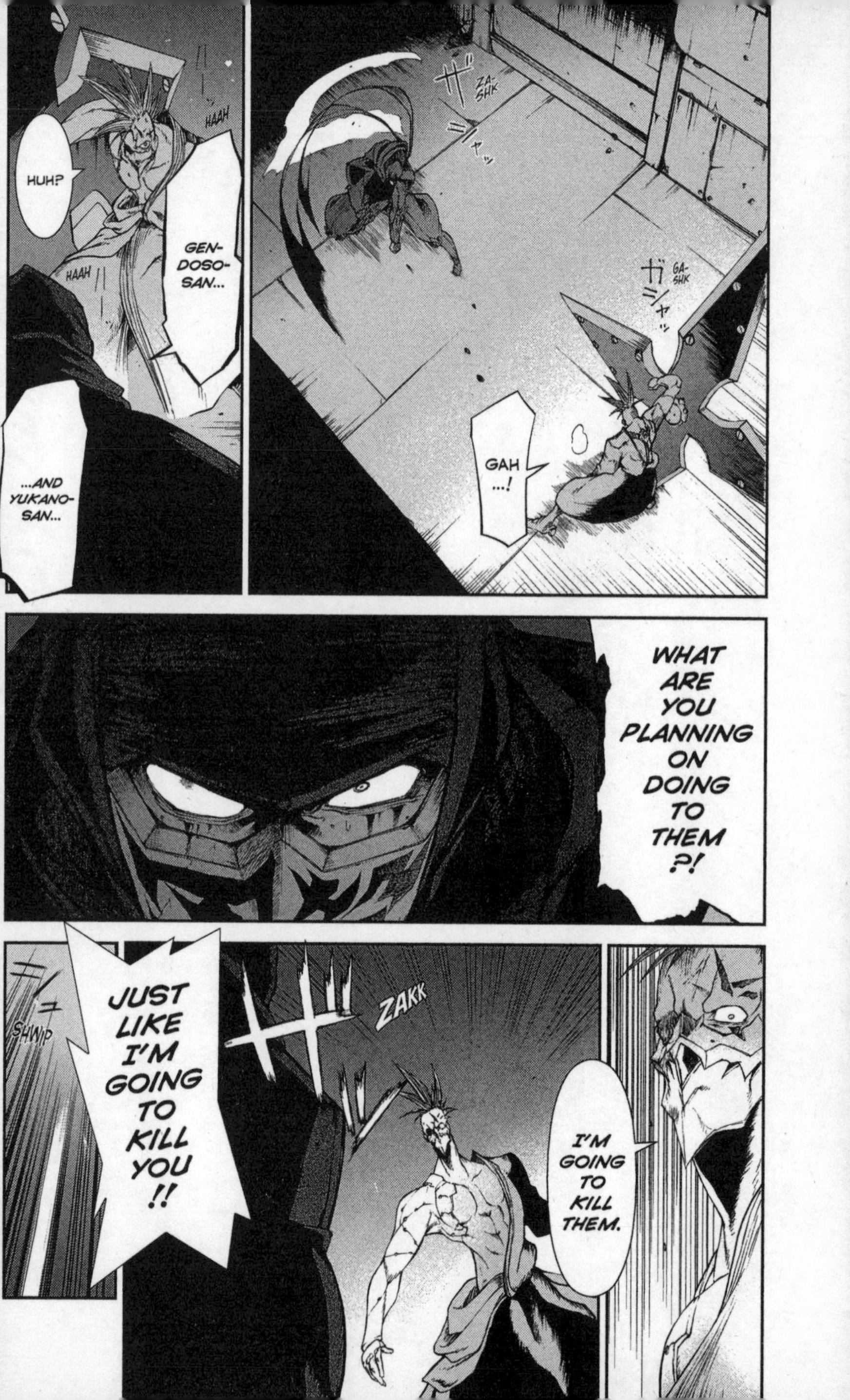
ザシャッ
ZA-SHK
ガシャッ
GA-SHK
GAH ...!
HUH?
HAAH
GEN-DOSO-SAN...
HAAH
...AND YUKANO-SAN...
WHAT ARE YOU PLANNING ON DOING TO THEM ?!
I'M GOING TO KILL THEM.
ZAKK
SHWIP
JUST LIKE I'M GOING TO KILL YOU !!

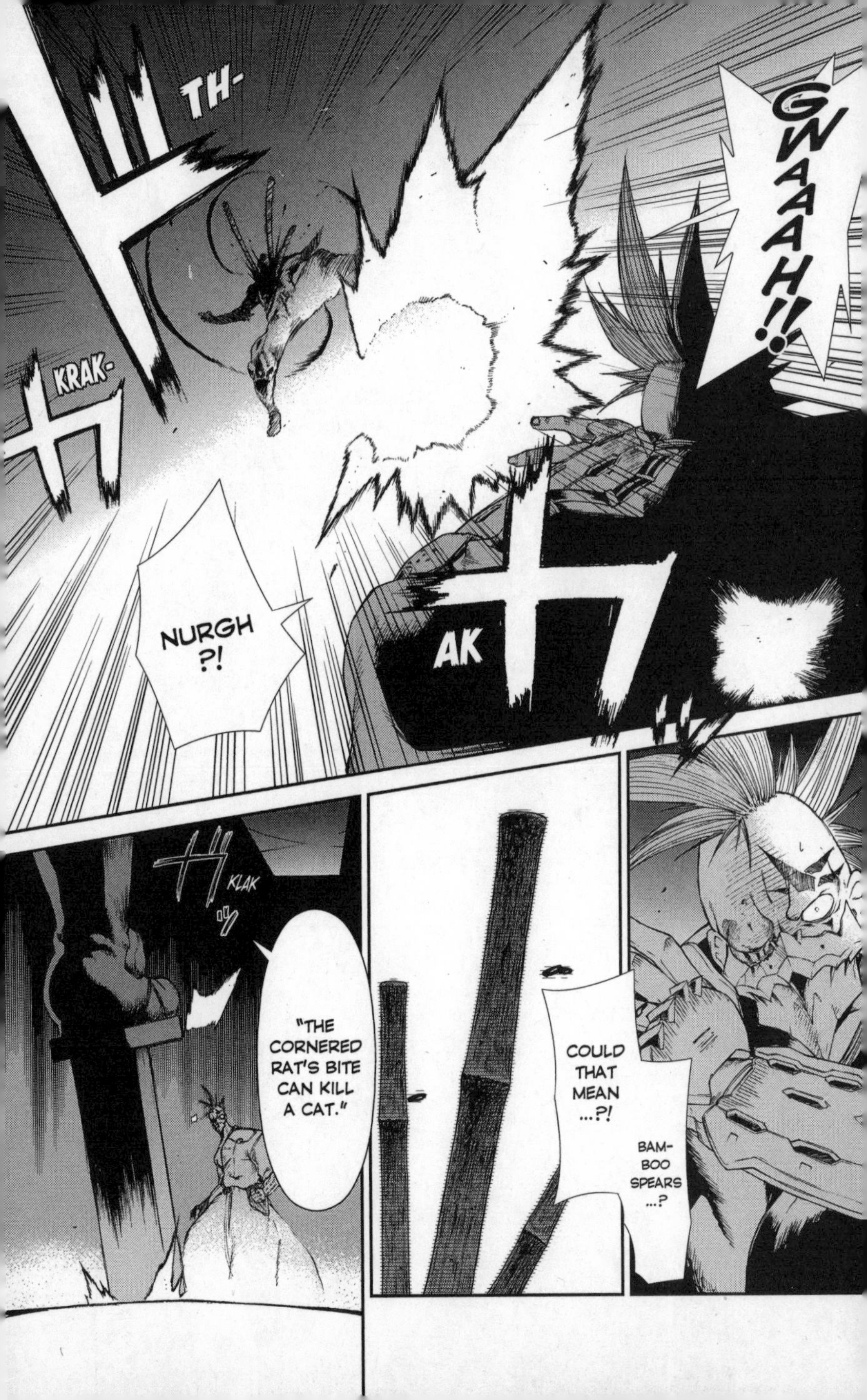
GWAAAH!!
TH-
KRAK-
AK
NURGH ?!
COULD THAT MEAN ...?!
BAM-BOO SPEARS ...?
KLAK
"THE CORNERED RAT'S BITE CAN KILL A CAT."

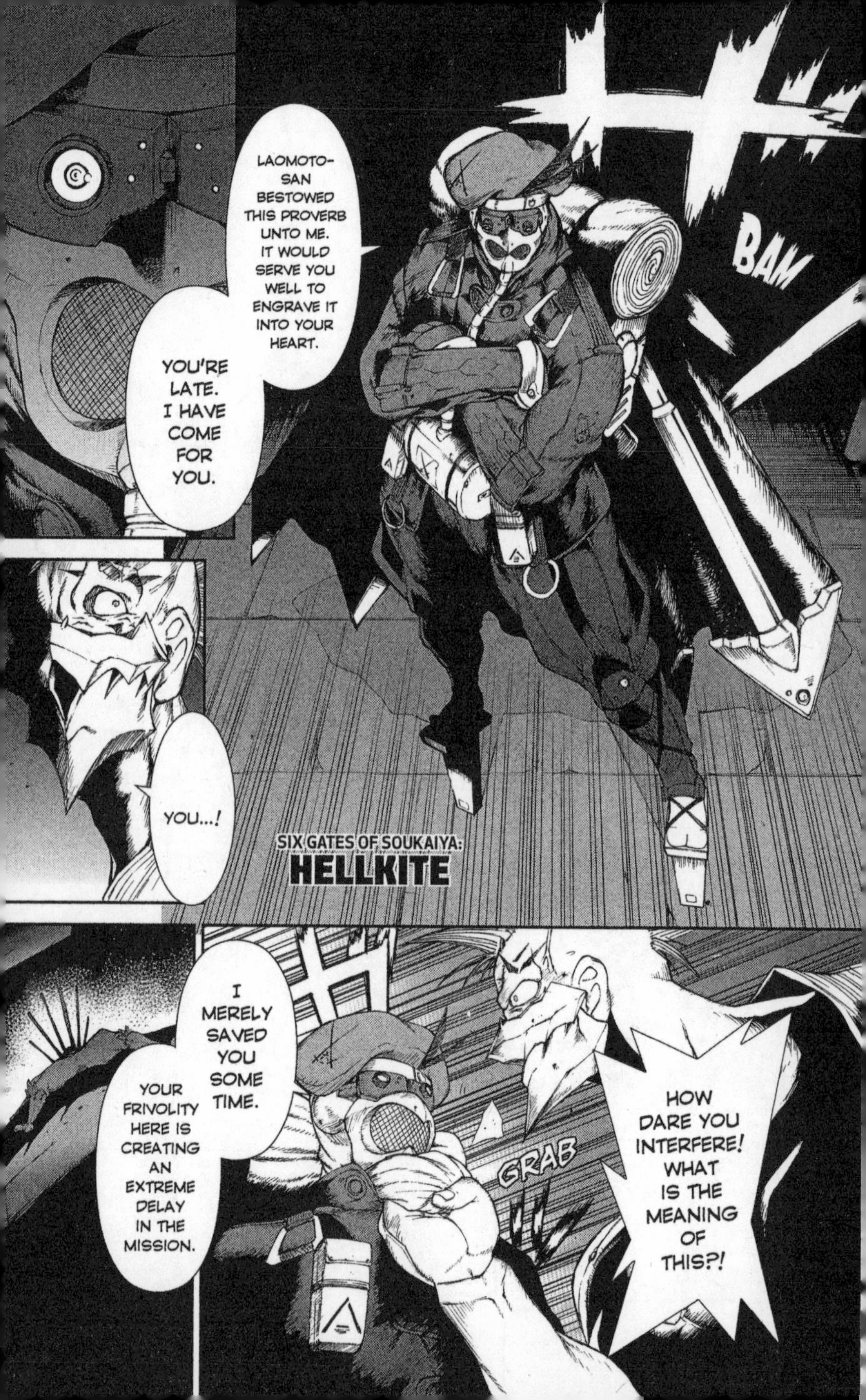
BAM
LAOMOTO-SAN BESTOWED THIS PROVERB UNTO ME. IT WOULD SERVE YOU WELL TO ENGRAVE IT INTO YOUR HEART.
YOU'RE LATE. I HAVE COME FOR YOU.
SIX GATES OF SOUKAIYA:
HELLKITE
YOU...!
HOW DARE YOU INTERFERE! WHAT IS THE MEANING OF THIS?!
GRAB
I MERELY SAVED YOU SOME TIME.
YOUR FRIVOLITY HERE IS CREATING AN EXTREME DELAY IN THE MISSION.

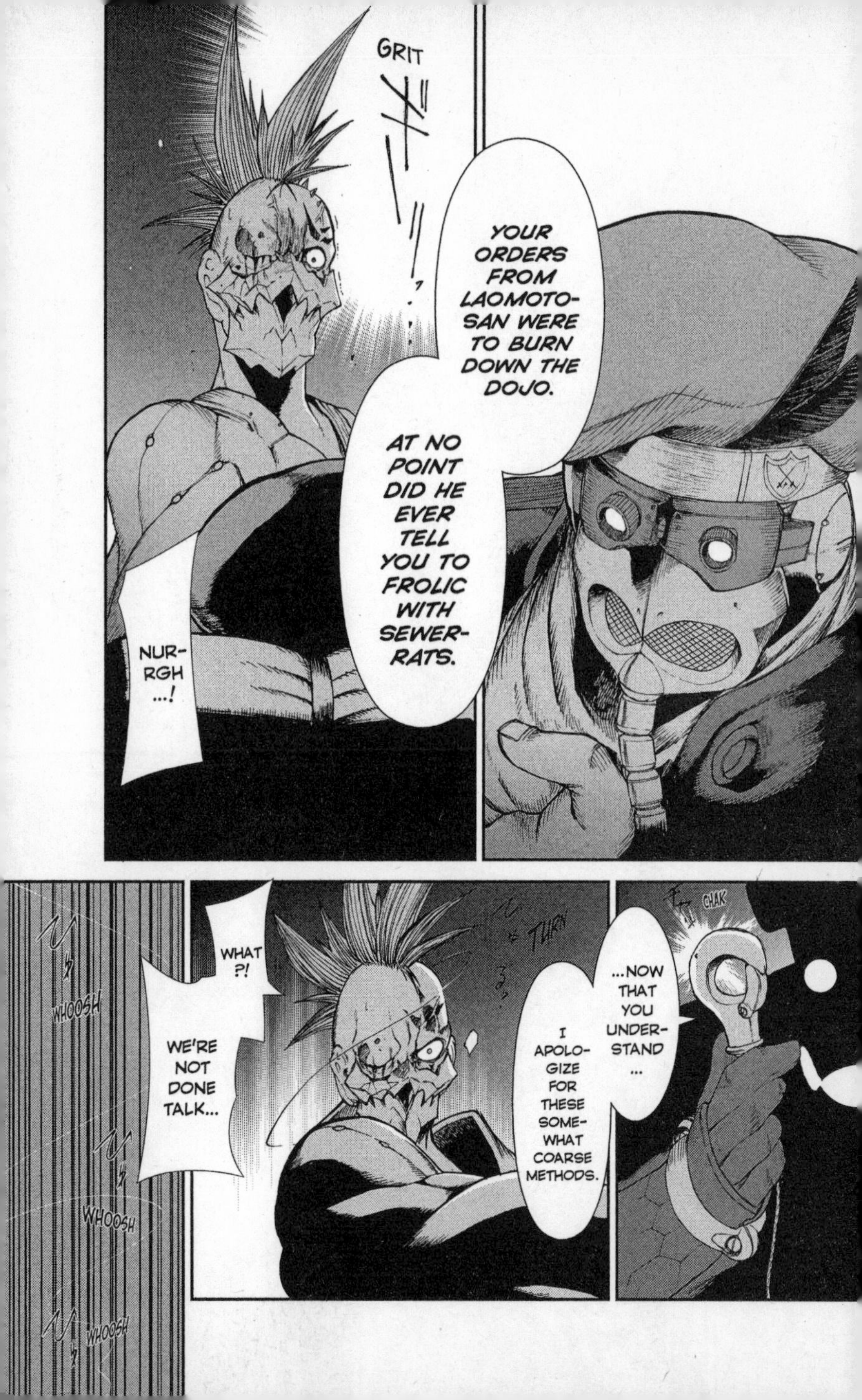
YOUR ORDERS FROM LAOMOTO-SAN WERE TO BURN DOWN THE DOJO.
AT NO POINT DID HE EVER TELL YOU TO FROLIC WITH SEWER-RATS.
GRIT
NUR-RGH ...!
CHAK
...NOW THAT YOU UNDER-STAND ...
I APOLO-GIZE FOR THESE SOME-WHAT COARSE METHODS.
TURN
WHAT ?!
WE'RE NOT DONE TALK...
WHOOSH
WHOOSH
WHOOSH

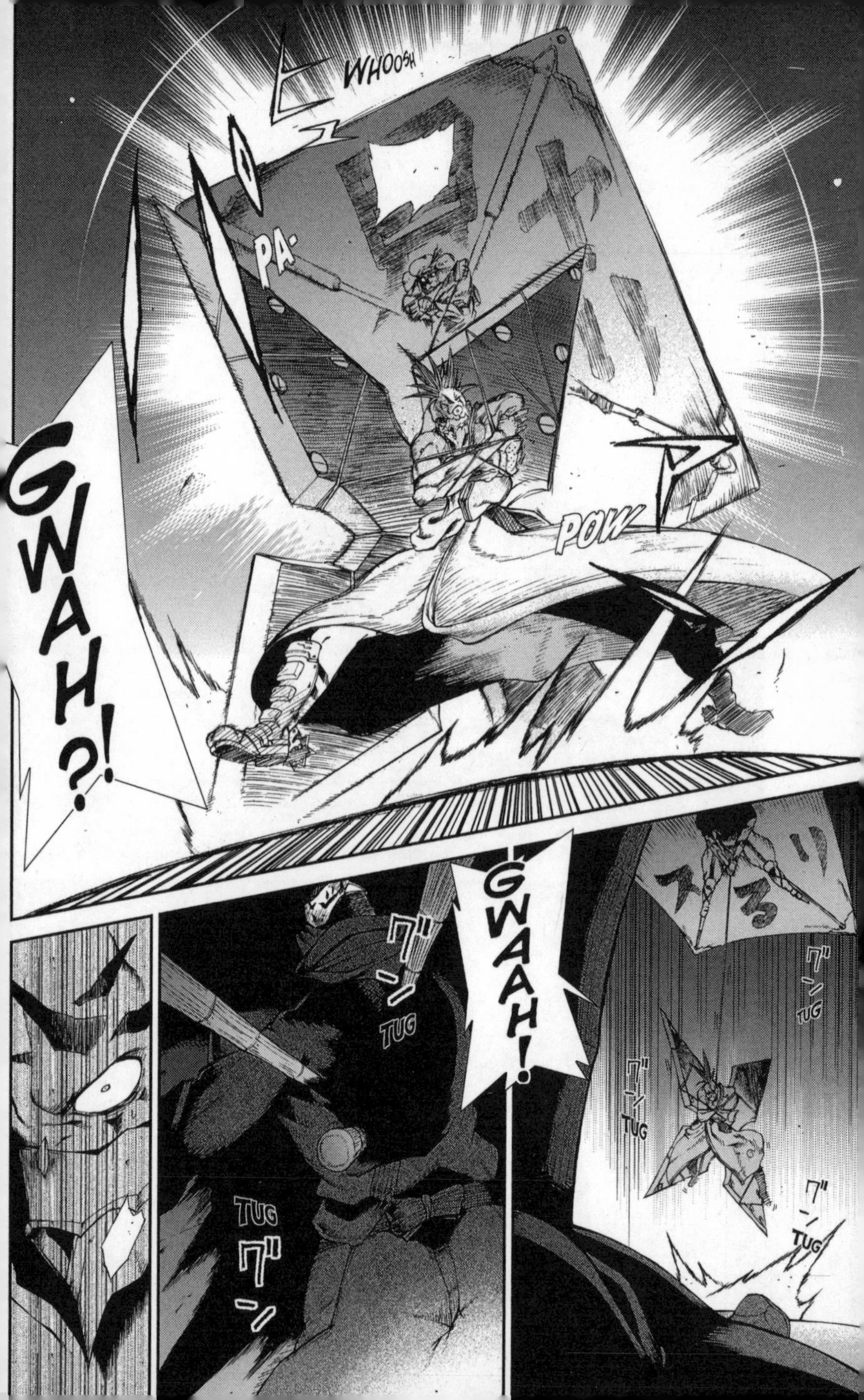
WHOOSH
PA-
POW
GWAH?!
TUG
TUG
TUG
GWAAH!
TUG
TUG

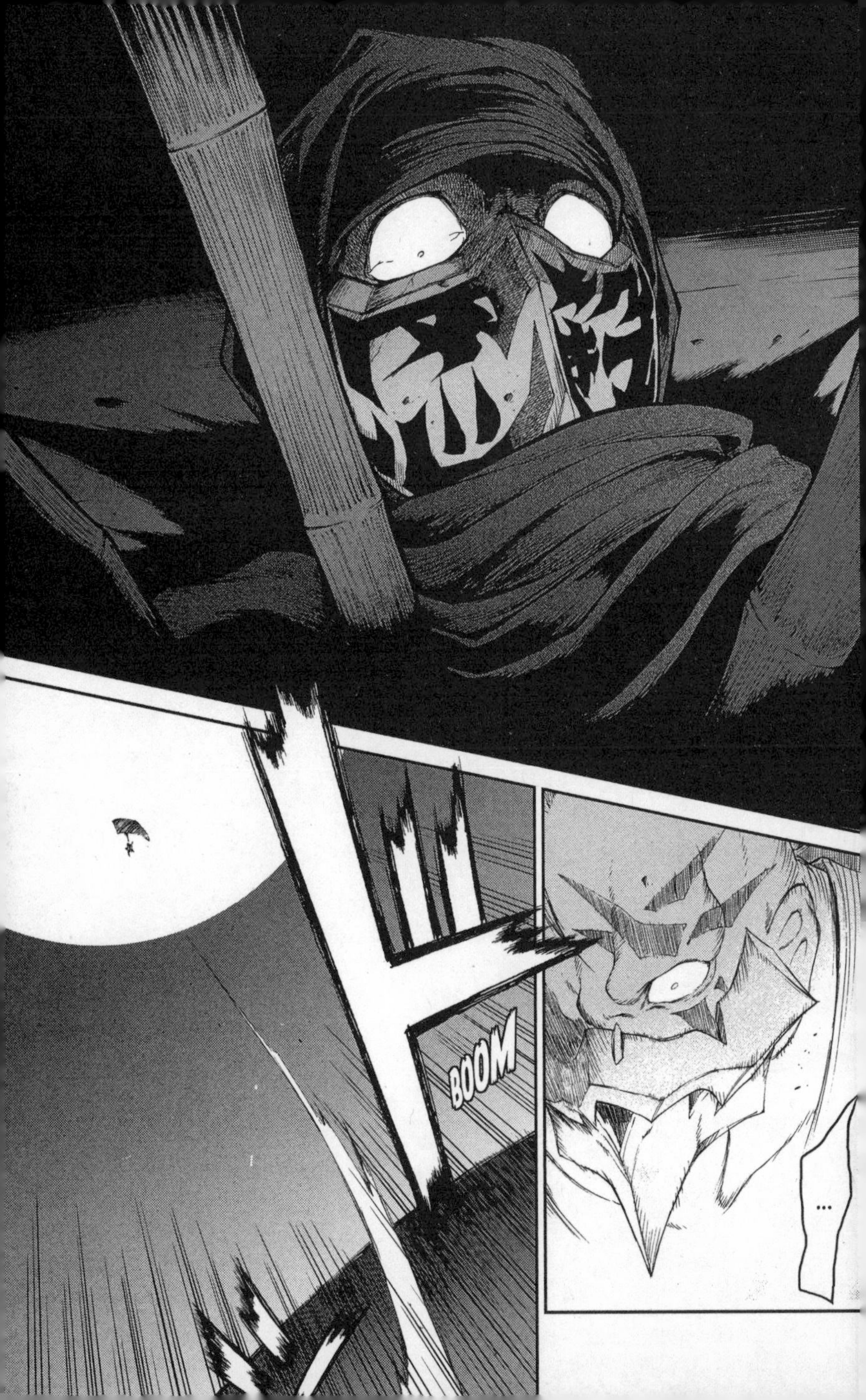
BOOM
...

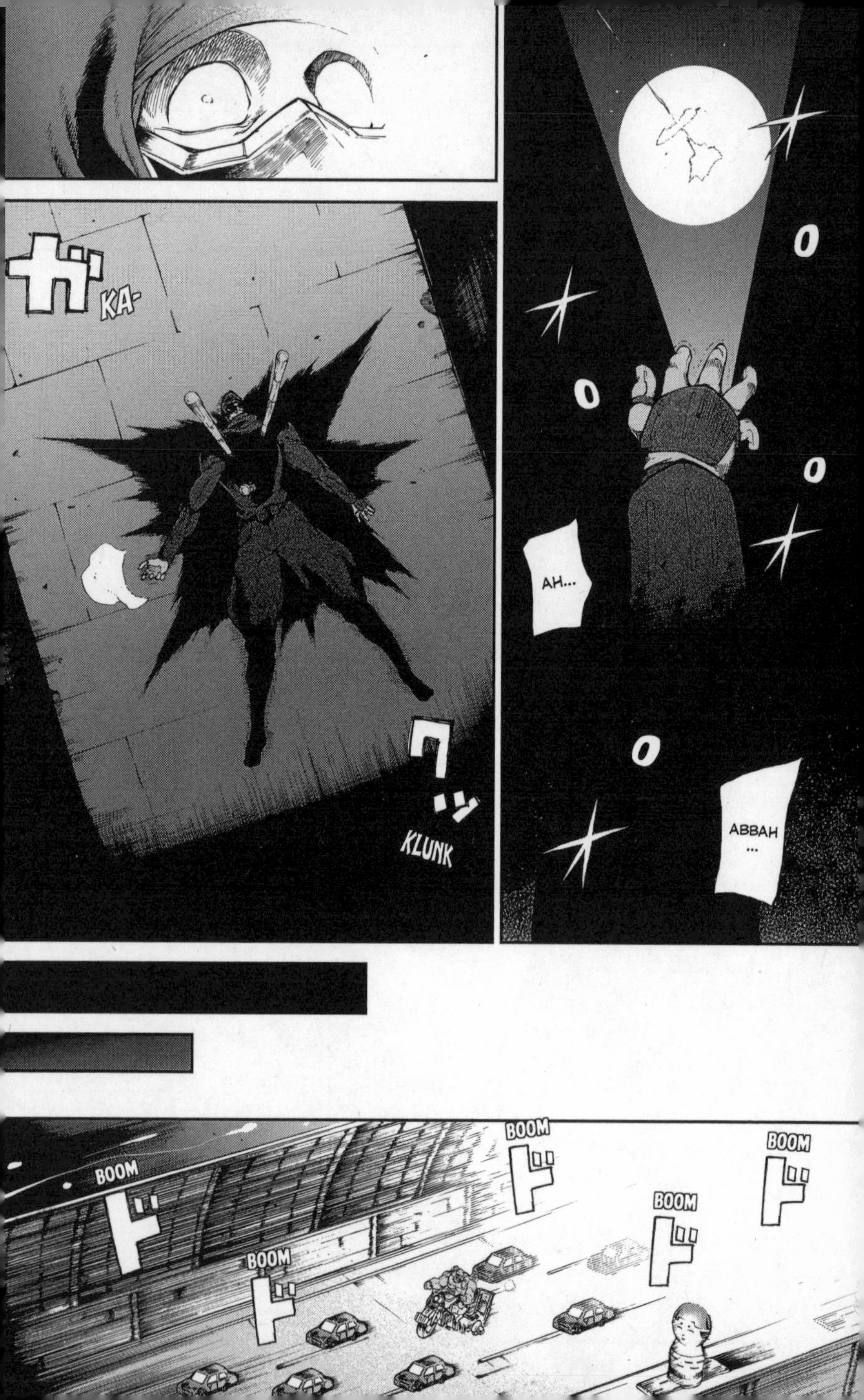
O
O
O
AH...
O
ABBAH ...
KA-
KLUNK
BOOM
BOOM
BOOM
BOOM
BOOM

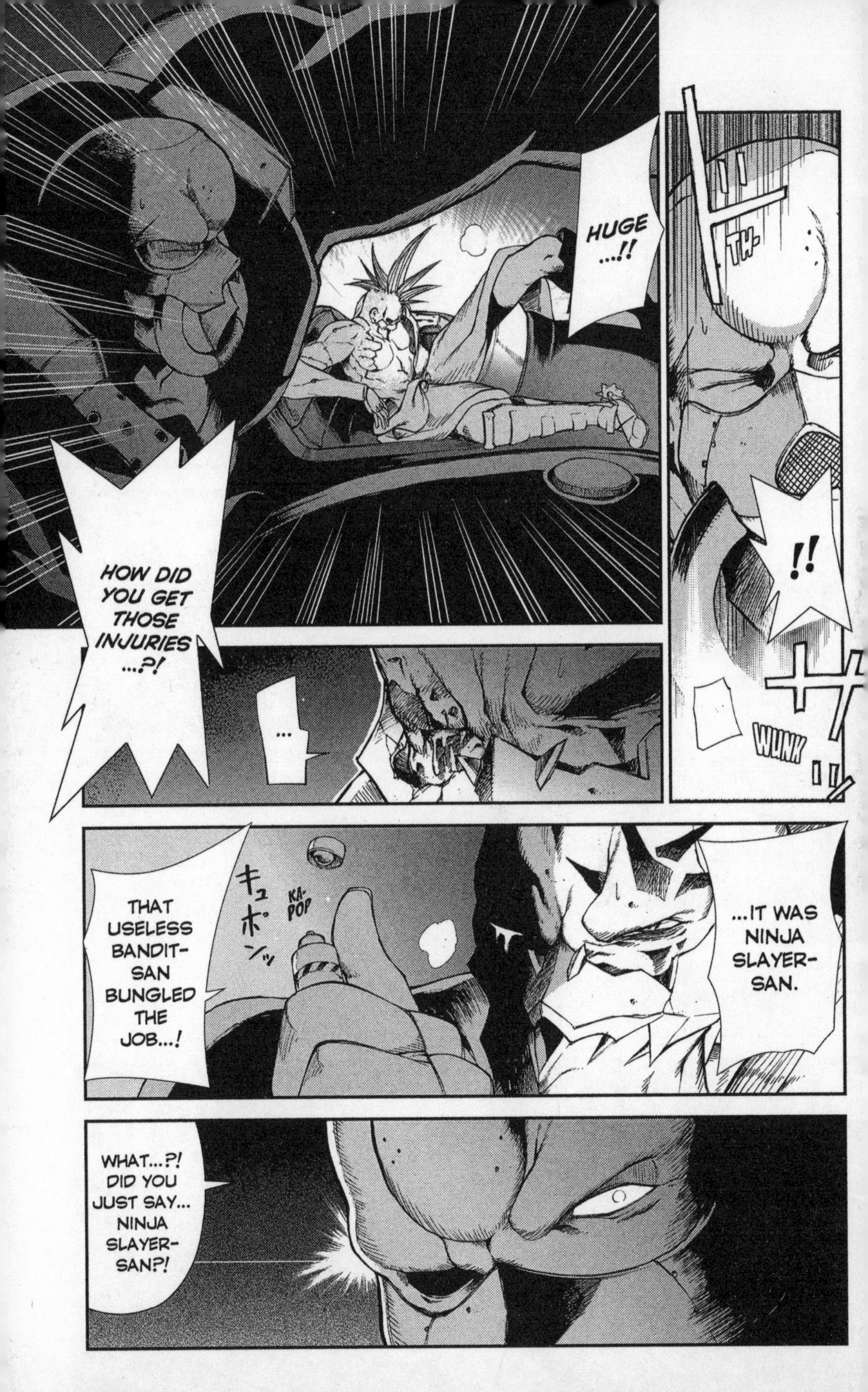
TH-
!!
WUNK
HUGE ...!!
HOW DID YOU GET THOSE INJURIES ...?!
...
...IT WAS NINJA SLAYER-SAN.
キュポンッ
KA-POP
THAT USELESS BANDIT-SAN BUNGLED THE JOB...!
WHAT...?! DID YOU JUST SAY... NINJA SLAYER-SAN?!

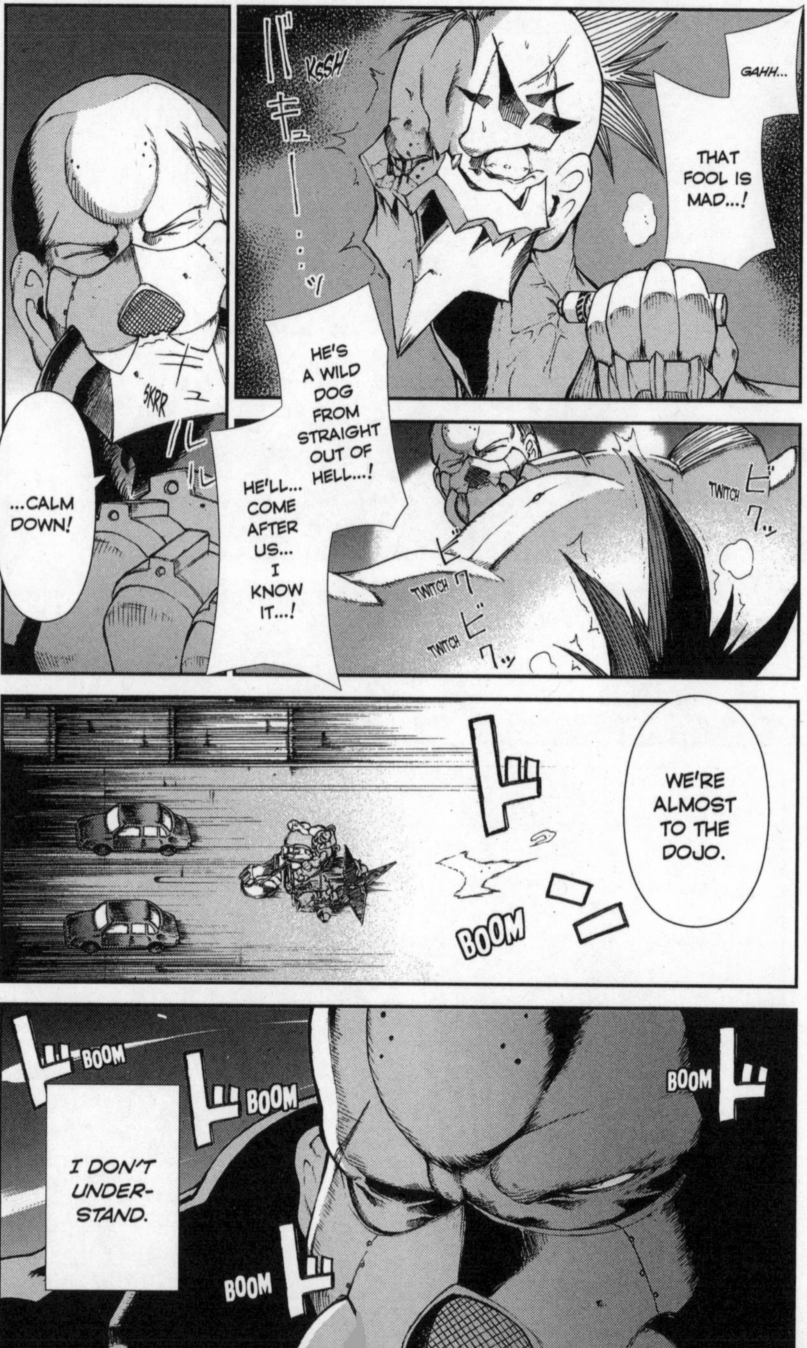
KSSH
GAHH...
THAT FOOL IS MAD...!
HE'S A WILD DOG FROM STRAIGHT OUT OF HELL...!
TWITCH
TWITCH
TWITCH
HE'LL... COME AFTER US... I KNOW IT...!
SKRR
...CALM DOWN!
WE'RE ALMOST TO THE DOJO.
BOOM
BOOM
BOOM
BOOM
I DON'T UNDER-STAND.
BOOM

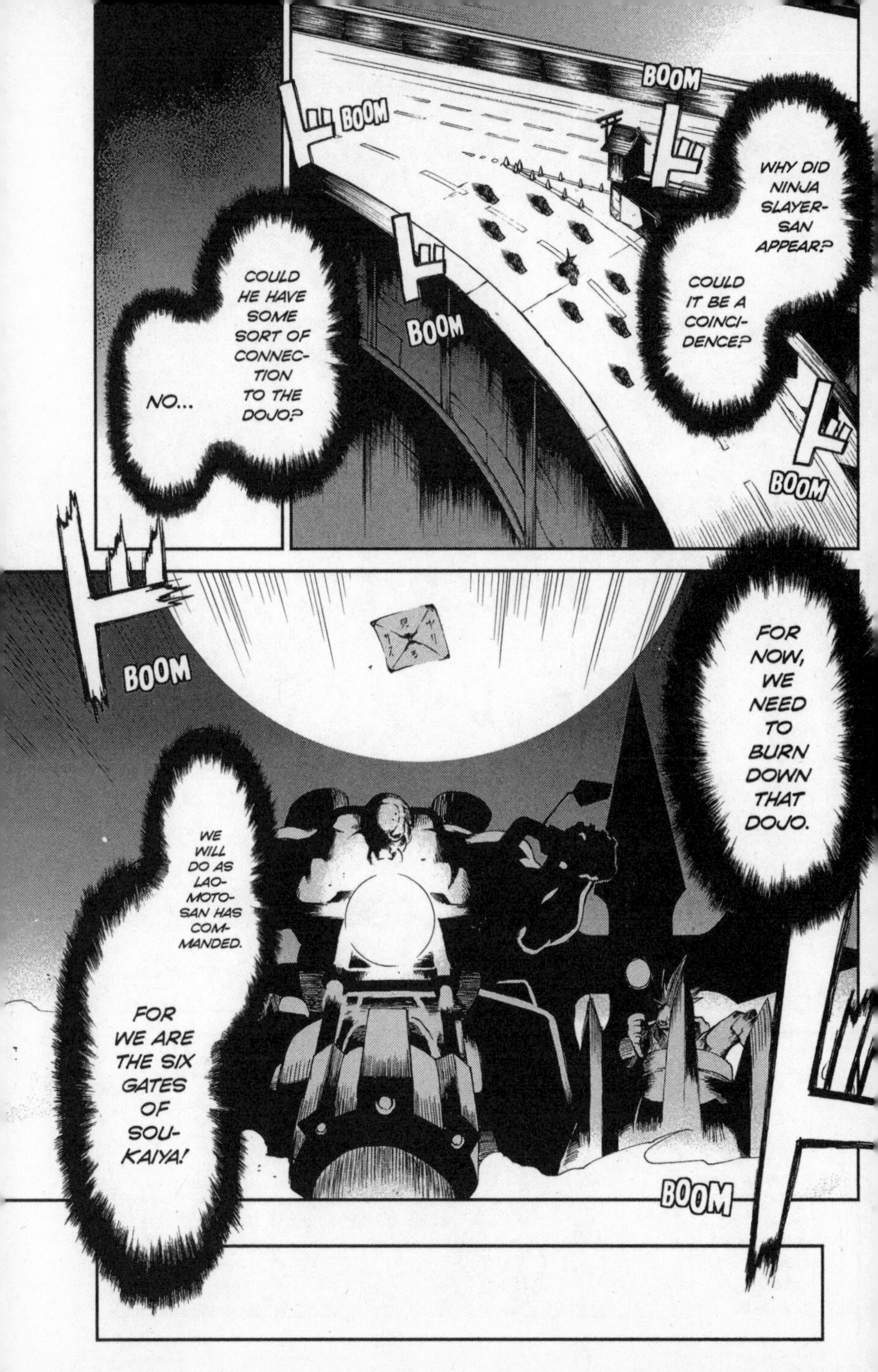
BOOM
WHY DID NINJA SLAYER-SAN APPEAR?
COULD IT BE A COINCIDENCE?
BOOM
BOOM
COULD HE HAVE SOME SORT OF CONNECTION TO THE DOJO?
NO...
BOOM
BOOM
FOR NOW, WE NEED TO BURN DOWN THAT DOJO.
BOOM
WE WILL DO AS LAO-MOTO-SAN HAS COM-MANDED.
FOR WE ARE THE SIX GATES OF SOU-KAIYA!
BOOM

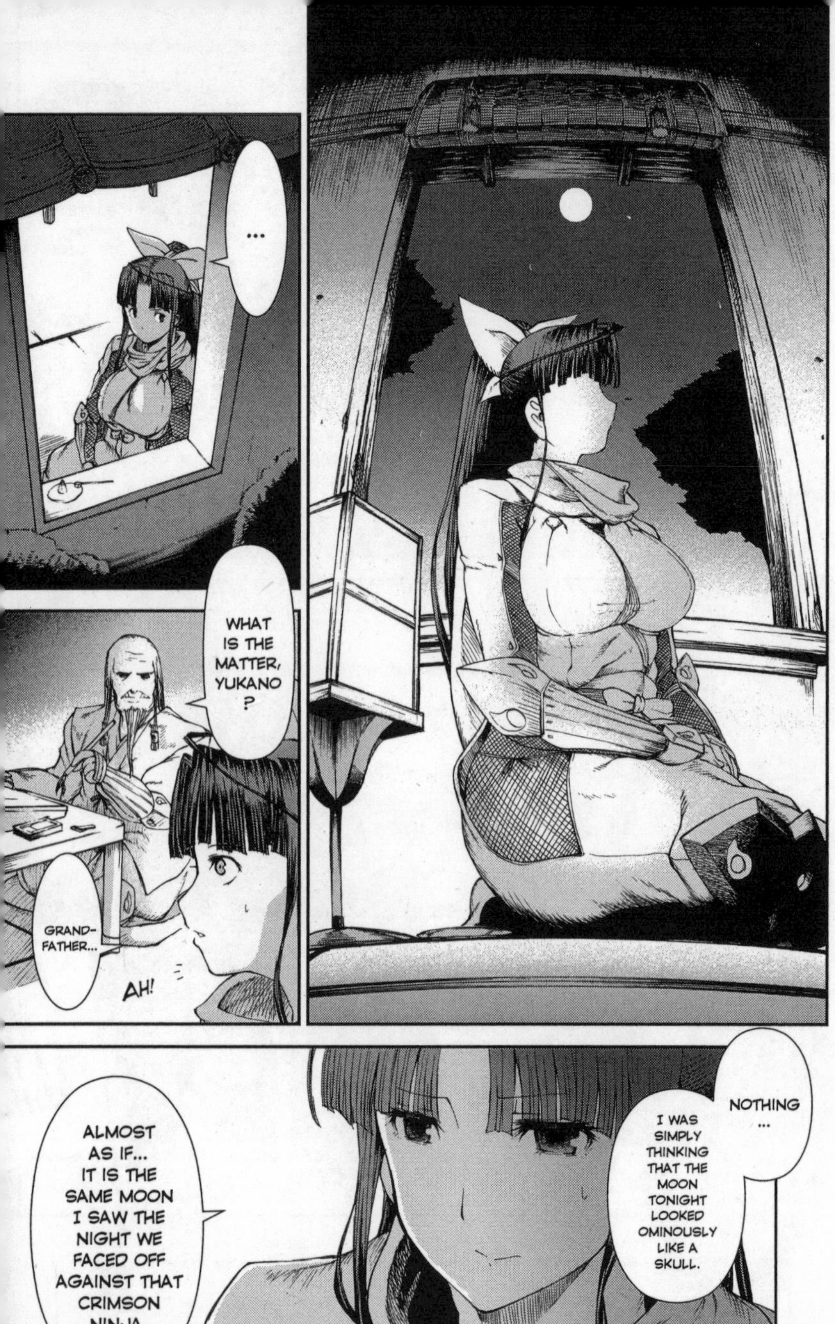
...
WHAT IS THE MATTER, YUKANO?
AH!
GRANDFATHER...
NOTHING...
I WAS SIMPLY THINKING THAT THE MOON TONIGHT LOOKED OMINOUSLY LIKE A SKULL.
ALMOST AS IF... IT IS THE SAME MOON I SAW THE NIGHT WE FACED OFF AGAINST THAT CRIMSON NINJA.

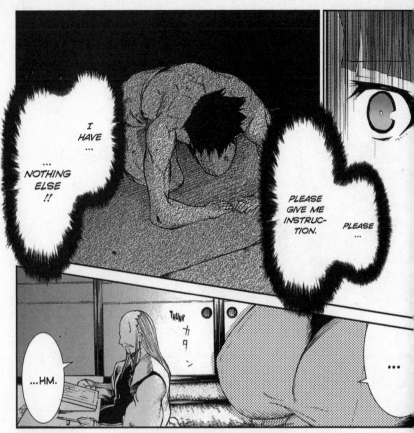

I HAVE
...

... NOTHING
ELSE !!

PLEASE
GIVE ME
INSTRUC-
TION.   PLEASE
...

...HM.

THUNK

...

NINJA
SLAYER-
SAN...   ...

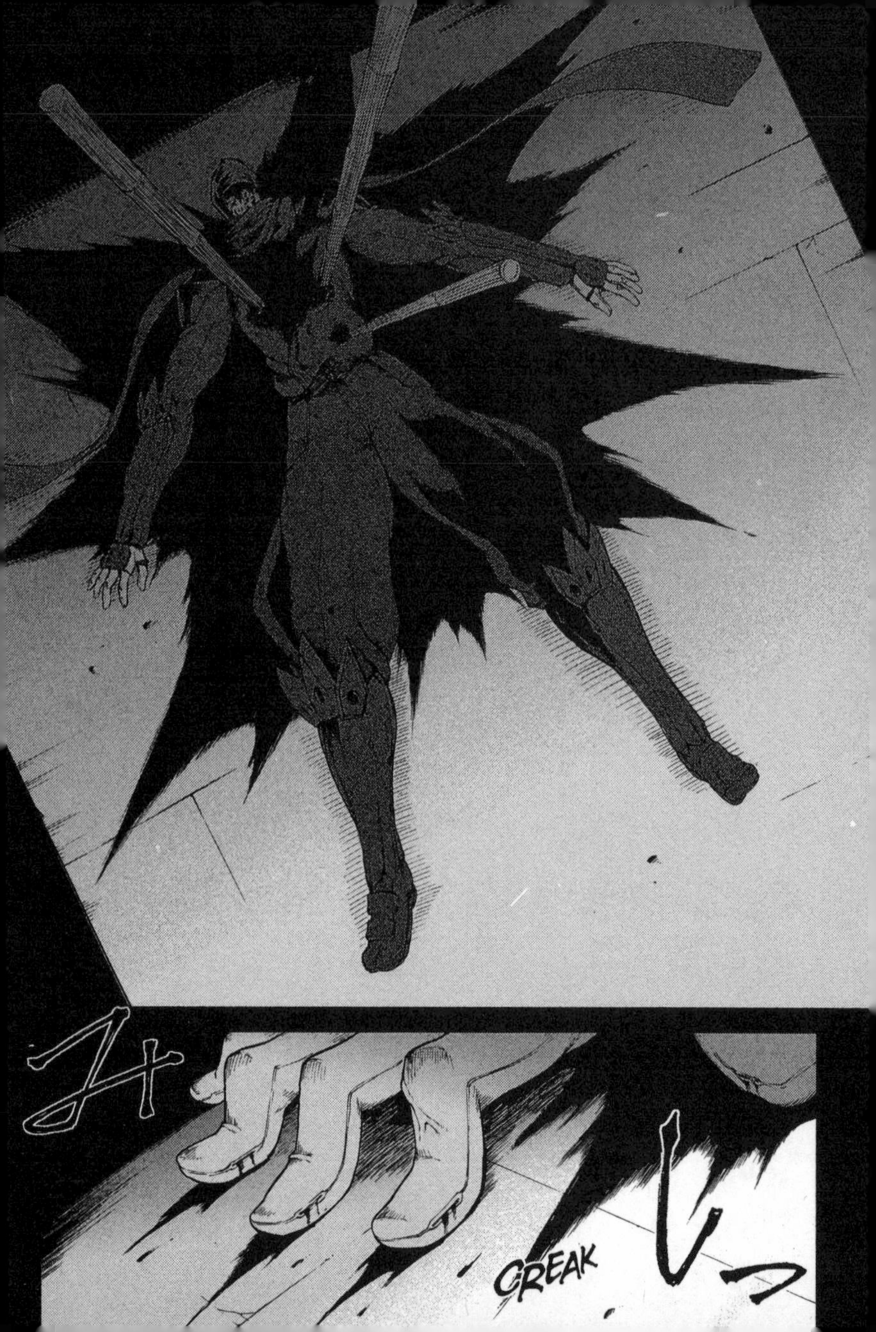
CREAK

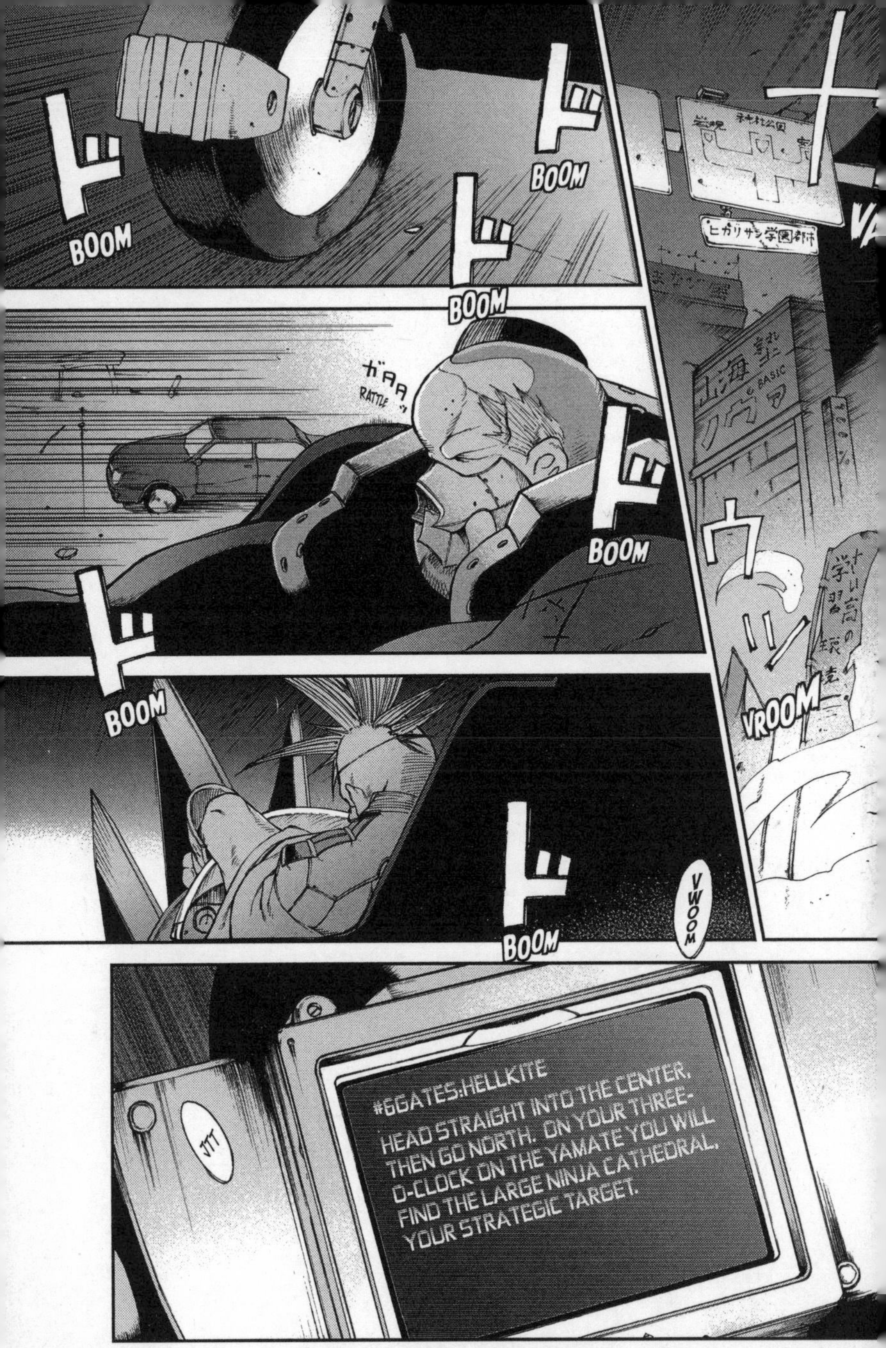
ヒカリサシ学園都市
VROOM
ド
BOOM
ド
BOOM
ド
BOOM
ガタタッ
RATTLE
ド
BOOM
ド
BOOM
ド
BOOM
VWOOM
JTT
#6GATES:HELLKITE
HEAD STRAIGHT INTO THE CENTER, THEN GO NORTH. ON YOUR THREE-O-CLOCK ON THE YAMATE YOU WILL FIND THE LARGE NINJA CATHEDRAL, YOUR STRATEGIC TARGET.

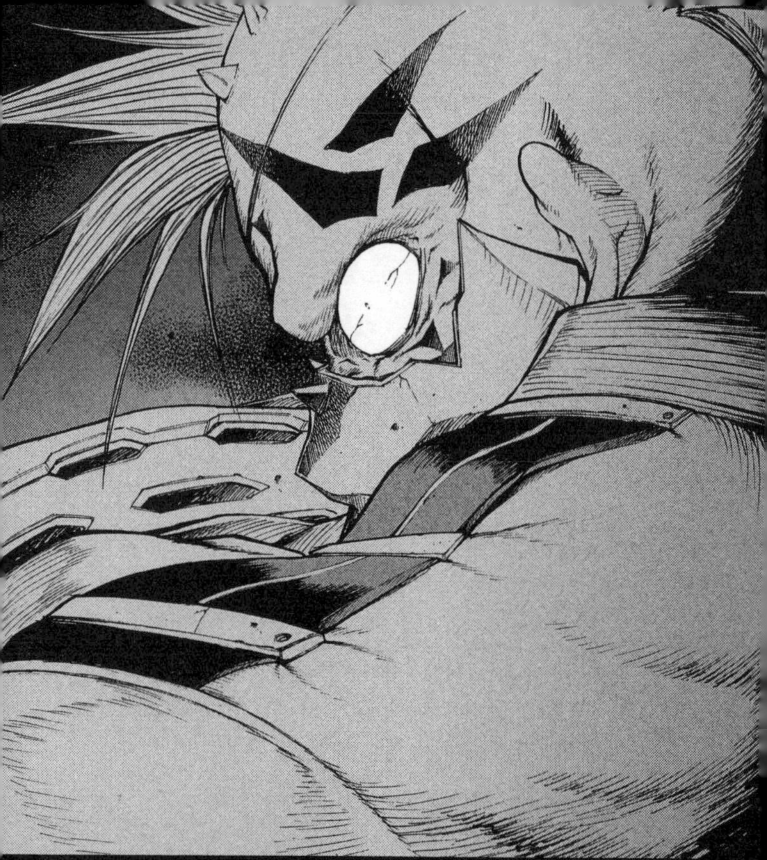

KILLs 017 ✦ SURPRISED DOJO PART 2

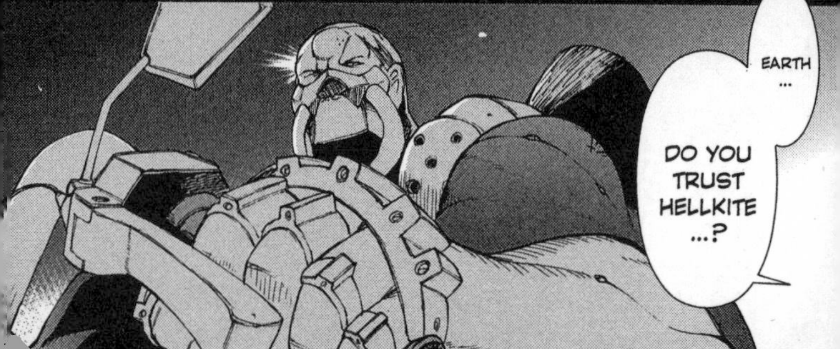
EARTH ...
DO YOU TRUST HELLKITE ...?

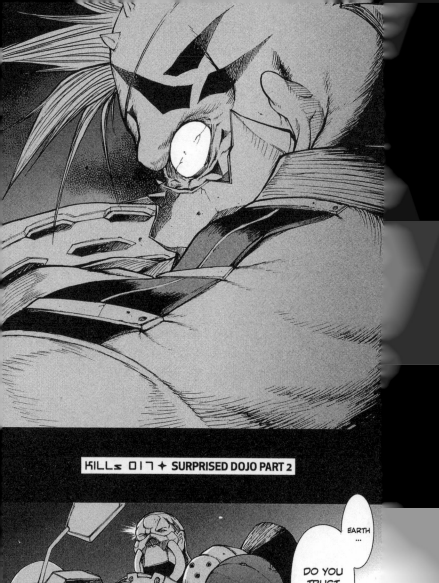

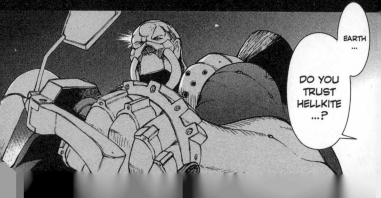

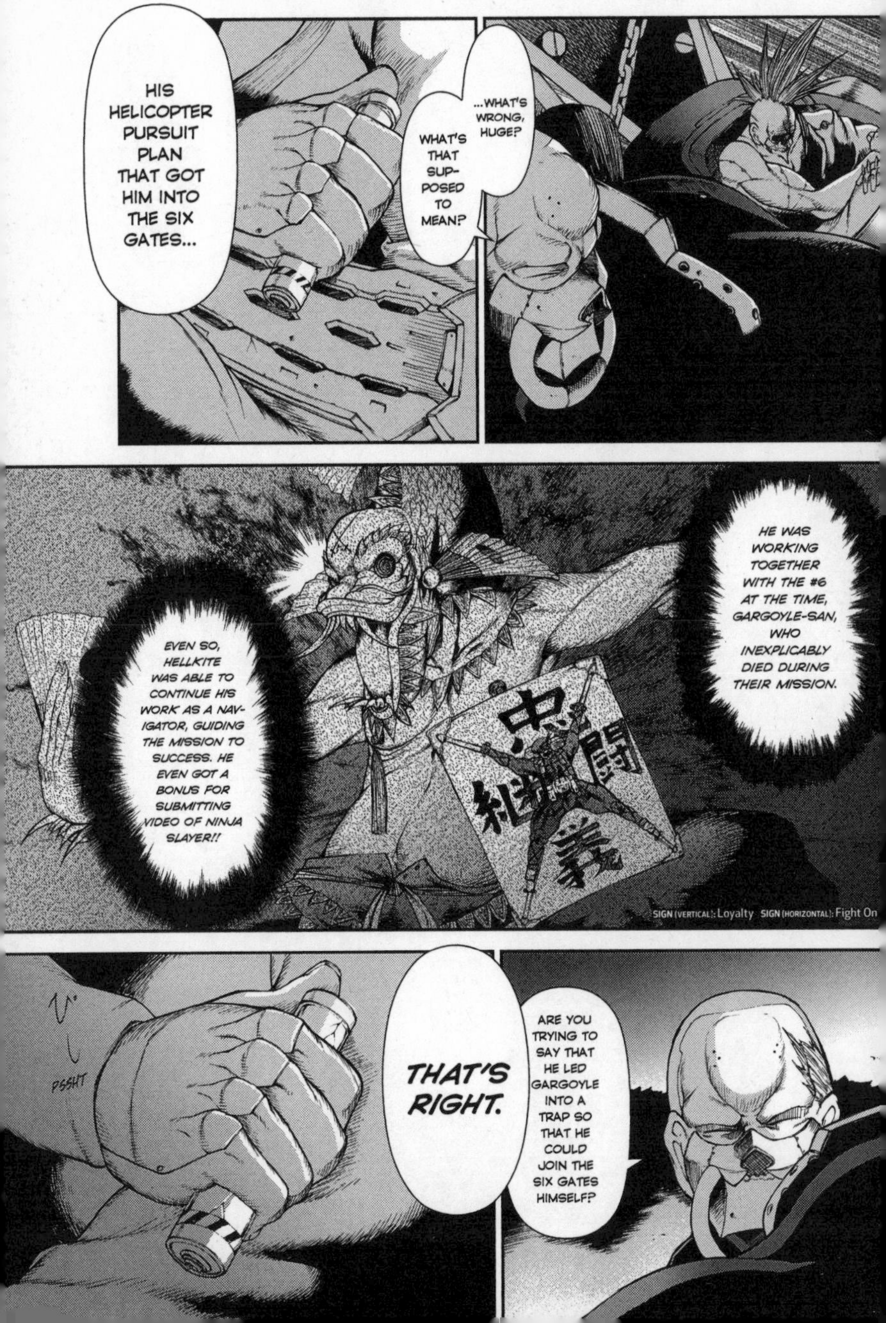
...WHAT'S WRONG, HUGE?
WHAT'S THAT SUP-POSED TO MEAN?
HIS HELICOPTER PURSUIT PLAN THAT GOT HIM INTO THE SIX GATES...
HE WAS WORKING TOGETHER WITH THE #6 AT THE TIME, GARGOYLE-SAN, WHO INEXPLICABLY DIED DURING THEIR MISSION.
EVEN SO, HELLKITE WAS ABLE TO CONTINUE HIS WORK AS A NAV-IGATOR, GUIDING THE MISSION TO SUCCESS. HE EVEN GOT A BONUS FOR SUBMITTING VIDEO OF NINJA SLAYER!!
SIGN (VERTICAL): Loyalty SIGN (HORIZONTAL): Fight On
ARE YOU TRYING TO SAY THAT HE LED GARGOYLE INTO A TRAP SO THAT HE COULD JOIN THE SIX GATES HIMSELF?
THAT'S RIGHT.
PSSHT

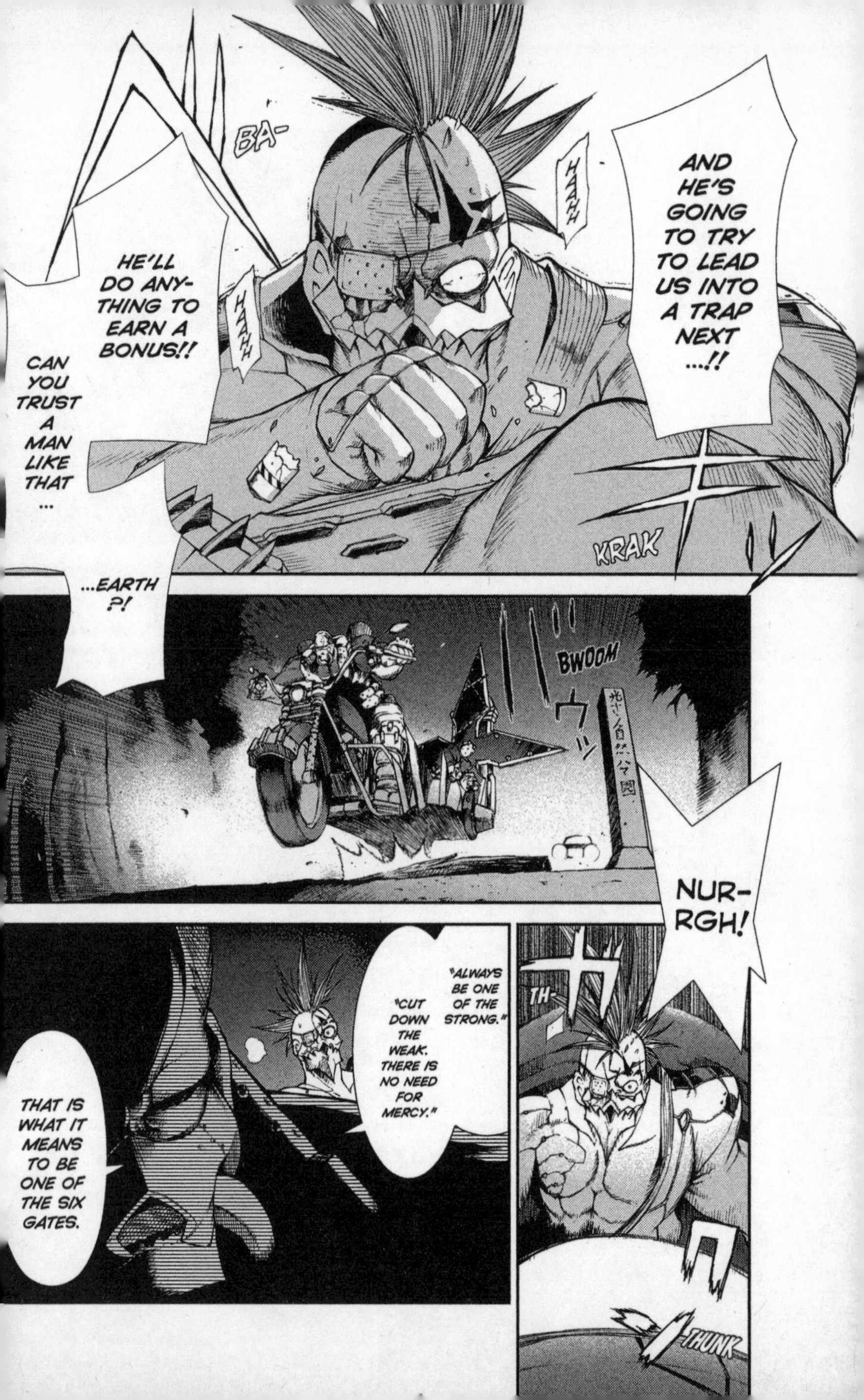
AND HE'S GOING TO TRY TO LEAD US INTO A TRAP NEXT ...!!
HAHHH
BA-
HAHHH
HE'LL DO ANY-THING TO EARN A BONUS!!
CAN YOU TRUST A MAN LIKE THAT ...
KRAK
...EARTH ?!
NUR-RGH!
BWOOM
ウッ
TH-
THUNK
"ALWAYS BE ONE OF THE STRONG."
"CUT DOWN THE WEAK. THERE IS NO NEED FOR MERCY."
THAT IS WHAT IT MEANS TO BE ONE OF THE SIX GATES.

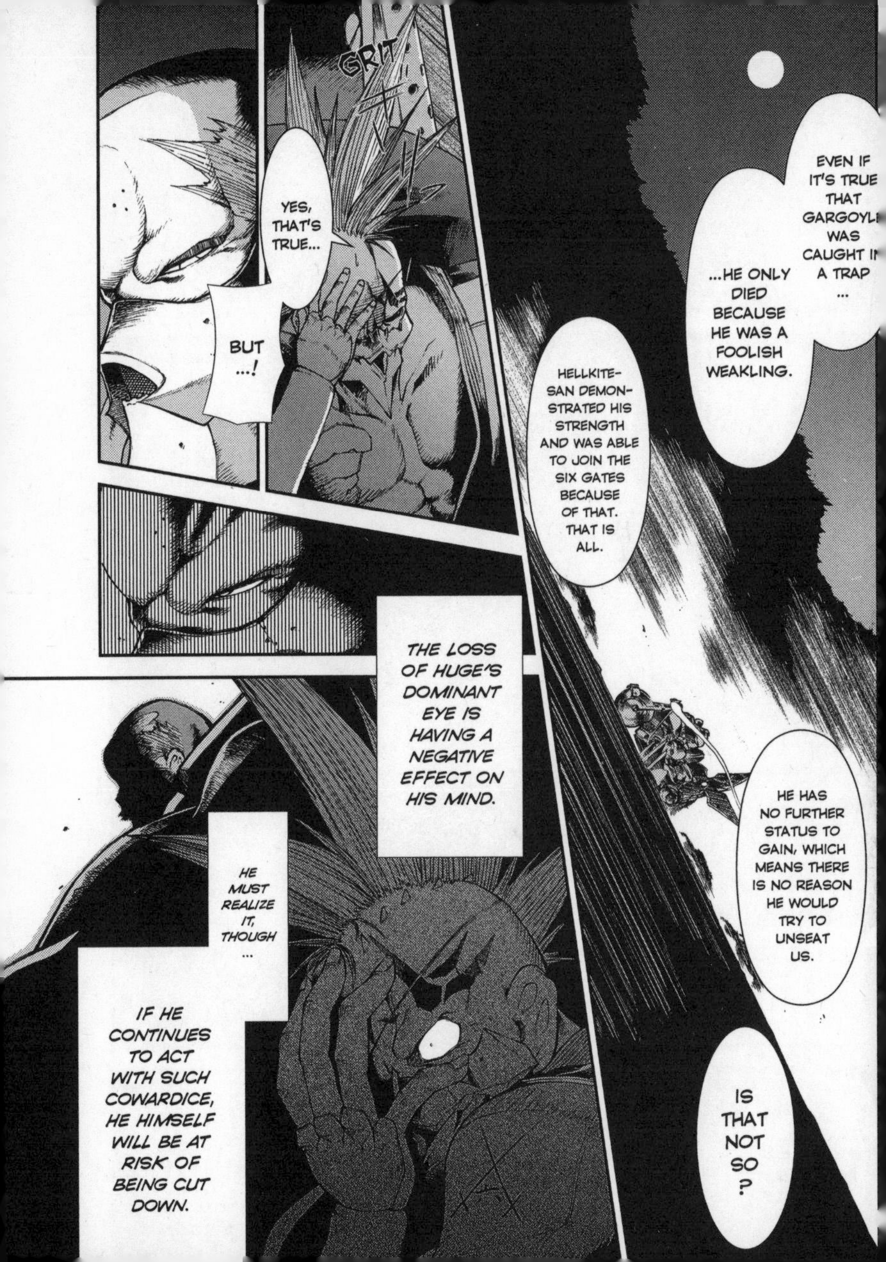
EVEN IF IT'S TRUE THAT GARGOYLE WAS CAUGHT IN A TRAP ...
...HE ONLY DIED BECAUSE HE WAS A FOOLISH WEAKLING.
HELLKITE-SAN DEMON-STRATED HIS STRENGTH AND WAS ABLE TO JOIN THE SIX GATES BECAUSE OF THAT. THAT IS ALL.
HE HAS NO FURTHER STATUS TO GAIN, WHICH MEANS THERE IS NO REASON HE WOULD TRY TO UNSEAT US.
IS THAT NOT SO?
GRIT
YES, THAT'S TRUE...
BUT ...!
THE LOSS OF HUGE'S DOMINANT EYE IS HAVING A NEGATIVE EFFECT ON HIS MIND.
HE MUST REALIZE IT, THOUGH ...
IF HE CONTINUES TO ACT WITH SUCH COWARDICE, HE HIMSELF WILL BE AT RISK OF BEING CUT DOWN.

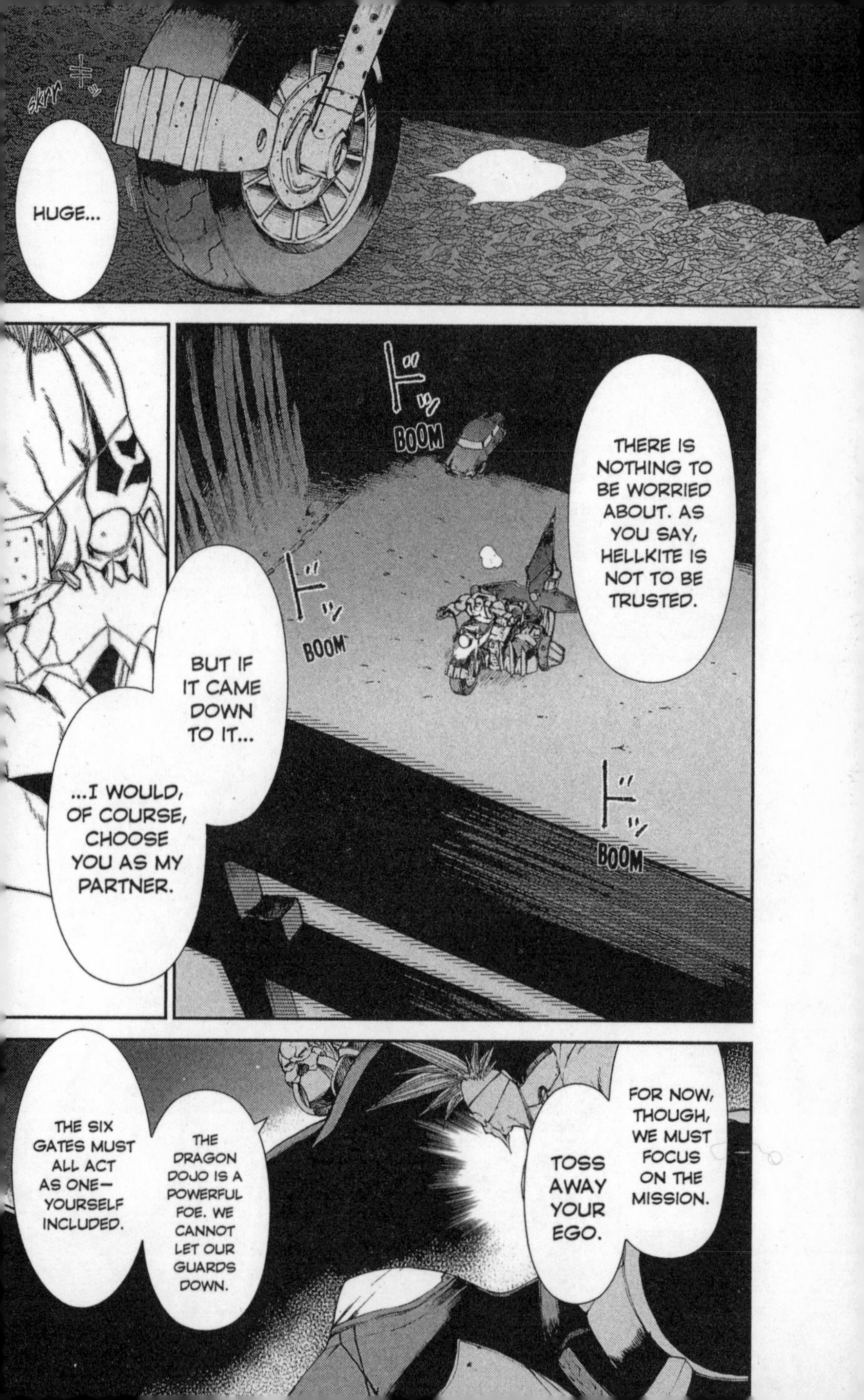
キッ
skrr
HUGE...
ドッ
BOOM
THERE IS NOTHING TO BE WORRIED ABOUT. AS YOU SAY, HELLKITE IS NOT TO BE TRUSTED.
ドッ
BOOM
ドッ
BOOM
BUT IF IT CAME DOWN TO IT...
...I WOULD, OF COURSE, CHOOSE YOU AS MY PARTNER.
FOR NOW, THOUGH, WE MUST FOCUS ON THE MISSION.
TOSS AWAY YOUR EGO.
THE DRAGON DOJO IS A POWERFUL FOE. WE CANNOT LET OUR GUARDS DOWN.
THE SIX GATES MUST ALL ACT AS ONE—YOURSELF INCLUDED.

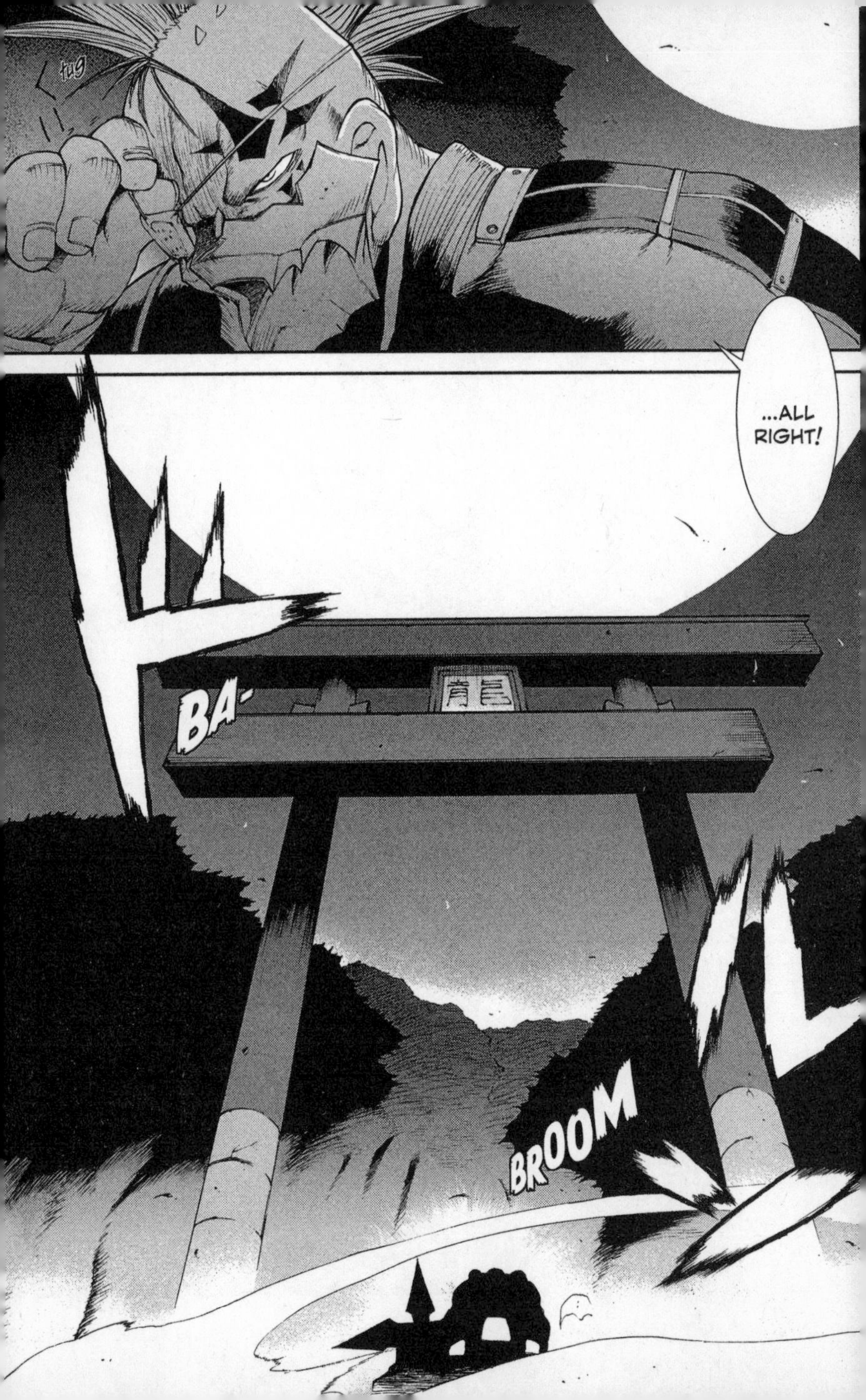
tug
...ALL RIGHT!
BA-
BROOM

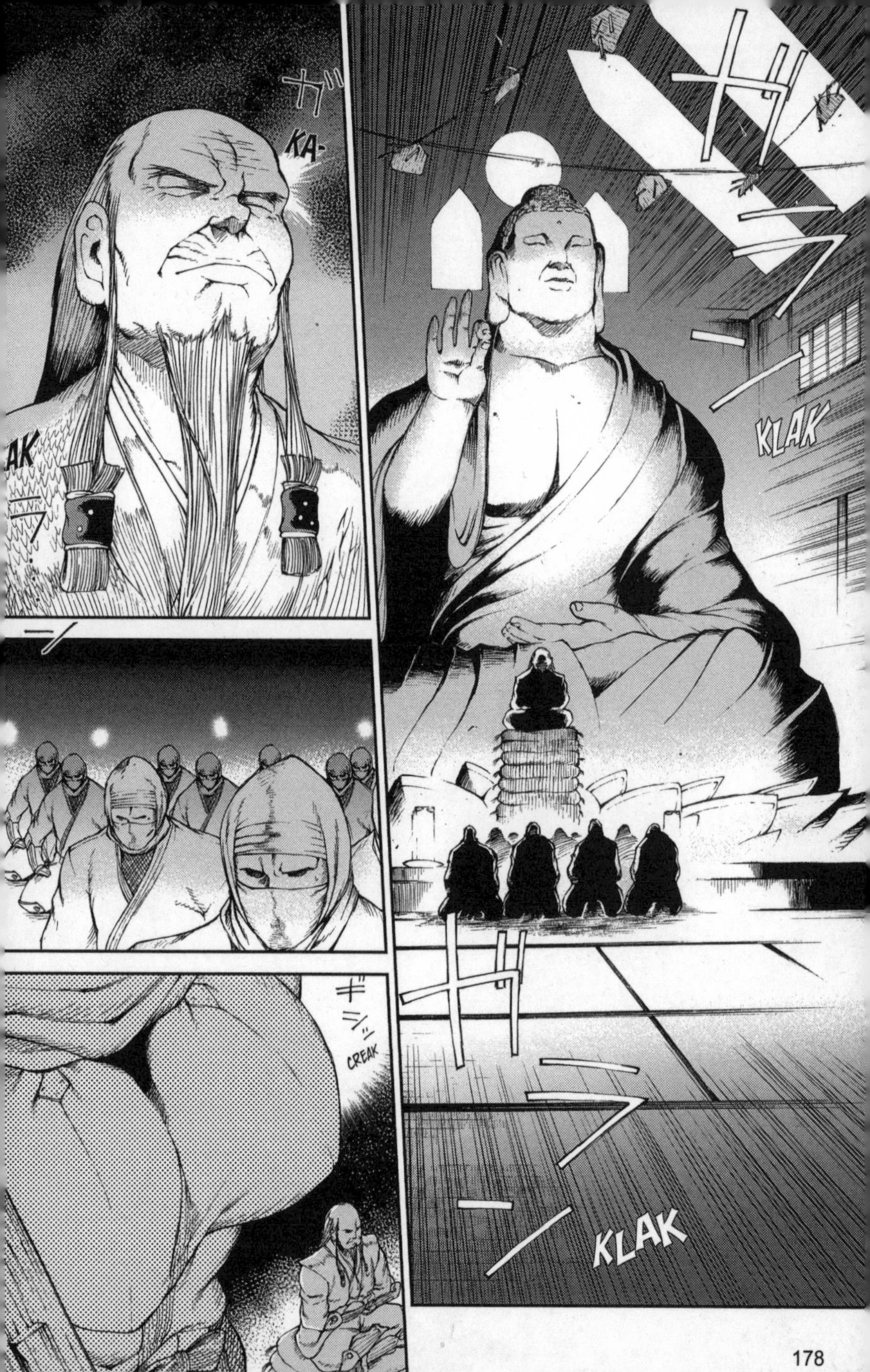
KLAK
KLAK
KA-
AK
CREAK

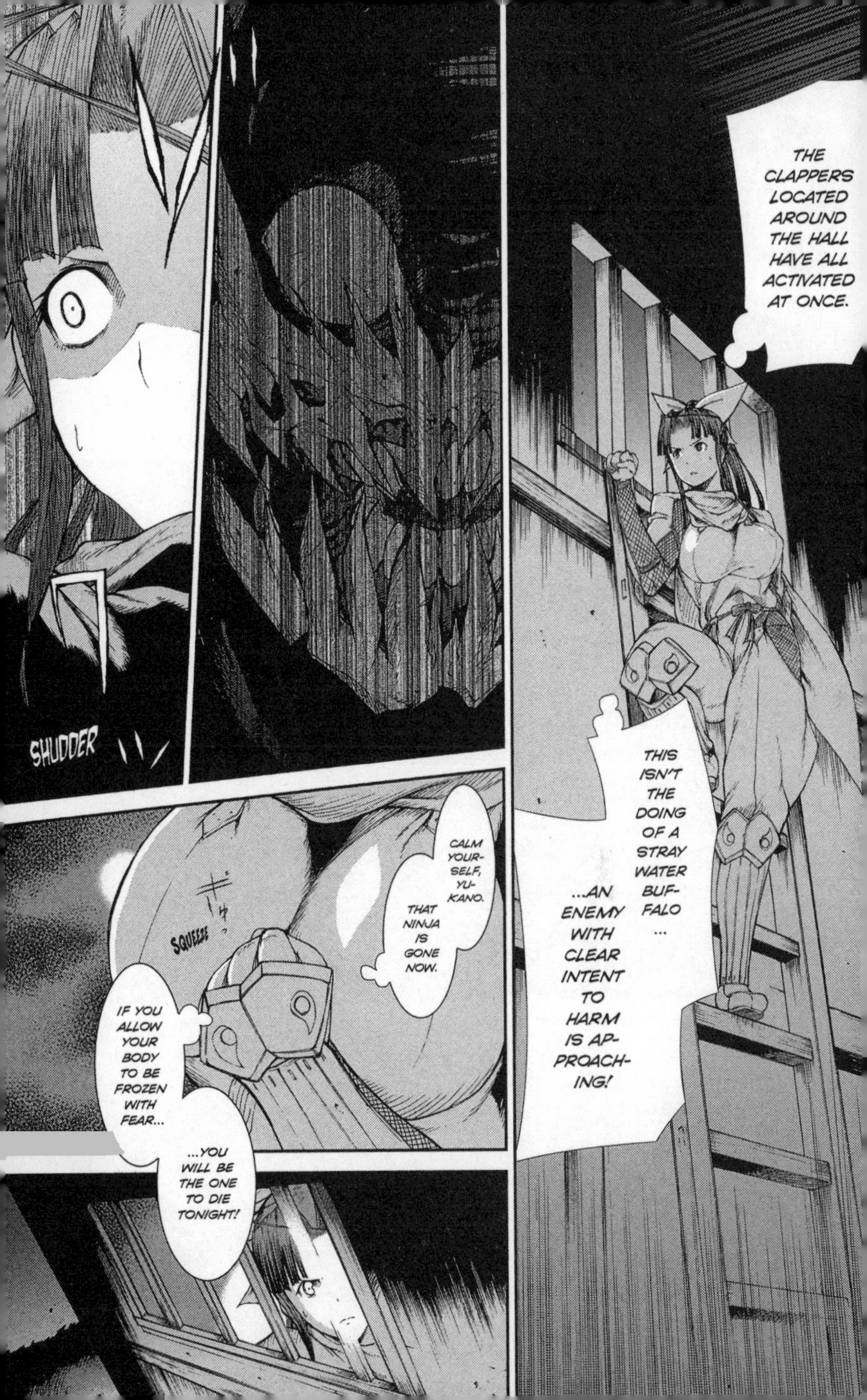
THE CLAPPERS LOCATED AROUND THE HALL HAVE ALL ACTIVATED AT ONCE.
THIS ISN'T THE DOING OF A STRAY WATER BUF-FALO...
...AN ENEMY WITH CLEAR INTENT TO HARM IS AP-PROACH-ING!
SHUDDER
CALM YOUR-SELF, YU-KANO.
THAT NINJA IS GONE NOW.
ギュッ
SQUEEZE
IF YOU ALLOW YOUR BODY TO BE FROZEN WITH FEAR...
...YOU WILL BE THE ONE TO DIE TONIGHT!

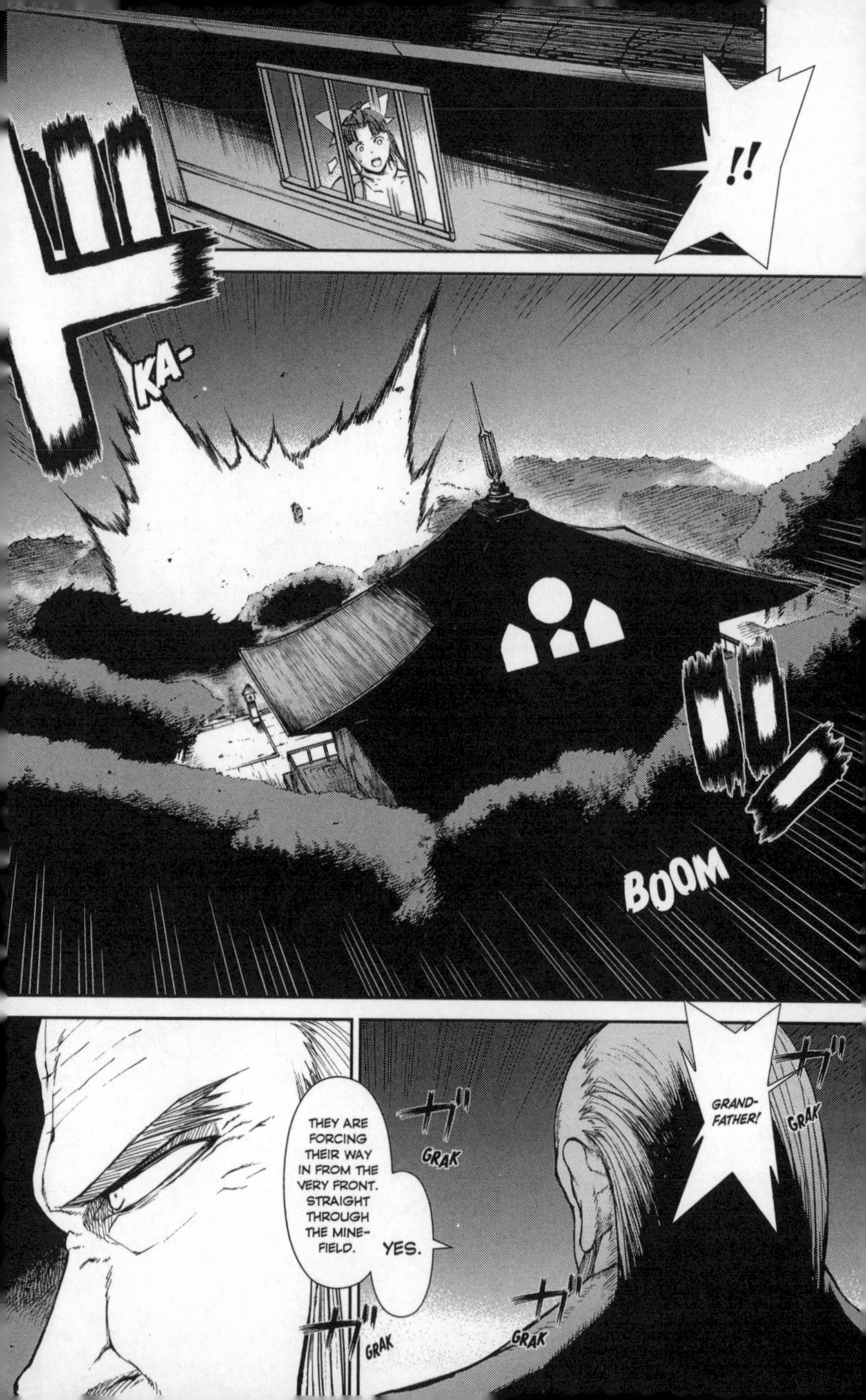

!!
KA-
BOOM
GRAND-FATHER!
GRAK
THEY ARE FORCING THEIR WAY IN FROM THE VERY FRONT. STRAIGHT THROUGH THE MINE-FIELD.
YES.
GRAK
GRAK
GRAK

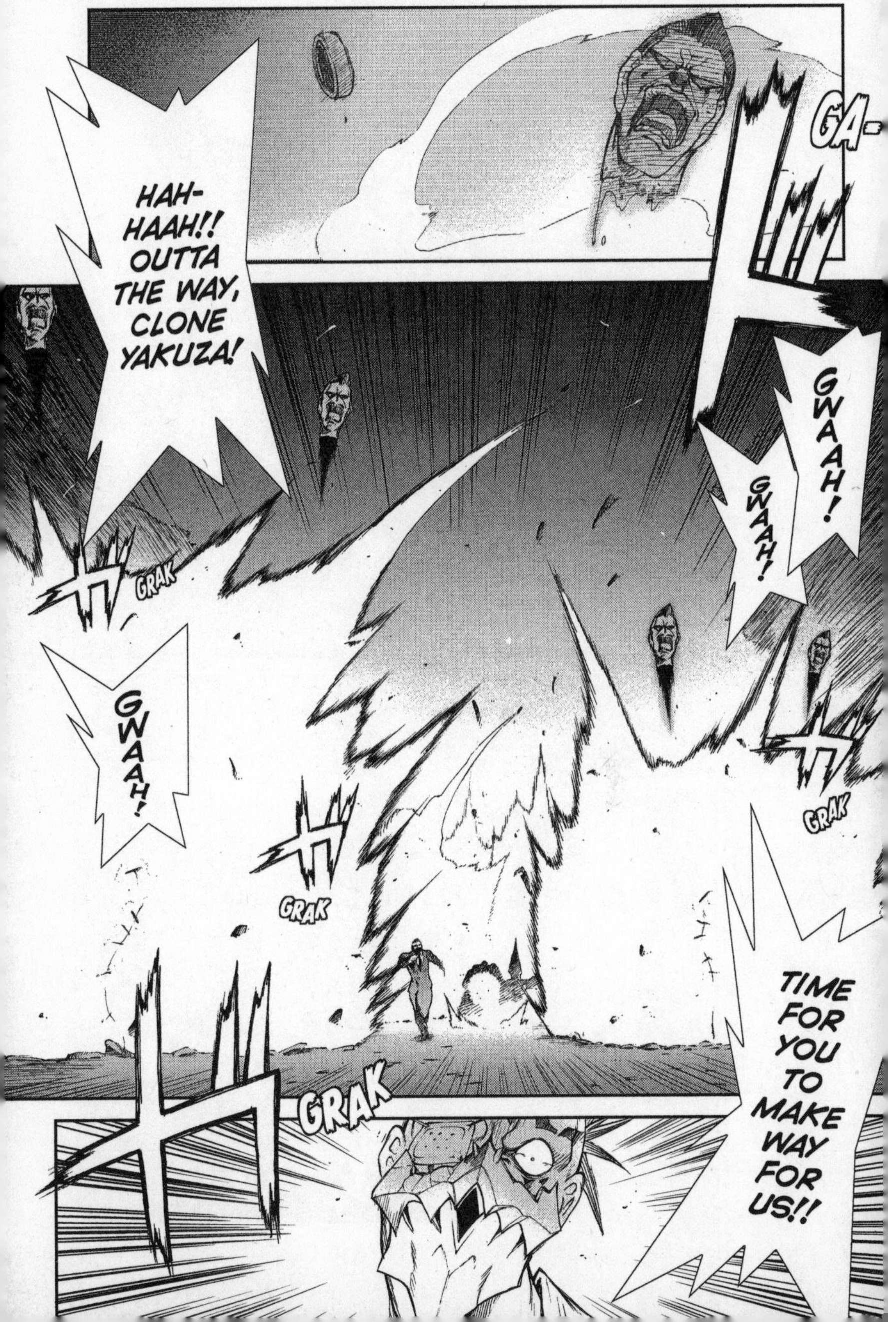
GA-
HAH-HAAH!! OUTTA THE WAY, CLONE YAKUZA!
GWAAH!
GWAAH!
GRAK
GRAK
GWAAH!
GRAK
TIME FOR YOU TO MAKE WAY FOR US!!
GRAK

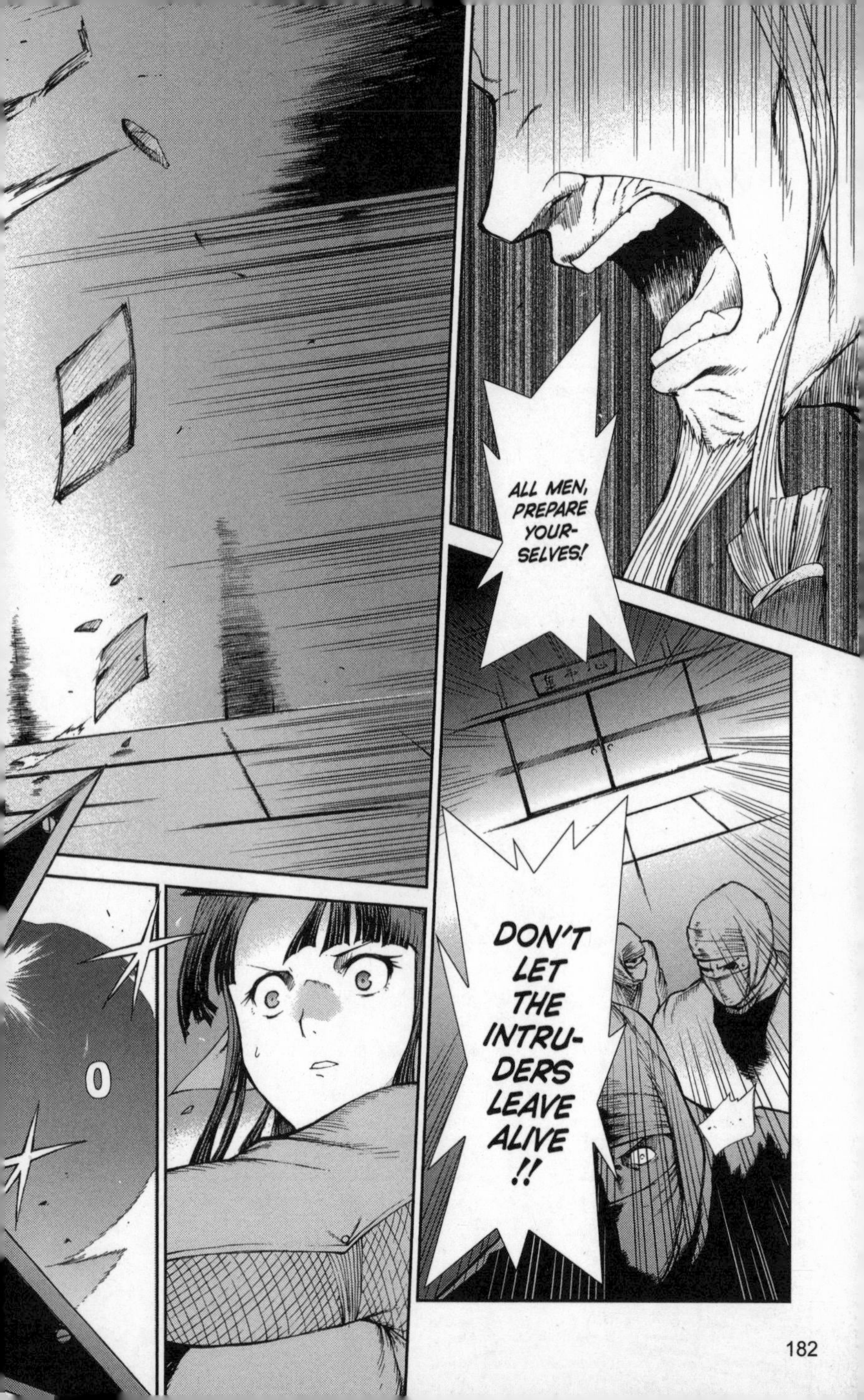
ALL MEN, PREPARE YOURSELVES!
DON'T LET THE INTRUDERS LEAVE ALIVE!!
O

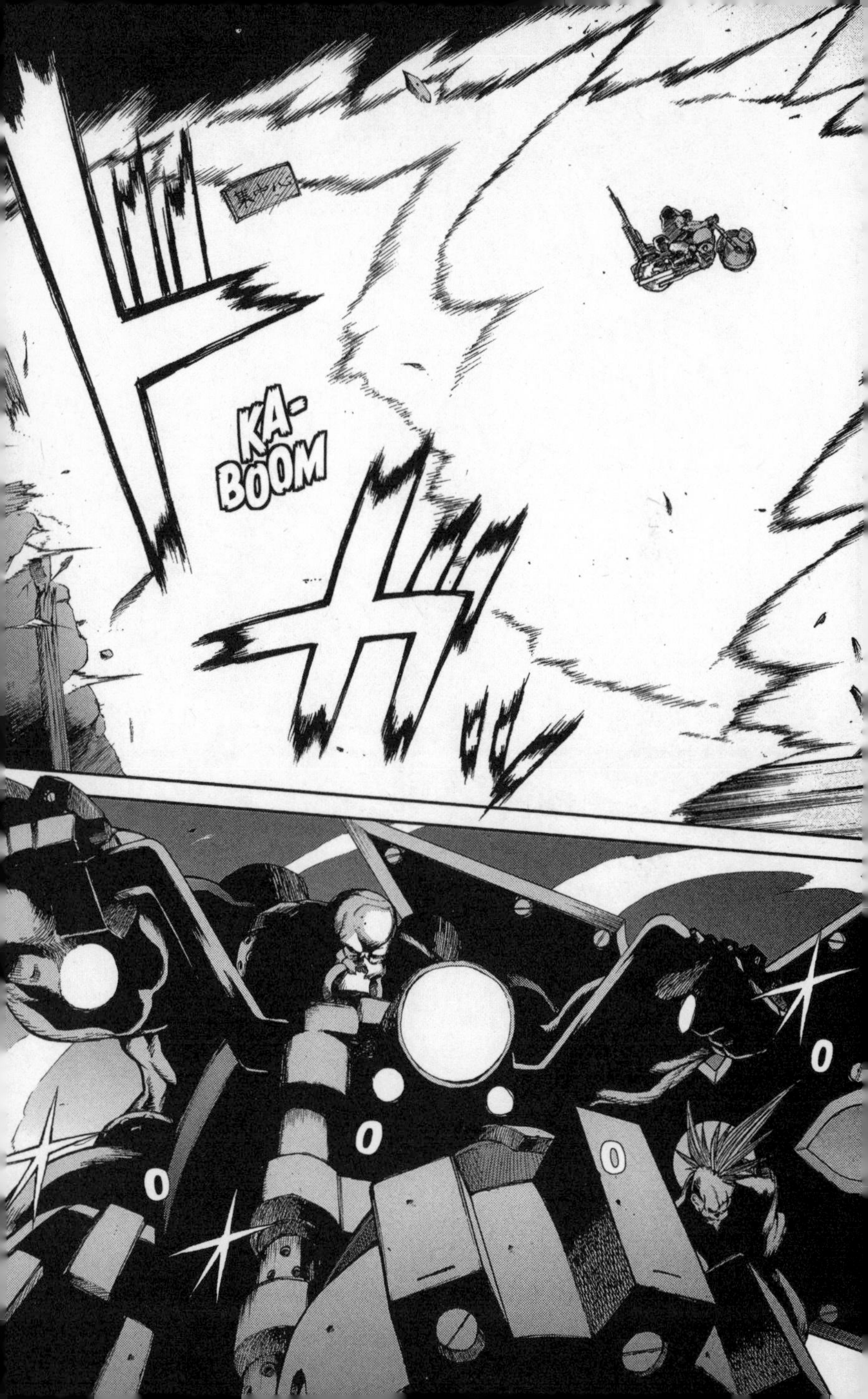
KA-BOOM

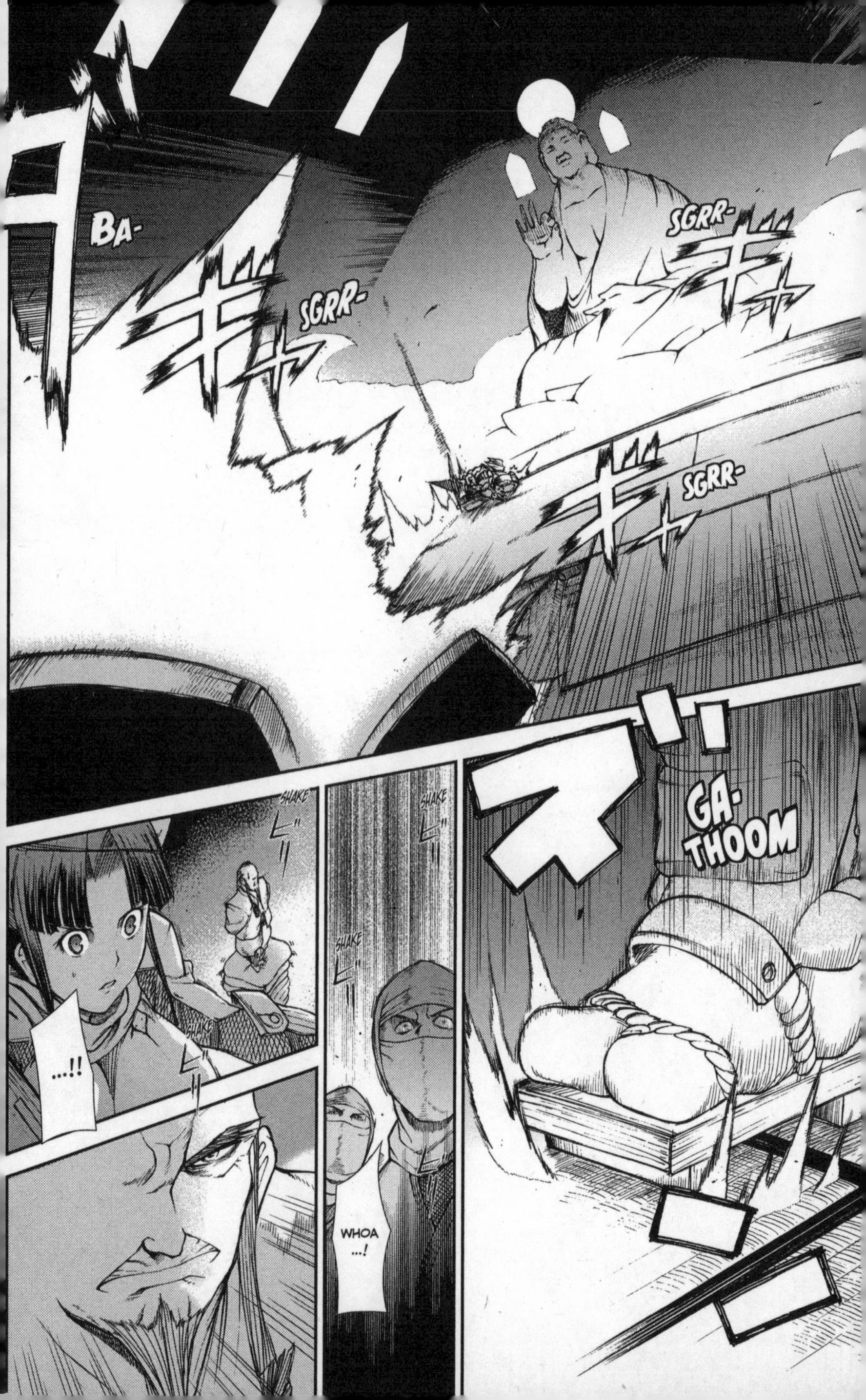
SGRR-
BA-
SGRR-
SGRR-
GA-
THOOM
SHAKE
SHAKE
WHOA
...!
SHAKE
SHAKE
...!!

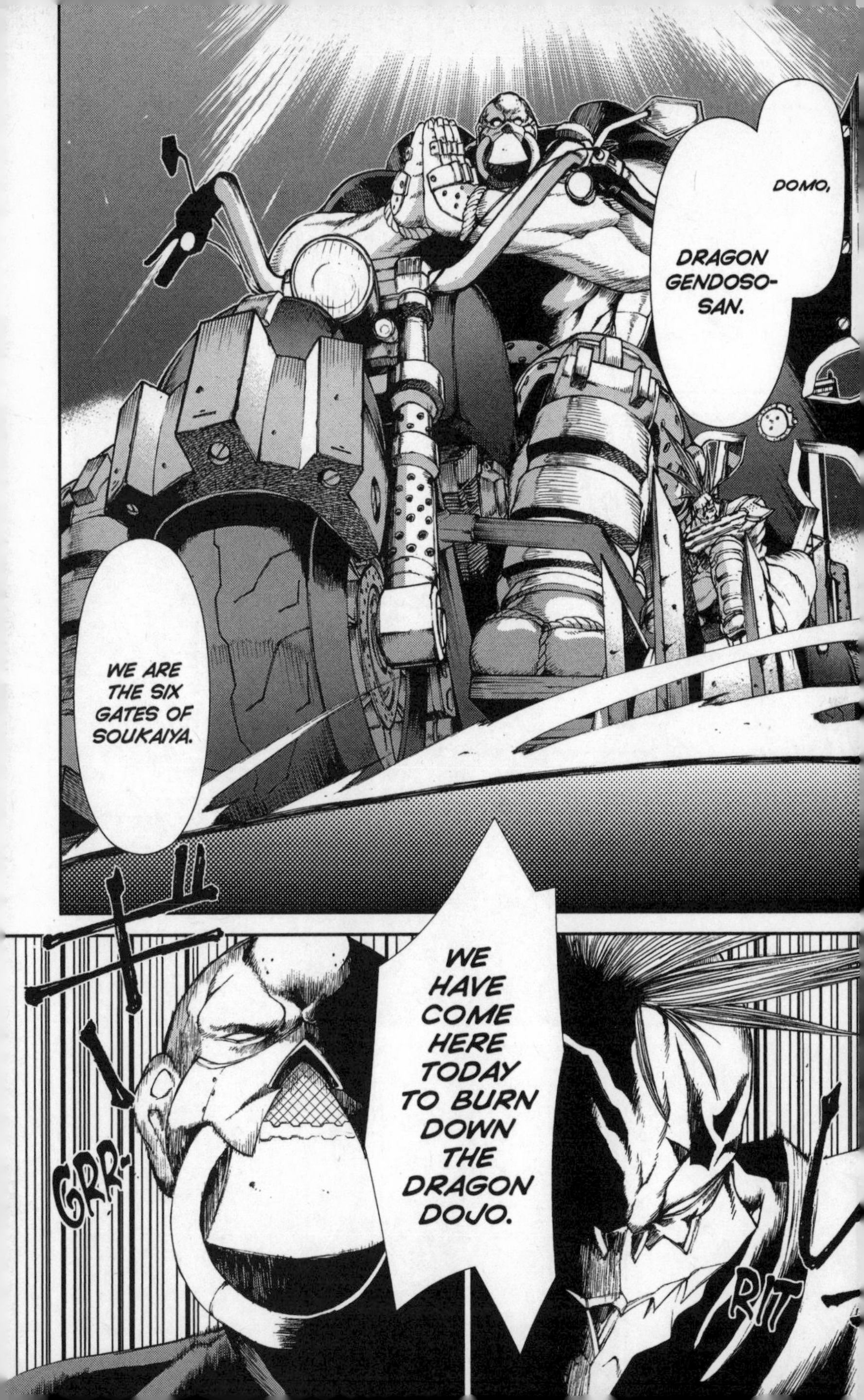
DOMO, DRAGON GENDOSO-SAN.
WE ARE THE SIX GATES OF SOUKAIYA.
WE HAVE COME HERE TODAY TO BURN DOWN THE DRAGON DOJO.
RIT
GRR-

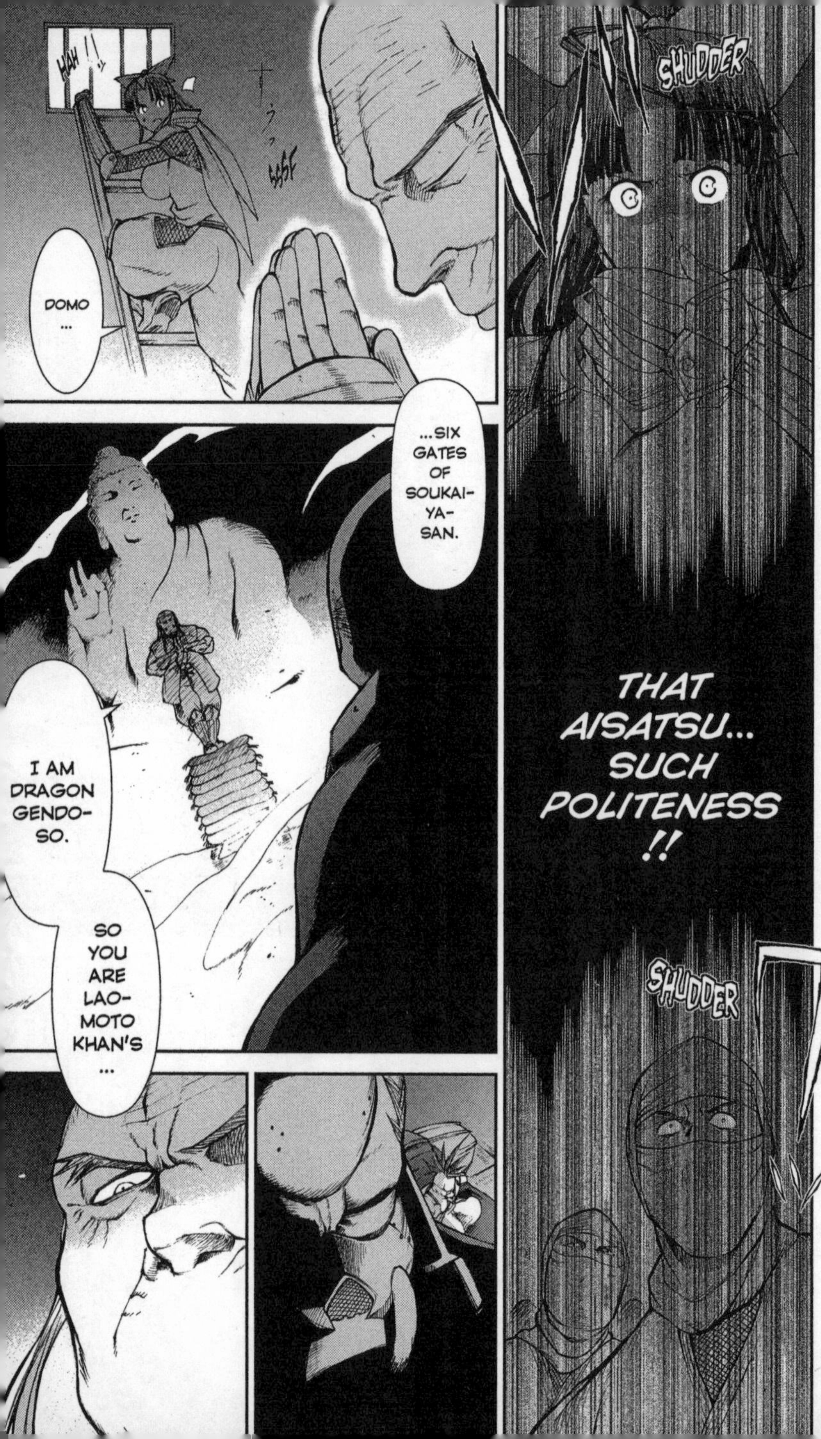
SHUDDER
THAT AISATSU... SUCH POLITENESS !!
SHUDDER
HAH !!
SSSF
DOMO ...
...SIX GATES OF SOUKAI-YA-SAN.
I AM DRAGON GENDO-SO.
SO YOU ARE LAO-MOTO KHAN'S ...

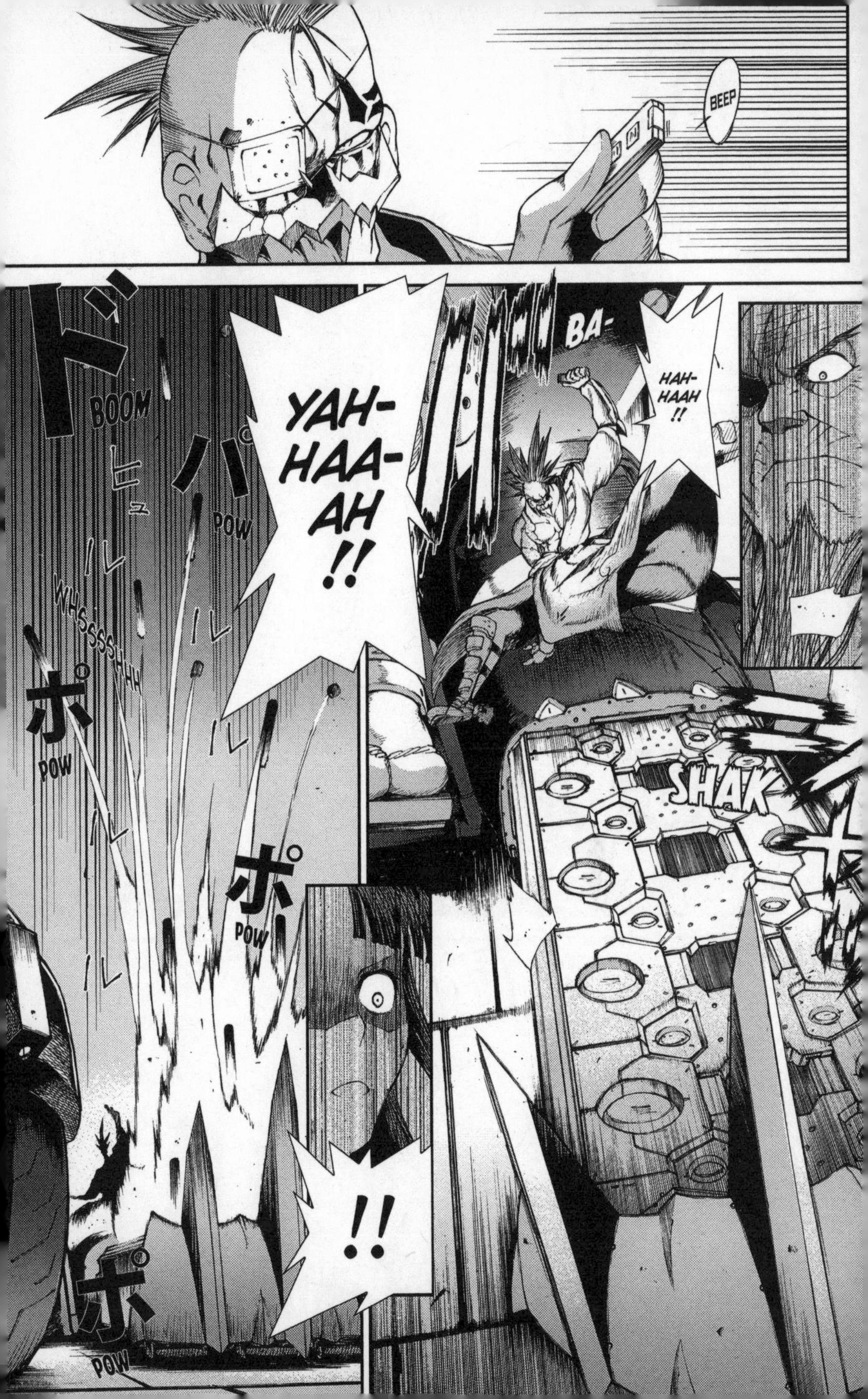
BEEP
BA-
HAH-HAAH!!
YAH-HAA-AH!!
ド
BOOM
パ
POW
ヒュ
WHSSSSSHHH
ポ
POW
ポ
POW
ポ
POW
SHAK
!!

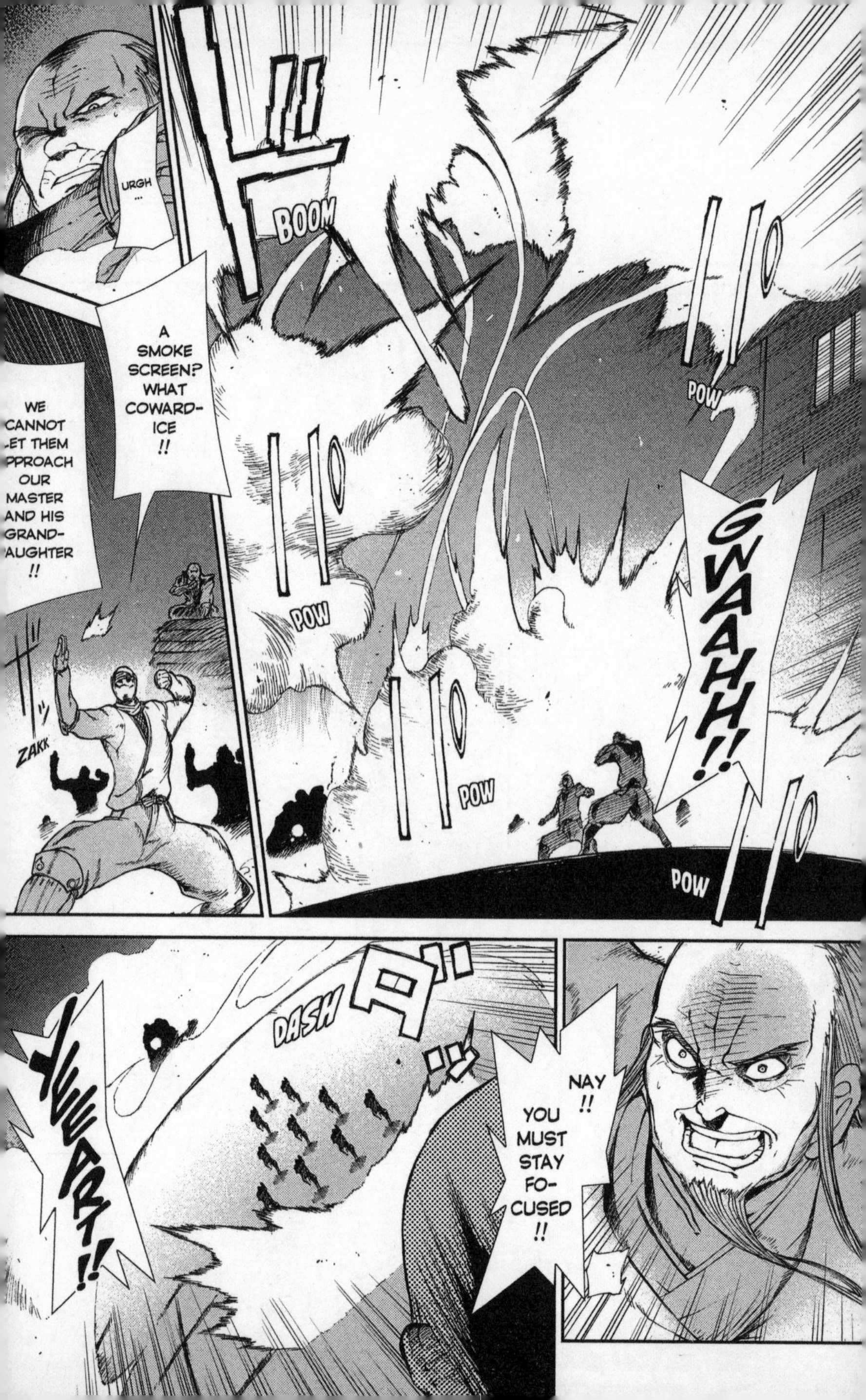
BOOM
POW
GWAAHH!!
POW
POW
POW
URGH...
A SMOKE SCREEN? WHAT COWARD-ICE!!
WE CANNOT ET THEM PPROACH OUR MASTER AND HIS GRAND-AUGHTER!!
ZAKK
NAY!! YOU MUST STAY FO-CUSED!!
DASH
HUWAART!!

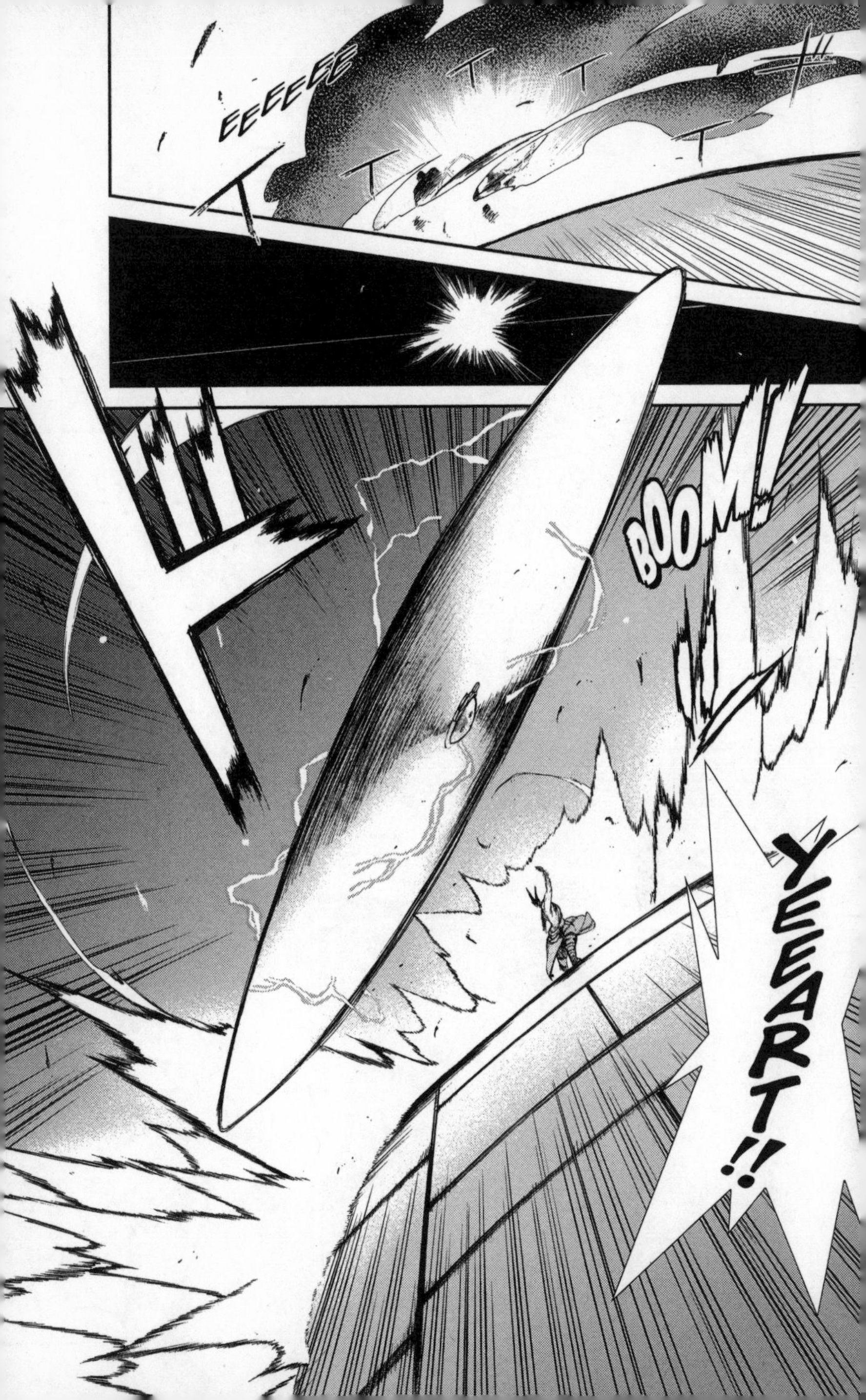
EEEEEEE
BOOM!
YEEART!!

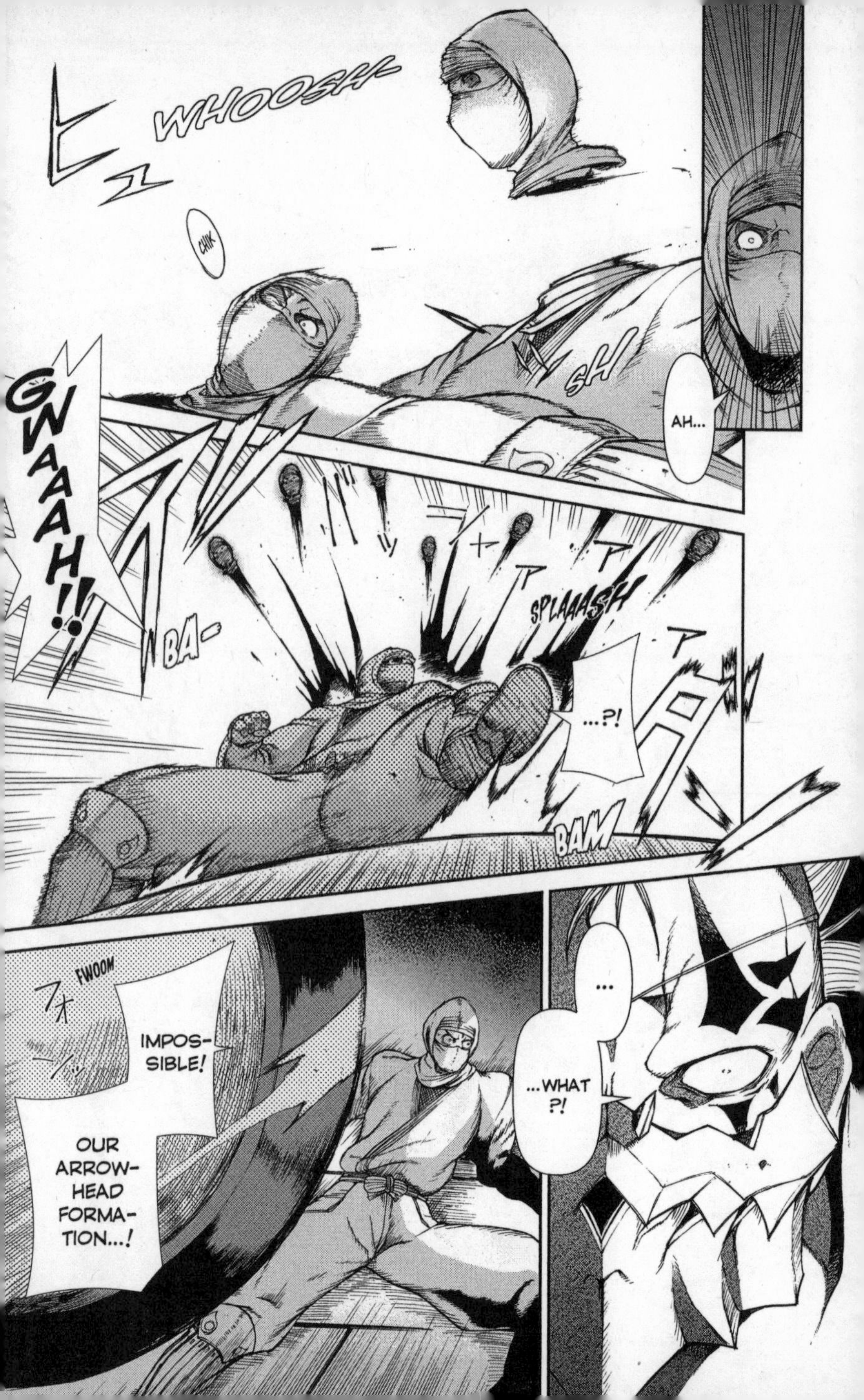
AH...
WHOOSH
CHIK
SH
GWAAAAH!!
...?!
SPLAAASH
BA-
BAM
...
...WHAT ?!
FWOOM
IMPOS-SIBLE!
OUR ARROW-HEAD FORMA-TION...!

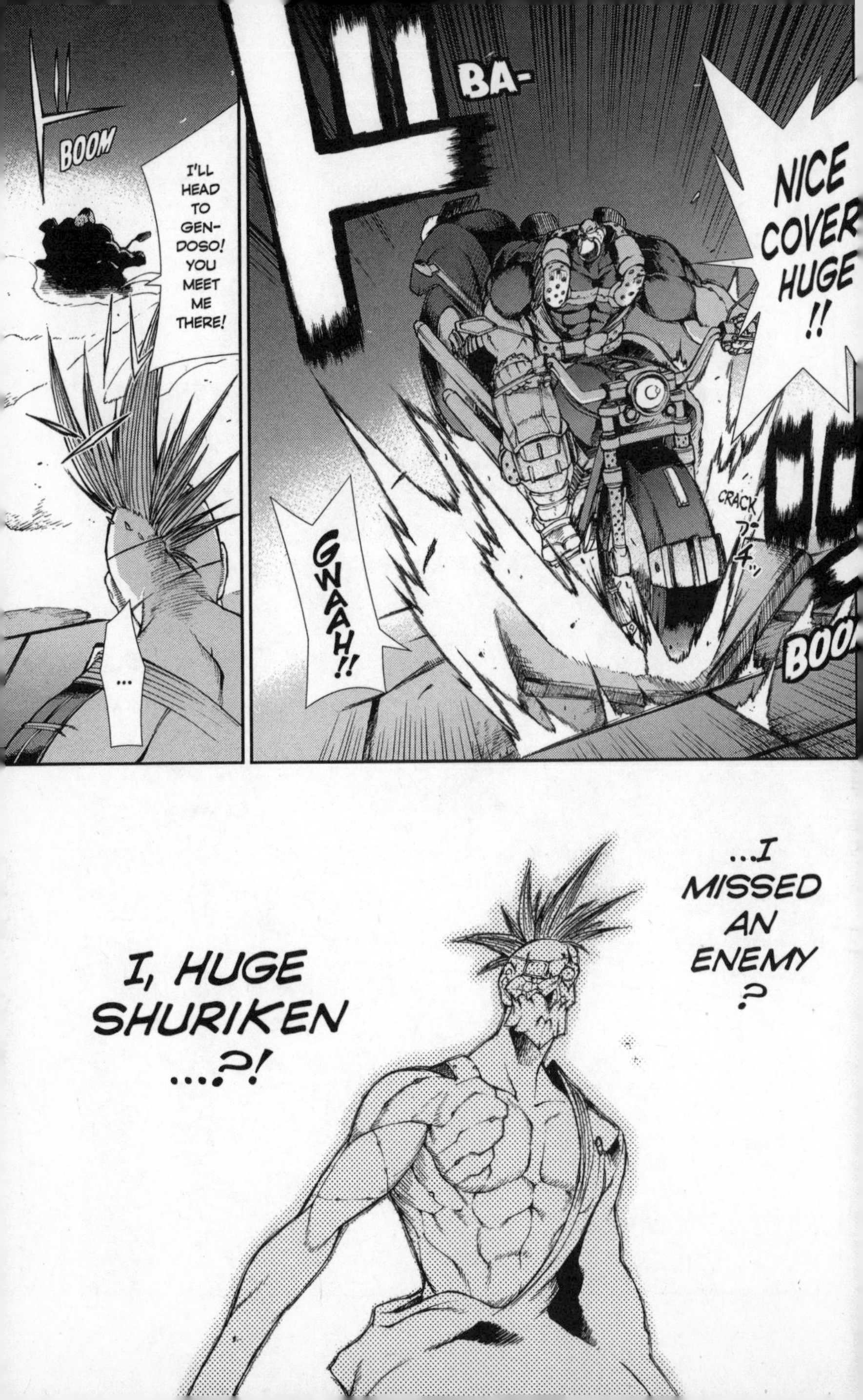
NICE COVER HUGE!!
BA-
CRACK
BOO
GWAAAH!!
BOOM
I'LL HEAD TO GEN-DOSO! YOU MEET ME THERE!
...
...I MISSED AN ENEMY?
I, HUGE SHURIKEN ...?!

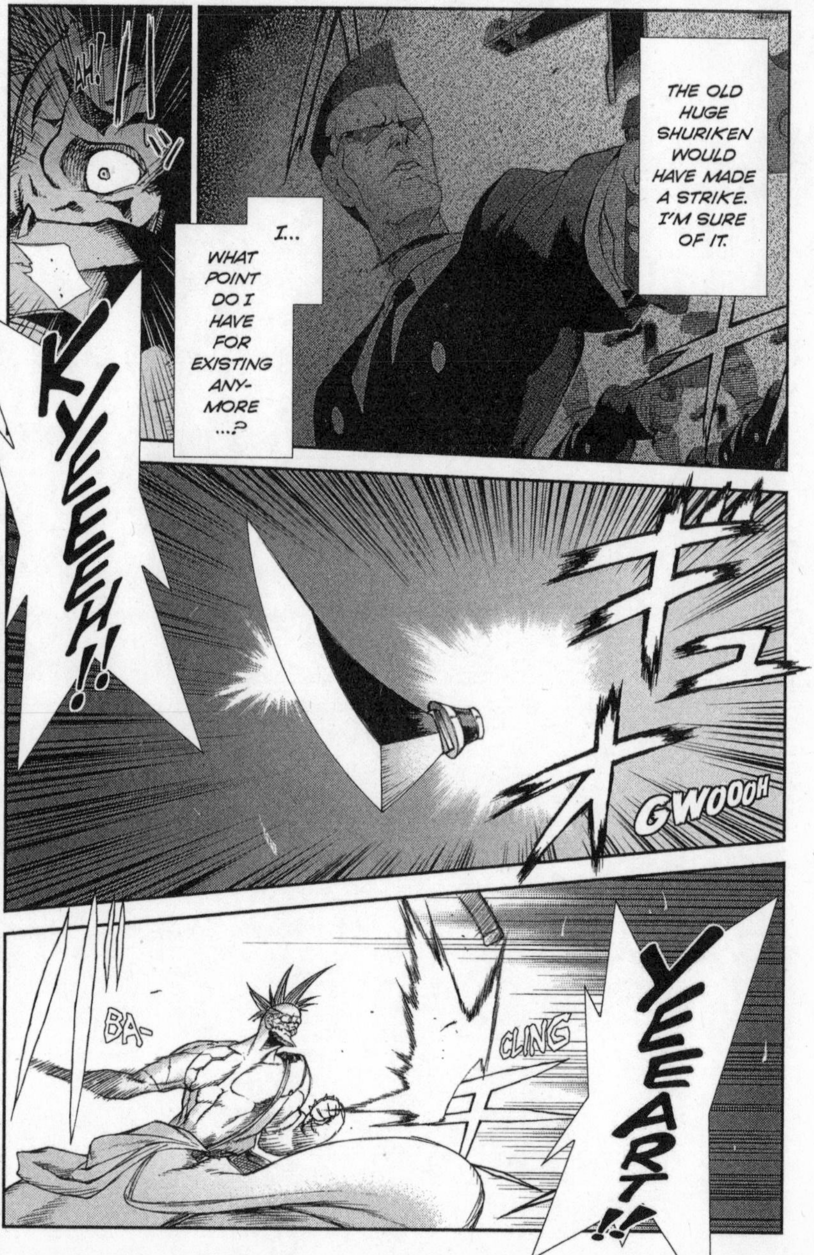
THE OLD HUGE SHURIKEN WOULD HAVE MADE A STRIKE. I'M SURE OF IT.
I... WHAT POINT DO I HAVE FOR EXISTING ANY-MORE ...?
AH!!
KYEEEEH!!
GWOOOH
YEEART!!
CLING
BA-

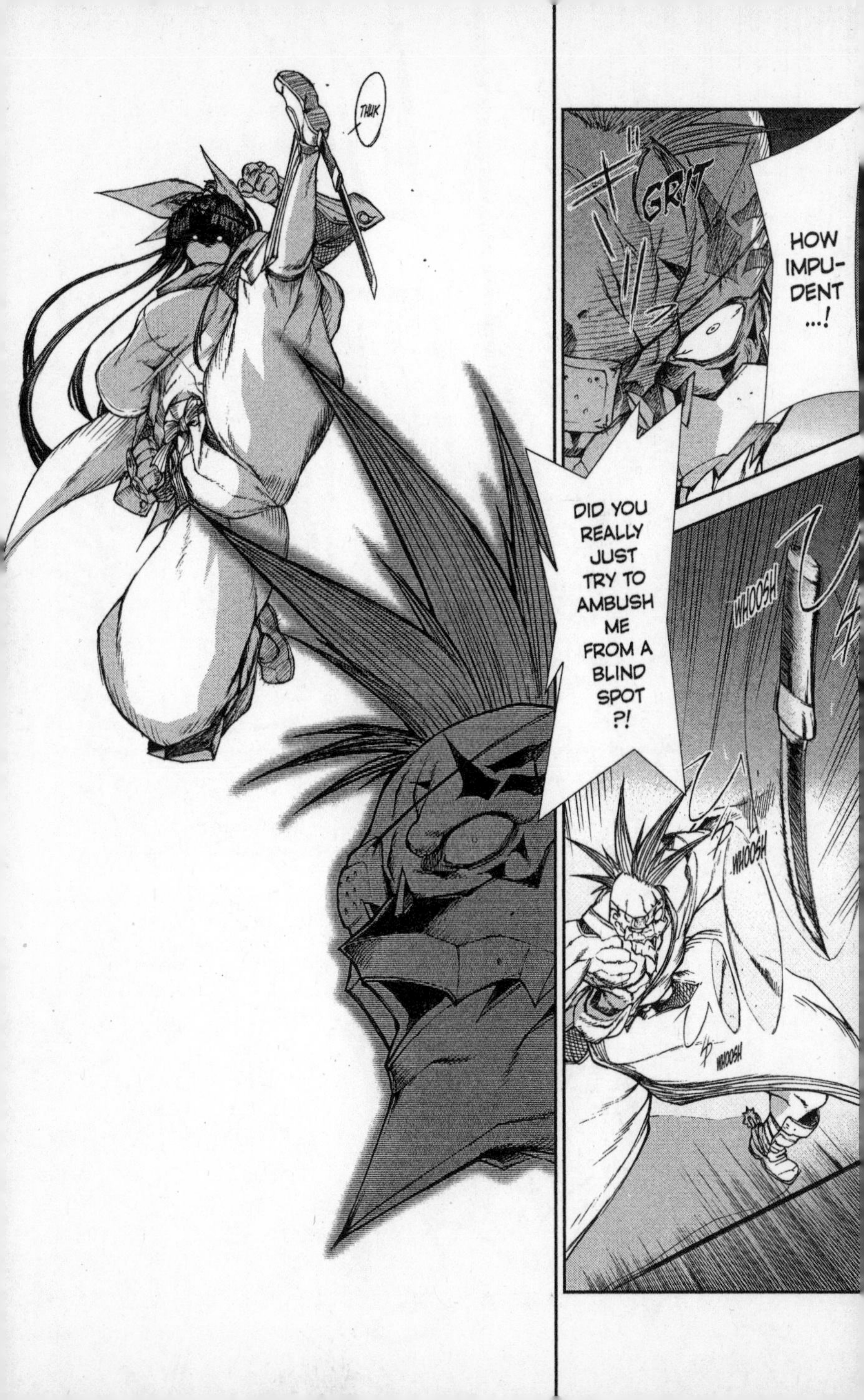
GRIT
HOW IMPUDENT...!
DID YOU REALLY JUST TRY TO AMBUSH ME FROM A BLIND SPOT?!
WHOOSH
WHOOSH
WHOOSH
THUK

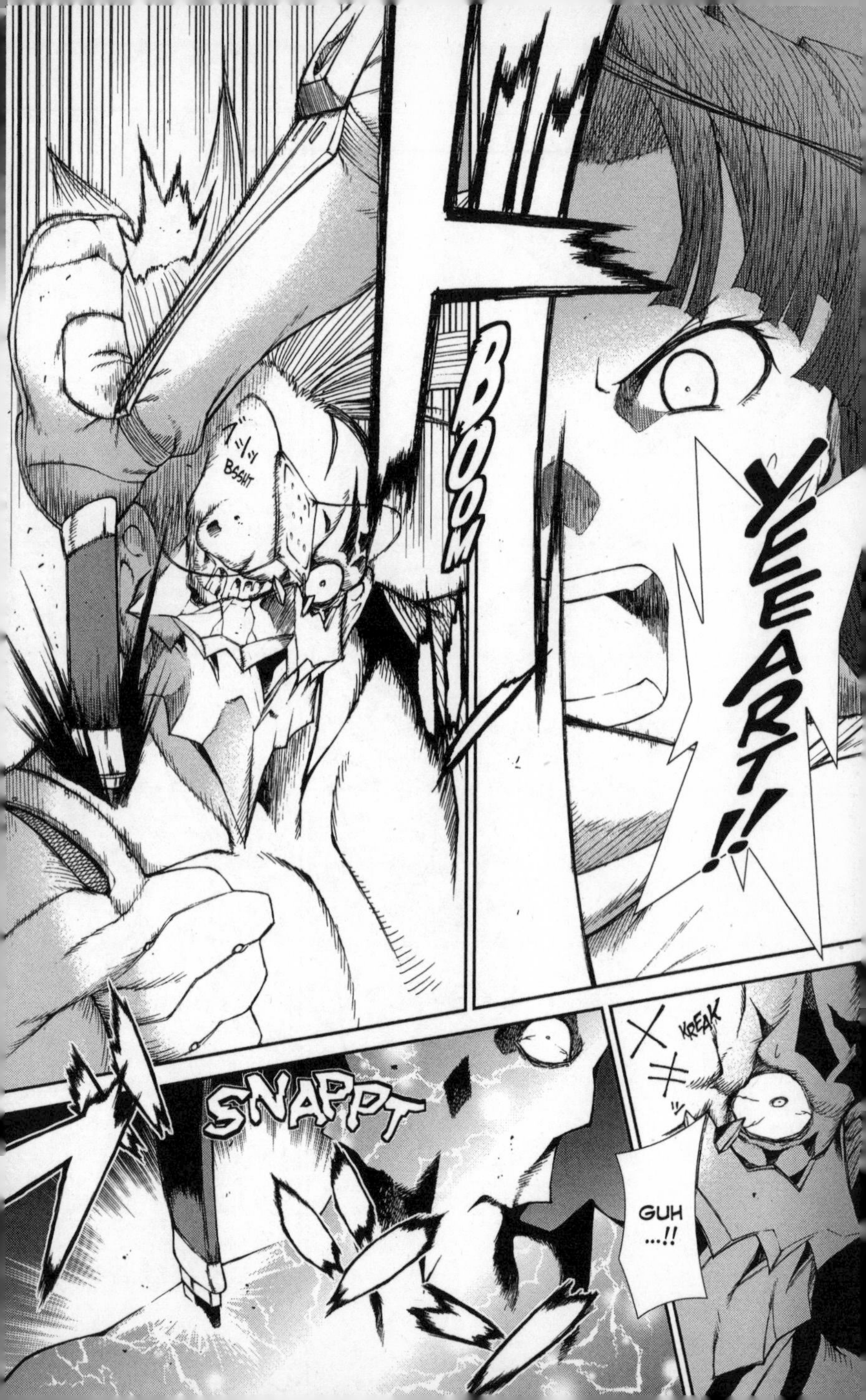
YEEART!!
BOOM
BSSHT
KREAK
GUH ...!!
SNAPPT

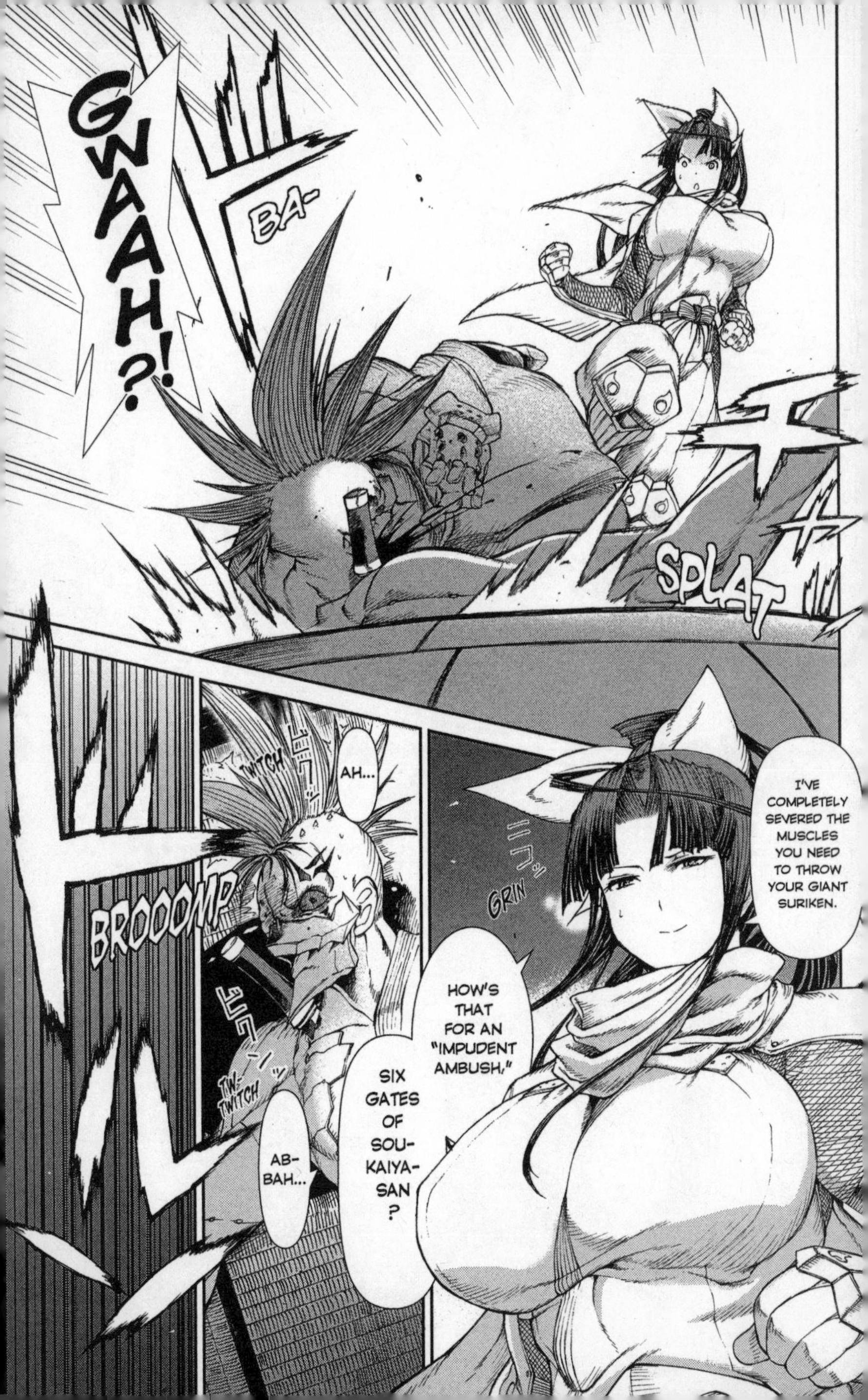
BA-
GWAAH?!
SPLAT
I'VE COMPLETELY SEVERED THE MUSCLES YOU NEED TO THROW YOUR GIANT SURIKEN.
GRIN
HOW'S THAT FOR AN "IMPUDENT AMBUSH,"
SIX GATES OF SOU-KAIYA-SAN?
TWITCH
AH...
TW-TWITCH
AB-BAH...
BROOOMP

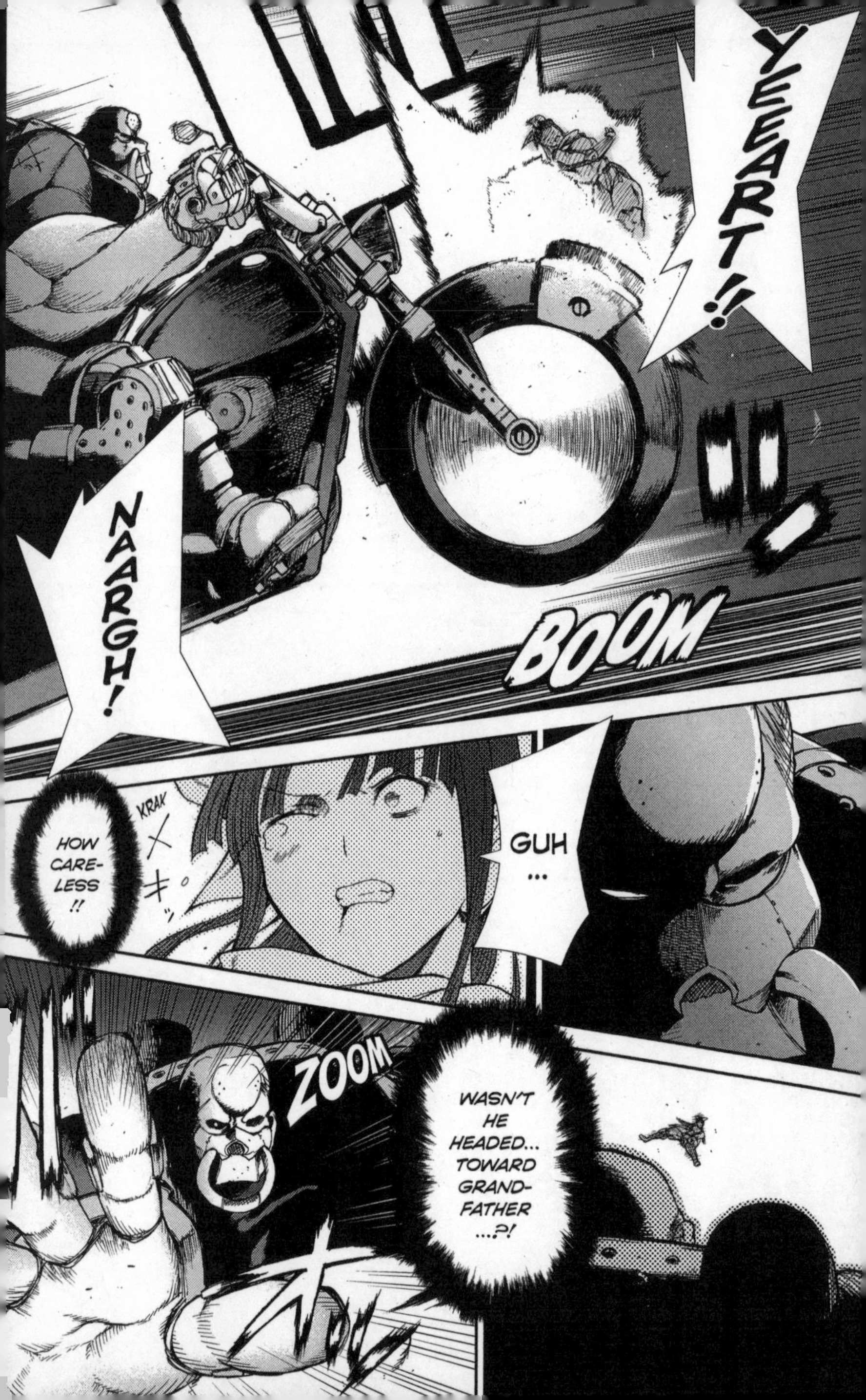
YEEART!!
BOOM
NAARGH!
GUH ...
KRAK
キッ
HOW CARE-LESS !!
WASN'T HE HEADED... TOWARD GRAND-FATHER ...?!
ZOOM

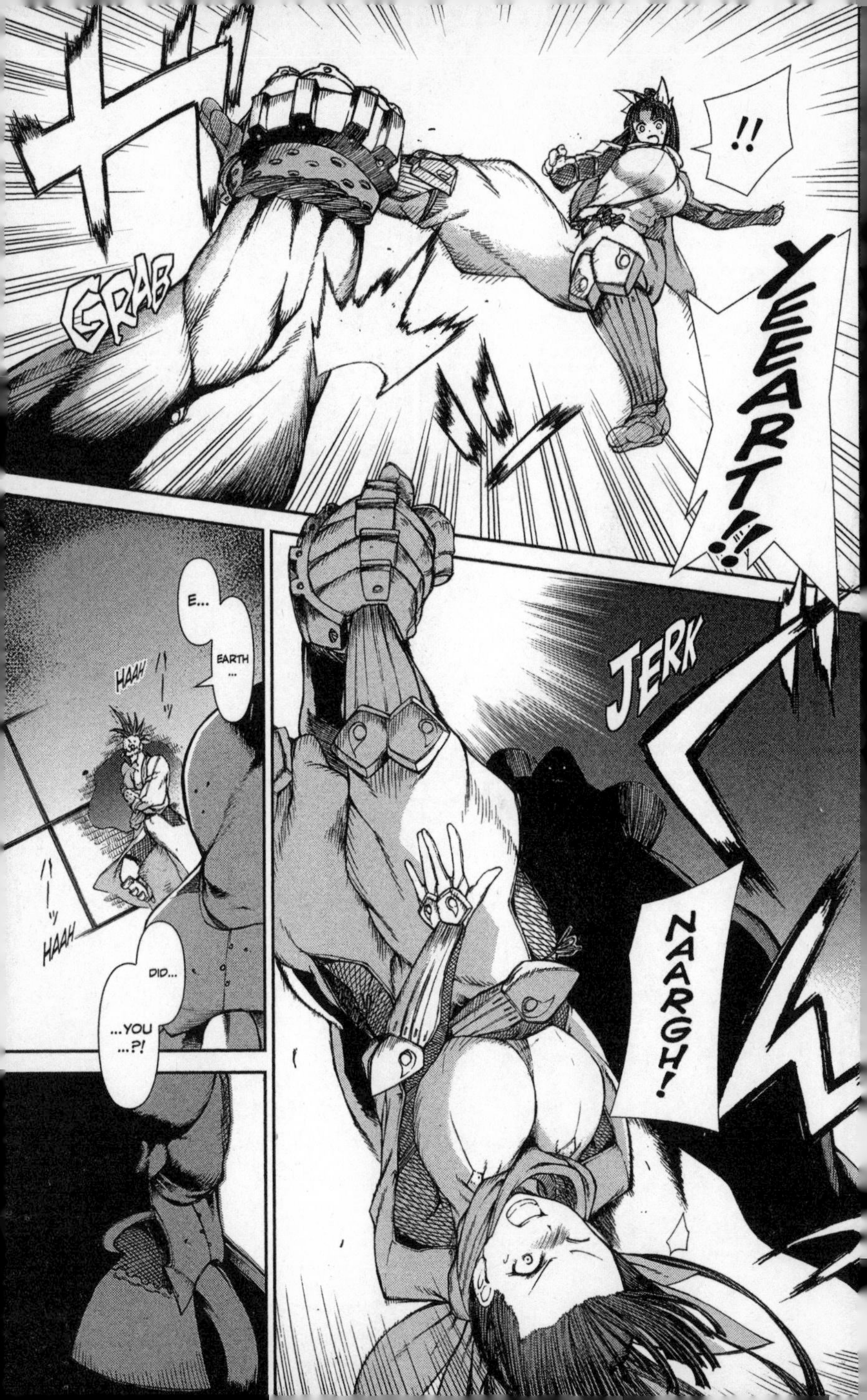
!!
YEEART!!
GRAB
JERK
NAARGH!
E...
EARTH...
HAAH
HAAH
DID...
...YOU ...?!

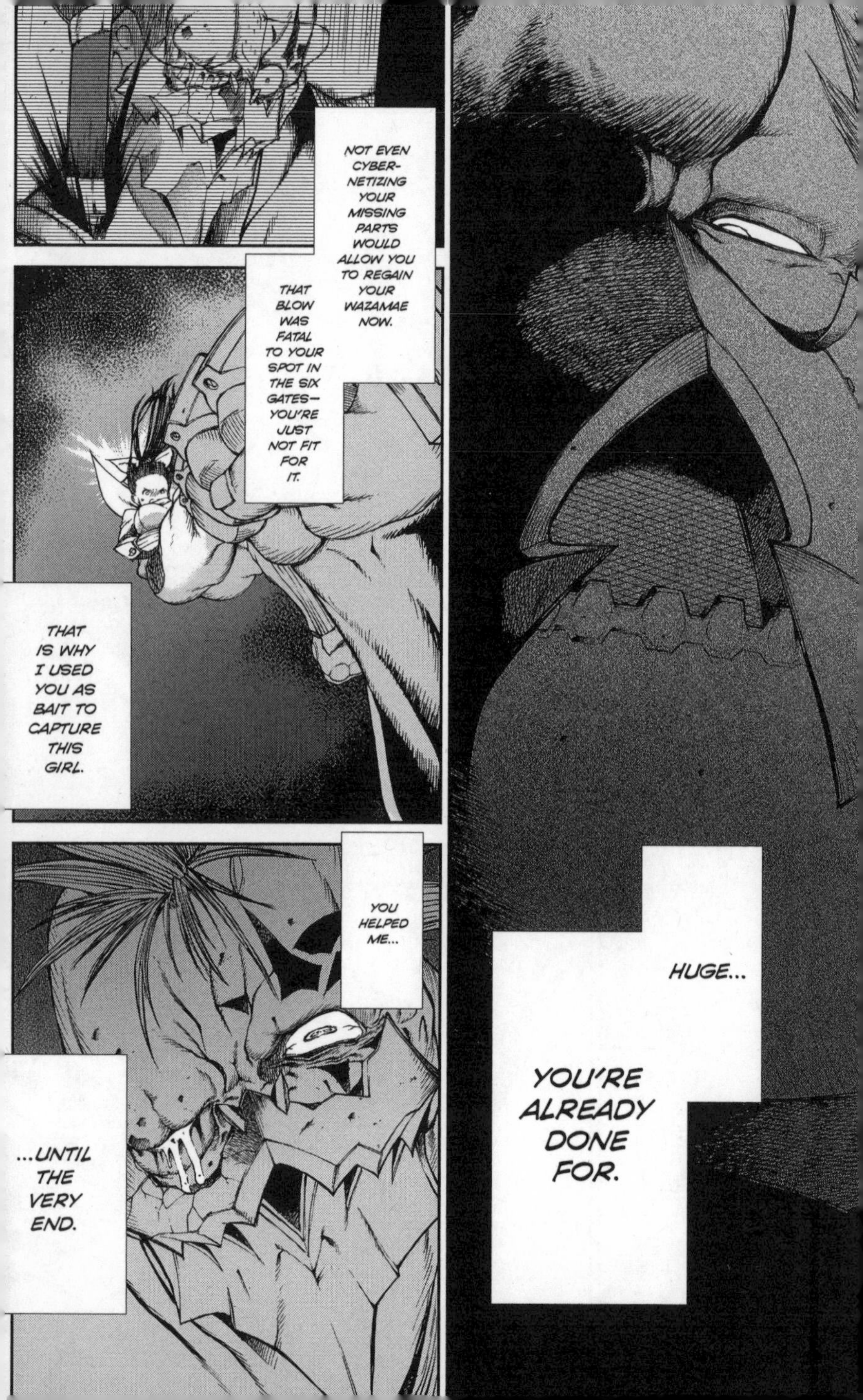
HUGE...
YOU'RE ALREADY DONE FOR.
NOT EVEN CYBER-NETIZING YOUR MISSING PARTS WOULD ALLOW YOU TO REGAIN YOUR WAZAMAE NOW.
THAT BLOW WAS FATAL TO YOUR SPOT IN THE SIX GATES— YOU'RE JUST NOT FIT FOR IT.
THAT IS WHY I USED YOU AS BAIT TO CAPTURE THIS GIRL.
YOU HELPED ME...
...UNTIL THE VERY END.

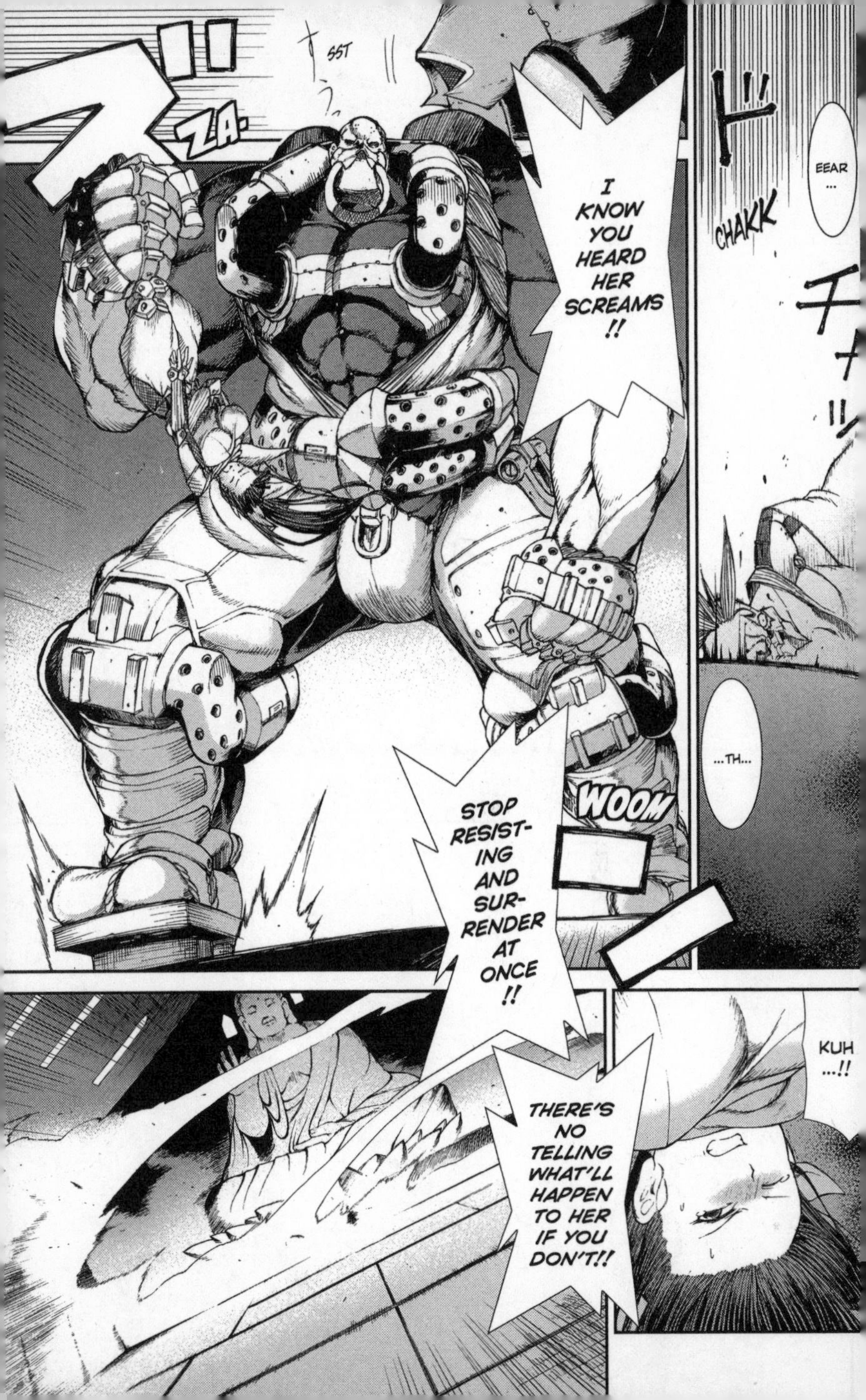
EEAR ...
CHAKK
...TH...
SST
ZA-
I KNOW YOU HEARD HER SCREAMS!!
WOOM
STOP RESISTING AND SURRENDER AT ONCE!!
KUH ...!!
THERE'S NO TELLING WHAT'LL HAPPEN TO HER IF YOU DON'T!!

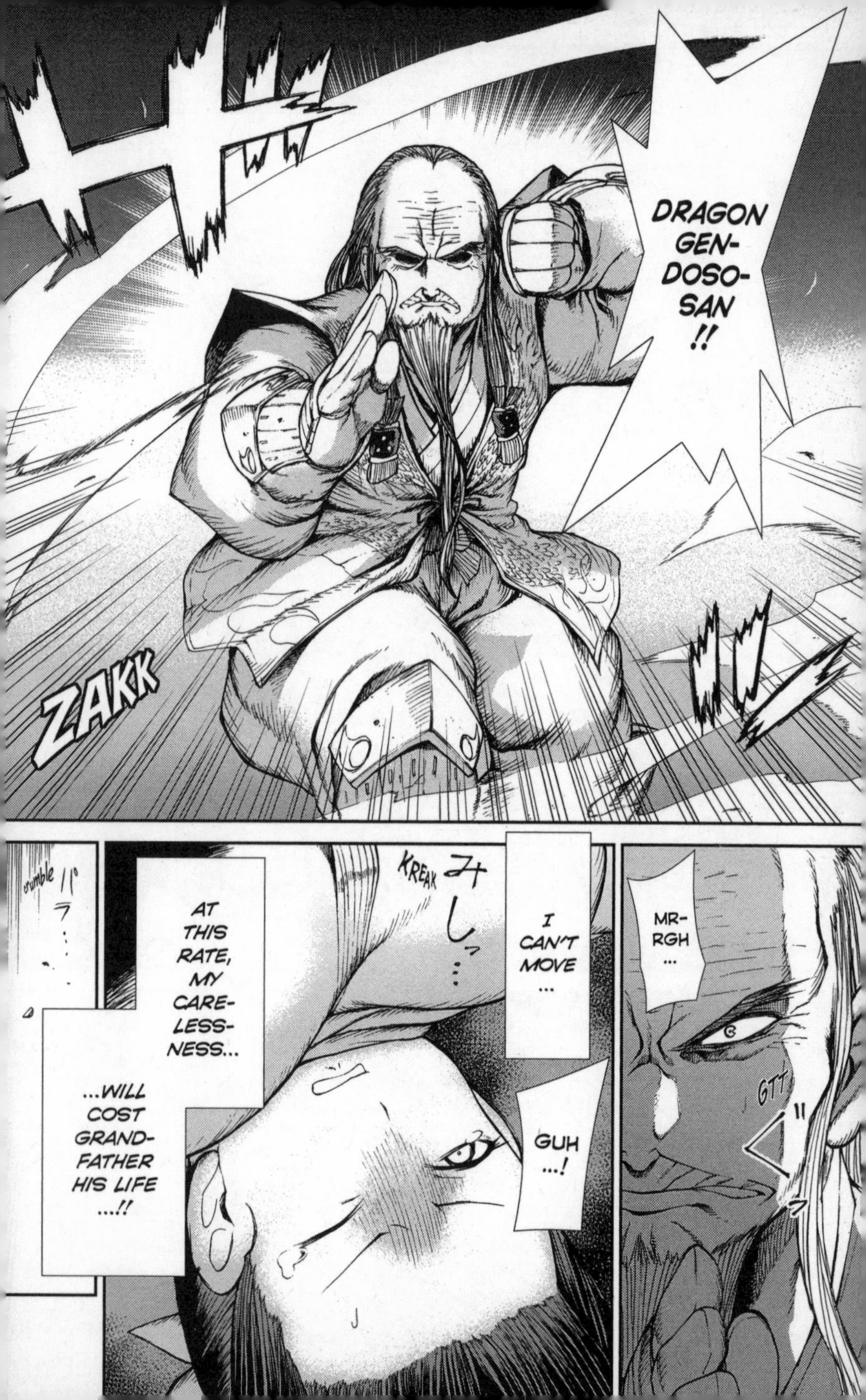
DRAGON GEN-DOSO-SAN !!
ZAKK
MR-RGH ...
GTT
I CAN'T MOVE ...
KREAK
GUH ...!
AT THIS RATE, MY CARE-LESS-NESS...
...WILL COST GRAND-FATHER HIS LIFE ....!!
crumble

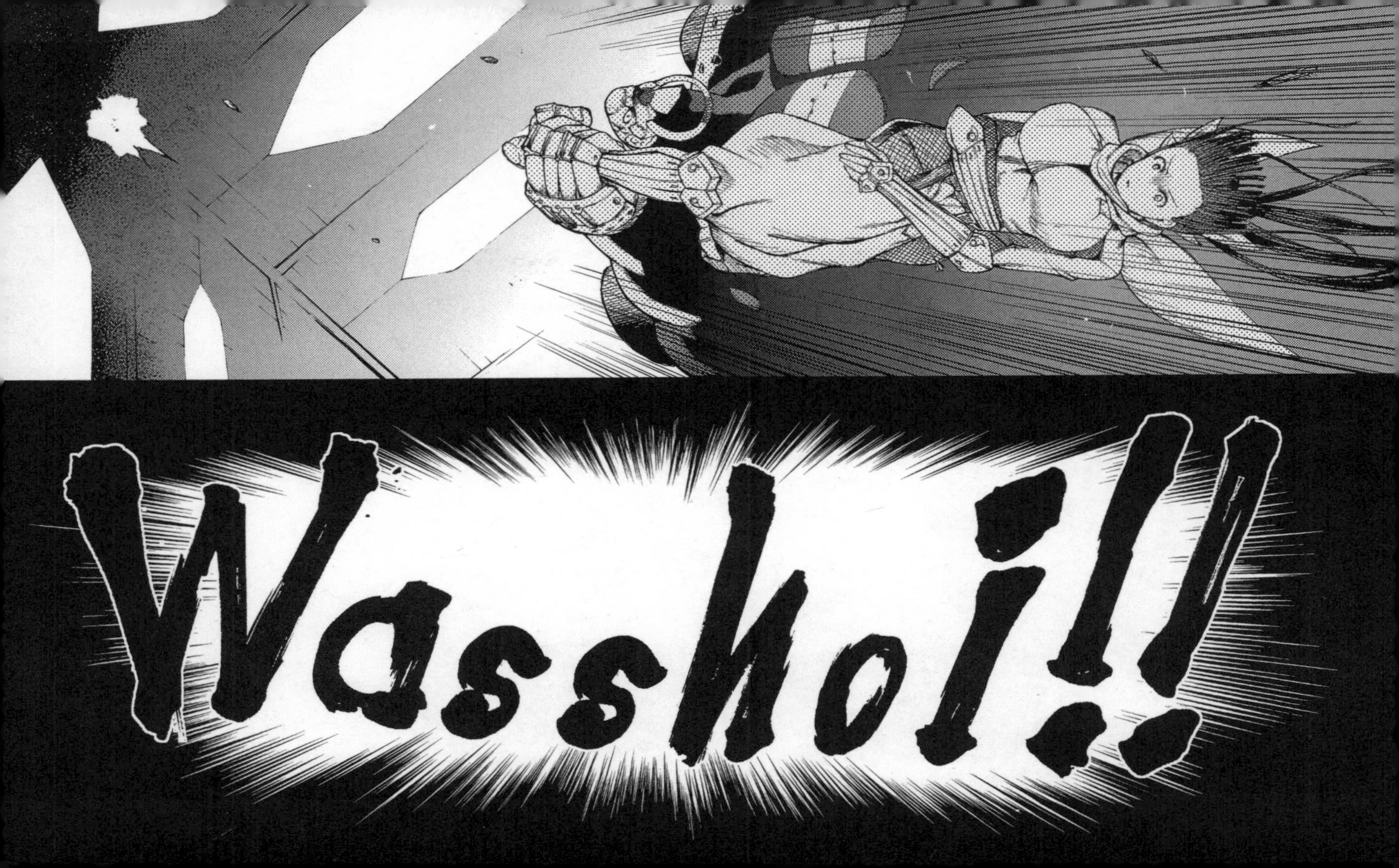
Wasshoi!!

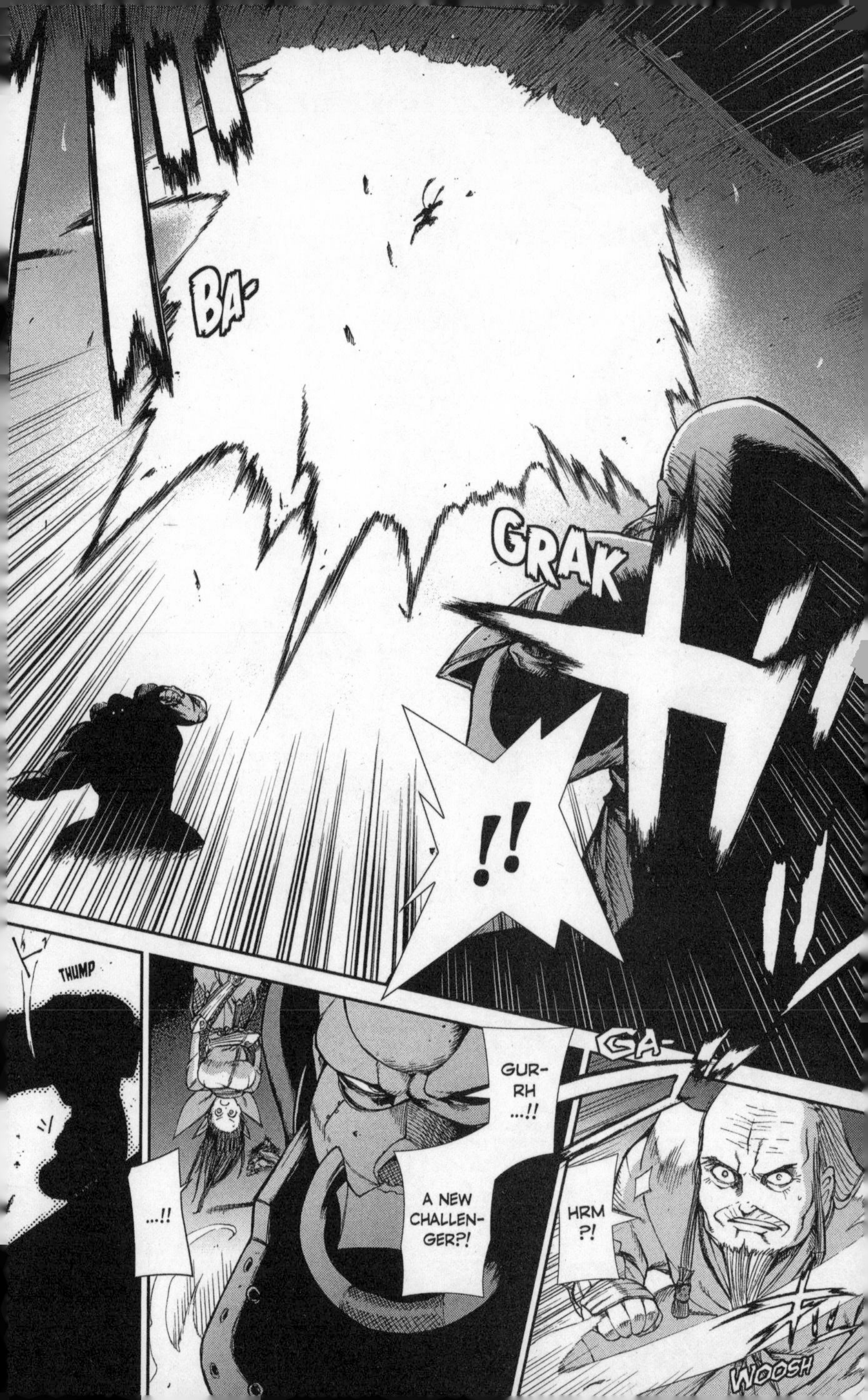
BA-
GRAK
!!
GA-
HRM ?!
WOOSH
GUR-RH ...!!
A NEW CHALLENGER?!
THUMP
...!!

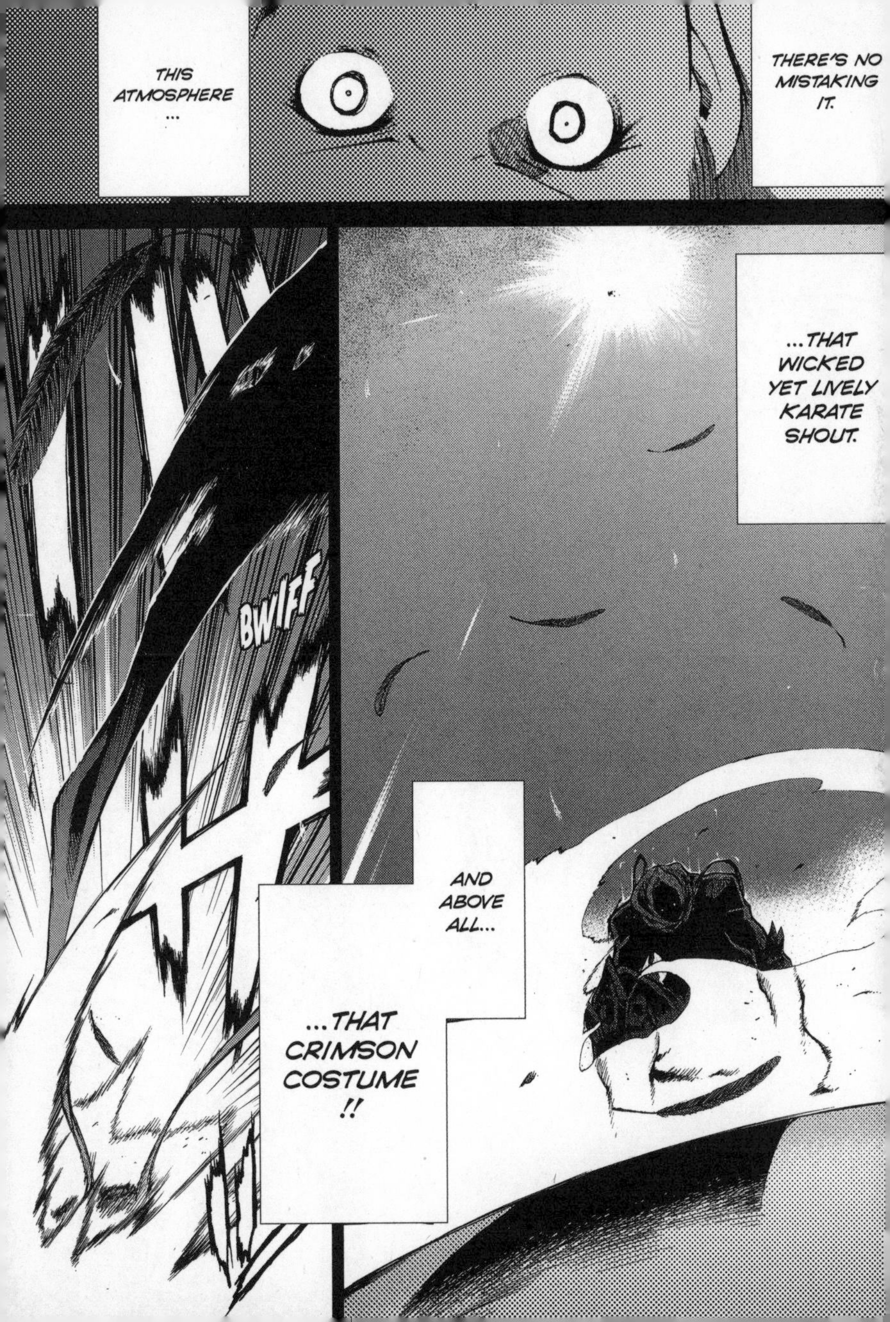
THERE'S NO MISTAKING IT.
THIS ATMOSPHERE ...
...THAT WICKED YET LIVELY KARATE SHOUT.
AND ABOVE ALL...
...THAT CRIMSON COSTUME !!
BWIFF

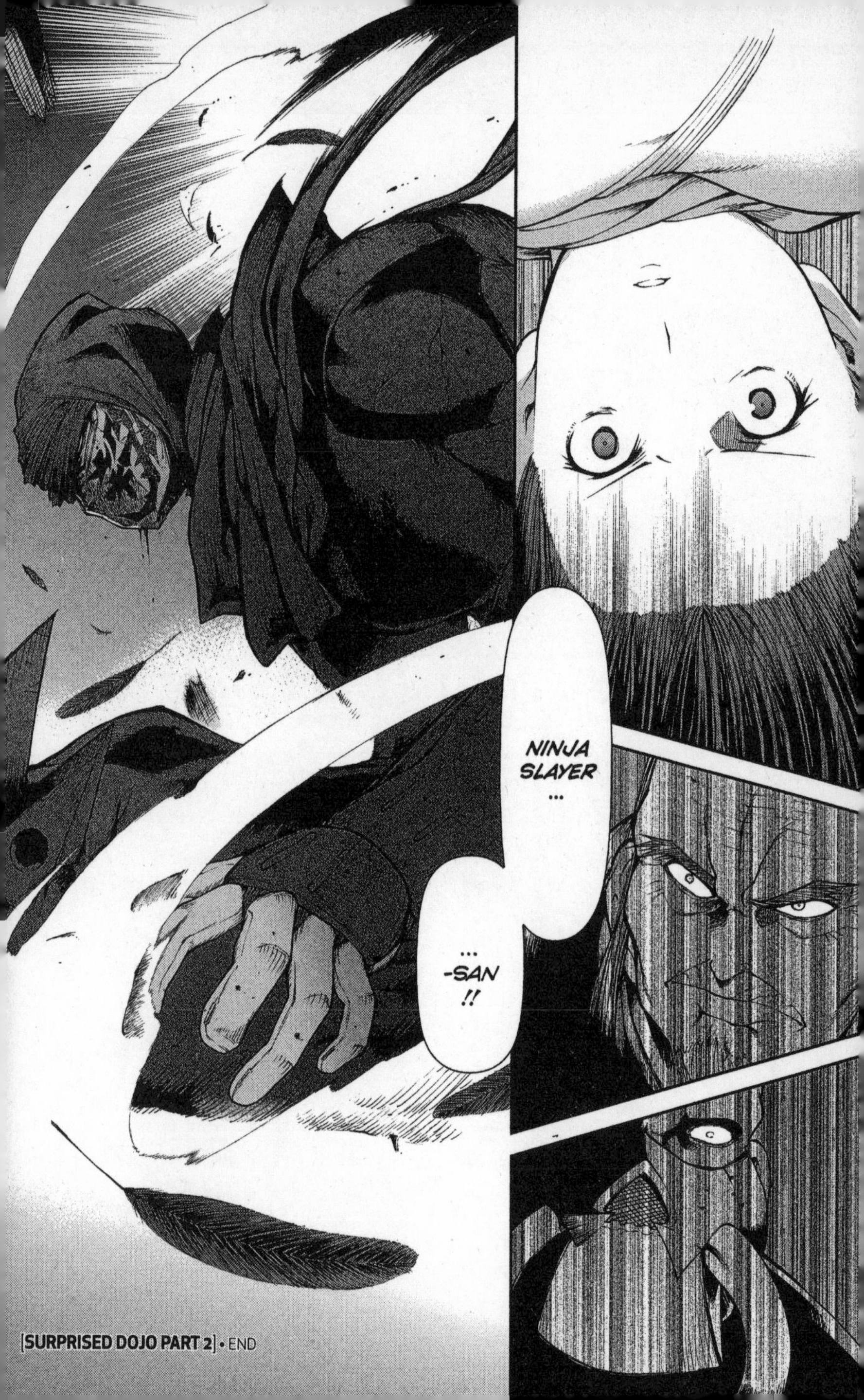
NINJA SLAYER ...
... -SAN !!

[SURPRISED DOJO PART 2] • END

TO BE CONTINUED

NINJA SLAYER KILLS!
ニンジャスレイヤー

SETTING DESIGN COLLECTION

COMMENTARY: KOUTAROU SEKINE

EARTHQUAKE

DOMINANT

PROTOTYPE NINJA SLAYER

HUGE SHURIKEN

GATEKEEPER

BANDIT

GARGOYLE

HELLKITE

PROTOTYPE NINJA SLAYER

This is a ninja costume cobbled together by Fujikido himself, so I drew it with the feel of an Iron Man Mark 1-style rivet-lined prototype. Other than that, I toned down the sharp edges of the original version of Ninja Slayer. The outfit is a mended judo outfit he picked up and dyed crimson, while the armored parts were refashioned as necessary from scrap lying around a factory. Though the equipment can't even stand up to a battle with a *sanshita* ninja, it must've been important for Fujikido to recreate Ninja Slayer from scratch.

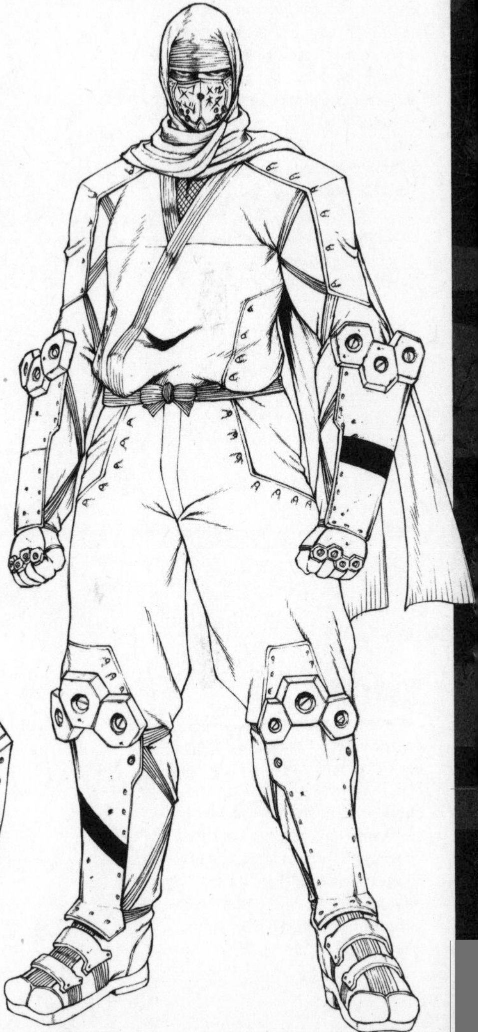

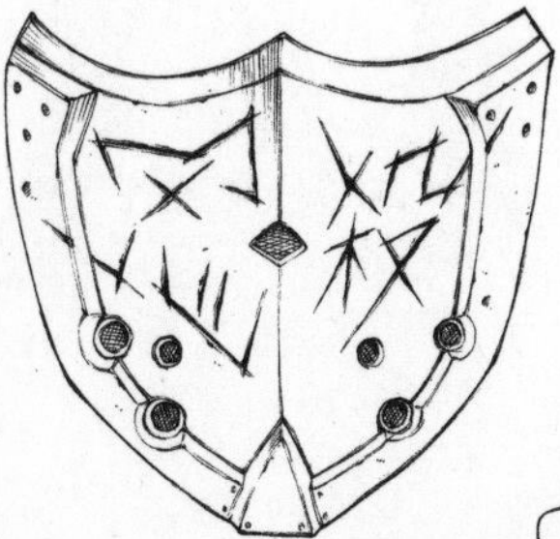

DOMINANT

Dominant is an up-and-coming, young Soukai ninja, so I gave him a prideful, arrogant, and handsome face. Dominant's outfit uses special experimental artificial muscles that react to his unique "Enhancement Jitsu" by increasing his physical capabilities. His mempo (mask) activates as his jitsu increases in intensity. The Emeici he uses as a weapon are held in storage units found on the left side of his waist and on his right knee. The unit on his right knee is meant to be used as a concealed weapon in emergency situations (fired during extreme close-quarters combat, etc.).

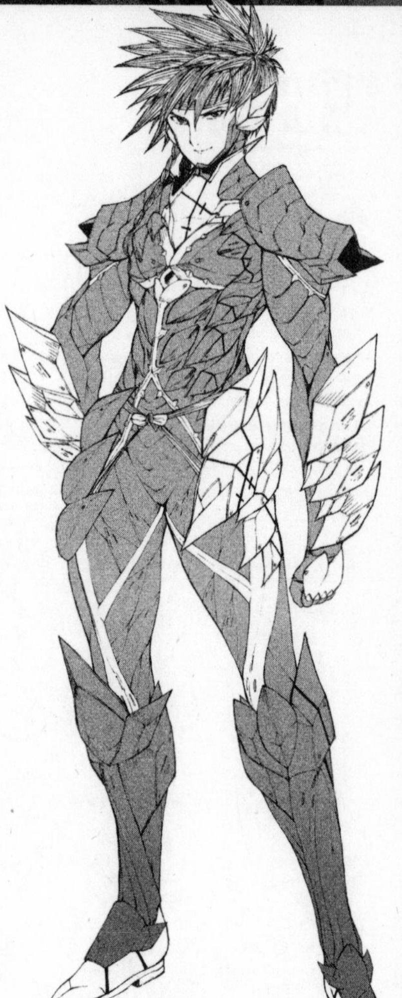

EMEICI

An assassination weapon said to have been once favored by ninja in the world of Ninja Slayer. It is attached to a ring on his middle finger when used and can be enhanced and remotely controlled by imbuing it with the azure light of his Enhancement Jitsu. The tips are rapidly rotating drills, which shred the target to pieces and make it difficult for the wounds it inflicts to heal.

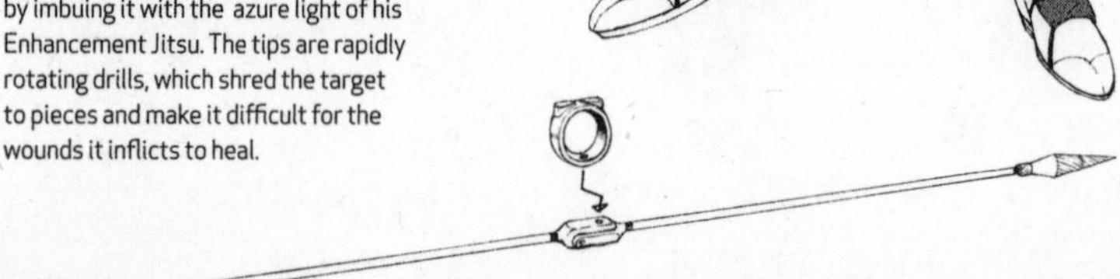

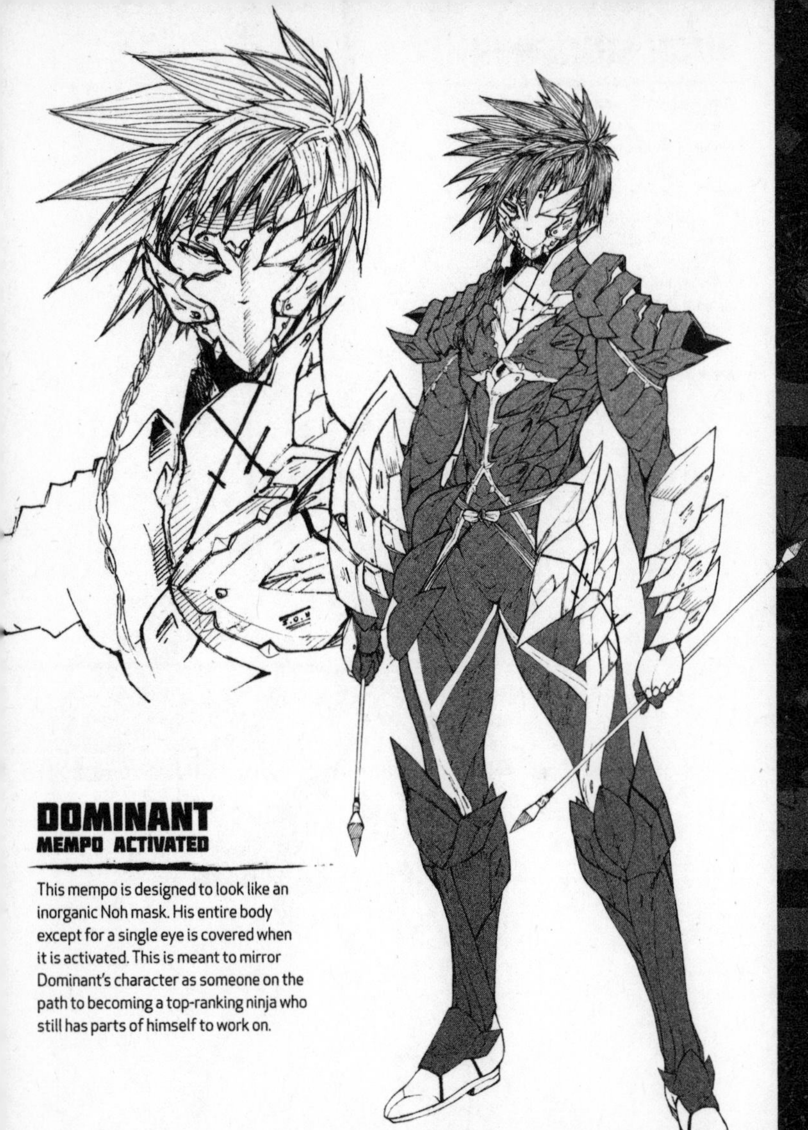

DOMINANT
MEMPO ACTIVATED

This mempo is designed to look like an inorganic Noh mask. His entire body except for a single eye is covered when it is activated. This is meant to mirror Dominant's character as someone on the path to becoming a top-ranking ninja who still has parts of himself to work on.

HUGE SHURIKEN

Huge Shuriken is meant to look like a scoundrel with a suriken motif decorating every aspect of his design, including his tattoo, hair, spurs, and so on. This is also why his mempo makes it look like he's whistling. The suriken-shaped eye patch over his dominant eye is, according to him, used for improved aim, but its actual efficacy is uncertain. It could just be a fashion statement. One can see on his exposed right arm an artificial muscle supporter used to assist his suriken throwing, while on his left arm is his secret attack bracer.

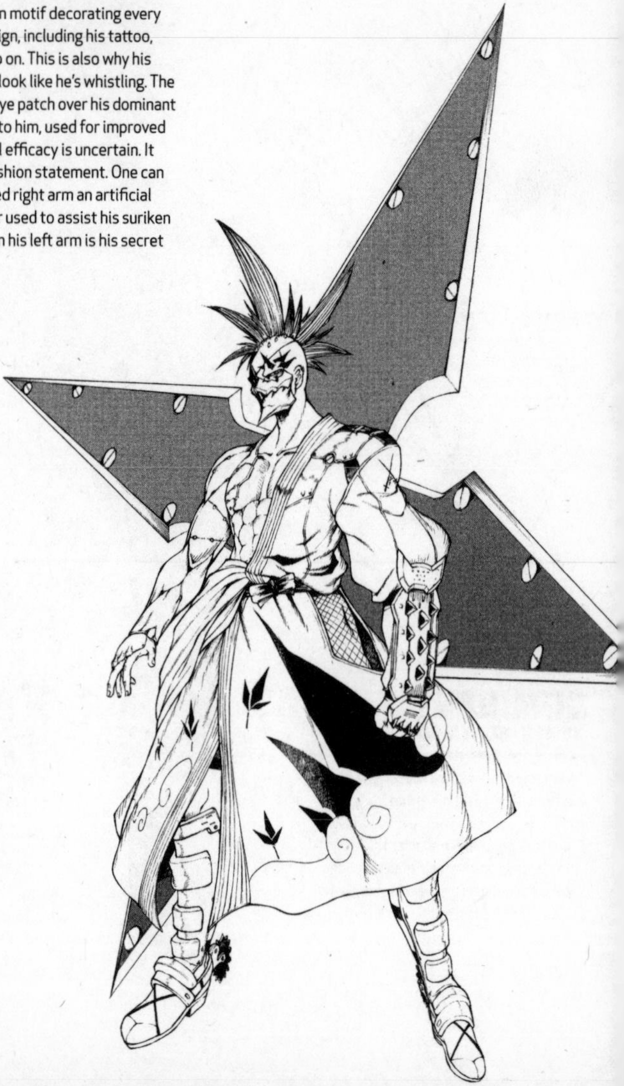

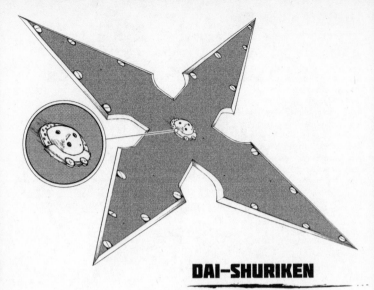

DAI-SHURIKEN

The central control unit is used to provide linear blade rotation acceleration
for improved stability and killing power.

SECRET ATTACK BRACER

Pulling the cord attached to this bracer causes gunpowder to
ignite, shooting out a flurry of small blades. As it was created with
a ninja's physical abilities in mind, the force of the explosion would
cause a mere mortal's arm to go flying if one ever tried to use it.

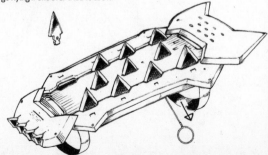

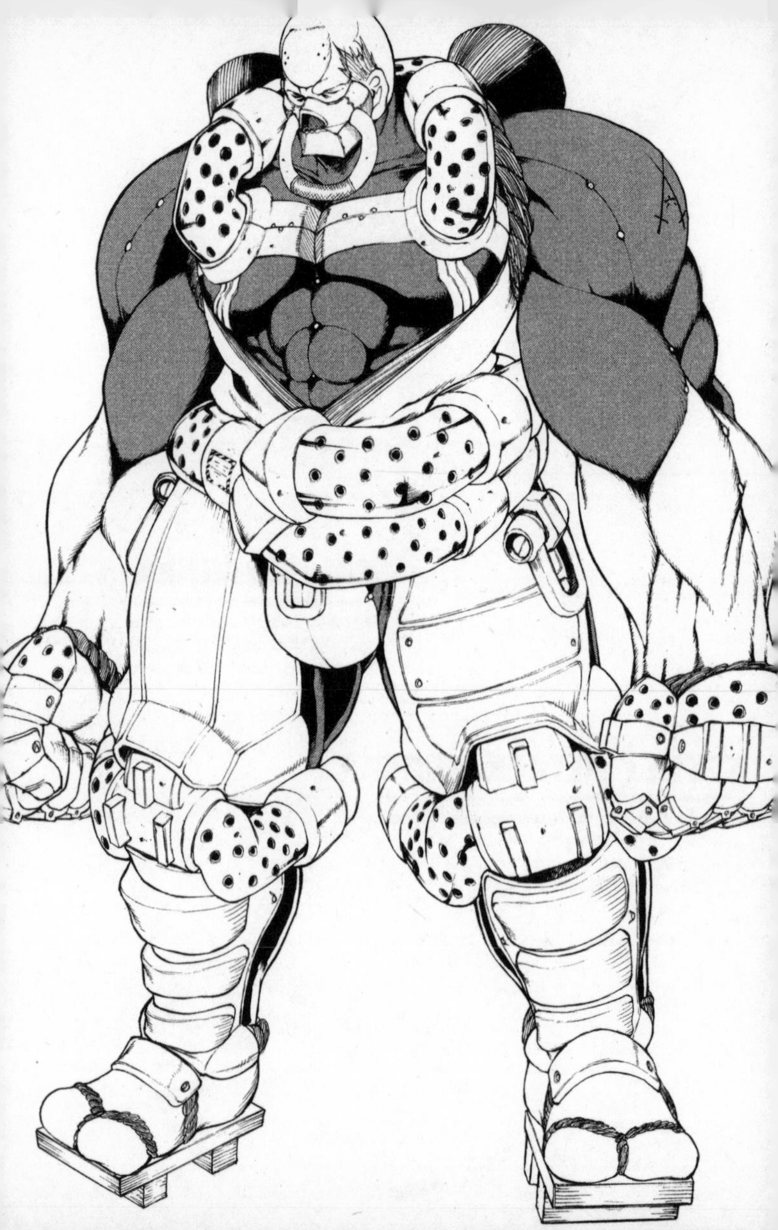

EARTHQUAKE

I think the *Animation* caused me to draw him a little too big, but bigger is cooler, after all… One of my base inspirations for Earth and Huge were Zhu Bajie and Sha Wujing from *Journey to the West*. On top of which, I added details from things like heavy machinery, motorcycles, and so on. The pipes across his body are used to effectively ventilate the karate heat generated when Earthquake gets serious. While Huge has a tendency to choose his equipment based on how cool it feels or looks, Earth chooses only the most barebones of gear.

Height comparison between Earthquake, Huge Shuriken, and Hellkite.

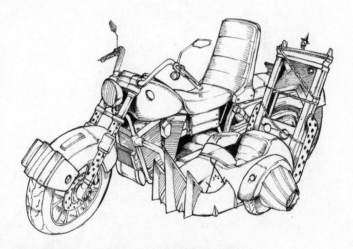

EARTHQUAKE'S MOTORCYCLE

I drew this right after watching *Mad Max: Fury Road*, which had converted me to the church of the V8. So naturally, I drew this like a child piling parts onto a model car, with a thought process along the lines of, "This bike won't kill a ninja, damn it! Let's put some brass knuckles on the front! And a triple blade! Now a shot from this thing will turn any regular ninja into mincemeat! But what if it gets attacked from the side?! Okay, then I'll put a spinny drilly thing on it!! I saw something like it in that *Crush Gear* anime!! And as a final touch, I'll add a guillotine to make it 100 million percent more deadly! Who cares how effective it is, I want a bike with looks that can slaughter any jelly-kneed, white-haired weakling that comes across it!!" But now that I look at it with more sober eyes, I think it turned out looking kind of classy. I guess in the end I'm just a simple resident of Saitama Prefecture, neither Mad nor Max…

HELLKITE

While much is said of his abilities in the story, I drew Hellkite in *Kills* with a Tengu-like military look. Some of my favorite flourishes include his eyes, as you can't tell what he's thinking, as well as the feathers in his beret cap. His tall single-toothed geta are worn so that he doesn't drag his kite on the ground.

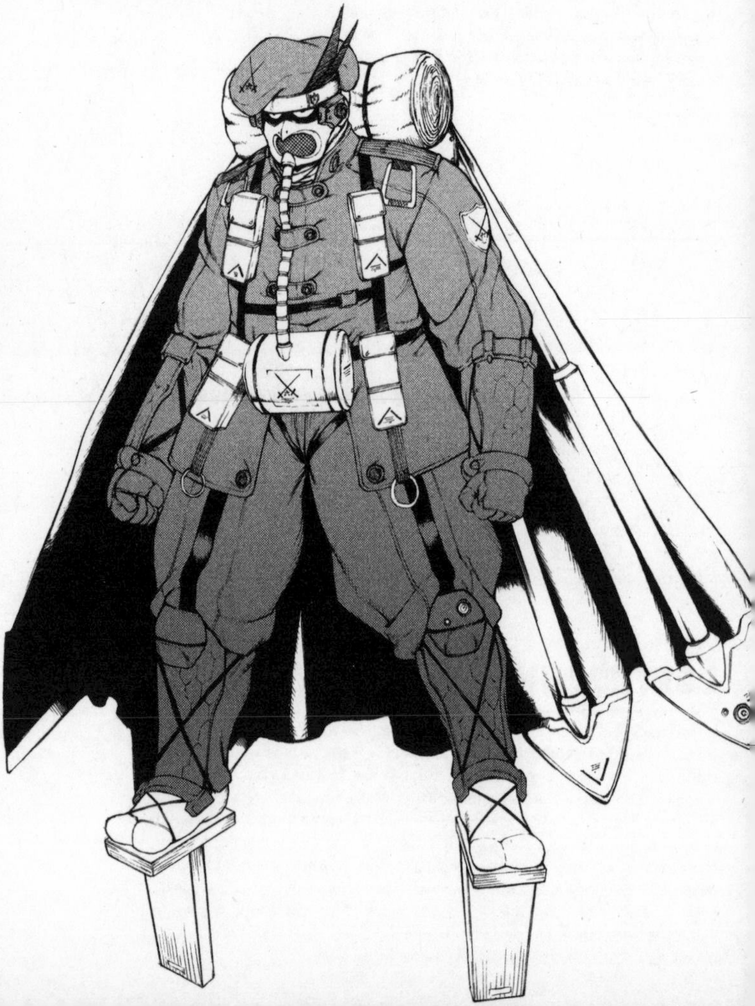

KITE WHEN ACTIVATED

GOGGLES

The multi-goggles Hellkite constantly wears are capable of folding out to the side. However, he generally does not activate his goggles in this way unless he is in Laomoto's presence.

GARGOYLE

If you're going to talk about gargoyles in Neo-Saitama, you're going to be talking about the shachihoko, which have the head of a tiger and the body of a carp. Gargoyle's shachihoko mempo also takes influence from the Balinese Rangda, and in fact his entire design is vaguely inspired by Balinese culture and Japanese water magic performers. He is able to release powerful currents of water from his fans, and he is able to use his unusually flexible body to become a true shachihoko gargoyle…or at least, that was probably the case while he was still alive.

BANDIT

I went all-out with the bandit imagery for this character because of his name. While he has an unusually prominent face for a scout, I needed to make him look strong. He is the Six Gates' top assassin in *Kills*, after all. It is said that Bandit's leg strength is three times a normal human's, and the frames around his legs can further improve it by activating to be used like competitive running blades. He didn't get a chance to show this off, though…

GATEKEEPER

Gatekeeper has been changed in *Kills* to act almost as Laomoto's butler, staying at his side to help him with whatever is necessary. For that reason, he simply wears a black suit and his mempo. I've always believed that any image looks tighter when a silver-haired gentleman is in it, which is why I've had him appear in *Kills* more often than he does in the original. Anyone who has Gatekeeper-san standing behind them will feel a serious thrill— even a soft, flabby salaryman.

AFTERWORD

The online broadcast of *Ninja Slayer from Animation* has come and gone, and it seems that its television broadcast is fast approaching. How have all of you been these days? This is Koutarou Sekine. It's been a while since the last compiled volume—nearly a year ago. I'm very sorry about that…

Whenever anyone asks me about what I've been doing over the past year, outside of drawing manga, I can't really say that anything dramatic has happened. Fujikido, on the other hand, takes his first steps on his own toward becoming Ninja Slayer, while Yukano poetically describes Fujikido's karate shout as "wicked yet lively" even as she's being dangled in the air… That about sums it up.

Yukano-san seems to be turning into a bit of a karate sommelier. Yukano-san, I know you've been put in a bit of a rough spot having to hang in the air like that until volume 4 comes out, but you can do it! Well, see you next volume…

関根光太郎
Koutarou Sekine

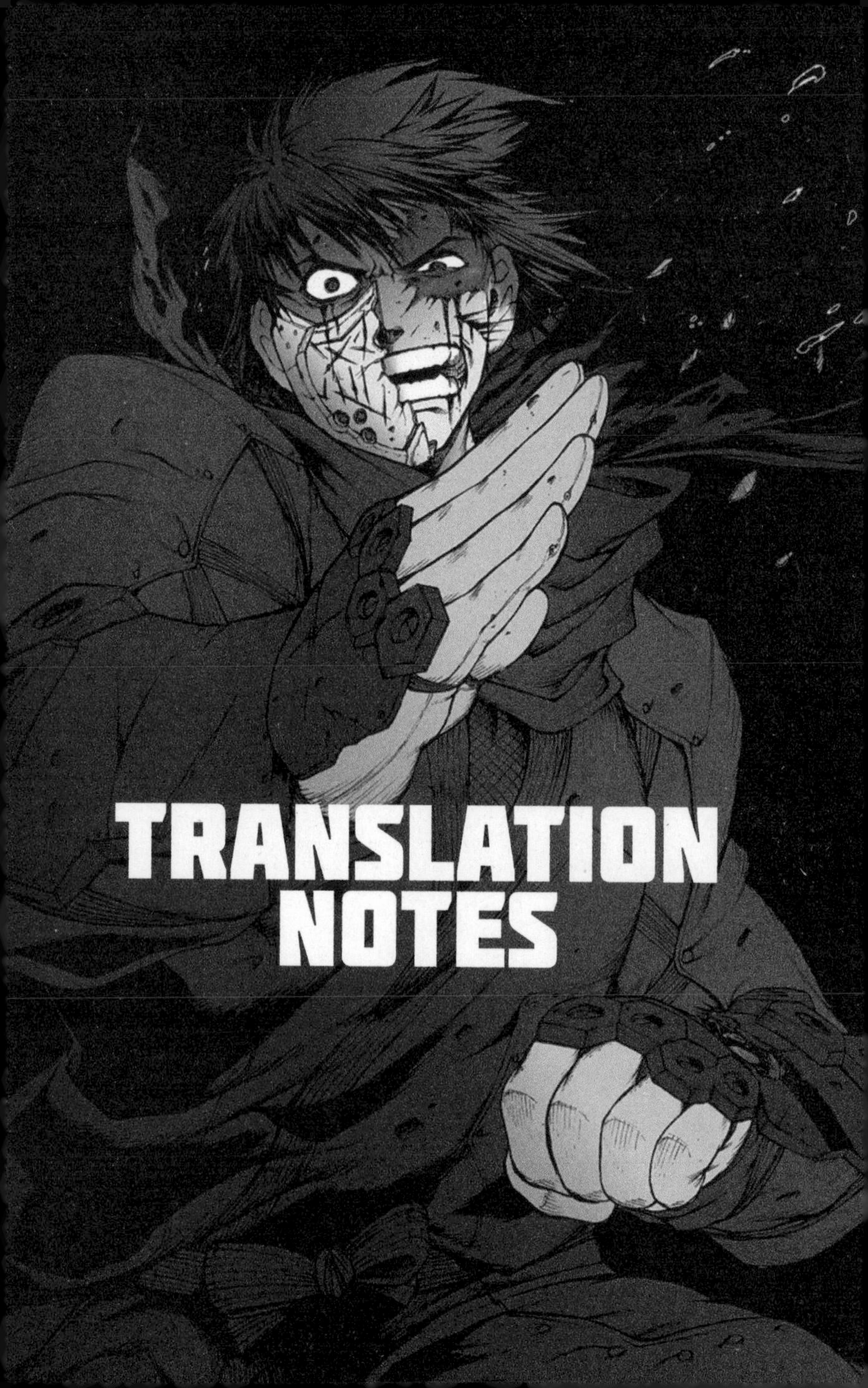
TRANSLATION NOTES

Zhu Bajie and Sha Wujing, page 213

Zhu Bajie (JP: Cho Hakkai) and Sha Wujing (JP: Sa Gojō) are both characters in the classic Chinese tale, *Journey to the West* (JP: *Saiyuki*). Both characters are helpers to the main character, the Buddhist monk Xuanzang (JP: Sanzōhōshi), as he makes a pilgrimage to the West to obtain and return with Buddhist sutras. Zhu Bajie is a half-pig/half-man who carries a large metal rake as a weapon and who, true to his swine-like appearance, is prone to laziness and gluttony. Sha Wujing is a large balding man with a halberd and a necklace made of skulls. Due to his appearance and association with water as a river monster, Sha Wujing is sometimes reinterpreted as a Japanese water imp, or Kappa.

Crush Gear, page 213

Crush Gear (full name: *Gekitō! Crush Gear Turbo*) is one of many toy-centric anime and manga series aimed at young boys. The series is about people who compete with modded toy vehicles by throwing the vehicles in a large ring to fight each other. The anime series ran from 2001-2003 and also resulted in an animated film and second TV series called *Crush Gear Nitro*.

Shachihoko, page 216

Shachihoko are half-fish, half-tiger creatures. Since they are believed to be able to produce great streams of water from their mouths, statues of shachihoko used to be placed on buildings in Japan as a charm against fire. The most famous shachihoko in Japan are the pair of golden ones on Nagoya Castle.

Rangda, page 216

According to Balinese legend, Rangda is the demon queen of the leyaks, fearsome creatures that consist of only a flying head with entrails dangling from its bottom. In Bali, she is seen as the embodiment of evil and is said to lead an army of witches against Barong, who represents good in Balinese mythology. When represented in costume for dances and other events, a mask with fangs, goggle eyes, and a long tongue is combined with a wig of almost body-length, blond hair and striped skin colored red, black, and white.

Japanese water magic, page 216

Japanese water magic (JP: *mizugei*) is an old style of entertainment that has been performed since the Edo period. A typical act consists of the performer manipulating water on a stage by stopping and starting the flow of a stream and making the water "dance" at the flick of the performers fan.

INUYASHIKI

A superhero like none you've ever seen, from the creator of "Gantz"!

ICHIRO INUYASHIKI IS DOWN ON HIS LUCK. HE LOOKS MUCH OLDER THAN HIS 58 YEARS, HIS CHILDREN DESPISE HIM, AND HIS WIFE THINKS HE'S A USELESS COWARD. SO WHEN HE'S DIAGNOSED WITH STOMACH CANCER AND GIVEN THREE MONTHS TO LIVE, IT SEEMS THE ONLY ONE WHO'LL MISS HIM IS HIS DOG.

THEN A BLINDING LIGHT FILLS THE SKY, AND THE OLD MAN IS KILLED... ONLY TO WAKE UP LATER IN A BODY HE ALMOST RECOGNIZES AS HIS OWN. CAN IT BE THAT ICHIRO INUYASHIKI IS NO LONGER HUMAN?

COMES IN EXTRA-LARGE EDITIONS WITH COLOR PAGES!

A Kodansha Comics Trade Paperback Original.

Ninja Slayer Kills volume 3 copyright © 2016 Ninj@ Entertainment & Koutarou Sekine
English translation copyright © 2016 Ninj@ Entertainment & Koutarou Sekine

Published in the United States by Kodansha Comics, an imprint of Kodansha USA Publishing, LLC, New York.

Publication rights for this English edition arranged through Kodansha Ltd., Tokyo.

First published in Japan in 2016 by Kodansha Ltd., Tokyo, as *Ninja Slayer Satsu (Kills)*, volume 3.

ISBN 978-1-63236-088-5

www.kodanshacomics.com

Localization: Ko Ransom
Lettering: Evan Hayden
Calligraphy for Kotodama: Megumi Fitzpatrick
Editing and additional material: Ajani Oloye
Kodansha Comics edition cover design: Phil Balsman